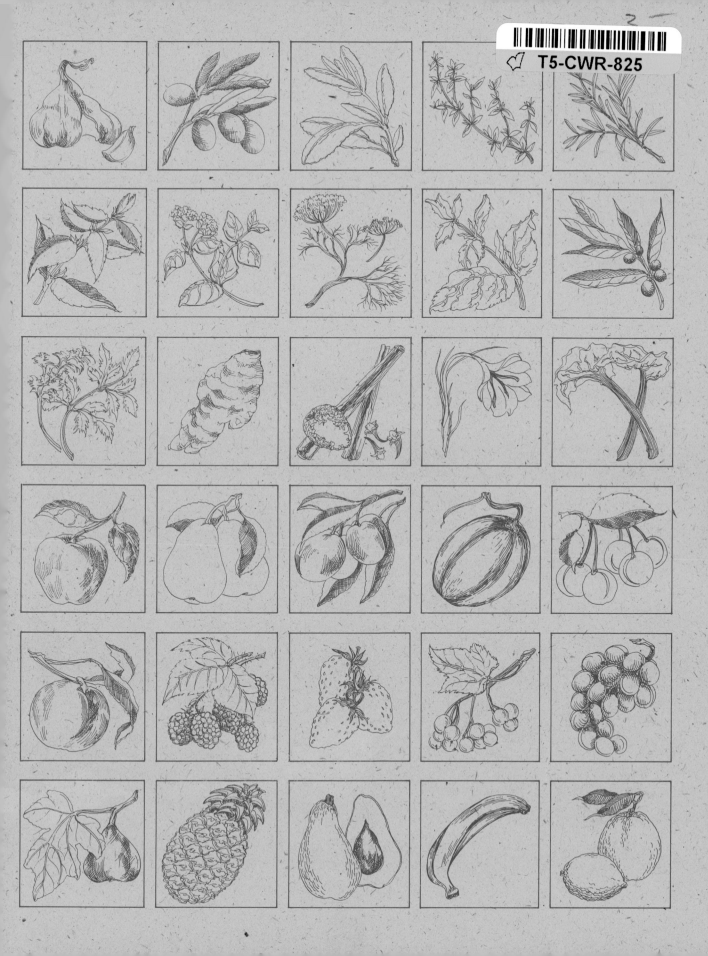

1988
FamilyCircle
C·O·O·K·B·O·O·K

Other Books by Family Circle:

The Best of Family Circle Cookbook
1986 Family Circle Cookbook
1987 Family Circle Cookbook

Family Circle Christmas Treasury
1987 Family Circle Christmas Treasury

Family Circle Favorite Needlecrafts

To order **FamilyCircle** books, write to Family Circle Books,
110 Fifth Avenue, 4th floor, New York, NY 10011.

To subscribe to **FamilyCircle** magazine, write to Family Circle Subscriptions,
110 Fifth Avenue, New York, NY 10011.

Editorial Staff

Editor, Book Development — Carol A. Guasti
Editorial/Production Coordinator — Kim Gayton

Project Staff

Project Editor — David Ricketts
Book Design — Bessen & Tully, Inc.
Illustrations — Lauren Jarrett
Typesetting — Gary S. Borden, Alison Chandler
Special Assistant — Kristen J. Keller

Marketing Staff

Manager, Marketing & Development — Margaret Chan-Yip
Project Coordinator — Judith Tashbook

Cover Photo — Debold

Photographers — Michael Clemente, Debold, Dennis Gottlieb, Richard Jeffrey,
James Kozyra, Lazlo, Maris/Semel, Bill McGinn, Rudy Muller, Tom Russell,
Ron Schwerin, Gordon E. Smith, Rene Velez.

Published by The Family Circle, Inc.
110 Fifth Avenue, New York, NY 10011

Copyright® 1987 by The Family Circle, Inc.

Manufactured in the United States of America

10 9 8 7 6 5 4 3 2 1

ISBN 0-933585-07-1
ISSN 0890-1481

1988

FamilyCircle

C·O·O·K·B·O·O·K

The Editors of Family Circle

Contents

I·N·T·R·O·D·U·C·T·I·O·N

You can make all these wonderful Mediterranean-style dishes from this cookbook! Our feast, clockwise from left: Rice Salad with Tuna and Shrimp (page 144), Cold Roast Pork with Garlic Mayonnaise (page 86), Cold Roast Turkey with Sweet and Sour Eggplant (page 100), Chicken with Provençal Vegetables (page 92), Spaghetti with Spinach (page 106).

*T*his is the busy 80's. Everywhere you look you see it in our eating habits: "grazing", or eating several small meals rather than three square; fast food chains offering expanded menus; the increased use of microwave ovens. And today, health is on everyone's mind. Americans are eating leaner, buying more fish, more poultry, more vegetables.

This cookbook is tailored to your busy lifestyle. We've highlighted all the low-calorie, low-sodium and quick-to-prepare recipes with symbols *(see below)* and provided a nutrient analysis as well.

You'll find some very special features here. Our Smart Eating chapter explains how to tailor your food and recipes to make them healthier; in Microwave Magic, see how beautiful microwave food can look, and how easy it is to prepare! You may even discover *new* uses for your microwave oven.

Of course, this cookbook isn't just a special features book. The first chapter features home-baked breads and muffins — and is there anything more satisfying to bake? In Tasty Accompaniments, you'll find a slew of appetizers, side dishes, soups and salads that add interest to a meal. Then flip to The Main Course chapter to whip up something sensational for dinner.

On warm, sunny days (or when you don't want to go near a stove), you'll find barbecue recipes, main dish salads, and even cooling drinks in the Warm Weather Dining chapter.

And what would life be without our just rewards — scrumptious pies, cakes, cookies, and even delicious frozen treats from Our Favorite Desserts chapter. So that's our 1988 Family Circle Cookbook — a guide to recipes for the Busy 80s.

Cooking Helps

Every recipe is coded with the following symbols:

N Quick

▨ Low-Calorie

LS Low-Sodium

Keep in mind that:
1. *Low-calorie* means main dish is 300 or fewer calories per serving; side dish is 100 or fewer calories; dessert is 150 or fewer calories; and condiments are 100 or fewer calories.
2. *Low-sodium* means main dish contains 140 or fewer milligrams of sodium per serving; side dish contains 100 or fewer milligrams; dessert, 50 or fewer milligrams; and condiments, 50 or fewer milligrams.
3. *Baking powder* is double action.
4. *Brown sugar* is firmly packed.
5. *Corn syrup,* unless specified, can be either light or dark.
6. Doubling recipes is not wise. It is best to make the recipe a second time.
7. *Eggs* are large.
8. *"Eggs, slightly beaten"* means just break the yolks.
9. *"Eggs, lightly beaten"* means create a smooth mixture.
10. Most commercial brands of cake or all-purpose flour come presifted from the manufacturer. Some of our recipes indicate additional sifting to produce a lighter product.
11. *Heavy cream* for whipping is 40 percent butterfat.
12. *Herbs and spices* are dried unless noted otherwise.
13. Measurements are level.
14. *Milk* is whole homogenized.
15. *Vegetable shortening* is used for greasing pans.
16. *Vinegar* is cider, unless otherwise noted.

Daily Nutrition Countdown Chart

	AVERAGE HEALTHY ADULT	
	Women	Men
Calories[1]	2,000	2,700
Protein[2]	44 g (176 cal.)	56 g (224 cal.)
Fat[3]	66 g (594 cal.)	90 g (810 cal.)
Sodium[4]	1,100–3,300 mg	1,100–3,300 mg
Cholesterol[5]	300 mg	300 mg

Calories (cal.) that do not come from protein or fat should be derived from complex carbohydrates found in whole grains, fresh fruits, vegetables, pasta, etc.

[1]RDA [2](8–12% of calories) RDA [3](30% of calories) RDA Amer. Heart Assoc. and Nat'l Acad. of Science [4](USDA) [5]Amer. Heart Assoc.

Due to rapid growth rate and body changes during the developmental years, nutritional needs for children vary more than for adults. Therefore, we suggest you supervise your children's daily dietary intake to make sure they're eating well-rounded meals and developing healthy eating habits. If you're not certain about specific dietary needs for your child, consult a registered dietitian or qualified doctor.

Important Measures

Dash or pinch	under ⅛ teaspoon
½ tablespoon	1½ teaspoons
1 tablespoon	3 teaspoons
1 ounce liquid	2 tablespoons
1 jigger	1½ ounces
¼ cup	4 tablespoons
⅓ cup	5 tablespoons plus 1 teaspoon
½ cup	8 tablespoons
⅔ cup	10 tablespoons plus 2 teaspoons
¾ cup	12 tablespoons
1 cup	16 tablespoons
1 pint	2 cups
1 quart	2 pints
1 gallon	4 quarts
1 pound	16 ounces

Measuring Equipment

MEASURING FLOUR
Measure the all-purpose flour called for in most of the recipes in this book by spooning flour from the bag or canister into a standard dry measuring cup, heaping slightly. (Note: The top of the cup is flat; there is no spout in a dry measure, as there is in a liquid measuring cup.)

   Place the heaping cup of flour over the bag of flour or canister and run the flat side of a long knife across the top to level off the cup. (Note: Use this technique for granulated sugar too.) Do not tap or shake the cup to level.

PACKING BROWN SUGAR
Measure light or dark brown sugar by packing it into a standard dry measuring cup, using the back of a tablespoon.

MEASURING SHORTENING
Measure vegetable shortening by scooping it with a rubber scraper into a standard dry measuring cup; run the flat blade of a long knife over the top, then scoop it out of the cup with a rubber scraper into the mixing bowl. Shortening can be measured before or after it is melted.

   One stick of butter or magarine equals 4 ounces; 4 sticks equal 1 pound or 2 cups.

MEASURING LIQUID
Place a standard liquid measuring cup on a flat surface and stoop to be at eye level with the measuring cup; pour the liquid to the desired measure printed on the side of the cup. (Note: When measuring a syrup, such as molasses or honey, grease the cup with butter or margarine. Then the syrup will pour out easily.)

Oven Temperatures

Very Slow	250°-275°
Slow	300°-325°
Moderate	350°-375°
Hot	400°-425°
Very Hot	450°-475°
Extremely Hot	Hot 500°+

Casserole Measurement Chart
Casseroles are international dishes created all over the world. Each country has its own system for measuring volume or quantity. The chart below will help you to convert your casserole's measurements from one system to another so that you can be assured your recipe will bake to perfection.

Cups	=	Pints	=	Quarts	=	Liters
1		½		¼		0.237
2		1*		½*		0.473
4		2*		1*		0.946
6		3		1½		1.419
8		4		2		1.892
10		5		2½		2.365
12		6		3		2.838

In Canada, 1 pint = 2½ cups; 1 quart = 5 cups.

Emergency Ingredient Substitutes

WHEN THE RECIPE CALLS FOR:	YOU MAY SUBSTITUTE:
1 square unsweetened chocolate	3 tablespoons unsweetened cocoa powder plus 1 tablespoon butter, margarine or vegetable shortening
1 cup *sifted* cake flour	⅞ cup *sifted* all-purpose flour (1 cup less 2 tablespoons)
2 tablespoons flour (for thickening)	1 tablespoon cornstarch
1 teaspoon baking powder	¼ teaspoon baking powder plus ⅝ teaspoon cream of tartar
1 cup corn syrup	1 cup sugar and ¼ cup liquid used in recipe
1 cup honey	1¼ cups sugar and ¼ cup liquid used in recipe
1 cup whole milk	½ cup evaporated milk plus ½ cup water
1 cup buttermilk	1 tablespoon vinegar plus enough sweet milk to make 1 cup; let stand 5 minutes
1 cup sour cream (in baking)	⅞ cup buttermilk or sour milk plus 3 tablespoons butter
1 egg (for custards)	2 egg yolks
1 cup brown sugar (packed)	1 cup sugar or 1 cup sugar plus 2 tablespoons molasses
1 teaspoon lemon juice	½ teaspoon vinegar
¼ cup chopped onion	1 tablespoon instant minced onion
1 clove garlic	⅛ teaspoon garlic powder
1 cup zucchini	1 cup summer squash
1 cup tomato juice	½ cup tomato sauce plus ½ cup water
2 cups tomato sauce	¾ cup tomato paste plus 1 cup water
1 tablespoon fresh snipped herbs	1 teaspoon dried herbs
1 tablespoon prepared mustard	1 teaspoon dry mustard
1 cup bread crumbs	¾ cup cracker crumbs

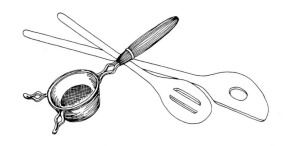

Emergency Baking Dish and Pan Substitutes

If you do not have the specific-size baking pan or mold called for in a recipe, substitute a pan of equal volume from the list below.
• If the pan you are substituting is made of glass, reduce the baking temperature by 25°.
• If you are substituting a pan that is shallower than the pan in the recipe, reduce the baking time by about one-quarter.
• If you are substituting a pan that is deeper than the pan in the recipe, increase baking time by one-quarter.

HANDY CHART OF KITCHEN MATH
You'll never have a cooking crisis when you use our handy charts. Need a 4- or 6-cup baking dish? Will your fancy mold be the right size for the recipe? See below for the answers, plus much more!

COMMON KITCHEN PANS TO USE AS CASSEROLES WHEN THE RECIPE CALLS FOR:

4-cup baking dish:
9-inch pie plate
8 x 1¼-inch round layer-cake pan — C
7⅜ x 3⅝ x 2⅝-inch loaf pan — A

6-cup baking dish:
10-inch pie plate
8 or 9 x 1½-inch round layer-cake pan — C
8½ x 3⅝ x 2⅝-inch loaf pan — A

8-cup baking dish:
8 x 8 x 2-inch square pan — D
11 x 7 x 1½-inch baking pan
9 x 5 x 3-inch loaf pan — A

10-cup baking dish:
9 x 9 x 2-inch square pan — D
11¾ x 7½ x 1¾-inch baking pan
15½ x 10½ x 1-inch jelly-roll pan

12-cup baking dish and over:
13½ x 8½ x 2-inch glass baking dish (12 cups)
13 x 9 x 2-inch metal baking pan (15 cups)
14 x 10½ x 2½-inch roasting pan (19 cups)

Three 8-inch round pans:
two 9 x 9 x 2-inch square cake pans

Two 9-inch round layer-cake pans:
two 8 x 8 x 2-inch square cake pans
13 x 9 x 2-inch pan

9 x 5 x 3-inch loaf pan:
9 x 9 x 2-inch square cake pan

9-inch angel-cake tube pan:
10 x 3¾-inch Bundt® pan
9 x 3½-inch fancy tube pan

TOTAL VOLUME OF VARIOUS SPECIAL BAKING PANS

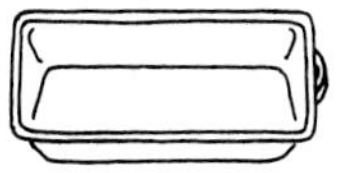

Tube pans:

7½ x 3-inch Bundt® tube pan — K	6 cups
9 x 3½-inch fancy tube or Bundt® pan — J or K	9 cups
9 x 3½-inch angel-cake or tube pan — I	12 cups
10 x 3¾-inch Bundt® or crownburst pan — K	12 cups
9 x 3½-inch fancy tube mold — J	12 cups
10 x 4-inch fancy tube mold (Kugelhopf) — J	16 cups
10 x 4-inch angel-cake or tube pan — I	18 cups

Melon Mold:

7 x 5½ x 4-inch mold — H	6 cups

Springform Pans:

8 x 3-inch pan — B	12 cups
9 x 3-inch pan — B	16 cups

Ring Molds:

8½ x 2¼-inch mold — E	4½ cups
9¼ x 2¾-inch mold — E	8 cups

Charlotte Mold:

6 x 4¼-inch mold — G	7½ cups

Brioche Pan:

9½ x 3¼-inch pan — F	8 cups

A
E
B
F
C
G
D
H 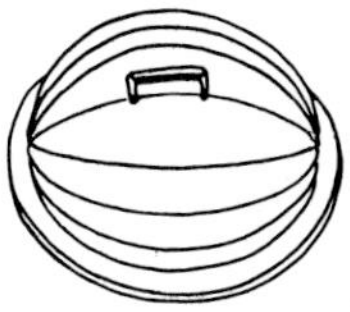
J 
I 
K

Food Equivalents

Berries, 1 pint 1¾ cups

Bread
1 pound, sliced 22 slices
Crumbs, soft, 1 cup 2 slices
Cubes, 1 cup 2 slices

Broth
Beef or Chicken, 1 cup 1 teaspoon instant bouillon or 1 envelope bouillon or 1 cube bouillon, dissolved in 1 cup boiling water

Butter or Margarine
½ stick ¼ cup or 4 tablespoons
1 pound 4 sticks or 2 cups

Cream and Milk
Cream, heavy, 1 cup 2 cups, whipped
Milk, evaporated, small can ⅔ cup
Milk, instant, nonfat dry, 1 pound 5 quarts liquid skim milk
Milk, sweetened condensed, 14-ounce can 1⅔ cups

Cheese
Blue, crumbled, 4 ounces 1 cup
Cheddar or Swiss, 1 pound, shredded 4 cups
Cottage, 8 ounces 1 cup
Cream, 8-ounce package 1 cup
Parmesan or Romano, ¼ pound, grated 1¼ cups

Chocolate
Unsweetened, 1 ounce 1 square
Semisweet pieces, 6-ounce package 1 cup

Coconut
Flaked, 3½-ounce can 1⅓ cups
Shredded, 4-ounce can 1⅓ cups

Cookies
Chocolate wafers, 1 cup crumbs 19 wafers
Graham crackers, 1 cup fine crumbs 14 square crackers
Vanilla wafers, 1 cup fine crumbs 22 wafers

Dried Beans and Peas
1 cup 2¼ cups, cooked

Eggs (large)
Whole, 1 cup 5 to 6
Whites, 1 cup 7 to 8
Yolks, 1 cup 13 to 14

Flour
All-purpose, sifted, 1 pound 4 cups
Cake, sifted, 1 pound 4¾ to 5 cups

Gelatin, unflavored, 1 envelope 1 tablespoon

Nuts
Almonds, 1 pound shelled 3½ cups
Peanuts, 1 pound, shelled 3 cups
Pecans, 1 pound, shelled 4 cups
Walnuts, 1 pound, shelled 4 cups

Pasta
Macaroni, elbow, uncooked, 8 ounces 4 cups, cooked
Noodles, medium width, uncooked, 8 ounces 3¾ cups, cooked
Spaghetti, uncooked, 8 ounces uncooked 4 cups, cooked

Rice
Enriched precooked rice, uncooked, 1 cup 2 cups, cooked
Long-grain white rice, uncooked, 1 cup 3 cups, cooked

Sugar
Brown, firmly packed, 1 pound 2¼ cups
Granulated, 1 pound 2 cups
10X (confectioners' powdered), sifted, 1 pound 3⅓ to 4 cups

Vegetables and Fruits
Apples, 1 pound 3 medium-size
Bananas, 1 pound 3 medium-size
Cabbage, 1 pound, shredded 4 cups
Carrots, 1 pound, sliced 2½ cups
Herbs, chopped fresh, 1 tablespoon 1 teaspoon dried
Lemon, 1 medium-size, grated 2 teaspoons lemon rind
Lemon, 1 medium-size, squeezed 2 tablespoons lemon juice
Mushrooms, 1 pound, sliced 3 cups
Onions, small white silverskins, 1 pound 12 to 14
Onions, yellow cooking, 1 pound 5 to 6 medium-size
Orange, 1 medium-size, grated 2 tablespoons orange rind
Orange, 1 medium-size, squeezed ⅓ to ½ cup orange juice
Peaches, 1 pound 4 medium-size
Potatoes, all-purpose, 1 pound 3 medium-size
Tomatoes, 1 pound
Large 2
Medium-size 3
Small 4

Maximum Cupboard Storage Times

Use foods within the times recommended in this chart. Foods stored longer than recommended are still good to eat, but may be less flavorful and nutritious.

Baking powder	18 months	**Nonfat dry milk powder**	6 months
Baking soda	18 months	**Oil***	
Barbecue sauce*	12 months	Olive	1 month
Bouillon cubes, instant	12 months	Vegetable	3 months
Cake Mixes	12 months	**Olives/pickles***	12 months
Canned foods*	12 months	**Pancake mixes**	6 months
Fruit, gravy, sauce, meat, poultry, milk, seafood, soup, vegetables		**Pasta**	12 months
		Peanut butter	6 months
Casserole mixes	18 months	**Piecrust mixes**	6 months
Catsup*	12 months	**Potato mixes** or instant	18 months
Cereal	6 months	**Pudding mixes**	12 months
Chili sauce*	12 months	**Rice**	
Chocolate for cooking	12 months	Brown, wild	12 months
Coconut*	12 months	Regular long-grain	24 months
Coffee*		**Salad dressing***	6 months
In vacuum-packed cans	12 months	**Shortening**	8 months
Instant ·	6 months	**Soup mixes**	6 months
Flour* all types	12 months	**Sugar**	
Frosting mixes or cans	8 months	Brown or 10X	4 months
Fruit, dried*	6 months	Granulated	24 months
Gelatin plain and sweet	18 months	**Syrup*** Corn, maple	12 months
Herbs/spices (refrigerate red spices)		**Tea**	
Ground	6 months	Bags or loose	6 months
Whole	12 months	Instant	12 months
Honey	12 months	**Vegetables**	
		Onions and potatoes	1 to 2 weeks
Jam/Jelly*	12 months	Winter squash	1 to 3 months
Molasses	24 months	**Yeast** active dry	follow package date

Refrigerate after opening

B·R·E·A·D·S & M·U·F·F·I·N·S

"Dad's" Frosted Whole-Wheat Raisin Bread (page 31) — *lots of raisins and rich icing make it extra-delicious.*

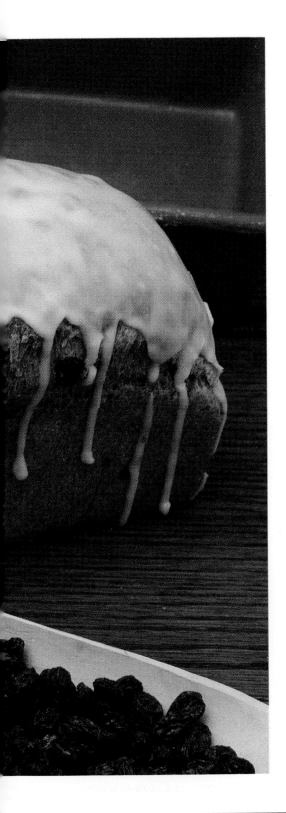

1

*B*reads and muffins fresh from the oven always bring a smile and an excited, "Can I have some?" Treat your family or friends, or just yourself. Why not plan a baking day, and prepare several different breads; some for now and some to freeze for upcoming days.

Yeast breads take the longest to make, but the results are worth it. Our Sunshine Carrot Bread *(page 23)* and Almond-Cheese Horseshoe *(page 24)* will help make a brunch or an afternoon with friends more leisurely. To shorten rising time by one-third to one-half, try using fast-rising dry yeast (see tips on *page 30*).

Quick breads are easy to prepare: no yeast, no rising time, no kneading, and they come in a virtually unlimited variety. On weekends, wake up the most reluctant sleepyhead with Banana Muffins with Brown Sugar-Pecan Topping *(page 12)* or Sunshine Muffins with Lemon Glaze *(page 11)* — just 30 minutes from start to finish. For dinner, surprise guests with Cheddar-Corn Muffins *(page 14)* or Zucchini-Dill Muffins with Parmesan Cheese Tops *(page 15)*.

At holiday time, our Coriander Gingerbread and No-Yeast Stollen *(page 19)* make thoughtful gifts. Let someone know you remember — there's nothing more welcome than something made by your hand, sent from your heart.

Q·U·I·C·K B·R·E·A·D·S

In the center of the bowl: Sunshine Muffin with Lemon Glaze; surrounded by Sour Cream and Onion Muffin (caviar-topped version is on small plate); Banana Muffin with Brown Sugar-Pecan Topping (page 12); Swedish Limpa Muffin (page 13); Pumpernickel-Raisin Muffin (page 14); and Cheddar-Corn Muffin (page 14).

Sunshine Muffins with Lemon Glaze

A breakfast pleaser.

Bake at 400° for 22 to 24 minutes.
Makes 12 muffins.

Nutrient Value Per Muffin: 136 calories, 2 g protein, 6 g fat, 20 g carbohydrate, 213 mg sodium, 25 mg cholesterol.

1¾ **cups unsifted all-purpose flour**
¼ **cup sugar**
3 **teaspoons baking powder**
½ **teaspoon salt**
1 **egg**
⅔ **cup milk**
⅓ **cup lemon juice**
¼ **cup vegetable oil**
2 **teaspoons grated lemon rind**

Lemon Glaze:
1 **cup sifted 10X (confectioners') sugar**
1 **teaspoon grated lemon rind**
2 **tablespoons milk**

1. Preheat the oven to hot (400°). Grease only the bottoms of twelve 2½-inch muffin-pan cups, or use paper liners. (The ungreased sides allow the batter to climb and form gently rounded tops while baking.)
2. Stir together the flour, sugar, baking powder and salt in a large bowl until well mixed.
3. Lightly beat the egg in a small bowl. Stir in the milk, lemon juice, oil and lemon rind until thoroughly combined.
4. Pour the liquid ingredients all at once into the dry ingredients. Stir the mixture briskly with a fork until all the ingredients are just evenly moistened; do not overstir. The batter will look lumpy.
5. Fill each prepared muffin-pan cup two-thirds full with the batter, using a large spoon and a rubber spatula to push the batter into the cups.
6. Bake the muffins in the preheated hot oven (400°) for 22 to 24 minutes or until the tops are light golden brown and a wooden pick inserted in the centers comes out clean.
7. While the muffins are baking, prepare the Lemon Glaze: Combine the 10X sugar and lemon rind in a small bowl. Stir in the milk until well combined and a good glazing consistency.
8. Remove the muffins from the pan to a wire rack. Make several holes with a wooden pick in the top of each muffin. Spoon the glaze over each muffin and serve while still warm.

10X (CONFECTIONERS') SUGAR GLAZE

Always start with the 10X sugar in a bowl. Slowly add the liquid called for in the recipe just until the mixture reaches a good glazing or spreading consistency.

IS YOUR BAKING POWDER FRESH?

Since the leavening power of baking powder diminishes with age, always test the powder: Place ½ teaspoon in ¼ cup of hot water. If the water bubbles actively, the powder is fresh.

Sour Cream and Onion Muffins with Caviar

A luxurious touch for a Sunday brunch, or serve as an hors d'oeuvre.

Bake at 400° for 14 to 16 minutes.
Makes 36 miniature muffins.

Nutrient Value Per Muffin: 56 calories, 1 g protein, 3 g fat, 6 g carbohydrate, 88 mg sodium, 13 mg cholesterol.

1¾ **cups unsifted all-purpose flour**
2 **tablespoons sugar**
3 **teaspoons baking powder**
½ **teaspoon salt**
¼ **teaspoon garlic powder**
1 **egg**
⅔ **cup dairy sour cream**
⅓ **cup milk**
¼ **cup vegetable oil**
3 **tablespoons chopped green onion**

Topping:
Dairy sour cream
Salmon caviar
Parsley sprigs

1. Preheat the oven to hot (400°). Grease only the bottoms of 36 miniature 1¾-inch muffin-pan cups, or use paper liners. (The ungreased sides allow the batter to climb and form gently rounded tops while baking.)

2. Stir together the flour, sugar, baking powder, salt and garlic powder in a large bowl until well mixed.
3. Lightly beat the egg in a small bowl. Stir in the sour cream, milk, oil and green onion until thoroughly combined.
4. Pour the liquid ingredients all at once into the dry ingredients. Stir the mixture briskly with a fork until all the ingredients are just evenly moistened; do not overstir. The batter will look lumpy.
5. Fill each prepared muffin-pan cup two-thirds full with the batter, using a small spoon and a rubber spatula to push the batter into the cups.
6. Bake the muffins in the preheated hot oven (400°) for 14 to 16 minutes or until the tops are light golden brown and a wooden pick inserted in the centers comes out clean. Remove the pan to a wire rack to cool slightly. Remove the muffins immediately and top each muffin with a small amount of sour cream, caviar and 1 small sprig of parsley. Serve the muffins while still warm.

Food for thought . . .

Webster's defines a muffin as "a quick bread made of batter containing egg and baked in a muffin pan."

A-1 MUFFINS

The perfect muffin has straight sides, a rounded top and a uniform grain.

MIXING MUFFINS: THREE IMPORTANT TIPS

● *Add the beaten liquid ingredients to the combined dry ingredients with a few, quick stirring strokes to just moisten the dry ingredients.*
● *The batter should be lumpy; if it pours smoothly from the spoon, you are guilty of overbeating.*
● *You can recognize overbeaten muffins by the coarse texture and the tunneling throughout.*

Banana Muffins with Brown Sugar-Pecan Topping

Sneak these sweet muffins into a lunch box for a special treat.

Bake at 400° for 22 to 24 minutes.
Makes 12 muffins.

Nutrient Value Per Muffin: 169 calories, 3 g protein, 6 g fat, 26 g carbohydrate, 210 mg sodium, 24 mg cholesterol.

1¾ **cups unsifted all-purpose flour**
 3 **teaspoons baking powder**
½ **teaspoon salt**
 1 **egg**
¾ **cup mashed banana (2 medium-size bananas)**
½ **cup milk**
¼ **cup vegetable oil**
½ **cup maple-flavored syrup**
  Brown sugar for topping
  Chopped pecans for topping

1. Preheat the oven to hot (400°). Grease only the bottoms of twelve 2½-inch muffin-pan cups, or use paper liners. (The ungreased sides allow the batter to climb and form gently rounded tops while baking.)
2. Stir together the flour, baking powder and salt in a large bowl until well mixed.
3. Lightly beat the egg in a medium-size bowl. Stir in the mashed banana, milk, oil and maple-flavored syrup until thoroughly combined.
4. Pour the liquid ingredients all at once into the dry ingredients. Stir the mixture briskly with a fork until all ingredients are just evenly moistened; do not overstir. The batter will look lumpy.
5. Fill each prepared muffin-pan cup two-thirds full

with the batter, using a large spoon and a rubber spatula to push the batter into the cups. Sprinkle the tops with a mixture of brown sugar and chopped pecans.

6. Bake the muffins in the preheated hot oven (400°) for 22 to 24 minutes or until lightly browned and a wooden pick inserted in the centers comes out clean. Remove the pan to a wire rack. Remove the muffins at once and serve piping hot.

Food for thought . . .

Quick breads are aptly named: they rely on baking powder, baking soda and eggs for leavening instead of yeast, so there is no waiting for yeast to proof or dough to rise. And, no kneading is required. Most quick breads can be mixed together in less than 15 minutes and baking times vary from 15 minutes for muffins to 1 hour for large, dense loaves.

QUICK BREAD TIPS

• *To prepare the ingredients ahead, mix the dry ingredients and liquid ingredients separately, then combine just before baking. Once the leavening agent comes in contact with the liquid, the leavening action begins and will be spent within a short period of time.*

• *Mix the batter gently but thoroughly with a fork or wooden spoon just until all the ingredients are evenly moistened.*

• *Prepare the entire recipe for muffins or quick-bread loaves and freeze what you don't use.*

• *You can freeze quick breads for up to 6 months. To thaw, heat the bread in an aluminum foil wrapping in a slow oven (325°) for about 25 minutes or until heated through.*

• *To store, allow freshly baked breads to cool in their pans for 10 minutes. Then remove to a wire rack to cool completely before wrapping in plastic wrap or aluminum foil.*

• *Add grated lemon, orange or lime rind to your favorite bread or muffin recipe for a little extra zest. Try about 2 teaspoons the first time around, then adjust according to your own taste.*

Swedish Limpa Muffins

Bake at 400° for 22 to 24 minutes.
Makes 10 muffins.

Nutrient Value Per Muffin: 128 calories, 3 g protein, 3 g fat, 23 g carbohydrate, 186 mg sodium, 30 mg cholesterol.

1   **cup buttermilk baking mix**
1   **cup rye flour**
2   **tablespoons firmly packed brown sugar**
2   **teaspoons caraway seeds**
1   **egg**
⅔   **cup milk**
2   **tablespoons molasses**
1   **teaspoon grated orange rind**
    Crystallized sugar for topping

1. Preheat the oven to hot (400°). Grease only the bottoms of ten 2½-inch muffin-pan cups, or use paper liners. (The ungreased sides allow the batter to climb and form gently rounded tops while baking.)
2. Stir together the baking mix, rye flour, brown sugar and caraway seeds in a large bowl until well mixed.
3. Lightly beat the egg in a small bowl. Stir in the milk, molasses and orange rind until thoroughly combined.
4. Pour the liquid ingredients all at once into the dry ingredients. Stir the mixture briskly with a fork, until all the ingredients are just evenly moistened; do not overstir. The batter will look lumpy.
5. Fill each prepared muffin-pan cup two-thirds full with the batter, using a large spoon and a rubber spatula to push the batter into the cups. Sprinkle the tops with a scattering of crystallized sugar.
6. Bake the muffins in the preheated hot oven (400°) for 22 to 24 minutes or until the tops are golden and a wooden pick inserted in the centers comes out clean. Remove the pan to a wire rack. Remove the muffins at once and serve piping hot.

Pumpernickel-Raisin Muffins

These muffins are particularly good when served with cream cheese, and they're superlative picnic fare.

Bake at 400° for 22 to 24 minutes.
Makes 12 muffins.

Nutrient Value Per Muffin: 156 calories, 3 g protein, 6 g fat, 24 g carbohydrate, 309 mg sodium, 26 mg cholesterol.

- ¾ **cup whole-wheat flour**
- ⅓ **cup rye flour**
- ⅓ **cup yellow cornmeal**
- ¼ **cup unsweetened cocoa powder**
- ¼ **cup lightly packed dark brown sugar**
- 3 **teaspoons baking powder**
- 1 **teaspoon salt**
- 1 **egg**
- 1 **cup milk**
- ¼ **cup vegetable oil**
- 2 **tablespoons molasses**
- ½ **cup golden raisins**

1. Preheat the oven to hot (400°). Grease only the bottoms of twelve 2½-inch muffin-pan cups, or use paper liners. (The ungreased sides allow the batter to climb and form gently rounded tops while baking.)
2. Stir together the whole-wheat and rye flours, cornmeal, cocoa, brown sugar, baking powder and salt in a large bowl until well mixed.
3. Lightly beat the egg in a small bowl. Stir in the milk, oil and molasses until thoroughly combined.
4. Pour the liquid ingredients all at once into the dry ingredients. Stir the mixture briskly with a fork until all the ingredients are just evenly moistened; do not overstir. Add the raisins; stir briefly to evenly distribute. The batter will look lumpy.
5. Fill each prepared muffin-pan cup two-thirds full with the batter, using a large spoon and a rubber spatula to push the batter into the cups.
6. Bake the muffins in the preheated hot oven (400°) for 22 to 24 minutes or until a wooden pick inserted in the centers comes out clean. Remove the muffins immediately from the pan to a wire rack. Serve piping hot.

WHOLE-WHEAT FLOUR

A coarse-textured flour ground from the entire kernel, whole-wheat flour has a small amount of gluten which results in baked goods heavier and denser than those made with all-purpose flour. For lighter baking results, mix the whole-wheat with a little all-purpose flour.

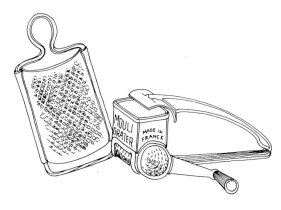

Cheddar-Corn Muffins

A delicious go-with to accent your favorite vegetable soup.

Bake at 400° for 25 minutes.
Makes 18 muffins.

Nutrient Value Per Muffin: 97 calories, 3 g protein, 5 g fat, 10 g carbohydrate, 181 mg sodium, 35 mg cholesterol.

- 1½ **cups yellow cornmeal**
- ½ **cup unsifted all-purpose flour**
- 2 **tablespoons sugar**
- 3 **teaspoons baking powder**
- ½ **teaspoon salt**
- 2 **eggs**
- 1½ **cups buttermilk**
- 1 **can (7 ounces) whole-kernel corn, drained**
- ½ **cup grated Cheddar cheese (2 ounces)**
- ⅓ **cup chopped green onion**
- ¼ **cup vegetable oil**
  Poppy seeds

1. Preheat the oven to hot (400°). Grease only the bottoms of eighteen 2½-inch muffin-pan cups, or use paper liners. (The ungreased sides allow the batter to climb and form gently rounded tops while baking.)
2. Stir together the cornmeal, flour, sugar, baking powder and salt in a large bowl until well mixed.

3. Lightly beat the eggs in a medium-size bowl. Stir in the buttermilk, corn, cheese, green onion and oil until well combined.
4. Pour the liquid ingredients all at once into the dry ingredients. Stir the mixture briskly with a fork until all the ingredients are just evenly moistened; do not overstir. The batter will look lumpy.
5. Fill each muffin-pan cup two-thirds full with the batter, using a large spoon and a rubber spatula to push the batter into the cups. Sprinkle the tops with the poppy seeds.
6. Bake the muffins in the preheated hot oven (400°) for 25 minutes or until the tops are golden brown and a wooden pick inserted in the centers comes out clean. Remove the pan to a wire rack. Remove the muffins at once and serve piping hot.

CULTURED BUTTERMILK POWDER

Dry buttermilk powder works the same as the liquid version to give baked goods a lighter, fluffier texture, and it offers the convenience and economy of being packaged in a shelf-stable form. To substitute the powder for the liquid in a recipe, mix ¼ cup powder for every 1 cup of liquid buttermilk, with the other dry ingredients. Then add 1 cup water when the recipe calls for the addition of the liquid buttermilk.

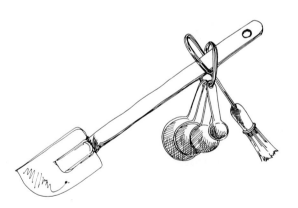

ADDING BAKING POWDER OR BAKING SODA

Be sure to thoroughly mix baking powder or baking soda with the other dry ingredients in the recipe by sifting together or stirring with a wire whisk for uniform leavening and texture.

Zucchini-Dill Muffins with Parmesan Cheese Tops

Yet another way to use up the end-of-the-summer zucchini surplus.

Bake at 400° for 22 to 24 minutes.
Makes 18 muffins.

Nutrient Value Per Muffin: 93 calories, 2 g protein, 4 g fat, 12 g carbohydrate, 210 mg sodium, 17 mg cholesterol.

1¾ **cups unsifted all-purpose flour**
  3 **tablespoons sugar**
  3 **teaspoons baking powder**
  1 **teaspoon salt**
  1 **egg**
 ¾ **cup milk**
 ¼ **cup vegetable oil**
  3 **tablespoons chopped fresh dill OR:**
    1 teaspoon dried dillweed
  1 **cup grated zucchini**
    Grated Parmesan cheese

1. Preheat the oven to hot (400°). Grease only the bottoms of eighteen 2½-inch muffin-pan cups, or use paper liners. (The ungreased sides allow the batter to climb and form gently rounded tops while baking.)
2. Stir together the flour, sugar, baking powder and salt in a large bowl until well mixed.
3. Lightly beat the egg in a medium-size bowl. Stir in the milk, oil, dill and grated zucchini until thoroughly combined.
4. Pour the liquid ingredients all at once into the dry ingredients. Stir the mixture briskly with a fork until all the ingredients are just evenly moistened; do not overstir. The batter will look lumpy.
5. Fill each prepared muffin-pan cup two-thirds full with the batter, using a large spoon and a rubber spatula to push the batter into the cups. Sprinkle the tops with the Parmesan cheese.
6. Bake the muffins in the preheated hot oven (400°) for 22 to 24 minutes or until the tops are golden brown and a wooden pick inserted in the centers comes out clean. Remove the pan to a wire rack. Remove the muffins at once and serve piping hot.

Chocolate Pecan Muffins

If you love chocolate, you'll want to make batches and batches of these chocolate muffins accented with orange.

Bake at 350° for 20 minutes.
Makes 2 dozen.

Nutrient Value Per Muffin: 190 calories, 3 g protein, 9 g fat, 27 g carbohydrate, 166 mg sodium, 11 mg cholesterol.

3	cups unsifted all-purpose flour
1	cup sugar
4	teaspoons baking powder
2	teaspoons pumpkin pie spice
1	teaspoon salt
1	package (6 ounces) semisweet chocolate pieces
½	cup chopped pecans
3	tablespoons grated orange rind
1	egg
1¼	cups orange juice
⅓	cup vegetable oil
	10X (confectioners') sugar
	Grated orange rind
	Whole pecans

1. Preheat the oven to moderate (350°). Grease bottoms and sides of 24 muffin-pan cups.
2. Sift together the flour, sugar, baking powder, pumpkin pie spice and salt into a large bowl. Add the chocolate pieces, pecans and orange rind and toss to blend well.
3. Beat the egg with a fork in a small bowl until foamy; stir in the orange juice and vegetable oil until blended.
4. Pour the egg mixture over the dry ingredients and stir with a fork, just until blended; do not overstir.
5. Spoon the batter into the prepared muffin-pan cups, dividing evenly.
6. Bake the muffins in the preheated moderate oven (350°) for 20 minutes or until a wooden pick inserted into the centers comes out clean. Remove the muffins from the pan to a wire rack. Sprinkle the tops with 10X sugar and garnish with the orange rind and a whole pecan.

Pineapple Whole-Wheat Muffins

Bake at 400° for 15 minutes.
Makes 12 muffins.

Nutrient Value Per Muffin: 126 calories, 4 g protein, 3 g fat, 22 g carbohydrate, 174 mg sodium, 23 mg cholesterol.

2	cups whole-wheat flour
½	cup instant nonfat dry milk powder
1	tablespoon baking powder
¼	teaspoon salt
1	can (8 ounces) crushed pineapple in its own juice
	Water
1	egg, slightly beaten
2	tablespoons safflower oil
2	tablespoons honey

1. Preheat the oven to hot (400°). Grease twelve 2½-inch muffin-pan cups.
2. Combine the whole-wheat flour, dry milk, baking powder and salt in a medium-size bowl; stir to mix well.
3. Drain the pineapple juice into a 2-cup measure. Add enough water to make 1 cup. Mix in the egg, oil and honey. Make a well in the center of the dry ingredients. Pour in the liquid mixture all at once. Stir gently just until the flour is moistened. Fold in the drained pineapple.
4. Spoon the mixture into the prepared muffin-pan cups, dividing equally.
5. Bake the muffins in the preheated hot oven (400°) for 15 minutes or until a wooden pick inserted in the centers comes out clean. Serve the muffins warm.

Summer Muffins

These lemony muffins are a "bright" taste for summer, or the gray days of winter.

Bake at 400° for 25 minutes.
Makes 12 muffins.

Nutrient Value Per Muffin: 184 calories, 4 g protein, 11 g fat, 18 g carbohydrate, 195 mg sodium, 39 mg cholesterol.

1¾	cups sifted all-purpose flour
3	tablespoons sugar
2½	teaspoons baking powder
½	teaspoon salt

1 **egg**
¾ **cup milk**
⅓ **cup unsalted butter, melted**
½ **teaspoon lemon extract**
⅛ **teaspoon vanilla**
¾ **cup chopped unblanched almonds**
2 **teaspoons grated fresh lemon rind**

1. Preheat the oven to hot (400°). Grease the bottoms only of twelve 2½-inch muffin-pan cups.
2. Sift together the flour, sugar, baking powder and salt into a large bowl.
3. Lightly beat the egg in a small bowl. Beat in the milk, butter, lemon extract and vanilla. Stir in the nuts and lemon rind. Pour all at once into the flour mixture. Stir briskly with a fork just until all the ingredients are evenly moistened; do not overstir. The batter will look lumpy.
4. Fill each prepared muffin-pan cup two-thirds full with the batter, using a large spoon and a rubber spatula to push the batter into the cups.
5. Bake the muffins in the preheated hot oven (400°) for 25 minutes or until golden brown and a wooden pick inserted in the centers comes out clean. Remove the pan to a wire rack. Loosen the muffins with a spatula and remove from the pan at once to prevent steaming. Serve the muffins piping hot.

Wheat and Cornmeal Rolls

A flavorful yeast-risen dinner roll that takes less time than you'd expect. The secret: fast-rising yeast.

Bake at 400° for 15 minutes.
Makes 24 rolls.

Nutrient Value Per Roll: 157 calories, 4 g protein, 5 g fat, 24 g carbohydrate, 143 mg sodium, 35 mg cholesterol.

1½ **cups water**
½ **cup yellow cornmeal**
1 **cup milk**
½ **cup (1 stick) butter**
¼ **cup honey**
2 **cups unsifted whole-wheat flour**
2¾ to 3 **cups unsifted all-purpose flour**
2 **packages fast-rising dry yeast**
1 **teaspoon salt**
2 **eggs**
2 **tablespoons water**

1. Combine the water and the cornmeal in a medium-size saucepan. Bring to boiling over medium heat, stirring constantly. Cook until thickened and bubbly, about 4 minutes. Stir in the milk, butter and honey. Remove from the heat; cool to very warm, about 125°.
2. Combine the whole-wheat flour, 1 cup of the all-purpose flour, the yeast and salt in the large bowl of a heavy-duty electric mixer.* At low speed, beat the cornmeal mixture into the dry ingredients just until well mixed. Increase the speed to medium; beat until the dough is smooth and elastic, about 5 minutes. (Or knead the dough by hand on a lightly floured board.)
3. Meanwhile, separate 1 of the eggs, placing the yolk in a small bowl or cup; reserve. Add the egg white and the remaining whole egg to the dough. Beat 2 minutes longer.
4. Stir in enough of the remaining all-purpose flour with a wooden spoon to make a soft dough; the dough should mound when dropped from the spoon. Cover with greased wax paper and a towel. Let rise in a warm place, away from drafts, for 30 to 40 minutes or until doubled in volume.
5. Preheat the oven to hot (400°). Grease twenty-four 2½-inch muffin-pan cups.**
6. Stir the dough down. Place about 2½ rounded tablespoons of the dough in each muffin-pan cup, mounding in the center. Let rise 15 minutes.
7. Beat the reserved egg yolk with the 2 tablespoons water. Lightly brush the tops of the rolls with the yolk mixture.
8. Bake the rolls in the preheated hot oven (400°) for 15 minutes or until a wooden pick inserted in the centers comes out clean. Remove the rolls from the pans immediately. Serve warm.

Notes: *If you don't have a heavy-duty mixer, use a regular mixer to combine the dry ingredients and the cornmeal mixture. Do the remaining mixing and kneading by hand.

**The muffins may be baked in 2 batches if you're short on muffin pans. Refrigerate half the dough in a bowl with plastic wrap pressed directly against the surface while you bake the first 12 muffins.

To Make Ahead: Bake the rolls, then cool on wire racks. Wrap the rolls in aluminum foil, or enclose in plastic bags. Freeze. To reheat, wrap the frozen rolls in aluminum foil. Bake in a preheated hot oven (400°) for about 15 minutes, unwrapping the rolls during the last few minutes to crisp the crust.

No-Yeast Stollen; Coriander Gingerbread; and spicy Cheese Twists (page 20).

No-Yeast Stollen

This bread improves with age, so it's an ideal gift to mail to relatives or friends at holiday time.

Bake at 350° for 40 to 50 minutes.
Makes 1 large loaf (about 20 slices).

Nutrient Value Per Slice: 170 calories, 3 g protein, 7 g fat, 23 g carbohydrate, 230 mg sodium, 32 mg cholesterol.

2½ **cups unsifted all-purpose flour**
¾ **cup sugar**
3 **teaspoons baking powder**
½ **teaspoon ground cardamom**
½ **teaspoon salt**
½ **cup (1 stick) butter, well chilled**
1 **cup creamy cottage cheese**
1 **egg**
1 **tablespoon vanilla**
½ **cup raisins**
3 **tablespoons butter, melted**

1. Preheat the oven to moderate (350°). Grease a baking sheet.
2. Sift together the flour, sugar, baking powder, cardamom and salt into a large bowl.
3. Cut the butter into the flour mixture with a pastry blender or 2 knives until coarse crumbs form.
4. Mix together the cottage cheese, egg and vanilla in a medium-size bowl. Add to the flour mixture along with the raisins. Stir the mixture until a dough forms. Turn out onto a lightly floured board. Knead about 10 turns, adding more flour, if necessary, to prevent sticking. The dough should be soft, not stiff.
5. Roll the dough into a 10-inch circle. Brush with 1 tablespoon of the melted butter. Fold the dough in half just off center. Place on a greased baking sheet.
6. Bake the stollen in the preheated moderate oven (350°) for 40 to 50 minutes or until golden brown. Brush with the remaining 2 tablespoons melted butter while still hot. Cool on a wire rack.
7. Wrap the stollen in aluminum foil or plastic wrap when completely cooled. Store at room temperature for 2 days before serving. Sprinkle with 10X (confectioners') sugar just before serving, if you wish. The stollen will keep for up to 1 week.

Coriander Gingerbread

The loaf becomes more flavorful as it ages.

Bake at 300° for 45 to 55 minutes.
Makes 4 small loaves (8 slices each).

Nutrient Value Per Slice: 114 calories, 2 g protein, 5 g fat, 16 g carbohydrate, 99 mg sodium, 37 mg cholesterol.

¾ **cup (1½ sticks) butter, softened**
¾ **cup sugar**
½ **cup light molasses**
3 **eggs**
2½ **cups unsifted all-purpose flour**
2 **teaspoons ground ginger**
2 **teaspoons ground coriander**
1½ **teaspoons baking powder**
¼ **teaspoon baking soda**
¼ **teaspoon salt**
½ **cup lowfat buttermilk**

1. Preheat the oven to slow (300°). Grease four 5¾ x 3½ x 2-inch disposable aluminum baby-loaf pans.
2. Beat together the butter and sugar in a large bowl until light and fluffy, about 2 minutes. Beat in the molasses until well blended. Add the eggs, one at a time, beating well after each addition.
3. Sift together the flour, ginger, coriander, baking powder, baking soda and salt into a medium-size bowl. Add half of the flour mixture to the egg-butter mixture. Beat with an electric mixer at low speed just until mixed. Add in the buttermilk at low speed. Add the remaining flour mixture and mix until just slightly blended; do not overbeat. Pour the batter into the prepared baby-loaf pans.
4. Bake the breads in the preheated slow oven (300°) for 45 to 55 minutes or until a wooden pick inserted in the centers comes out clean. Cool the breads in the pans on a wire rack. The gingerbread can be stored, tightly wrapped in the pans with plastic wrap, for up to 1 week.

BAKING SODA NEEDS ACID

Baking soda (bicarbonate of soda) works when combined with an acid substance, such as baking powder mixtures, or with an acidic liquid, such as buttermilk, sour milk, chocolate, corn syrup or molasses.

Cheese Twists

Bake at 400° for 10 to 12 minutes.
Makes 4½ dozen.

Nutrient Value Per Twist: 26 calories, 1 g protein, 2 g fat, 2 g carbohydrate, 34 mg sodium, 5 mg cholesterol.

---

1   **cup unsifted all-purpose flour**
¼   **teaspoon salt**
¼   **teaspoon ground hot red pepper**
5   **tablespoons butter, well chilled (margarine won't work)**
4   **ounces Cheddar cheese, shredded (about 1 cup)**
2   **tablespoons ice water**
1   **teaspoon lemon juice**

1. Preheat the oven to hot (400°).
2. Sift together the flour, salt and pepper into a large bowl. Cut in the butter with a pastry blender or 2 knives until coarse crumbs are formed. Add the cheese; toss to combine.
3. Combine the water and the lemon juice in a small bowl. Add to the flour mixture, stirring with a fork until the mixture forms a dough and comes together. Add another 1 teaspoon of water, if necessary, to make the dough hold together.
4. Divide the dough in half. Keep one half covered. Roll the other half out on a lightly floured surface into a 10 x 7-inch rectangle. Cut the dough in half to form two 7 x 5-inch rectangles. Cut each half into fourteen 5 x ½-inch strips. Twist each strip 3 or 4 times. Place the twists on an ungreased baking sheet.
5. Bake the twists in the preheated hot oven (400°) for 10 to 12 minutes or until golden brown. Cool the twists on a wire rack. Repeat with the remaining dough.
6. The twists can be stored in an airtight container at room temperature for up to 1 week.

Garlic Bread

Flavorful crusty bread adds a finishing touch to barbecued or broiled meats.

Bake at 350° for 15 to 20 minutes.
Makes 8 servings.

Nutrient Value Per Serving: 216 calories, 5 g protein, 7 g fat, 32 g carbohydrate, 388 mg sodium, 17 mg cholesterol.

---

1   **loaf French, Italian or sourdough bread**
¼   **cup (½ stick) butter or margarine**
1   **clove garlic, mashed**

1. Preheat the oven to moderate (350°).
2. Cut the bread into ½-inch-thick slices and keep the slices in order.
3. Melt the butter or margarine and garlic in a small saucepan. Brush the butter generously over each slice of bread. Reshape the loaf on a large sheet of heavy-duty aluminum foil; wrap the loaf.
4. Heat the bread in the preheated moderate oven (350°) until hot and crisp around the edges, 15 to 20 minutes. Loosen the foil packet for serving, but keep the bread in the foil to keep warm.

Oatmeal Pancakes

Delightful alone or served with maple syrup or warm honey.

Makes 8 four-inch pancakes.

Nutrient Value Per Pancake: 94 calories, 4 g protein, 3 g fat, 12 g carbohydrate, 119 mg sodium, 35 mg cholesterol.

1½ **cups rolled oats**
½   **teaspoon baking powder**
¼   **teaspoon salt**
1   **egg**
1   **cup skim milk**
1   **tablespoon corn oil margarine**

1. Place the oats in a container of an electric blender or food processor. Whirl for 1 minute, or until the consistency of flour. Combine the oat flour, baking powder and salt in a large mixing bowl.
2. Combine the egg and the skim milk in a separate bowl. Pour the liquid into the dry ingredients and mix until just moist.
3. Heat a cast-iron skillet or a non-stick pan and add the margarine; melt; spread on the pan with paper toweling. Spoon about 3 tablespoons of the batter into the pan for each pancake.
4. Cook over medium heat until bubbles form on the surface and the underside is lightly browned. Flip and cook until the other side is lightly browned. Keep warm and repeat with the remaining batter.

THE PATH TO PERFECT PANCAKES

- *Mix the liquid ingredients quickly into the dry ingredients; do not overbeat. Lumps are OK.*
- *Be sure your griddle is hot enough. To test, sprinkle several drops of water on the griddle; if they sputter and dance about, you're ready to go.*
- *For equal-size pancakes, measure the batter onto the griddle. A scant ¼ cup makes a 4-inch round. Since the batter spreads, be sure to leave enough space between the pancakes.*
- *When bubbles appear on the top sides, but before they break, and the undersides are golden and puffy, flip over with a wide spatula. The second side will take half as long as the first, and will never be as evenly browned.*

Potato Pancakes

Serve with roast or grilled meats, or with a dab of yogurt or sour cream as a warming winter brunch dish.

Makes 6 large servings.

Nutrient Value Per Serving: 168 calories, 5 g protein, 7 g fat, 23 g carbohydrate, 30 mg sodium, 91 mg cholesterol.

4 **large baking potatoes (about 2 pounds), pared**
1 **small onion**
2 **eggs**
2 **tablespoons all-purpose flour**
   Salt and pepper to taste
   Dash ground nutmeg
   Vegetable oil for skillet

1. Grate the potatoes and the onion into a large bowl. Add the eggs; beat until well blended. Stir in the flour, and add the salt, pepper and nutmeg to taste.
2. Oil an electric skillet, griddle or large, heavy skillet. Heat the electric skillet to 375°, or the griddle or skillet over medium-high heat. Drop the batter by tablespoons onto the hot skillet. Cook the pancakes for about 3 minutes per side until golden brown. Remove the pancakes with a spatula to a platter; keep warm. Repeat with the remaining batter to make a total of 12 to 14 pancakes.

Tortilla Foldups

For a Southwestern change of pace, offer dinner guests a basket of warm tortillas instead of bread or chips alongside your chili, beef stew, grilled steak or spicy chicken curry.

Warm at 250° until serving time.
Makes enough for 16 servings.

Nutrient Value Per Serving: 214 calories, 6 g protein, 4 g fat, 39 g carbohydrate, 0 mg sodium, 0 mg cholesterol.

3 **packages (1 dozen each) flour tortillas**

1. Preheat the oven to very slow (250°).
2. Separate the tortillas, one package at a time, into individual tortillas.
3. Heat a flat griddle over medium heat until very warm, but not too hot.
4. Place the tortillas, one at a time, on the griddle and heat, 30 seconds to a side. Fold the tortillas and lay between layers of dampened paper toweling on a cookie sheet.
5. Keep warm in the preheated very slow oven (250°) until serving time. Arrange the folded tortillas in a napkin-lined basket and serve warm.

Y·E·A·S·T B·R·E·A·D·S

Homemade treats, from bottom: Sunshine Carrot Bread; Almond-Cheese Horseshoe (page 24); and Kielbasa Ring (page 25).

Sunshine Carrot Bread

The addition of orange juice gives this carrot bread a special flavor. Try a little toasted for breakfast.

Bake at 350° for 35 to 45 minutes.
Makes 2 loaves (10 slices each).

Nutrient Value Per Slice: 157 calories, 4 g protein, 1 g fat, 32 g carbohydrate, 121 mg sodium, 41 mg cholesterol.

- ½   **cup warm water (105° to 115°)**
- 2   **envelopes active dry yeast**
- ⅓   **cup sugar**
- 1   **tablespoon grated orange rind**
- ½   **cup orange juice, at room temperature**
- 1   **cup shredded carrots**
- ½   **cup raisins**
- 2   **teaspoons ground cinnamon**
- 1   **teaspoon salt**
- 2   **eggs**
- 4½   **cups unsifted all-purpose flour**
- 1   **egg yolk**
- 1   **tablespoon water**
  Orange Glaze (recipe follows)

1. Pour the warm water into a large bowl. Sprinkle the yeast and 1 tablespoon of the sugar over the water; stir to dissolve the yeast. Let the mixture stand for 5 minutes.
2. Add the remaining sugar, orange rind, orange juice, carrots, raisins, cinnamon, salt, eggs and 2 cups of the flour. Beat with an electric mixer at low speed until thoroughly blended. Increase the speed to medium and beat for 2 more minutes. Mix in 2 cups more of the flour, ½ cup at a time.
3. Turn the dough out onto a lightly floured surface. Knead about 5 minutes, adding up to ½ cup of the remaining flour, until the dough is smooth and elastic. Place the dough in an oiled large bowl; turn to coat. Cover with oiled wax paper and a towel. Let rise in a warm place, away from drafts, until doubled in volume, about 1 hour.
4. Punch the dough down; knead briefly. Divide the dough into 6 equal portions. Shape each into a ball. Place 3 balls side by side in each of 2 greased 8½ x 4½-inch loaf pans. Cover with oiled wax paper and a towel. Let rise in a warm place, away from drafts, until doubled in volume, about 45 minutes.
5. Combine the egg yolk and the water in a small cup. Brush the mixture evenly over the tops of the loaves.
6. Preheat the oven to moderate (350°).
7. Bake the bread in the preheated moderate oven (350°) for 35 to 45 minutes or until golden brown. Remove the breads from the pans and cool on wire racks. Drizzle the top of the bread with the Orange Glaze.

Orange Glaze: Place ½ cup *un*sifted 10X (confectioners') sugar in a small bowl. Gradually stir in 2 to 3 teaspoons orange juice until the mixture is a good glazing consistency.

WHAT IS ALL-PURPOSE FLOUR?

It's a blend of soft and hard flours, the latter containing a greater amount of tougher gluten which produces a more elastic and porous result. Bleached and unbleached all-purpose flours may be used interchangeably, but remember unbleached has a higher nutritional value.

KNEADING YEAST DOUGH

When the dough is first turned out onto the work surface, it will be sticky. Reflouring your hands and the surface as you work the dough will help reduce the stickiness. Kneading develops the gluten in flour and causes the dough to become smooth and elastic. Avoid overkneading, however, which results in coarse-textured breads.

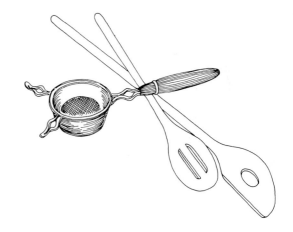

Almond-Cheese Horseshoe

The almond-flavored cream cheese filling is especially delicious when this coffeecake is served warm.

Bake at 375° for 15 to 20 minutes.
Makes 2 loaves (8 slices each).

Nutrient Value Per Slice: 383 calories, 7 g protein, 19 g fat, 47 g carbohydrate, 222 mg sodium, 98 mg cholesterol.

½ cup warm water (105° to 115°)
2 envelopes active dry yeast
½ cup sugar
½ teaspoon salt
½ cup (1 stick) butter or margarine, softened
2 eggs
3½ to 4 cups unsifted all-purpose flour
**   Almond-Cheese Filling (recipe follows)**
**   Glaze (recipe follows)**

1. Pour the warm water into a large bowl. Sprinkle the yeast over the water; stir to dissolve the yeast. Let the mixture stand 5 minutes.
2. Add the sugar, salt, butter, eggs and 2 cups of the flour. Beat with an electric mixer at low speed until thoroughly blended. Increase the speed to medium and beat 2 more minutes. Mix in 1 cup more of the flour, ½ cup at a time.
3. Turn the dough out onto a lightly floured surface. Knead the dough about 5 minutes, adding up to 1 cup of the remaining flour, until the dough is smooth and elastic. Place the dough in an oiled large bowl; turn to coat. Cover with oiled wax paper and a towel. Let rise in a warm place, away from drafts, until the dough is doubled in volume, about 1 hour.
4. Punch the dough down; knead briefly. Divide the dough in half. Roll one half into a 15 x 10-inch rectangle. Spread the dough with half of the Almond-Cheese Filling, leaving a ½-inch border on all sides. Starting with a long side, roll the dough up jelly-roll fashion. Tuck and seal the ends; seal the long seam. Place the roll, seam-side down, on a greased cookie sheet. Shape into a horseshoe. Repeat with the remaining dough and filling. Cut slits with scissors through the top of the dough at 2-inch intervals. Cover the dough with oiled wax paper and a towel. Let rise in a warm place, away from drafts, until doubled in volume, about 45 minutes.
5. Preheat the oven to moderate (375°).
6. Bake the horseshoe in the preheated moderate oven (375°) for 15 to 20 minutes or until golden brown. Cool slightly on a wire rack.
7. Drizzle the top of the horseshoe with the Glaze.

Almond-Cheese Filling: Combine 2 packages (8 ounces each) softened cream cheese, ½ cup sugar, ½ cup almond paste (not marzipan) and 1 egg yolk in a food processor or an electric mixer. Mix until smooth. Refrigerate the filling until you are ready to use it.

Glaze: Combine 1 cup *un*sifted 10X (confectioners') sugar, ½ teaspoon vanilla and ⅛ teaspoon almond extract in a small bowl. Gradually mix in 1 to 2 tablespoons milk until the mixture is a good spreading consistency.

BREAD DONENESS CHECK

Check breads for doneness at the end of the suggested baking time — they should be nicely browned and sound hollow when lightly tapped on top. Remove the loaves from the pans so they do not become soggy. Cool completely on wire racks.

HINTS FOR BETTER BREADS

- *Use the pan size called for in the recipe. Too large a pan will yield a flat bread, and too small a pan will cause the dough to overflow.*
- *The material the pan is made of will affect the baking time. Uncoated metal pans need longer baking. Black metal pans will cause breads to brown quicker. Glass and enamel pans need a lower oven temperature; lower the oven temperature in the recipe by 25°.*
- *For a shiny crust, brush the dough with an egg beaten with a little water.*

Kielbasa Ring

A whole kielbasa is hidden in the center of this golden tube bread.

Bake at 375° for 45 minutes.
Makes one 10-inch tube bread (12 slices).

Nutrient Value Per Slice: 375 calories, 13 g protein, 19 g fat, 39 g carbohydrate, 612 mg sodium, 117 mg cholesterol.

1   pound Polish kielbasa sausage, about
    18 inches long
    Water for cooking sausage
⅓   cup butter or margarine
1   cup water
1   tablespoon sugar
2   envelopes active dry yeast
⅓   cup instant nonfat dry milk powder
1   teaspoon salt
3   eggs
4½   cups unsifted all-purpose flour
1   egg yolk
1   tablespoon water

1. Arrange the sausage in a circle in an 8-inch skillet. Cover the sausage with water. Bring to boiling. Lower the heat and simmer for 5 minutes. Let the sausage cool in the skillet. Drain the sausage.
2. Combine the butter and the 1 cup water in a small saucepan. Heat until small bubbles appear around the edge of the pan (butter need not be melted). Pour the liquid into a large bowl. Mix in the sugar. Cool the mixture to 105° to 115°.
3. Sprinkle the yeast over the warm water mixture; stir to dissolve the yeast. Let stand for 5 minutes. Add the dry milk, salt, eggs and 2 cups of the flour. Beat with an electric mixer at low speed until thoroughly blended. Increase the speed to medium and beat 2 more minutes. Mix in 2 more cups of the flour, ½ cup at a time.
4. Turn the dough out onto a lightly floured surface. Knead about 5 minutes, adding up to ½ cup of the remaining flour, until the dough is smooth and elastic. Place the dough in an oiled large bowl; turn to coat. Cover with oiled wax paper and a towel. Let rise in a warm place, away from drafts, until doubled in volume, about 1 hour.
5. Punch the dough down; knead briefly. Divide the dough in half. Cut away one-quarter of one-half of the dough to use for making the ropes for the top of the bread. Roll the largest piece of dough into a 13-inch circle; cut a 2-inch cross in the center. Place the dough in a greased 10-inch tube pan, fitting the cross over the tube and the dough up the sides of the pan. Set the sausage in the pan over the dough. Roll the second largest piece of dough into a 9-inch circle; cut a 1½-inch cross in the center. Place over the sausage; seal the edges together.
6. Divide the remaining portion of the dough in half. Roll each half into two 26-inch long ropes. Twist the ropes together.
7. Mix together the egg yolk and the 1 tablespoon water in a small bowl. Brush the top of the dough in the pan with the egg mixture. Arrange the rope in a circle on top of the bread around the edge of the pan, stretching if necessary so the ends meet; pinch the ends together. Brush the rope with the mixture. Cover with greased wax paper and a towel. Let rise in a warm place, away from drafts, until the dough is doubled in volume, about 45 minutes.
8. Preheat the oven to moderate (375°).
9. Bake the bread in the preheated moderate oven (375°) for 45 minutes or until golden. Unmold the bread onto a wire rack. Invert the bread, right-side up. Serve warm or at room temperature.

TO SIFT OR NOT TO SIFT

Most commercial brands of flour come presifted from the manufacturer, making additional sifting unnecessary in most cases. Some of our recipes indicate additional sifting to produce a lighter product. Do not sift unless the recipe specifically calls for it.

Almond and Apricot Family Tea Ring

Delicious for breakfast or with afternoon tea.

Bake at 325° for 30 to 40 minutes.
Makes 1 coffee cake (14 slices).

Nutrient Value Per Slice: 322 calories, 7 g protein, 10 g fat, 54 g carbohydrate, 185 mg sodium, 25 mg cholesterol.

1 **cup warm water (105° to 115°)**
1 **envelope active dry yeast**
⅓ **cup instant nonfat dry milk powder**
¼ **cup sugar**
1 **teaspoon salt**
1 **egg**
¼ **cup vegetable shortening**
3½ **cups unsifted all-purpose flour**
   Almond Filling (recipe follows)
   Cooked Apricots (recipe follows)
1 **tablespoon brown sugar**
½ **teaspoon ground cinnamon**
   Almond Icing (recipe follows)
   Sliced almonds for garnish (optional)

1. Pour the warm water into a large bowl. Sprinkle the yeast over the water; stir to dissolve the yeast. Let the mixture stand for 5 minutes. Add the dry milk, sugar, salt, egg, shortening and 2 cups of the flour. Beat with an electric mixer at low speed until thoroughly blended. Increase mixer speed to medium and beat for 2 minutes. Mix in 1 more cup of the flour, ½ cup at a time.
2. Turn the dough out onto a lightly floured surface. Knead the dough for 5 minutes, adding up to ½

cup of the remaining flour, until the dough is smooth and elastic. Place the dough in a large oiled bowl; turn the dough to coat with the oil. Cover with oiled wax paper and a towel. Let rise in a warm place, away from drafts, until doubled in volume, about 1 hour.

3. Punch the dough down; knead briefly. Roll into a 16 x 12-inch rectangle. Spread the Almond Filling lengthwise down half of the dough. Sprinkle the other half of the dough with the Cooked Apricots. Combine the brown sugar and cinnamon in a small bowl; sprinkle the mixture evenly over all the dough.
4. Starting with a long side, roll up the dough jelly-roll fashion; seal the long seam. Form the tube of dough into a circle, sealing the ends together. Place the circle, seam-side down, on a greased cookie sheet. Using scissors, cut slashes two-thirds through the dough at 1-inch intervals around the outside of the circle. Turn each section cut-side up. Cover the dough with greased wax paper and a towel. Let rise in a warm place, away from drafts, until doubled in volume, about 45 minutes.
5. Preheat the oven to slow (325°).
6. Bake the ring in the preheated slow oven (325°) for 30 to 40 minutes or until golden brown on top. Cool the ring on a wire rack.
7. Frost the top with the Almond Icing and sprinkle with sliced almonds, if you wish.

Almond Filling: Combine ½ cup almond paste (not marzipan), ¼ cup 10X (confectioners') sugar, ¼ cup ground almonds and 2 tablespoons heavy cream in a food processor. Whirl until smooth.

Cooked Apricots: Combine 1 cup chopped dried apricots and ½ cup of water in a small saucepan. Simmer, covered, until the apricots are very soft, about 10 mintues. Drain and let cool.

Almond Icing: Combine 1 cup 10X (confectioners') sugar, 1 tablespoon soft butter and ½ teaspoon almond extract in a small bowl. Gradually mix in 1 to 2 tablespoons milk until the icing is a good spreading consistency.

HOW TO KNEAD AND SHAPE BREAD

1. Turn soft dough out on a floured board. (Place a damp towel under the board to prevent it from moving.) Flour hands lightly, then pat dough to flatten slightly. Begin to knead this way. Pick up the edge of the dough with your fingers and fold over toward you.

2. Push the dough away from you with the heels of both hands. If the dough sticks to the board, have a metal spatula handy to scrape the board clean; then re-flour and continue.

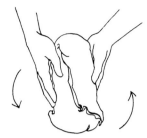

3. Give the dough a quarter turn, then repeat folding, pushing, turning. As you knead, you will develop your own speed. You'll find that well-kneaded bread dough is satiny, elastic and smooth.

4. An easy way to determine when dough has doubled in volume: Press the dough flat in a bowl, mark its level, then remove the dough. Fill the bowl with water to double the first mark; mark the level.

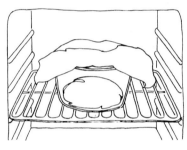

5. For a warm, draft-free place to let dough rise, use the oven with the door closed. If the oven is electric, warm to 200°, then turn off and let cool for 5 minutes. If gas, the pilot light will keep the dough warm with oven door ajar.

6. To shape a handsome loaf of bread: Roll or pat the dough out to a rectangle with the short side equal to the length of a bread pan. Roll up the dough, in jelly-roll style, pressing the turns firmly.

7. When the loaf has been shaped, make sure the dough is even on both ends. Then, with your fingers, pinch long seam firmly — to seal and keep from unrolling. Put in the pan, with the seam on the bottom.

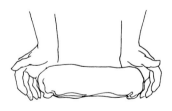

8. How to smooth the end of the loaf: Press the dough down on each end of the loaf with the sides of your hands. Tuck the thin strips formed under the loaf. Lift the loaf to the pan without stretching.

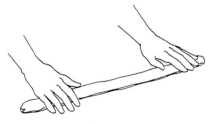

9. To shape a long loaf of bread: Roll up, in jelly-roll style, pinching the seam, as in Fig. 7. Then, with the palms of your hands, taper the ends by rolling the loaf back and forth on a board.

HOW TO SHAPE YEAST ROLLS

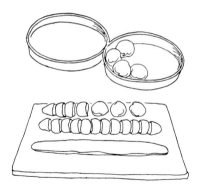

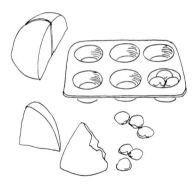

Pan Rolls: Divide the dough into three equal parts and shape each into a fat roll, 12 inches long. Slice each roll crosswise every inch; roll the slices into balls; place ¼ inch apart in greased 9-inch-round layer-cake pans.

Parker House Rolls: Divide the dough in three equal parts; roll, one part at a time, on a floured board into a circle 9 inches across. Cut into rounds with a lightly floured, 2½-inch biscuit cutter; brush each round with softened butter or margarine, make a crease across each slightly to one side of center, then fold the smaller "half" over the larger, forming half-moons, and place on greased baking sheets 1 inch apart. Pinch the edges lightly to seal.

Cloverleaf Rolls: Divide the dough into four equal parts, then working with one part at a time, pinch off small pieces of dough; shape into balls about the size of marbles. Place three balls of dough in each cup of greased muffin pans, forming "three-leaf clovers."

Pinwheels: Divide the dough into three equal parts and roll, one part at a time, on a floured board into a 16 x 8-inch rectangle. Spread with softened butter or margarine, and, if you like, cinnamon-sugar, jam or other filling. Roll up from the long side, jelly-roll fashion; slice 1-inch thick. Place, cut-sides up, in greased muffin-pan cups.

Quick Cloverleafs: Pinch off pieces of the dough and shape into balls slightly larger than golf balls. Place in greased muffin-pan cups, then with kitchen shears, snip a cross into the top of each roll, forming "four-leaf clovers."

Fans-Tans: Divide the dough into three equal parts and roll each part on a floured board into a 15 x 9-inch rectangle; cut crosswise into strips 1½ inches wide, then make a stack by piling 6 strips on top of one another. Cut the stack crosswise into squares and place, cut-side down, in greased muffin-pan cups.

Raisin-Orange Bread

Bake at 375° for 35 minutes.
Makes 2 loaves (12 slices).

Nutrient Value Per Slice: 393 calories, 12 g protein, 7 g fat, 73 g carbohydrate, 493 mg sodium, 59 mg cholesterol.

- **4 to 5 cups unsifted bread flour**
- **2 teaspoons salt**
- **2 envelopes active dry yeast**
- **1 teaspoon ground allspice**
- **½ teaspoon ground cardamom**
- **1 cup orange juice**
- **½ cup honey**
- **¼ cup (½ stick) butter**
- **1 cup creamy cottage cheese**
- **Grated zest of 1 orange**
- **2 eggs, slightly beaten**
- **1 cup whole-wheat flour**
- **½ cup rolled oats**
- **1 cup raisins**
- **Confectioners' Glaze (optional; recipe follows)**

1. Combine 2 cups of the bread flour, salt, yeast, allspice and cardamom in a large bowl until well mixed.
2. Heat the orange juice, honey, butter, cottage cheese and zest in a small saucepan until very warm. Add the warm liquid and the eggs to the flour mixture. Beat with an electric mixer at low speed until the ingredients are moistened. Increase the speed to medium and beat for 3 minutes. Stir in by hand the whole-wheat flour, oats, raisins and enough of the bread flour to form a stiff dough.
3. Turn the dough out onto a floured surface. Knead until smooth and elastic, about 10 minutes. Place the dough in a greased bowl; turn to coat. Cover with greased wax paper and a towel. Let rise in a warm place, away from drafts, until the dough is doubled in volume.
4. Punch the dough down. Divide in half. Cover with greased wax paper and a towel. Let rest for 15 minutes.
5. Shape each half into a loaf. Place each in a greased 9 x 5-inch loaf pan. Cover and let rise until doubled in volume.
6. Preheat the oven to moderate (375°).
7. Bake the bread in the preheated moderate oven (375°) for about 35 minutes or until browned and the bread sounds hollow when tapped with fingertips. Remove the breads from the pans and cool completely on a wire rack.
8. Drizzle the tops of the breads with the

Confectioners' Glaze, if you wish.

Confectioners' Glaze: Place 1 cup *un*sifted 10X (confectioners') sugar in a small bowl. Gradually stir in 1 to 2 tablespoons milk until the mixture is a good spreading consistency.

FLOUR RANGE IN BREAD RECIPES

Many bread recipes indicate a range of flour since the results will be affected by several variables — the type and brand of flour, the moisture in the flour and in the air, the heat of the kitchen, the size of the eggs and the vigor with which the bread is kneaded.

Food for thought . . .

Yeasts are actually tiny plants — an estimated 3200 billion to the pound. They feed on sugar and produce two products: alcohol, which gives a "yeasty flavor;" and the gas carbon dioxide which causes dough to rise.

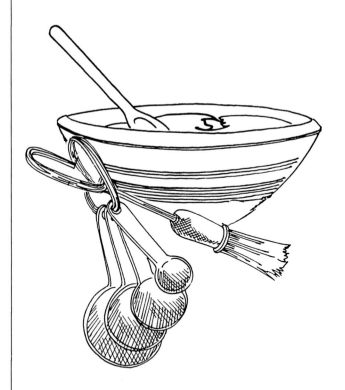

YEAST POINTERS

Active dry yeast is a granular form of yeast that comes packaged in an airtight, moisture-proof envelope (1 scant tablespoon) and 4-ounce vacuum-packed jars. Store in a cool place for up to 6 months, or in the refrigerator for a bit longer. To be sure your yeast has retained its freshness and power, use before the date indicated on the envelope. To activate, dry yeast needs a warm liquid, 105° to 115°.

TO TEST DRY YEAST FOR FRESHNESS

Add a small amount of sugar to the yeast while it is dissolving in the warm liquid. Within 10 minutes, the liquid will be bubbly — if not, start with another envelope of yeast.

FAST-RISING DRY YEAST

Using this granular dry yeast in bread recipes will decrease the dough rising time by one-third and in some cases by one-half. To substitute fast-rising yeast for regular active dry, keep the following in mind:

● *Always include water in the ingredients. If your recipe calls for liquid with no water included, decrease the amount of liquid by ¼ cup per envelope of fast-rising yeast used, and substitute an equal amount of water.*

● *No need to dissolve the yeast in liquid first. Combine the yeast with about two-thirds of the flour and the other dry ingredients.*

● *Fast-rising dry yeast requires a hotter liquid than regular to activate. Be sure to heat the liquid and solid or liquid fats (but not the eggs!) until hot to the touch, 130°.*

● *Stir the hot liquids into the dry ingredients (including the yeast). Blend at low speed with an electric mixer; then beat at medium speed for 3 minutes. Stir in enough of the remaining flour to make a soft dough.*

● *Follow the recipe directions as if you were using regular active dry yeast, for kneading and rising, but start checking the dough halfway through the suggested rising time.*

"Dad's" Frosted Whole-Wheat Raisin Bread

This bread makes delicious toast!

Bake at 325° for 50 minutes.
Makes 1 loaf (16 slices).

Nutrient Value Per Slice: 187 calories, 5 g protein, 2 g fat, 38 g carbohydrate, 156 mg sodium, 18 mg cholesterol.

1½ **cups water**
1½ **cups raisins**
1 **tablespoon sugar**
1 **package active dry yeast**
2 **cups whole-wheat flour**
1½ to 2 **cups unsifted all-purpose flour**
½ **cup dry nonfat milk powder**
1 **teaspoon salt**
1 **egg**
1½ **tablespoons vegetable oil**

Glaze:
¾ **cup sifted 10X (confectioners') sugar**
⅛ **teaspoon vanilla**
2 **to 3 teaspoons water**

1. Combine the water, raisins and sugar in a small saucepan. Bring to boiling to plump the raisins. Strain the liquid into a large bowl; reserve the raisins separately. Cool the liquid to 110°.
2. Stir the yeast into the liquid to dissolve. Let the yeast mixture stand until bubbly, about 10 minutes.
3. Stir together the whole-wheat flour, 1½ cups of the white flour, the milk powder and salt in a medium-size bowl.
4. Mix the egg and the oil into the yeast mixture. Stir in the flour mixture and enough of the white flour to make a soft dough.
5. Turn the dough out onto a lightly floured surface. Knead the dough until smooth and elastic, about 10 minutes, adding only enough white flour to prevent sticking.
6. Place the dough in an oiled bowl. Turn the dough to coat. Cover with a damp towel. Let the dough rise in a warm place, away from drafts, for 1½ hours or until doubled in volume.
7. Punch the dough down. Roll the dough out to ¾-inch thickness. Sprinkle the dough with the reserved raisins. Roll the dough up. Shape into a loaf. Place the loaf in a lightly greased 9 x 5 x 3-inch loaf pan. Cover with a damp towel; let rise for 1 hour or until doubled in volume.
8. Preheat the oven to slow (325°).
9. Bake the loaf in the preheated slow oven (325°) for 50 minutes or until the loaf is browned and sounds hollow when tapped with your fingertip. Remove the loaf from the pan to a wire rack to cool for 10 minutes.
10. Meanwhile, prepare the Glaze: Place the 10X (confectioners') sugar in a small bowl. Stir in the vanilla and the 2 to 3 teaspoons water until the mixture is smooth and a good glazing consistency.
11. Spread the cooled bread with the Glaze. Let the bread cool to room temperature.

Warm from the oven: Prosciutto Braid and Walnut-Pesto "Pizzas".

Prosciutto Braid

Using prepared dough shortens your time in the kitchen.

Bake at 375° for 40 minutes.
Makes 1 large loaf; 16 slices.

Nutrient Value Per Slice: 272 calories, 8 g protein, 8 g fat, 41 g carbohydrate, 543 mg sodium, 28 mg cholesterol.

3	**pounds prepared Italian or French bread dough***
1	**small onion, halved and sliced crosswise**
1	**tablespoon vegetable oil**
¼	**pound prosciutto, thinly sliced and slivered OR: salami, thinly sliced and slivered**
1	**egg yolk**
1	**tablespoon cream or milk**

1. Thaw the dough if frozen, following the package directions.
2. Meanwhile, sauté the onion in the oil in a small skillet over medium heat until soft and transparent. Drain well.
3. Punch the dough down. Knead in the sautéed onion and slivered prosciutto or salami on a lightly floured pastry board or cloth, adding additional flour to prevent any sticking. Cover the dough with an inverted bowl. Let the dough rest for 10 to 15 minutes.
4. Divide the dough in thirds. Roll each into a 15-inch-long rope. Place the ropes together on a lightly greased large cookie sheet. Braid the ropes together, avoiding stretching. Pinch the ends together to secure; tuck the ends under. Cover the dough. Let rise for 45 minutes or until the dough is double in bulk. Just before baking, stir together the egg yolk and cream in a small cup. Brush the top of the loaf with the glaze.
5. Preheat the oven to moderate (375°).
6. Bake the loaf in the preheated moderate oven (375°) for 40 minutes or until the loaf is golden brown and sounds hollow when tapped with your fingertip. Remove the loaf to a wire rack to cool completely.

*Note: Prepared dough is available frozen in some markets, or by the pound from some local bakeries.

Walnut-Pesto "Pizzas"

For a variation, add slivered boiled ham before sprinkling the pastry rounds with mozzarella.

Bake at 425° for 13 minutes.
Makes 36 "pizza" wedges.

Nutrient Value Per Wedge: 58 calories, 1 g protein, 4 g fat, 3 g carbohydrate, 60 mg sodium, 11 mg cholesterol.

1	**package (10 ounces) frozen patty shells**
1	**egg, beaten**
½	**cup chopped walnuts**
¼	**cup finely chopped green onion**
1	**tablespoon butter or margarine**
2	**tablespoons prepared pesto sauce (optional)**
1	**tablespoon grated Parmesan cheese**
	Pinch salt
	Pinch nutmeg
1	**cup shredded mozzarella cheese (4 ounces)**

1. Thaw the patty shells until soft enough to work with, but still cold, for about 30 minutes. Roll out each shell into a 6-inch round on a very lightly floured board. Place the rounds on ungreased baking sheets. Prick the shells with a fork.
2. Brush the surfaces with the beaten egg. Sprinkle with chopped walnuts to within about ½ inch of the edge.
3. Preheat the oven to hot (425°).
4. Bake the rounds on the center rack of the preheated hot oven (425°) for 8 minutes or until the pastries are lightly golden. Leave the oven on 425°.
5. Meanwhile, sauté the green onion in butter or margarine in a small saucepan over moderate-high heat until soft but not browned. Remove the saucepan from the heat. Add the pesto sauce, if using, the Parmesan cheese, salt and nutmeg. Spread about 1 tablespoon of the green onion mixture over each pastry. Top with the mozzarella cheese, dividing equally.
6. Bake the "pizzas" for 5 minutes longer or until the cheese melts and the pastries are golden. Cut each "pizza" into six wedges. Serve hot.

Note: The pastries may be prepared ahead up to Step 5. Cover lightly with plastic wrap and refrigerate until 15 minutes before serving time. Let the "pizzas" stand at room temperature for 10 minutes. Bake in a preheated hot oven (425°) for 5 minutes.

Variation: For a Mexican version, substitute chopped ripe olives for the chopped walnuts and bottled taco sauce for the pesto sauce.

T·A·S·T·Y
A·C·C·O·M·P·A·N·I·M·E·N·T·S

Perfect for a party or buffet dinner: Warm Shrimp Appetizer Salad (page 53).

2

*A*dd variety to your meals! Surround some of your favorite main dishes with new "friends" — appetizers, soups and salads that add pizzazz to your plate.

Begin a meal with teasers — that is, appetizers that whet the palate. Or, serve them with cocktails, as party munchies or even as midnight snacks. Something simple but really good would be our popular Spinach Dip *(page 42),* for dressing up raw vegetables. And if there's a special occasion, try our California Hors d'Oeuvre Cheesecake *(page 37)* or Tri-Vegetable Paté *(page 41)*. They're impressive and delicious!

As for soups and salads, there's no limit to their versatility. Forego tomato or chicken noodle soup once in a while to sample Gingered Carrot Soup *(page 45)* — a perfect complement to roasted and grilled meats, or Apple and Potato Chowder *(page 46),* an excellent partner to roast chicken. Serve salads before, during or after the meal — whether it's assorted greens or a more daring Endive Watercress and Walnut Salad with Raspberry Vinaigrette *(page 49)*. Heartier dishes such as Lentil Salad with Goat Cheese *(page 52)* are great for lunch.

To really break old routines, serve a variety of teasers and salads for dinner. Add side-of-the-plate fillers too, such as Home-Style Potatoes Anna *(page 67)*. A great meal for families on the run.

T·E·A·S·E·R·S

Something wonderful for a party: Caviar and Cream Mold

Caviar and Cream Mold

Red and black caviar, resting on a molded cream cheese and sour cream mixture, create a spectacular buffet centerpiece.

Makes 24 servings.

Nutrient Value Per Serving: 128 calories, 5 g protein, 11 g fat, 4 g carbohydrate, 171 mg sodium, 115 mg cholesterol.

2   **envelopes unflavored gelatin**
1   **cup cold water**
1   **cup light cream**
2   **packages (8 ounces each) cream cheese, softened**
½   **cup dairy sour cream (from a ½-pint container)**
1   **tablespoon grated onion**
1   **teaspoon Worcestershire sauce**
½   **teaspoon grated lemon rind**
1   **jar (2 ounces) black caviar**
1   **jar (2 ounces) red caviar**
    Yolks from 6 hard-cooked eggs, sieved

1. Soften the gelatin in the cold water in a medium-size saucepan; let stand for 1 minute.
2. Cook over medium heat, stirring constantly, until the gelatin dissolves completely, about 2 minutes. Remove the saucepan from the heat. Stir in the cream.
3. Beat together the cream cheese and the sour cream in a medium-size bowl until well blended. Stir in the onion, Worcestershire sauce and lemon rind. Then gradually blend in the gelatin mixture.
4. Pour the mixture into a moistened 4-cup bowl or mold. Refrigerate for 4 hours or overnight.
5. To unmold, run a thin-bladed knife around the edge of the bowl. Quickly immerse the bowl in a bowl of hot water. Invert the mold onto a moistened plate; remove the bowl. Cover the cheese mold with plastic wrap. Refrigerate until 1 hour before party time.
6. At party time, arrange concentric circles of caviar on top of the mold. Fill in with the sieved egg yolk. Surround the base of the mold with the remaining egg yolk.

California Hors d'Oeuvre Cheesecake

Create your own unique design of vegetables on top of this appetizer pie.

Bake pastry at 425° for 12 to 15 minutes.
Makes 12 appetizer servings.

Nutrient Value Per Serving: 277 calories, 6 g protein, 23 g fat, 13 g carbohydrate, 288 mg sodium, 76 mg cholesterol.

Pastry:
1½   **cups** sifted **all-purpose flour**
2   **tablespoons grated Parmesan cheese**
¼   **teaspoon salt**
½   **cup (1 stick) chilled butter or margarine**
1   **egg, lightly beaten**
3   **to 4 tablespoons cold water**

Filling:
1   **package (8 ounces)** plus **1 package (3 ounces) cream cheese, softened**
1   **cup chopped, drained tofu (6 ounces)**
⅓   **cup mayonnaise OR: mayonnaise-type salad dressing**
1   **tablespoon finely chopped shallot**
2   **to 3 teaspoons Dijon-style mustard**

Garnish suggestions:
   Sliced cherry tomatoes, chopped parsley, sliced mushrooms, sliced green onion, chopped hard-cooked egg, sliced ripe olives.

1. Prepare the Pastry: Stir together the flour, Parmesan cheese and salt in a medium-size bowl. Cut in the butter until the mixture is crumbly. Stir in the beaten egg and enough water just to moisten the mixture; gather into a ball. Cover with plastic wrap and chill 1 hour.
2. Preheat the oven to hot (425°).
3. Roll out the dough on a lightly floured surface to a 12-inch circle. Fit into a 9½- or 10-inch tart pan with a removable bottom. Prick the bottom of the pastry with a fork.
4. Bake the crust in the preheated hot oven (425°) for 12 to 15 minutes or until light golden brown. Cool the crust on a wire rack.
5. Meanwhile, prepare the Filling: Combine the cream cheese, tofu, mayonnaise, shallot and mustard in the container of a food processor or blender. Cover; whirl until very smooth. Turn the mixture into the cooled pastry shell; spread the filling evenly to the edges with a rubber spatula. Cover with plastic wrap and chill at least 2 hours or overnight.

6. To serve, arrange vegetables of your choice in concentric circles on the top of the pie. Cut the pie into wedges to serve.

Food for thought . . .

Tofu, or bean curd, is made from soybean milk and is an excellent source of protein. Almost tasteless and with a cheeselike consistency, tofu adds textural contrast to salads and soups. To give tofu a little more flavor, let soak briefly in a marinade, salad dressing, barbecue sauce or other sharply flavored liquid. Look for tofu, plastic wrapped, in the produce or refrigerator sections of your supermarket, or in its fresher form, in small plastic containers immersed in water, in some specialty grocery shops. Refrigerate at home for no more than a few days.

Vegetable Sesame Turnovers

Bake at 375° for 30 minutes.
Makes 6 large or 12 small turnovers.

Nutrient Value Per Large Turnover: 461 calories, 7 g protein, 33 g fat, 36 g carbohydrate, 986 mg sodium, 111 mg cholesterol.

Dough*:
- 2 **cups** sifted **all-purpose flour**
- 1 **teaspoon salt**
- ⅔ **cup plus 2 tablespoons butter, cut into small pieces**
- 4 **tablespoons water**

Filling:
- 1 **small onion, chopped (¼ cup)**
- 2 **cloves garlic, chopped**
- 3 **tablespoons olive oil**
- 1 **small eggplant, cut into ½-inch dice (about 3 cups)**
- 1 **small sweet red pepper, cut into ½-inch dice (about 1 cup)**
- ½ **teaspoon leaf marjoram, crumbled**
- ½ **teaspoon ground cinnamon**
- ½ **teaspoon crushed red pepper flakes**
- 1 **cup canned tomatoes**
- ¾ **teaspoon salt**
- 1 **egg, slightly beaten**
- 1 **tablespoon sesame seeds**

1. Prepare the Dough: Combine the flour and the salt in a medium-size bowl. Mix in the butter with your fingertips until the mixture resembles coarse meal. Stir in enough water, mixing with your fingers, until the dough forms a ball. Cover the dough with plastic wrap and refrigerate while preparing the filling.

2. Prepare the Filling: Sauté the onion and the garlic in the olive oil in a large skillet over medium heat until the onion is softened, about 5 minutes. Add the eggplant; cook another 5 minutes. Add the sweet red pepper, marjoram, cinnamon and red pepper flakes. Cook another 5 minutes. Add the tomatoes. Increase heat to medium-high and cook 5 more minutes. Add the salt. Remove the skillet from the heat and let cool. Both the dough and the filling can be made ahead and refrigerated for up to 48 hours or frozen for up to 3 months.

3. Preheat the oven to moderate (375°).

4. Divide the dough into 6 equal pieces. Roll out each piece on a well-floured board into a circle about 7 inches in diameter. Place ¼ cup of the filling in the center of each pastry circle. Brush the edges of the pastry with the beaten egg. Fold one half of the circle over the filling to form a half-moon turnover. Crimp the edges to seal. Place the turnovers on a baking sheet; brush with the remaining egg. Sprinkle with the sesame seeds.

5. Bake the turnovers in the preheated moderate oven (375°) for 30 minutes or until golden brown. Cool on a wire rack. Serve at room temperature.

Note: One and a half packages piecrust mix can be substituted. Prepare according to the package directions.

SESAME SEEDS

To preserve freshness, store sesame seeds in the refrigerator for up to 1 month, or even better, in the freezer for up to 6 months.

Endive Hors d'Oeuvre Hawaiian

An easy, unusual appetizer.

Makes about 2 dozen appetizer servings.

Nutrient Value Per Serving: 17 calories, 0 g protein, 1 g fat, 1 g carbohydrate, 11 mg sodium, 4 mg cholesterol.

2   **Belgian endive**
1   **package (3 ounces) cream cheese, softened**
1   **kiwi fruit, peeled and coarsely chopped**
¼   **cup canned crushed pineapple, drained**
1   **small shallot, finely chopped**
    Alfalfa sprouts for garnish

Dipping Sauce (optional):
⅓   **cup bottled Italian dressing**
1   **ounce macadamia nuts, finely chopped**
    (¼ cup)

1. Trim about ½ inch from the bottom of the endive; separate the leaves. Wash the leaves; drain well on paper toweling.

2. Stir together the cream cheese, kiwi, pineapple and shallot until well combined. Spoon about 1 teaspoon of the mixture on the bottom of each leaf. Garnish the tops of the leaves with the sprouts. Arrange the endive leaves on a platter. Cover the platter with plastic wrap and chill until serving time.

3. Just before serving, stir together the Italian dressing and the nuts in a small bowl, if you wish, to serve as dipping sauce with the endive.

Scandinavian Creamed Herring Salad

A Scandinavian tradition for any celebration.

Makes 12 servings.

Nutrient Value Per Serving: 300 calories, 13 g protein, 25 g fat, 8 g carbohydrate, 63 mg sodium, 61 mg cholesterol.

1½ **pounds green beans**
1   **large zucchini, trimmed and sliced**
1   **large yellow squash, trimmed and sliced**
⅔   **cup vegetable oil**
⅓   **cup cider vinegar**
¼   **cup snipped fresh dill**
    Salt and pepper, to taste
    Romaine lettuce leaves
3   **jars (12 ounces each) herring in cream sauce**
1   **medium-size red onion, cut into rings**

1. Trim the beans; cut into 2-inch lengths. Bring a large saucepan of salted water to boiling. Add the green beans and cook 5 to 8 minutes or until tender but crisp. Drain in a colander and run under cold water to stop the cooking process. Drain again. Place the beans in a pile in a shallow dish. Arrange the zucchini and squash slices in piles in another dish.

2. Combine the oil, vinegar, dill and salt and pepper to taste in a small jar with a screw-top. Cover and shake until the dressing is well blended. Pour over the beans and the zucchini and squash. Cover the vegetables with plastic wrap. Refrigerate for several hours or overnight to blend flavors.

3. At serving time, line a bowl with the lettuce leaves. Place the herring in the center. Surround with the green beans, zucchini and squash slices and onion rings. Garnish with dill, if desired. Refrigerate until serving time.

HOW TO HARD-COOK AN EGG

The classic hard-cooked egg used for stuffed eggs, potato salad and other cold salads simmers for 10 minutes (never boil!). Arrange the eggs in a single layer in the bottom of a saucepan and add enough cold water to cover the eggs by at least 1 inch. Place over medium-high heat and as soon as large bubbles begin to bubble from the bottom to the surface, start timing. Lower the heat so the water simmers and simmer for 10 minutes for a hard-cooked egg with a white and yolk that are firmly set. If overcooked, the white will be rubbery and the yolk dry and crumbly with a characteristic green ring. Remove the eggs with a slotted spoon to a bowl of cold water to stop the cooking. Refrigerate the eggs for no more than 1 week.

LS

Marinated Asparagus Spears

Use these as part of your party antipasto platter, or wrap several spears with prosciutto or ham and serve as a first course.

Makes 12 servings.

Nutrient Value Per Serving: 41 calories, 2 g protein, 3 g fat, 2 g carbohydrate, 1 mg sodium, 0 mg cholesterol.

- **3 pounds fresh asparagus, trimmed OR: 3 packages (10 ounces each) frozen asparagus spears**
- **⅓ cup olive or vegetable oil**
- **2 tablespoons red wine vinegar**
  Salt and pepper, to taste
- **1 clove garlic, crushed**
  Pinch dry mustard

1. Cook the fresh or frozen asparagus spears in a large saucepan of boiling salted water until barely tender. Drain well in a colander; rinse under cold water to stop the cooking process. Drain again on paper toweling. Place in a shallow glass or ceramic dish.
2. Combine the oil, vinegar, salt and pepper, garlic and dry mustard in a small jar with a screw-top. Cover and shake vigorously. Pour the dressing over the asparagus spears. Cover with plastic wrap. Refrigerate several hours or overnight to blend flavors.
3. At serving time, drain the asparagus and arrange on a serving platter.

Marinated Artichoke Hearts

Frozen artichoke hearts are cooked in a marinade, then cooled and refrigerated. Drain them just before serving.

Makes 12 servings.

Nutrient Value Per Serving: 58 calories, 1 g protein, 5 g fat, 4 g carbohydrate, 65 mg sodium, 0 mg cholesterol.

- **2 packages (9 ounces each) frozen artichoke hearts**
- **1 cup water**
  Juice of 1 lemon
- **¼ cup olive or vegetable oil**
- **2 cloves garlic, crushed but left whole**
- **¼ teaspoon salt**
  Pinch ground pepper
  Few coriander seeds
- **½ teaspoon leaf thyme, crumbled**
  Chopped fresh parsley

1. Combine the artichoke hearts, water, lemon juice, oil, garlic, salt, pepper, coriander seeds and thyme in a medium-size saucepan. Bring to boiling over medium heat, gently separating the artichoke hearts with a long fork. Lower the heat. Cover the saucepan and simmer, following package directions, until the artichoke hearts are tender. Remove the saucepan from the heat. Cool to room temperature. Refrigerate, covered, several hours or overnight.
2. At serving time, drain the artichoke hearts, reserving the marinade for another use. Place the artichokes on a serving platter. Sprinkle with the chopped parsley.

Delicious and colorful Tri-Vegetable Pâté.

Tri-Vegetable Pâté

Spinach, carrots, sliced green onions and a tangy yogurt mixture are combined to make this chilled loaf.

Bake at 350° for 1½ hours.
Makes 10 servings.

Nutrient Value Per Serving: 121 calories, 7 g protein, 8 g fat, 9 g carbohydrate, 163 mg sodium, 123 mg cholesterol.

    3 packages (10 ounces each) frozen chopped
         spinach, thawed
    3 large carrots, pared
   ¼ cup (½ stick) butter
    2 bunches green onions, thinly sliced (1 cup)
    1 container (8 ounces) plain lowfat yogurt
 1½ teaspoons salt
   ¼ teaspoon ground hot red pepper
   ⅛ teaspoon ground nutmeg
    4 eggs, lightly beaten

1. Line an 8½ x 4½-inch loaf pan with wax paper; grease the paper.
2. Squeeze the spinach to remove as much liquid as possible. Place in the container of a food processor. Cover and process until the spinach is finely chopped.
3. Cook the whole carrots in a large saucepan of boiling water for 5 minutes or until crisp-tender; drain the carrots.
4. Melt the butter in a saucepan over medium heat. Add the sliced green onions and cook until limp, stirring frequently. Add the chopped spinach, yogurt, salt, red pepper and nutmeg; heat the mixture just to boiling. Remove the saucepan from the heat. Stir in the eggs until well blended.
5. Preheat the oven to moderate (350°).

6. Pour half of the spinach mixture into the prepared loaf pan. Arrange the whole carrots lengthwise over the mixture in the center of the pan, pushing in slightly. Pour the remaining mixture on top of the carrots, patting down slightly and smoothing the top with a rubber spatula. Cover the top with a sheet of aluminum foil. Place a large pan on the middle rack of the oven. Place the loaf pan in the large pan. Fill the large pan with enough water to come 1 inch up the side of the loaf pan.
7. Bake the pâté in the preheated moderate oven (350°) for 1½ hours or until a cake tester comes out clean. Cool the pâté on a wire rack. Refrigerate 6 hours or overnight.
8. Remove the pâté from the refrigerator 15 minutes before serving. Cut into thin slices and serve with a tomato wedge as a garnish, if you wish.

Zippy Beef Spread on Colorful Vegetables

A creamy horseradish sauce turns leftover cooked beef into today's classy appetizer spread.

Makes 1½ cups spread.

Nutrient Value Per Tablespoon: 22 calories, 2 g protein, 1 g fat, 1 g carbohydrate, 53 mg sodium, 7 mg cholesterol.

    6 ounces lean cooked beef, cut into 1-inch
         pieces
   ¼ cup dairy sour cream
   ¼ cup finely chopped red onion
    2 tablespoons bottled horseradish
   ½ teaspoon leaf rosemary, crumbled
   ½ teaspoon salt
  12 thin cucumber slices
  12 thin yellow squash slices
    1 large sweet red pepper, halved, seeded and
         cut into 1¼-inch squares

1. Place the cooked beef in the container of a food processor fitted with the steel blade. Process for 15 to 20 seconds, using on/off pulses until the beef is ground.
2. Add the sour cream, onion, horseradish, rosemary and salt. Process just until blended, using on/off pulses.
3. Transfer the spread to a bowl, and cover with plastic wrap. Refrigerate until serving time. Serve the spread with the cucumber slices, yellow squash slices and red pepper squares.

Garden Patch Dip

Even fussy vegetable eaters will munch a bunch of celery sticks when they have this delectable dip.

Makes 8 servings.

Nutrient Value Per Tablespoon: 30 calories, 1 g protein, 3 g fat, 1 g carbohydrate, 26 mg sodium, 3 mg cholesterol.

> 1   container (8 ounces) plain yogurt
> ⅓   cup mayonnaise OR: salad dressing
> ¼   cup chopped parsley
> 2   tablespoons chopped chives
>   Seasoned salt and pepper
>   Celery sticks, carrot sticks and cucumber
>   sticks

1. Combine the yogurt, mayonnaise or salad dressing, parsley and chives in a small bowl until well blended. Taste and season with the seasoned salt and pepper. Cover the bowl with plastic wrap and refrigerate at least 2 hours for flavors to blend.
2. At party time, pile the yogurt dip into a bowl. Place on a platter and arrange the vegetable sticks in piles around the dip.

Spinach Dip

Delicious as a dip; scrumptious as a salad dressing.

Makes 3 cups.

Nutrient Value Per Tablespoon: 53 calories, 1 g protein, 5 g fat, 2 g carbohydrate, 130 mg sodium, 6 mg cholesterol.

> 1   package (10 ounces) frozen chopped
>   spinach, thawed
> 1   container (16 ounces) dairy sour cream
> ¾   cup mayonnaise OR: salad dressing
> 1   package dry leek soup mix
> 2   teaspoons dry Italian dressing mix
> 2   tablespoons chopped fresh parsley

Drain the spinach; squeeze out excess liquid. Combine the sour cream, mayonnaise, leek soup mix, Italian dressing mix and parsley in the container of an electric blender. Cover and whirl until smooth. Pour into a serving bowl. Stir in the spinach until well blended. Chill. Serve with assorted raw vegetables for dipping. Mushrooms, cherry tomatoes, broccoli, zucchini strips, sweet red and green pepper strips and cucumber slices are especially good. The dip will keep in the refrigerator for up to 1 week in a covered bowl.

Guacamole Picante

Green chili peppers give punch to a favorite dip.

Makes about 3 cups.

Nutrient Value per ¼ Cup: 85 calories, 1 g protein, 8 g fat, 5 g carbohydrate, 160 mg sodium, 0 mg cholesterol.

> 3   ripe avocados
> 1   green chili, seeded and chopped OR: 1 can
>   (4 ounces) jalapeño peppers, seeded and
>   chopped
> 1   ripe tomato, chopped
> 2   tablespoons finely chopped onion
> 1   tablespoon lemon juice
> 1   teaspoon garlic salt
>   Broccoli flowerets
>   Cauliflower flowerets
>   Radishes, cut into roses (optional)

1. Halve, pit and peel the avocados. Cut the avocados into cubes. Place in a large glass or ceramic bowl. Mash with a potato masher until the avocados are very smooth.
2. Stir in the chili or jalapeño peppers, tomato, onion, lemon juice and garlic salt until well blended. Cover the bowl with plastic wrap. Refrigerate the dip at least 2 hours to develop the flavors.
3. To serve, pile the avocado mixture into a serving container. Surround with the broccoli, cauliflower and radishes.

Chili Con Queso

The translation is "chili with cheese." Serve with flour tortilla or corn chips.

Makes about 4 cups.

Nutrient Value Per Tablespoon: 48 calories, 2 g protein, 3 g fat, 2 g carbohydrate, 195 mg sodium, 9 mg cholesterol.

- 1 **large onion, chopped (1 cup)**
- 2 **cloves garlic, finely chopped**
- 2 **tablespoons butter or margarine**
- 6 **fresh green chilies OR: 2 cans (4 ounces each) jalapeño peppers**
- 2 **large tomatoes, peeled and diced**
- 1½ **teaspoons leaf oregano, crumbled**
- 1 **to 2 teaspoons ground cumin**
- 2 **pounds pasteurized American cheese, shredded**
  Liquid red-pepper seasoning, to taste
  Corn chips

1. Sauté the onion and garlic in the butter in a large saucepan until soft.
2. Halve, seed and dice the fresh chilies, or drain, seed and dice the canned peppers. Add to the saucepan with the tomatoes, oregano and cumin; stir to blend well. Simmer for 10 minutes.
3. Stir in the shredded cheese, a part at a time, until the cheese melts and the mixture is well blended. Season to taste with the liquid red-pepper seasoning. Serve warm with the corn chips.

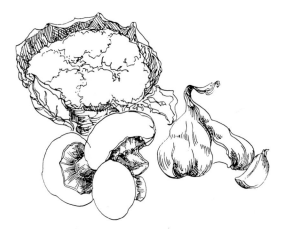

Salsa Diablo

Potent but delicious! Serve with corn chips.

Makes 6 to 8 cups salsa.

Nutrient Value Per ¼ Cup: 11 calories, 0 g protein, 0 g fat, 3 g carbohydrate, 8 mg sodium, 0 mg cholesterol.

- 8 **large fresh tomatoes**
- 10 **radishes**
- ½ **bunch of cilantro (fresh coriander), no stems**
- 3 **small fresh jalapeño peppers (green or yellow, including the spicy seeds)**
  Juice of 1 large lemon
  Juice of 1 large lime
- 3 **tablespoons vinegar**
- 1 **teaspoon salt**
- ½ **teaspoon pepper**
  Pinch garlic salt
  Pinch leaf oregano

Cut the tomatoes, radishes, cilantro and peppers into a small dice. Mix all the ingredients together in a large bowl. Add the lemon and lime juices, vinegar, salt, pepper, garlic salt and oregano. Mix well. Refrigerate, covered, before serving.

Food for thought . . .

Medium to dark green, the jalapeño chili has a smooth surface and is usually rounded at the tip rather than pointed. It usually measures 2½ inches long and about ¾ inch at its widest part. Remember, it's the seeds that provide the fire.

Sensational Salsa

This sauce is great with eggs, Heŭvos Rancheros or just as a dip for tortilla chips. And this recipe makes enough for a crowd.

Makes ¾ gallon.

Nutrient Value Per ¼ Cup: 14 calories, 1 g protein, 1 g fat, 3 g carbohydrate, 149 mg sodium, 0 mg cholesterol.

- 6 **medium-size to large fresh tomatoes (5 if large), diced**
- 1 **large white or yellow onion, diced**
- 1 **bunch green onions (at least 6), diced**
- 2 **cans (16 ounces each) stewed tomatoes, drained and diced**
- 1 **can (16 ounces) tomato sauce**
- ½ **to 1 bunch cilantro (fresh coriander), chopped**
- 1 **can (7 ounces) diced green chilies (optional: add up to 7 more ounces chilies, according to taste)**
- ½ **of 4-ounce can jalapeño peppers, diced**
- 2 **to 3 cloves garlic, pressed**
  Salt and pepper, to taste (more pepper than salt
- ½ **teaspoon ground cumin**
- 1 **teaspoon leaf oregano, crumbled**
- ⅛ **to ¼ cup white vinegar**

Steam or boil the fresh tomatoes briefly just to loosen the skin. Remove the skins. Squeeze the tomatoes to drain the excess water and remove the seeds. Mix all the ingredients in a large bowl; stir to blend well. Refrigerate overnight for flavors to blend. (The salsa taste will improve after 2 or 3 days). Keep the finished salsa in a glass container. This salsa will keep in the refrigerator for up to 2 weeks.

WORKING WITH FRESH CHILIES

Select chilies that are still green and have a smooth, unwrinkled skin. Wrap the chilies in paper toweling, place in a brown paper bag and store in the refrigerator. When cutting, seeding or otherwise working with chilies, wear rubber gloves, especially if you have sensitive skin. Never touch your fingers or hands to your face or eyes, and be sure to wash your hands thoroughly when you're finished. To "deheat" fresh chilies, remove and discard the seeds.

CILANTRO

Also known as coriander, Chinese parsley and Mexican parsley, this green leafy herb is used in Asian, Middle Eastern, Mexican and Central and South American cuisines. When shopping for cilantro, look for fresh, leafy plants with the roots still attached if possible. To store, place the roots in a small jar of water, enclose the leaves in a plastic bag and refrigerate for up to 1 week. If your cilantro is rootless, wrap the stem ends in damp paper toweling, enclose the whole bunch in a plastic bag and store in the crisper section of your refrigerator. Use cilantro to flavor chili, soups, fish, chicken or any other dish in which you think its distinctive flavor would add interest.

S·O·U·P·S

White Spanish Gazpacho

Makes 6 servings.

Nutrient Value Per Serving: 377 calories, 10 g protein, 31 g fat, 18 g carbohydrate, 471 mg sodium, 51 mg cholesterol.

3	**medium-size cucumbers**
	Salt
1	**clove garlic, crushed**
3	**cups chicken broth**
3	**cups dairy sour cream**
3	**tablespoons vinegar**
4	**medium-size tomatoes, peeled and chopped**
½	**cup finely chopped parsley**
½	**cup chopped green onions**
½	**cup shredded carrot**
½	**cup sliced radish**
¾	**cup sliced blanched almonds, toasted**

1. Peel and seed the cucumbers. Cut into pieces and place in a colander. Sprinkle with salt. Let stand over a bowl for ½ hour. Drain the cucumbers and rinse well.
2. Place the cucumber and garlic in the container of an electric blender. Whirl until the mixture is smooth. Add a little chicken broth. Continue blending, adding the broth to the cucumber mixture until all the broth is used up; work in batches, if necessary.
3. Transfer the cucumber-garlic-broth mixture to a large bowl. Stir in the sour cream until well blended. Season with the vinegar and salt to taste. Cover and refrigerate until well chilled.
4. Fill 6 small bowls with each of the following: chopped tomatoes; chopped parsley; chopped green onions; shredded carrot; sliced radish; and toasted almonds.
5. To serve: Ladle the soup into wide shallow bowls nestled, if possible, in a bed of crushed ice. Pass around the 6 bowls of vegetables and nuts and have your guests sprinkle their own garnishes over the soup. Or for a more dramatic presentation, ladle the soup into a large serving bowl. Arrange the garnishes in sections over the top of the soup.

Gingered Carrot Soup

Fresh orange juice and ginger give this soup its special flavor.

Makes 6 servings.

Nutrient Value Per Serving: 153 calories, 4 g protein, 9 g fat, 14 g carbohydrate, 620 mg sodium, 21 mg cholesterol.

¼	**cup (½ stick) butter or margarine**
1	**pound carrots, pared and sliced**
1	**medium-size onion, sliced (½ cup)**
4	**cups chicken broth**
1	**tablespoon finely chopped fresh gingerroot OR: 1 teaspoon ground ginger**
	Salt, to taste
	Pinch ground hot red pepper
	Pinch ground nutmeg (freshly grated, if possible)
1	**cup freshly squeezed orange juice**
2	**tablespoons Cointreau OR: other orange-flavored liqueur**
2	**tablespoons chopped fresh mint (optional)**

1. Melt the margarine or butter in a large saucepan. Add the carrots and onion and toss to coat. Cover the pan and cook over low heat for 10 minutes.
2. Add the chicken broth, ginger, salt, red pepper and nutmeg; stir to combine. Simmer, uncovered, until the carrots are soft enough to mash against the side of the pan.
3. Transfer the mixture to the container of an electric blender or food processor. Whirl until smooth. Pour into a large mixing bowl. Blend in the orange juice and Cointreau.
4. Cover the bowl and refrigerate for 6 hours, or until thoroughly chilled. Serve in clear glass bowls garnished with mint, if you wish.

PURÉE VEGETABLE SOUPS

Even when made from scratch, these soups can be prepared in 30 minutes or less. And they're ideal for cleaning out leftover vegetables from the refrigerator. First, cook the cut-up vegetables in water or stock or a combination. Strain, reserving the cooking liquid. Purée the solids in a blender, food processor or food mill. Add enough of the strained liquid to reach the consistency you like. For extra richness, stir in a little milk, cream or butter.

Summer Zucchini Soup

You can serve this soup either hot or cold.

Makes 6 servings.

Nutrient Value Per Serving: 123 calories, 5 g protein, 9 g fat, 7 g carbohydrate, 647 mg sodium, 21 mg cholesterol.

¼	**cup (½ stick) butter**
2	**pounds small zucchini, thinly sliced**
5	**tablespoons finely chopped shallots (about 3) OR: finely chopped green onion**
4	**cups chicken broth**
1½	**teaspoons curry powder**
⅛	**teaspoon salt**
⅛	**teaspoon ground hot red pepper**

Garnish:
⅓   **cup croutons, if serving hot OR:**
      2 tablespoons chopped fresh chives,
      if serving cold.

1. Melt the butter in a large skillet. Add the zucchini and shallots; cover the skillet and cook 10 to 15 minutes, stirring often, until the zucchini is soft but not browned.
2. Combine half of the zucchini mixture, 2 cups of the chicken broth, the curry powder, salt and red pepper in a food processor or blender. Whirl until puréed. Pour into a saucepan if serving hot, or into a large bowl, if serving cold.
3. Repeat puréeing with the remaining zucchini mixture and chicken broth. Combine the batches.
4. If serving the soup hot, heat in the saucepan and garnish with croutons. If serving cold, chill for 2 hours. Garnish with chives.

JAZZING UP SOUPS

Use these garnishes to dress up simple broth soups (chicken, beef, vegetable or fish) or to "disguise" leftovers.

Fresh Herbs *— chopped parsley, tarragon, dill, rosemary, basil, chives, mint or coriander, or a mixture.*
Shredded Greens *— finely shredded arugula, spinach, bok choy, romaine, endive or sorrel.*
Citrus Rind *— thin strips of or finely grated lemon, lime or orange rind.*
Sliced Mushrooms *— simmer thinly sliced mushrooms in the soup for a few minutes.*
Pasta or Rice *— simmer small or broken-up pieces of noodles, pasta, macaroni, rice or pastina in the soup until tender.*
Grated Cheese *— sprinkle soup with grated Parmesan or Romano or float thin shavings of a hard cheese on top.*
Mixed Vegetables *— simmer thin slivers or matchstick pieces of carrot, turnip, sweet pepper, celery, green onion or whole peas in the soup to add color and crunch.*

Apple and Potato Chowder

The apple adds a touch of sweetness to this cool weather soup.

Makes 6 servings.

Nutrient Value Per Serving: 270 calories, 6 g protein, 17 g fat, 24 g carbohydrate, 656 mg sodium, 33 mg cholesterol.

¼	**pound salt pork OR: smoky bacon**
2	**medium-size onions, finely chopped (about 1 cup)**
1	**or 2 boiling potatoes (about ¾ pound), pared and cut into ½-inch dice**
3	**large Granny Smith apples (about 1½ pounds)**
4	**cups chicken broth**
¼	**teaspoon pepper**
½	**pint (1 cup) light cream OR: half-and-half**
¼	**cup thinly sliced green onion tops OR: chives**

1. Trim the rind from the salt pork. Cut the pork into ¼-inch dice. Gently cook the pork in a medium-size saucepan over medium heat until the fat is rendered out and the pork is browned and crispy. Remove the cracklings from the fat

with a slotted spoon to paper toweling to drain.

2. Add the onion to the bacon drippings in the saucepan. Cook for 2 minutes, scraping up any browned bits from the bottom of the pan with a wooden spoon. Add the potatoes. Cook, stirring occasionally, for 5 minutes.

3. Meanwhile, pare and core the apples. Cut into ½-inch dice.

4. Add the apple and chicken broth to the saucepan. Bring to boiling. Season with the pepper. Lower the heat and simmer 25 minutes or until the potato and apple are very soft. Stir several times with a whisk to purée some of the apple and potato, but still leaving the soup very chunky. Add the cream. Gently heat over medium-low heat to serving temperature.

5. Reheat the cracklings in a small skillet.

6. To serve, ladle the chowder into soup bowls. Sprinkle each serving with the cracklings and green onion.

SHALLOTS

A member of the onion family, the shallot has a flavor somewhere between a regular onion and garlic. In fact, it resembles garlic in appearance, but the bulb cluster or cloves are not as compact and the outer paper skin is brown. Select plump heads and gently squeeze them to make sure they are firm. Use finely chopped shallots instead of regular onions in sauces and skillet-sautéed foods for a more delicate taste.

Bacon-Corn Chowder

Makes 4 servings.

Nutrient Value Per Serving: 248 calories, 11 g protein, 8 g fat, 36 g carbohydrate, 470 mg sodium, 20 mg cholesterol.

- 2 **slices bacon, chopped**
- ½ **cup chopped onion (1 medium-size)**
- ½ **cup chopped celery**
- 3 **tablespoons coarsely chopped sweet green pepper**
- 2 **cups water**
- 2 **cups pared diced potato, ½-inch pieces (2 medium-size)**
- ½ **teaspoon salt**
- ½ **teaspoon coarsely ground pepper**
- ½ **teaspoon leaf basil, crumbled**
- 1 **bay leaf**
- 1 **cup skim milk**
- 2 **cups frozen corn kernels, partially thawed**

- ½ **cup shredded sharp Cheddar cheese (2 ounces)**
- **Chopped parsley (optional)**

1. Sauté the bacon in a medium-size nonstick saucepan over medium heat until crisp. Remove the bacon with a slotted spoon to paper toweling to drain. Drain all but 1 teaspoon of the fat from the saucepan.

2. Add the onion, celery and green pepper to the saucepan. Sauté over medium-high heat until the onion is golden, for 5 minutes. Add the water, potatoes, salt, pepper, basil and bay leaf. Bring to boiling. Lower the heat and simmer for 10 to 15 minutes or until the potatoes are tender.

3. Stir in the milk and corn. Cook for 5 minutes or until the soup is heated through. Stir in the cheese until melted. Remove the bay leaf.

4. Ladle the chowder into soup cups. Sprinkle each serving with crisp bacon, and chopped parsley, if you wish.

Speedy Corn Chowder

Makes 8 servings.

Nutrient Value Per Serving: 223 calories, 6 g protein, 11 g fat, 26 g carbohydrate, 515 mg sodium, 26 mg cholesterol.

- 2 **slices bacon, cut into small pieces**
- 1 **large onion, chopped (1 cup)**
- 2 **medium-size all-purpose potatoes (about ¾ pound)**
- 1 **can (13¾ ounces) chicken broth**
- 4 **cups fresh corn kernels (6 ears)**
- 1 **pint half-and-half**
- ¾ **teaspoon salt**
- ½ **teaspoon white pepper**
- 2 **tablespoons chopped parsley**

1. Sauté the bacon in a large saucepan until crisp. Remove the bacon with a slotted spoon to paper toweling to drain; reserve. Add the onion to the bacon drippings in the saucepan; sauté, stirring often, until the onion is softened, about 5 minutes.

2. Meanwhile, pare the potatoes. Cut into ½-inch cubes. Add to the onion along with the chicken broth. Bring to boiling. Lower the heat; cover and simmer 15 minutes. Add the corn. Cook 5 more minutes or until the potatoes and corn are tender. Stir in the half-and-half, salt and pepper. Gently heat over medium-low to serving temperature.

3. Ladle the chowder into soup plates. Sprinkle with the reserved bacon and parsley.

S·A·L·A·D·S A·N·D D·R·E·S·S·I·N·G·S

Fresh and crunchy delights: Marinated Vegetables in a basket of crisp garden greens.

Platter of Marinated Vegetables

Brilliantly colored vegetables, cooked till just crisp-tender, are marinated overnight for this tasty dish.

Makes 12 servings.

Nutrient Value Per Serving: 364 calories, 6 g protein, 27 g fat, 29 g carbohydrate, 249 mg sodium, 0 mg cholesterol.

- 2 **cups cooked, sliced, peeled potatoes**
- 2 **cups cooked corn kernels**
- 2 **cups marinated artichoke hearts**
- 4 **sweet red peppers, halved, seeded and cut into squares**
- 1 **pound medium-size mushrooms, sliced**
- 4 **large tomatoes, cored and sliced**
- 2 **cups cooked, sliced carrots**
- 2 **cups cooked broccoli flowerets**
- ¾ **pound green beans, trimmed and cooked**
- 1 **pound asparagus, trimmed, cooked, and stalk ends peeled if woody**
- 2 **medium-size yellow squash, cut into chunks and cooked**
- 2 **yellow turnips, peeled, cut into chunks and cooked**
  Classic Vinaigrette (recipe follows)
  Salad greens

1. Prepare all the vegetables.
2. Prepare the Classic Vinaigrette.
3. Drizzle each vegetable with a little of the vinaigrette and place each in its own plastic bag. Refrigerate overnight.
4. At serving time, arrange the salad greens on an attractive serving platter and arrange the vegetables over the greens.

Classic Vinaigrette: Mix ⅔ cup red or white wine vinegar, 1 teaspoon salt and ¼ teaspoon white pepper in a large jar with a screw-top. Add 1⅓ cups olive or vegetable oil or a mix. Shake until the dressing is well blended and thickened slightly.

FRESH HERB AND VEGETABLE COMBOS

Basil — *tomatoes and asparagus*
Chive — *potatoes and turnips*
Coriander — *tomatoes and summer squash*
Dill — *carrots and mushrooms*
Marjoram — *green beans and broccoli*
Thyme — *artichokes and sweet red peppers*

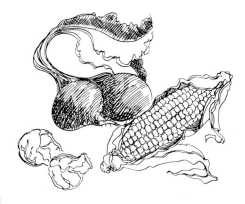

Endive, Watercress and Walnut Salad

This salad, which combines Belgian endive, walnuts, pears and blue cheese, is dressed with a tantalizing raspberry vinaigrette.

Makes 6 servings.

Nutrient Value Per Serving (without dressing): 164 calories, 5 g protein, 12 g fat, 12 g carbohydrate, 132 mg sodium, 6 mg cholesterol.

- 2 **heads Belgian endive**
- 2 **pears, cored and thinly sliced**
- 1 **bunch watercress**
- 6 **tablespoons crumbled blue cheese**
- ¾ **cup walnuts, toasted***
  Raspberry Vinaigrette (recipe follows)

For each serving: Fan 3 leaves of Belgian endive over half of a salad plate. Fan the slices from one-third of a pear over the opposite half of the plate. Place 4 sprigs of watercress in the center. Sprinkle 1 tablespoon of blue cheese, then 2 tablespoons of toasted walnuts over the pear. Ladle 2 to 2½ tablespoons Raspberry Vinaigrette around the plate.

Raspberry Vinaigrette: Combine ½ teaspoon minced shallots and ¼ teaspoon Dijon-style mustard in a small bowl. Slowly whisk in ¼ cup raspberry vinegar. Whisking rapidly, gradually add ¾ cup walnut oil. Mix in 1 tablespoon lemon juice. Season with salt and pepper to taste. Makes about 1 cup. *Nutrient Value Per Tablespoon: 97 calories, 0 g protein, 10 g fat, 0 g carbohydrate, 3 mg sodium, 0 mg cholesterol.*

Note: To toast walnuts, spread the shelled walnuts in a shallow pan. Bake in a preheated moderate oven (350°), stirring often, for 10 to 12 minutes or until golden. Shake the walnuts in a colander to remove any loose skins, if desired. Cool the walnuts.

S·A·L·A·D·S

A Gallery of Salad Greens *From crunchy iceberg to peppery cress, here are the tossings of superb salads. For contrast, toss two together. Better yet, three.*

Chicory (or **Curly Endive**) Sprawling, frilly, green head, sharp flavor, medium-crisp. Season: Year-round.

Sorrel Also known as **Dock.** Bright green, tongue-shaped leaves, pleasantly sour in flavor. Season: Year-round.

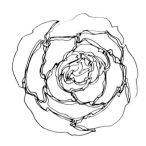

Bibb Lettuce Also known as **Limestone Lettuce.** The tiny dark-green heads have buttery leaves. Season: Year-round.

Belgian Endive Small, chunky, ivory-hued heads with mellow to bitter flavor. Softly crisp, but not crunchy. Season: Fall to spring.

Watercress Has peppery, medium-crisp, medium-green leaves branching from slender stalks. Season: Year-round.

Romaine Also known as **Cos Lettuce.** Cylindrical, medium-green head with crisp, delicate leaves. Season: Year-round.

Iceberg Lettuce Compact, crisp head with pale- to medium-green leaves. Season: Year-round.

Chinese Cabbage Also called **Celery Cabbage.** Has tight, long, pale-green to ivory head. Delicate. Season: Year-round.

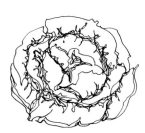

Boston Lettuce Also known as **Butterhead.** Soft, loose head. Tender, delicate leaves ranging from yellow to green. Season: Year-round.

Field Salad Also known as **Lamb's Quarter.** Dark-green, small, spoonlike leaves with radish-sharp flavor. Season: Fall, winter.

Leaf Lettuce Also known as **Garden Lettuce.** Has sprawling, ruffled leaves; pale green and delicate. Season: March to July.

Escarole A cross between leaf lettuce and chicory. Curly green leaves, medium-crisp, mildly bitter flavor. Season: Year-round.

Great luncheon idea: Bok Choy Salad.

Bok Choy Salad

In this recipe, cold Chinese noodles are combined with bok choy and unsalted cashews to create an Oriental-style main-dish.

Makes 6 servings.

Nutrient Value Per Serving: 281 calories, 7 g protein, 17 g fat, 27 g carbohydrate, 352 mg sodium, 27 mg cholesterol.

1   **medium-size bunch bok choy**
⅓   **cup vegetable oil**
8   **large mushrooms, sliced**
3   **green onions, sliced (both white and green parts)**
¼   **cup water**
2   **tablespoons rice vinegar**
2   **tablespoons soy sauce**
1   **teaspoon Oriental (dark) sesame oil**
6   **ounces Chinese noodles, boiled and drained**
¼   **cup unsalted cashews, coarsely chopped**
1   **tablespoon chopped fresh cilantro (Chinese parsley)**
   Sweet red pepper rings, for garnish (optional)

1. Trim the stem end and thinly slice the bunch of bok choy. Heat 3 tablespoons of the vegetable oil in a wok or large skillet over high heat. Add the bok choy and toss to coat evenly. Stir until the bok choy is limp.
2. Add the mushrooms and onions and pour on the water. Continue stirring over high heat until the water is evaporated. Remove the wok from the heat.
3. Whisk together the remaining 3 tablespoons of vegetable oil, the rice vinegar, soy sauce and sesame oil in a small bowl. Pour over the bok choy and toss to coat.
4. Add the drained noodles, nuts and cilantro to the bok choy mixture. Toss to combine.
5. Refrigerate, covered, for 4 hours or until thoroughly chilled. Serve on glass salad plates. Garnish with red pepper rings, if you wish.

Food for thought . . .

Similar to Swiss chard in appearance, bok choy has long, broad white stems with dark green leaves, formed together in a loose bunch. The crisp stalks have a mild, somewhat sweet taste while the green leaves are softer, more cabbagelike. Bok choy can·be eaten raw in salads or cooked in stir-fry dishes.

Food for thought . . .

Oriental sesame oil is much different from the light golden sesame oil often found in healthfood stores. Made from toasted sesame seeds, the Oriental oil has a characteristic dark brown color and a rich flavor and aroma. Since the oil burns at a low temperature, it is used primarily as a seasoning oil rather than for cooking. Store the oil in a cool dark place. Small bottles of the oil are usually available in the Oriental section of the supermarket or specialty food shops.

Lentil Salad with Goat Cheese

Serve as an elegant first course or as the main dish for a summer lunch.

Makes 4 servings.

Nutrient Value Per Serving: 153 calories, 9 g protein, 3 g fat, 24 g carbohydrate, 372 mg sodium, 9 mg cholesterol.

- ½ **cup dried lentils**
- 2 **cups water**
- 1 **bay leaf**
- ¼ **teaspoon leaf thyme, crumbled**
- 1 **teaspoon finely chopped garlic**
- 2 **pinches ground cloves**
- ¼ **pound carrot slices**
- ½ **pound red onion slices**
- ½ **cup chopped celery**
- ¼ **cup Italian dressing**
- 4 **teaspoons red wine vinegar**
- 2 **teaspoons lemon juice**
- ¼ **teaspoon pepper**
- 1½ **ounces goat cheese, crumbled**

1. Combine the lentils, water, bay leaf, thyme, garlic and cloves in a medium-size saucepan. Bring to boiling.
2. Meanwhile, coarsely chop the carrot and onion. Set aside ¼ cup of the chopped onion and ¼ cup of the chopped celery. Add all of the carrot and the remaining onion and celery to the lentils. Lower the heat and simmer, covered, for 20 minutes or until the lentils are tender. Drain the lentil mixture in a colander. Discard the bay leaf.
3. Combine the warm lentils with the salad dressing, vinegar, lemon juice and pepper in a medium-size bowl. To serve, stir in the goat cheese and the reserved onion and celery.

BASIC VINAIGRETTE DRESSING

Whisk together 2 parts oil with 1 part vinegar or citrus juice in a small bowl. For jazzier versions, add chopped fresh herbs, mustard, garlic, honey or any other ingredient that suits the salad you are dressing. Experiment with the wide range of oils and vinegars that are now available.
Quick Tip: For dressings in no time at all, combine all the ingredients in a food processor or blender and whirl until well mixed.

Green Salad with Apples and Orange Vinaigrette

Makes 6 servings.

Nutrient Value Per Serving: 167 calories, 2 g protein, 13 g fat, 16 g carbohydrate, 274 mg sodium, 0 mg cholesterol.

Orange-Mustard Dressing:
- 1 **large navel orange**
- ⅓ **cup olive oil**
- 3 **tablespoons red wine vinegar**
- 1 **teaspoon Dijon-style mustard**
- ½ **teaspoon salt**
- ¼ **teaspoon pepper**

- 1 **Golden Delicious apple**
- 1 **Red Delicious apple**
- 12 **cups mixed torn salad greens, preferably half curly endive and half romaine**

1. Prepare the Orange-Mustard Dressing: Grate the rind from the orange directly into a salad bowl. Add the olive oil, vinegar, mustard, salt and pepper; whisk together until creamy.
2. Cut the white pith from the orange. Separate the orange into segments, letting them fall into the salad bowl.
3. Core both apples; leave the skin on. Cut the apples into ½-inch dice. Add to the dressing; toss to coat the apple pieces. The salad can be prepared up to 1 hour ahead to this point.
4. To serve, place the greens in the salad bowl. Toss all the ingredients together. The apple will fall to the bottom, so place the greens on the plates first; then arrange the apple on top of the greens.

Marinated Broccoli and Red Peppers

Soy vinaigrette is a tangy marinade for this colorful salad.

Makes 6 servings.

Nutrient Value Per Serving: 96 calories, 5 g protein, 5 g fat, 10 g carbohydrate, 385 mg sodium, 0 mg cholesterol.

- 1 **bunch broccoli**
- 3 **sweet red peppers**
- 2 **tablespoons peanut or vegetable oil**
- 2 **tablespoons soy sauce**
- 2 **tablespoons red wine vinegar**
- 2 **tablespoons Oriental sesame oil (optional)**

1. Remove the stalks from the broccoli; reserve the stalks for another use. Cut the remaining broccoli into flowerets.
2. Halve, seed and slice the peppers. Combine with the broccoli flowerets in a large bowl.
3. Place the peanut oil, soy sauce, vinegar and sesame oil, if using, in a small jar with a screw-top. Cover and shake vigorously to blend the marinade. Pour the marinade over the broccoli and red peppers; toss gently to evenly coat the vegetables. Cover the bowl with plastic wrap and let stand for 1 hour at room temperature to blend the flavors.

Warm Shrimp Appetizer Salad

Most of the ingredients can be prepared a day ahead; the shrimp topping is quickly cooked just before serving.

Makes 16 servings.

Nutrient Value Per Serving: 141 calories, 8 g protein, 11 g fat, 4 g carbohydrate, 136 mg sodium, 53 mg cholesterol.

2	*heads Belgian endive*
1	*medium-size head romaine lettuce*
1	*small head chicory*
2	*zucchini (about 8 ounces each)*
1	*bag (6 ounces) red radishes*
2	*small red onions*
½	*cup extra-virgin olive oil*
⅓	*cup fresh lemon juice (2 to 3 lemons)*
1	*tablespoon Worcestershire sauce*
1	*teaspoon dry mustard*
½	*teaspoon salt*
¼	*teaspoon white pepper*
¼	*cup vegetable oil*
1½	*pounds uncooked medium-size shrimp in the shell (1¼ pounds peeled and cleaned)*
2	*cloves garlic, finely chopped*

1. Trim off the stem end of the Belgian endive. Cut the endive lengthwise into quarters. Separate the quarters into individual leaves. Wrap the leaves in paper toweling; place in a plastic bag and store in the refrigerator.
2. Separate the romaine and chicory into leaves. Wash the leaves and dry with paper toweling. Tear the leaves into bite-size pieces. Wrap the greens in paper toweling; place in plastic bags and refrigerate.

3. Cut the zucchini into 2½ x ½-inch strips. Cut each radish into 4 or 6 wedges. Halve the red onions and slice crosswise. Wrap each vegetable separately in plastic bags and refrigerate.
4. Combine the olive oil, lemon juice, Worcestershire sauce, mustard, salt and pepper in a jar with a tight-fitting lid. Shake well to blend the dressing; set aside.
5. Just before serving, heat the vegetable oil in a large skillet. Add the shrimp and garlic; sauté over medium-high heat just until the shrimp are pink and tender, about 3 minutes. Remove with a slotted spoon to a bowl. Add the zucchini strips to the skillet; sauté until crisp-tender, about 4 minutes. Remove the skillet from the heat. Stir the red onion slices and radishes into the zucchini. Return the shrimp and its juices to the skillet. Shake the dressing and add to the shrimp mixture. Stir to mix well. Place the greens in a large, shallow salad bowl. Spoon the shrimp mixture over the greens. Toss and serve.

King Crab Cocktails

Serve with our Creamy Seafood Dressing or your own favorite tangy cocktail sauce.

Makes 8 servings.

Nutrient Value Per Serving (without dressing): 128 calories, 24 g protein, 3 g fat, 1 g carbohydrate, 286 mg sodium, 136 mg cholesterol.

2	*tablespoons shrimp boiling mix*
3	*lemon slices*
	Water
4	*pounds frozen King crab legs*
	Creamy Seafood Dressing (recipe follows)
	Lime wedges

1. Combine the shrimp boiling mix and lemon slices in a large pot of water. Bring to boiling. Add the frozen crab legs and return to boiling. Lower the heat and simmer for 5 minutes.
2. Remove the crab legs from the water with tongs. If you want to remove the shells, cool the crab legs until lukewarm. Cut along the side of each

crab leg with kitchen shears and remove the crab in whole pieces. Cover with plastic wrap. Refrigerate until serving time.
3. Prepare the Creamy Seafood Dressing. Cover and refrigerate.
4. At serving time, fill a serving bowl with cracked ice. Pile the crab legs and lime wedges on top. Serve with the Creamy Seafood Dressing.

Creamy Seafood Dressing: Combine ¾ cup mayonnaise or salad dressing, ¼ cup sliced green onion, ¼ cup parsley leaves, 1 tablespoon prepared horseradish and 1 tablespoon lime juice in the container of an electric blender or food processor. Cover and whirl on medium speed for 30 seconds or until the mixture is creamy. Pour into a glass bowl and fold in ½ cup dairy sour cream and ¼ teaspoon freshly ground pepper. Makes about 1½ cups. *Nutrient Value Per Tablespoon: 60 calories, 0 g protein, 6 g fat, 1 g carbohydrate, 43 mg sodium, 6 mg cholesterol.*

Shrimp Louis

Instead of a tomato cocktail sauce with chilled shrimp, try this spicy mustard Louis dressing.

Makes 6 appetizer servings.

Nutrient Value Per Serving: 172 calories, 13 g protein, 12 g fat, 2 g carbohydrate, 288 mg sodium, 95 mg cholesterol.

3   *cups water*
2   *bay leaves*
1   *teaspoon leaf thyme, crumbled*
1   *teaspoon garlic powder*
     Dash ground hot red pepper
1   *pound fresh or frozen shelled and deveined shrimp*
1   *head leaf lettuce*
¾   *cup Louis Dressing (recipe follows)*

1. Combine the water, bay leaves, leaf thyme, garlic powder and red pepper in a large skillet. Bring to boiling. Lower the heat and simmer for 3 minutes.
2. Add the shrimp; return to boiling and then lower the heat and simmer for 3 minutes or until the shrimp turn pink. Drain the shrimp in a colander. Place in a bowl and refrigerate, covered.
3. Place a lettuce leaf in each serving dish. Shred the remaining lettuce and pile into the lettuce cups. Arrange the chilled shrimp on top of the lettuce. Spoon the Louis Dressing over the shrimp, dividing evenly.

Louis Dressing

Makes about 1 cup.

Nutrient Value Per Tablespoon: 54 calories, 0 g protein, 6 g fat, 1 g carbohydrate, 80 mg sodium, 4 mg cholesterol.

½   *cup mayonnaise OR: salad dressing*
1   *tablespoon catsup*
1   *tablespoon Dijon-style mustard*
½   *teaspoon lemon juice*
¼   *cup finely chopped celery*
¼   *cup finely chopped green onion*
2   *tablespoons chopped parsley*
1   *tablespoon paprika*

Combine the mayonnaise or salad dressing, catsup, mustard and lemon juice in the container of an electric blender or food processor. Add the celery, green onion, parsley and paprika. Cover and process on high until the dressing is smooth and creamy.

Creamy Blue Cheese Dressing

Makes about 1 cup.

Nutrient Value Per Tablespoon: 76 calories, 2 g protein, 8 g fat, 1 g carbohydrate, 150 mg sodium, 10 mg cholesterol.

½   *cup mayonnaise*
¼   *cup buttermilk*
4   *ounces blue cheese, crumbled*
1   *teaspoon red wine vinegar*
½   *teaspoon dry mustard*
¼   *teaspoon pepper*
     Pinch Worcestershire sauce
     Pinch salt

Blend all the ingredients together in a bowl with a fork until enough lumps of the cheese are incorporated throughout the dressing.

MAKE YOUR OWN CROUTONS

Add a flavorful crunch to soups and salads with home-made croutons. Cut day-old white bread into small cubes. Sauté in a little olive oil and butter in a skillet over medium heat, tossing frequently, until crisp and golden, about 5 minutes. For extra flavor, add a little finely chopped garlic or chopped fresh herbs.

Easy "House" Dressing

A quick and easy dressing when time is at a minimum.

Makes 2 cups.

Nutrient Value Per Tablespoon: 92 calories, 0 g protein, 10 g fat, 0 g carbohydrate, 28 mg sodium, 0 mg cholesterol.

- ½ **teaspoon salt**
- ½ **teaspoon white pepper**
- ¼ **teaspoon leaf tarragon, crumbled**
- ¼ **teaspoon chopped shallot**
- ¼ **teaspoon chopped garlic**
- 2 **tablespoons Dijon-style mustard**
- ½ **cup red wine vinegar**
- 1½ **cups vegetable oil**

Combine the salt, pepper, tarragon, shallot, garlic, mustard and vinegar in a bowl and mix well. Whisk in the oil until smooth. Toss a small amount with your favorite assortment of salad greens.

Italian Salad Dressing or Marinade

Use as a dressing for crisp salad greens or as a marinade for poultry.

Makes about 1 cup.

Nutrient Value Per Tablespoon: 46 calories, 0 g protein, 5 g fat, 0 g carbohydrate, 42 mg sodium, 0 mg cholesterol.

- 6 **tablespooons olive oil**
- 3 **tablespoons red wine vinegar**
- 2 **tablespoons tomato juice (shake well before adding)**
- 1 **clove garlic, pressed**
- ¼ **teaspoon salt**
- ⅛ **teaspoon pepper**
- ¼ **teaspoon dried parsley flakes**
- ¼ **teaspoon leaf oregano, crumbled**
- ½ **teaspoon grated Parmesan cheese**

Combine all the ingredients in a screw-top jar or any jar that can be tightly covered. Shake well. For best results, make a day ahead so the flavors can blend. Shake well before serving.

Variation: Spicy Italian Dressing

Add Dijon-style mustard to taste, or substitute ground hot red pepper to taste for the black pepper. Or used crushed red pepper flakes.

Avocado-Anchovy Salad Dressing

Makes about 2 cups.

Nutrient Value Per Tablespoon: 76 calories, 0 g protein, 8 g fat, 1 g carbohydrate, 20 mg sodium, 17 mg cholesterol.

- 2 **egg yolks**
- 1 **tablespoon Dijon-style mustard**
- 1 **cup olive oil**
- 1 **ripe avocado, peeled, pitted and puréed**
- 1 **clove garlic, mashed**
- 4 **canned, flat anchovy fillets, mashed and puréed**
- 1 **tablespoon lemon juice**
- 1 **sprig parsley, chopped**
- 2 **tablespoons prepared horseradish**
  Salt and pepper, to taste

Whisk the egg yolks and mustard together in a bowl. Then slowly whisk in the oil to make a mayonnaise; when this consistency is reached, add all the remaining ingredients. Mix until well blended. Let the dressing stand a few minutes to let the flavors blend.

Lemon Country Dressing

Adjust the lemon so there is just a hint, or enough to pucker the mouth, if you wish. This dressing pairs nicely with crisp romaine leaves.

Makes about 2 cups.

Nutrient Value Per Tablespoon: 63 calories, 0 g protein, 7 g fat, 0 g carbohydrate, 67 mg sodium, 13 mg cholesterol.

- 1 **teaspoon imported mustard powder**
- 1 **cup heavy cream**
- 2 **tablespoons fresh lemon juice, or to taste**
- ½ **teaspoon salt**
- ⅛ **teaspoon liquid red-pepper seasoning**
- ¾ **cup mayonnaise**

Combine the mustard powder, heavy cream, lemon juice, salt, liquid red-pepper seasoning and mayonnaise in a medium-size bowl and mix with a whisk or fork until well blended. Cover the bowl with plastic wrap and refrigerate until ready to use. Whisk again just before using.

Three-Bean Salad for a Crowd

A classic combination, equally at home with other antipasto ingredients or with hamburgers and franks.

Makes 12 servings.

Nutrient Value Per Serving: 181 calories, 5 g protein, 9 g fat, 21 g carbohydrate, 438 mg sodium, 0 mg cholesterol.

- 2 **cans (1 pound each) red kidney beans, rinsed and drained**
- 1 **pound green beans, cooked, drained and cut into 2-inch lengths**
- 1 **pound wax beans, cooked, drained and cut into 2-inch lengths**
- ½ **cup vegetable oil**
- ½ **cup cider vinegar**
- ⅛ **to ¼ cup sugar**
- 1 **teaspoon salt**
- 1 **medium-size onion, sliced (optional)**

1. Combine the kidney beans, green beans and wax beans in a large bowl.
2. Mix together the oil, vinegar, sugar and salt in a small saucepan. Bring to boiling over moderate heat. Pour over the beans and toss to blend.

Cover the bowl with plastic wrap. Refrigerate several hours or overnight.
3. At serving time, remove the beans from the marinade with a slotted spoon to the serving platter. Top with the onion rings, if you wish.

Irish Potato Salad

Every outdoor party needs a good potato salad.

Makes 8 servings.

Nutrient Value Per Serving: 446 calories, 5 g protein, 33 g fat, 34 g carbohydrate, 540 mg sodium, 26 mg cholesterol.

- 4 **pounds medium-size potatoes**
- ¾ **cup chopped celery**
- ¾ **cup diced carrot**
- ½ **cup sliced green onion**
- 1½ **cups mayonnaise OR: salad dressing**
- 6 **tablespoons milk**
- 2 **tablespoons snipped chives (optional)**
- 1 **teaspoon salt**
  Freshly ground pepper
  Leaf lettuce
  Hard-cooked egg wedges

1. Cook the potatoes in enough boiling salted water to cover the potatoes in a large saucepan, covered, for 30 minutes or just until tender. Drain the potatoes and cool. Then peel and cube the potatoes and combine with the celery, carrot and green onion in a large bowl.
2. Blend together the mayonnaise or salad dressing, milk, chives, if using, salt and pepper to taste in a small bowl. Fold the dressing into the potato mixture.
3. Cover the bowl with plastic wrap and refrigerate for several hours to blend the flavors.
4. At serving time, line a serving bowl with lettuce; fill the bowl with the potato salad. Garnish with the egg wedges.

S·I·D·E O·F T·H·E P·L·A·T·E F·I·L·L·E·R·S

Sweet Potato-Parsnip Timbale (page 59) *with Sautéed Mixed Vegetables* (page 60).

Cheese-Topped French Fries

Oven-fried frozen potatoes are so easy to prepare and become so crisp.

Bake at 425° for 15 minutes.
Makes 8 servings.

Nutrient Value Per Serving: 239 calories, 6 g protein, 12 g fat, 29 g carbohydrate, 305 mg sodium, 13 mg cholesterol.

1 **bag (32 ounces) frozen French fries**
 Seasoned salt
 Shredded American cheese

1. Preheat the oven to hot (425°).
2. Spread the potatoes in a single layer in a large jelly-roll pan.
3. Bake the French fries in the preheated hot oven (425°) for 15 minutes or until golden brown. Sprinkle the fries with the seasoned salt. Pile the fries in a napkin-lined basket. Sprinkle the fries while still hot with the cheese and serve them immediately.

Fabulous Fried Onion Rings

Our favorite recipe for crisp and delicate fried onion rings. The perfect accompaniment to grilled steak, burgers or chops.

Makes 6 servings.

Nutrient Value Per Serving: 311 calories, 5 g protein, 18 g fat, 34 g carbohydrate, 7 mg sodium, 0 mg cholesterol.

1½ **cups all-purpose flour**
 1 **can (12 ounces) beer**
 1 **teaspoon leaf sage, crumbled**
 3 **very large yellow onions**
 3 **to 4 cups vegetable shortening**
 Salt and pepper, to taste

1. Combine the flour, beer and sage in a large glass or ceramic bowl with a wire whisk until well blended. Cover the bowl with plastic wrap. Let the batter rest at room temperature for at least 3 hours. (This makes the batter extra light.)
2. Cut the onions into ¼-inch-thick slices; separate the slices into rings and remove the skin from the rings.
3. Melt enough shortening in a 10-inch heavy skillet over low heat to a depth of 2 inches. Heat the oil

until it registers 375° on a deep-fat frying thermometer.
4. Dip a few onion rings into the batter, using metal tongs; let the excess batter drip off back into the bowl. Carefully place a few of the onion rings at a time in the hot fat.
5. Fry the rings, turning once or twice, for 3 minutes or until the onion rings are golden. Transfer the rings to a paper towel-lined cookie sheet. Keep warm in a preheated very slow oven (250°). Continue frying until all the onion rings are fried.

Note: To freeze, fry the rings and drain on paper toweling at room termperature. Arrange the rings on a cookie sheet and freeze. When frozen, pack the rings in plastic bags and return to the freezer. To reheat: Arrange the onion rings on a cookie sheet. Heat the onion rings in a preheated hot oven (400°) for 4 to 6 minutes or until hot.

Stuffed Mushrooms

Accompany classy outdoor-grilled steak with this elegant side dish.

Makes 1 dozen.

Nutrient Value Per Mushroom: 32 calories, 1 g protein, 1 g fat, 4 g carbohydrate, 36 mg sodium, 0 mg cholesterol.

12 **medium-size mushrooms (about ½ pound)**
 1 **tablespoon vegetable oil**
 2 **teaspoons grated onion**
 3 **slices bread, crumbled**
 2 **tablespoons chopped parsley**
 1 **tablespoon beef broth**
 1 **teaspoon leaf basil, crumbled**
 Watercress

1. Wipe the mushrooms well with a damp cloth. Remove the stems and chop the stems only. Set the chopped stems aside for making the filling.
2. Sauté the mushroom caps in the oil in a medium-size skillet for 2 minutes or just until the caps are heated through. Place the caps on a metal plate.
3. Sauté the chopped stems with the grated onion in the same skillet just until soft. Place the mixture in a small bowl; stir in the bread crumbs, parsley, beef broth and basil until blended.
4. Pile the filling into the mushroom caps. Keep warm in a preheated slow oven (275°) until ready to serve. Garnish each mushroom with a sprig of watercress, just before serving.

HOW TO HANDLE MUSHROOMS

Select mushrooms with caps that are tightly closed so the gills on the underside are not visible. Mushrooms contain a lot of water, so as they age, the water evaporates and the underside opens up and the top shrivels. Store mushrooms, unwashed, in a ventilated container or a brown paper bag in the refrigerator. Rich in vitamin D, mushrooms are practically without calories. To clean, wipe the caps with damp paper toweling. If a lot of dirt clings to the underside, swish in a bowl of cold water; drain and pat dry. Wash only the mushrooms you're going to use immediately and never soak them.

Herbed Tomatoes

Bake at 400° for 10 to 15 minutes.
Makes 6 servings.

Nutrient Value Per Serving: 95 calories, 3 g protein, 7 g fat, 7 g carbohydrate, 52 mg sodium, 7 mg cholesterol.

6   large firm tomatoes
     Salt and pepper, to taste
2   tablespoons olive or vegetable oil
¼   cup chopped parsley
⅓   cup grated Cheddar cheese

1. Preheat the oven to hot (400°).
2. Cut the tomatoes into wedges. Season with salt and pepper. Drain the tomatoes on paper toweling for 10 minutes.
3. Arrange the tomatoes in a heavy metal baking pan. Drizzle the tomatoes with the oil and sprinkle with the chopped parsley. Cover the pan with heavy-duty aluminum foil.
4. Bake the tomatoes in the preheated hot oven (400°) for 10 minutes or until the tomatoes are tender. Sprinkle them with the cheese. Serve the tomatoes hot or at room temperature.

Sweet Potato-Parsnip Timbale

For an attractive presentation, fill the center with the Sautéed Mixed Vegetables (see recipe, page 60).

Bake at 350° for 1 hour.
Makes 12 servings.

Nutrient Value Per Serving: 222 calories, 4 g protein, 11 g fat, 27 g carbohydrate, 230 mg sodium, 125 mg cholesterol.

3   pounds sweet potatoes, peeled
1   pound parsnips, peeled
1¼ cups heavy cream
4   eggs
1   teaspoon salt
⅛   teaspoon ground nutmeg, plus a pinch
¼   teaspoon pepper

1. Cut the sweet potatoes into 2-inch pieces. Cook the potatoes in boiling water to cover in a large saucepan until the potatoes are tender.
2. Cut the parsnips into 1-inch pieces. Cook the parsnips in boiling water to cover in another saucepan until tender.
3. Drain the sweet potatoes. Place half of the pieces in the container of a food processor.* Add ½ cup of the cream. Cover; whirl until a smooth purée. Scrape the purée into a bowl. Repeat with the other half of the potatoes and ½ cup of the cream. Add to the potato purée 3 of the eggs, ¾ teaspoon of the salt, the nutmeg and ⅛ teaspoon of the pepper; mix well. Set aside.
4. Wash the container of the food processor. Drain the parsnips. Combine the parsnips, ¼ cup of the cream, the remaining egg, the pinch nutmeg, ¼ teaspoon of the salt and ⅛ teaspoon of the pepper in the container of the food processor. Cover; whirl until a smooth purée.
5. Preheat the oven to moderate (350°). Generously butter a 6½-cup ring mold.
6. Spoon half of the sweet potato mixture in an even layer in the prepared mold, smoothing the top with the back of a small spoon. Add all of the parsnip mixture, spreading it in an even layer. Top with the remaining sweet potato mixture; the mold should be full to the top.
7. Place the mold in a shallow baking pan; place on the oven rack. Pour boiling water into the pan until it comes halfway up the side of the mold.
8. Bake the mold in the preheated moderate oven (350°) for about 1 hour or until the mold is set and the top feels firm to the touch. Remove the mold from the water and cool on a wire rack for 20 minutes.
9. To unmold, run a knife around the edges to

loosen the timbale. Invert a plate over the mold; holding the plate and mold together, invert and carefully lift off the mold. Garnish the timbale with the Sautéed Mixed Vegetables *(see recipe this page),* if you wish.

*Note: To purée the sweet potato and the parsnip in an electric blender instead of a food processor, use the following procedure: Pour ⅓ cup of the cream into the blender container; add about one-third of the sweet potato; break in 1 of the eggs. Cover; whirl at low speed using on/off pulses. Scrape down the sides of the container with a rubber spatula several times. Transfer the mixture to a bowl. Repeat the puréeing process two more times. Season the purée with salt, nutmeg and pepper. Wash the blender container. Pour in the remaining ¼ cup of cream; add the parsnips and the remaining egg. Cover; whirl until smooth and scrape down the sides as above.

MAKE-AHEAD TIP

Prepare and bake the timbale the day before you plan to serve it. Do not unmold. Refrigerate the ring, covered. To reheat, remove the mold from the refrigerator and let stand at room temperature for 3 hours. Place the mold in a water bath and place in a preheated hot oven (400°) for 20 minutes or until heated through. Unmold and serve. To reheat the timbale in a microwave oven, unmold the cold timbale directly from the refrigerator onto a microwave-safe serving plate. Cover the top of the timbale with a piece of wax paper and microwave at full power for 9 to 10 minutes, rotating the plate one-quarter turn after 5 minutes. Let the timbale stand for 5 minutes before serving.

Sautéed Mixed Vegetables

Makes 12 servings.

Nutrient Value Per Serving: 51 calories, 2 g protein, 3 g fat, 4 g carbohydrate, 107 mg sodium, 3 mg cholesterol.

- **1 pound fresh snow peas OR: green beans**
- **1 small bunch broccoli (about 12 ounces)**
- **1 small sweet red pepper**
- **2 tablespoons vegetable oil**
- **1 tablespoon butter or margarine**
- **½ teaspoon salt**
- **⅛ teaspoon pepper**

1. Remove the strings and tips from the snow peas or the green beans. Cut the flowerets off the broccoli stalks in 2½-inch lengths. Split the large flowerets in half. Peel the tough outer woody layer off the broccoli stalks. Diagonally slice the broccoli stalks. If using green beans, cut each in half. Cut the red pepper into 2 x ¼-inch strips.
2. Cook the broccoli stalk slices in a large pot of boiling water for 1 minute. (If using green beans instead of snow peas, cook the beans with the broccoli slices.) Add the flowerets and cook for 1½ minutes longer. Add the snow peas and cook for 30 seconds. Drain the vegetables in a colander under cold running water to prevent any further cooking.
3. Heat the oil and butter in a large skillet. Add the sweet red pepper and sauté over medium-high heat just until the pepper is wilted, for about 2 minutes. Add the blanched vegetables, salt and pepper. Cook until all the vegetables are heated through.

Note: To make ahead, the vegetables may be blanched hours in advance, cooled, drained and refrigerated. Reheating will take a little longer if the vegetables are used directly from the refrigerator.

V·E·G·E·T·A·B·L·E·S

Fresh Fruit and Vegetable Availability

The following fruits and vegetables (thanks to refrigeration and efficient transportation) are usually available all year:

Apples	Corn, sweet	Parsley and
Artichokes	Cucumbers	herbs
Avocados	Eggplant	Parsnips
Bananas	Escarole	Pears
Beans, green	Garlic	Peas, green
Beets	Grapefruit	Peppers, sweet
Broccoli	Grapes	Pineapples
Brussels	Greens	Plantains
sprouts	Lemons	Potatoes
Cabbage	Lettuce	Radishes
Carrots	Limes	Spinach
Cauliflower	Mushrooms	Squash
Celery	Onions	Strawberries
Chinese	Onion, green	Sweet potatoes
cabbage	Oranges	Tomatoes
Coconuts	Papayas	Turnips-rutabagas

The following are widely available in the markets during the months indicated, although a variety of fruits may be imported from other countries, making them available during "off" seasons.

Apricots — June to August
Asparagus — March to July
Blueberries — June to August
Cantaloupes — April to October
Cherries — May to August
Cranberries — September to December
Honeydews — February to October
Mangoes — March to August
Nectarines — January and February/June to
  September
Okra — April to November
Peaches — May to September
Persimmons — October to February
Plums and Prunes — June to October
Pomegranates — September to December
Pumpkins — September to December
Tangelos — October to February
Tangerines — November to March
Watermelons — April to September

Selecting Fresh Fruits and Vegetables

• Take time to look for the freshest of the fresh. Select fruits and vegetables that are of characteristic color, shape and size. Misshapen fruits and vegetables are often inferior, taste bad and are difficult to prepare.
• Use fruits and vegetables as soon as possible. Avoid buying too much at once.
• Enjoy the fresh produce of the season for flavor and price. When supplies are abundant, the prices are low.

Refrigeration of Fresh Fruits and Vegetables

Fruits and vegetables may be stored in the refrigerator for several days. The longer they are refrigerated, the greater the vitamin loss, so it is best to eat them as soon after purchase as possible.

Asparagus, broccoli, cabbage, cauliflower, celery, cucumbers, green beans, green onions, sweet green and red peppers and radishes should be promptly refrigerated in a covered container, moisture-proof bag or a vegetable crisper. Greens (kale, spinach, turnip greens, chard and salad greens) should first be wrapped in paper toweling and then refrigerated.

Apples, apricots, berries, cherries, corn (in husks), grapes, nectarines, peaches, pears, peas (in shell) and plums should be refrigerated loosely covered or in a plastic produce bag with air holes.

Vegetable Preparation Techniques

• **Don't overcook!** Vegetables should be cooked only until tender.
• **Boil:** Use a small amount of water, cover with a tight-fitting lid and cook over low heat to minimize loss of vitamins and minerals. Cook until tender.
• **Blanch:** Bring plenty of water to a rolling boil, immerse vegetables and bring water back to a boil for 2 to 4 minutes. Refresh vegetables under icy water and use in salads.
• **Steam:** Place a steaming basket, colander or bamboo steamer over 1½ to 2 inches of boiling water and place the prepared vegetables on the rack. Cover the pan, reduce the heat but keep the water boiling and cook until just tender.
• **Stir-Fry:** Place the wok or wide skillet over high heat; when hot, add vegetable oil and heat. Then add the cut-up vegetables. Cook, uncovered, stirring constantly, just until the vegetables have been lightly coated and slightly cooked (approximately 1 to 2 minutes). Add approximately ¼ cup of broth to 4 cups of vegetables; then cover and cook, stirring occasionally, until tender. Add more broth if necessary.

• **Microwave:** Cook all vegetables on 100% HIGH power, following the manufacturer's directions. Cover the microwave-safe cooking dish with a casserole lid or microwave-safe plastic wrap. Cooking time depends on the freshness, moisture content and maturity of the vegetable. Remove the vegetables from the microwave after the shortest recommended time, let stand and test for doneness. If the vegetables are still too crisp, microwave in 1 minute segments.

THE WINTER PRODUCE STALL

Besides the year-round favorites (such as bananas, cabbage, carrots, celery, onions, lettuce, sweet red and green peppers and potatoes), winter features an abundance of apples, pears, avocados, grapes, citrus fruits, broccoli, cauliflower, Brussels sprouts, peas, spinach, winter squash and sweet potatoes.

The Roots Revisited

Don't ignore the earthy goodness of the following root vegetables.

Beets: Cook without trimming the stems or roots too closely, or they'll "bleed." Prepare vitamin A-rich tops as you would spinach. Serve hot sliced beets in an orange glaze, spiced with cloves.

Carrots: Add to soups and stews. Scrub very well; peeling is not necessary. Toss grated carrots with lemon juice, sherry, raisins and chopped nuts. Cut carrots into 2-inch chunks; boil until barely tender. Drain well and roll in orange-mint butter, then in dry bread crumbs; bake.

Parsnips: Parsnips are sweeter after prolonged exposure to cold temperatures; that's why they're best during the winter months. Steam them to bring out their rich nutty flavor. Toss diced cooked parsnips with a thin white sauce; sprinkle with crisp bacon bits and chopped parsley.

Radishes: Serve crisp radishes with butter, coarse salt, pumpernickle bread and icy cold beer.

Rutabagas and Turnips: Rutabagas, also called Swedes or Swedish turnips, are golden and larger than white turnips. Rutabaga tops, unlike turnip tops, are not eaten as a separate vegetable. Add a teaspoonful of sugar to the cooking water to improve the mild flavor and sweetness. Mix mashed cooked rutabaga with apple-sauce. Toss diced cooked turnip with heavy cream and grated Parmesan cheese.

Salsify: Similar in appearance to parsnips, but with grass-like tops, salsify is also called Oyster plant. Serve gratinée, with minced chives or shallots. Or mash until creamy; season with butter, salt and pepper.

Celeriac: Also known as celery root. Peel before cooking, adding vinegar to the water. Marinate raw celeriac in a vinaigrette dressing and serve over sliced tomatoes.

A FRUITFUL WINTER

Pears, bananas, oranges, grapefruit, apples, tangerines and cranberries are plentiful in winter.

• Fill apples with sugar, grated orange rind and coconut. Place in a baking pan; squeeze orange juice over tops. Bake until tender, basting often.

• Top grapefruit halves with honey, rum and ground cinnamon; broil.

• Fill individual shortcakes with a cranberry relish; top with sweetened whipped cream.

• Sauté halved bananas in butter until golden. Sprinkle with brown sugar and brandy; serve with ice cream.

• Add chopped orange to sweetened whipped cream cheese; use to top toasted pound cake.

• Combine diced pear with tangerine sections, whole almonds and ground ginger; toss with lemon juice and 10X (confectioners') sugar. Serve icy cold.

REUSE VEGETABLE LEFTOVERS

Toss leftover cooked vegetables into salads, purée for chilled soups or warm sauces, or coarsely chop and mix with mayonnaise for sandwich makings.

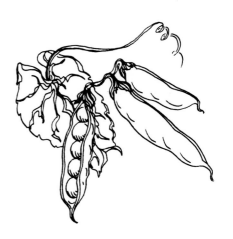

Squash and Onion Combo

Onion combines equally well with yellow or zucchini squash.

Makes 4 servings.

Nutrient Value Per Serving: 36 calories, 1 g protein, 1 g fat, 6 g carbohydrate, 276 mg sodium, 0 mg cholesterol.

- 1 **small onion, thinly sliced**
- 1 **clove garlic, finely chopped**
- 1 **teaspoon vegetable oil**
- 1 **pound yellow squash or zucchini squash, sliced ¼ inch thick**
- 2 **tablespoons water**
- ½ **teaspoon salt**
  Pepper (optional)

1. Sauté the onion and garlic in the oil in a large non-stick skillet over medium heat for 4 minutes or until tender.
2. Add the squash and water. Cover the skillet tightly and continue cooking for 7 minutes or until the squash is crisp-tender. Season with the salt and pepper, if you wish.

Spade Ranch Beans

Pintos have been grown in large quantities for centuries in the semi-arid climate of New Mexico and provide at low cost an excellent source of energy.

Makes 10 to 12 servings.

Nutrient Value Per Serving: 204 calories, 10 g protein, 6 g fat, 27 g carbohydrate, 277 mg sodium, 7 mg cholesterol.

- 1 **pound pinto beans, picked over and soaked overnight**
- 2 **quarts hot water**
- ¼ **pound bacon, diced**
- 4 **cloves garlic, peeled**
- 1 **teaspoon salt**
- 1 **teaspoon chili powder OR: ground hot red pepper**

1. Rinse the pre-soaked beans in cold water. Put the beans in a large black iron pot or other large pot and add the hot water. Bring the water just to boiling over high heat. Reduce the heat; add the bacon, garlic and seasonings. Cover the pot and simmer (do not boil) for about 3 hours. Check from time to time and add more water if necessary.
2. You want the cooked bean juice to be fairly thick. The beans are done when the skin is almost as tender as the inside of the bean, but the skin should not be broken. Taste and correct the seasonings as desired, adding more chili powder or red pepper, if you wish.

Pilaf with Peas and Mushrooms

Makes 4 servings.

Nutrient Value Per Serving: 275 calories, 8 g protein, 4 g fat, 49 g carbohydrate, 493 mg sodium, 0 mg cholesterol.

- ½ **cup chopped onions, frozen or fresh**
- 1 **tablespoon olive oil**
- 1 **can (13¾ ounces) chicken broth**
- 1 **cup uncooked long-grain converted white rice**
- ¼ **cup freeze-dried mushrooms**
- 1 **package (10 ounces) frozen peas**
  Pinch white pepper
- 2 **tablespoons chopped parsley**

1. Sauté the onion in the oil in a medium-size saucepan until tender, about 5 minutes.
2. Pour the chicken broth into a 4-cup liquid measure. Add enough water to make a total of 2½ cups liquid. Add the liquid to the onion along with the rice and mushrooms. Bring the mixture to boiling over high heat. Lower the heat and simmer, covered, stirring the mixture occasionally, for 15 minutes.
3. Add the frozen peas and pepper. Simmer for 10 minutes or until the liquid is absorbed and the rice is tender. Stir in the parsley.

A ROSTER OF RICE

White Rice It's dubbed "regular" because it is the most familiar and popular. Hull, bran and polishings have been removed, leaving a snow-white grain. The size regulates the price: *Short-grain or medium-grain* rice are the thriftiest. These cook moist and tender and are an ideal choice for casseroles, puddings and croquettes. *Long-grain* rice, at a few pennies more a pound, cooks fluffier and flakier and is preferred for serving as a vegetable or as a base for curry. Most white rice is enriched, but let the label be your guide.

Processed White Rice The term *"parboiled"* or *"converted"* on the package of rice simply means that the grains have been partly cooked before milling, with special care taken to protect the vitamins and minerals in the outer layer. This rice is long grain with a light golden color and it cooks the same as regular rice.

Precooked White Rice It's called *"instant"* because it needs only the briefest cooking. It is milled from special long-grain rice, is enriched and comes plain and seasoned.

Brown Rice This is whole-grain rice with only the outer hull removed. The cooking time for brown rice is longer than for regular rice and its savory, nut-like flavor makes it a perfect partner for meat or game.

Wild Rice This is not a true rice, but is the seed of a water grass native to some of our northern states. When cooked, these long, slender, gray-brown grains have a sweet, nut-like flavor. Wild rice is available as is or mixed with long-grain white rice.

Seasoned Rice These are quick-to-fix, convenience foods. The seasonings are mixed with the rice before packaging or included in a separate packet. Take your pick of beef, chicken, chili, cheese, curry, herb, pilaf or saffron (yellow) rice flavors. Frozen seasoned rice is the easiest to fix; just heat and serve.

How Much Rice Should You Cook?

Rice swells 3 to 4 times as it cooks. Use this chart for reference

Rice	Uncooked	Cooked	Servings
Long-Grain White Rice	1 cup	3 cups	3 to 4
Processed Converted White Rice	1 cup	4 cups	4 to 6
Precooked Instant White Rice	1 cup	2 cups	2 to 3
Brown Rice	1 cup	4 cups	4 to 6
Wild Rice	1 cup	4 cups	4 to 6

Sauce Primavera

Use whatever combination of vegetables you like. Serve over pasta, baked potatoes or toast points.

Makes 4 cups.

Nutrient Value Per ½ Cup: 135 calories, 9 g protein, 38 g fat, 17 g carbohydrate, 587 mg sodium, 127 mg cholesterol.

- **1   large stalk broccoli, cut into tiny flowerets (about 2 cups)**
- **1   large zucchini, trimmed, halved lengthwise and sliced crosswise (about 1 cup)**
- **1   large yellow squash, trimmed, halved lengthwise and sliced crosswise (about 1 cup)**
- **1   large carrot, peeled and sliced crosswise (about ¾ cup)**
- **½   cup (1 stick) butter or margarine**
- **1   large onion, chopped (1 cup)**
- **½   cup all-purpose flour**
- **2   envelopes or 2 teaspoons instant chicken broth powder**
- **¼   teaspoon grated nutmeg**
- **2   cups milk**
- **2   cups heavy cream**
- **⅔   cup grated Parmesan cheese**
  White pepper, to taste

1. Bring salted water to boiling in a large saucepan. Blanch the broccoli, then the zucchini and squash, and then the carrot, just until barely tender; remove each batch with a slotted spoon to a bowl of ice water before adding the next vegetable. Drain the vegetables well. Discard the water.

Sauce Primavera

2. Melt the butter or margarine in a large saucepan. Add the onion and sauté until soft and transparent. Stir in the flour, instant chicken broth and nutmeg. Cook, stirring constantly, until the mixture thickens and bubbles for 2 minutes.
3. Add the milk and cream. Cook the sauce, stirring constantly, until thickened and bubbly, for about 3 minutes. Stir in the Parmesan cheese and white pepper to taste. Add the drained vegetables.
4. Keep the sauce warm, stirring occasionally.

POTATOES TURNING DARK?

To prevent potatoes turning dark after peeling, completely immerse in a bowl of cold water, until ready to use.

Pommes Dauphinoise

Rich and delicious scalloped potatoes.

Bake at 300° for 2 hours.
Makes 6 servings.

Nutrient Value Per Serving: 481 calories, 10 g protein, 34 g fat, 36 g carbohydrate, 372 mg sodium, 126 mg cholesterol.

- **6   large baking potatoes (3 pounds)**
- **2   large cloves garlic, finely chopped**
- **¾   teaspoon salt**
- **½   teaspoon pepper**
- **2   cups heavy cream**
- **1¼   cups milk (about)**
- **½   cup shredded Gruyère or Swiss cheese (2 ounces)**

1. Preheat the oven to slow (300°). Butter a 10-cup flame-proof baking dish. Place a sheet of aluminum foil on the oven floor to catch any drips.
2. Peel the potatoes and drop them into a bowl of cold water.
3. Place the prepared dish over low heat. Dry and thinly slice 1 potato at a time. Spread the slices evenly in the dish. When half of the potatoes are in the dish, sprinkle with the garlic and half of the salt and pepper. Add enough cream to barely cover the potatoes. Let the cream heat slowly, while slicing and layering the remaining potatoes.
4. When all the potatoes are in the dish, add the remaining cream and enough of the milk to just

cover the potatoes. Sprinkle the potatoes with the remaining salt and pepper. Bring the mixture to a gentle boiling. Sprinkle the top with the cheese.

5. Bake the potatoes in the preheated slow oven (300°) for 2 hours or until the potatoes are tender when pierced with a knife.

Country-Fried Potatoes

Crispy on the outside and tender within, these potatoes are a great texture contrast to serve with any meat that is sauced.

Makes 6 servings.

Nutrient Value Per Serving: 271 calories, 4 g protein, 16 g fat, 31 g carbohydrate, 167 mg sodium, 41 mg cholesterol.

  6 large baking potatoes (about 3 pounds)
½ cup (1 stick) butter
     Salt and white pepper, to taste
½ cup chopped chives OR: chopped green
     onion, green part only

1. Peel the potatoes. Halve the potatoes lengthwise and drop into a large saucepan with enough water to cover the potatoes. Bring the water to boiling. Boil for about 15 minutes or until the potatoes are just barely tender. Drain the potatoes and return to the saucepan. Shake over heat to dry the potatoes.
2. Melt the butter in a large skillet, or in 2 medium-size skillets, dividing the butter. Arrange the halved potatoes, cut-side down, in the skillet. Cook the potatoes over medium-low heat for about 20 minutes or until the potatoes are golden and crusty.
3. Turn the potatoes curved-side down, being careful not to break them. Sprinkle the potatoes with salt and pepper to taste. Cook the potatoes for another 20 to 30 minutes until they are tender.
4. Lift the potatoes carefully into a serving dish. Sprinkle with the chives.

Swiss-Fried Potatoes

These crusty pan-browned potatoes are an excellent accompaniment to any pan-fried or charcoal-broiled meat.

Makes 6 servings.

Nutrient Value Per Serving: 234 calories, 3 g protein, 15 g fat, 22 g carbohydrate, 163 mg sodium, 41 mg cholesterol.

  4 large baking potatoes, with skins left on
     (about 2 pounds)
½ cup (1 stick) butter OR: half butter and
     half bacon drippings
  2 medium-size onions, finely chopped
     Salt and pepper, to taste

1. Place the potatoes in a large saucepan with enough water to cover the potatoes. Bring the water to boiling. Boil just until the potatoes are barely tender, 10 to 15 minutes; do not overcook the potatoes.
2. Drain the potatoes. Peel the potatoes while still hot. (If you stick one potato at a time on a fork, you won't burn your fingers.)
3. As soon as the potatoes are cool enough to handle, cut into thin strips or shred on a coarse grater.
4. Heat the butter in a 10-inch skillet. Add the potatoes. Sprinkle with the onion and the salt and pepper to taste. Cook the potatoes over medium heat, turning and tossing frequently until they are lightly browned on all sides, about 25 minutes.
5. Lower the heat. Press the potatoes firmly into a cake shape with a pancake turner. Cook the potatoes for 8 to 10 minutes longer or until a crust forms on the bottom. Turn out the potatoes, crust-side up, onto a serving plate.

Sweet Potato Special

Makes 4 servings.

Nutrient Value Per Serving: 198 calories, 3 g protein, 2 g fat, 42 g carbohydrate, 41 mg sodium, 5 mg cholesterol.

4   **sweet potatoes or yams (about 2 pounds)**
2   **teaspoons butter or margarine**
⅓   **cup orange juice**
     Maple syrup OR: fruit-flavored yogurt

1. Scrub the sweet potatoes. Cook the potatoes in a large saucepan of boiling water until almost tender, about 25 minutes. Drain the potatoes in a colander and cool.
2. Peel off the skins. Cut the sweet potatoes into small cubes.
3. Melt the butter in a large nonstick skillet. Add the sweet potatoes and cook over medium-low heat, stirring often, until the potatoes are heated through and slightly browned. Pour the orange juice into the skillet. Cook until all the liquid evaporates. Serve with maple syrup or fruit-flavored yogurt.

Home-Style Potatoes Anna

Makes 6 servings.

Nutrient Value Per Serving: 171 calories, 2 g protein, 12 g fat, 16 g carbohydrate, 122 mg sodium, 31 mg cholesterol.

3   **large baking potatoes (about 1½ pounds)**
6   **tablespoons butter**
2   **cloves garlic, finely chopped**
     Salt and pepper, to taste

1. Peel the potatoes and drop into a large bowl of cold water. Slice 2 potatoes crosswise as thinly as possible. Blot the slices dry with paper toweling.
2. Melt 3 tablespoons of the butter in a heavy 12-inch skillet. Arrange the potato slices in the bottom of the skillet in a spiral pattern, overlapping the slices, until the bottom of the skillet is completely covered. Sprinkle the potato slices with the garlic, salt and pepper. Slice the remaining potato; pat dry with paper toweling. Continue arranging the potato slices in a spiral pattern on top of the first layer. Sprinkle the potatoes with salt and pepper. Dot the top with the remaining butter.
3. Cover the skillet. Cook the potato circle over medium heat until the bottom is brown and crusty, about 8 minutes. Peek occasionally to make sure the heat is not too high and the potatoes are browning, not burning.
4. With a sharp knife, cut the potato layers in half. Lift one-half of the potatoes with a pancake turner and return to the skillet, crusty-side up. Repeat with the other half of the potatoes. Or carefully place a large, oiled cookie sheet or pizza pan over the skillet and invert both the pan and the skillet. Return the skillet to the heat. Slide the potato circle back into the skillet, crusty-side up. Lower the heat. Cook the potatoes, uncovered, until brown and crusty on the bottom, about 8 minutes. Cut each half into 3 equal wedges and serve.

Delicious ways to use apples: Potato-Apple Gratin, Cranberry-Apple Tart (page 167) *and mini Apple-Nut Torte* (page 177).

Potato-Apple Gratin

A lighter-than-usual version of scalloped potatoes. Serve with roast ham or chicken.

Bake at 300° for 1 hour.
Makes 6 servings.

Nutrient Value Per Serving: 278 calories, 10 g protein, 16 g fat, 26 g carbohydrate, 380 mg sodium, 57 mg cholesterol.

2 **Russet or baking potatoes (about 1¼ pounds), peeled, halved lengthwise and thinly sliced crosswise**
1 **medium-size onion, halved lengthwise, thinly sliced crosswise and slices separated**
1 **clove garlic, crushed**
1½ cups milk
¾ teaspoon salt
¼ teaspoon pepper
1 **tablespoon all-purpose flour**
2 **large Golden Delicious apples (about ¾ pound)**
½ cup heavy cream
¼ pound Gruyère cheese, shredded (1 cup)

1. Preheat the oven to slow (300°).
2. Combine the potato, onion, garlic, milk, salt and pepper in a medium-size heavy-bottomed saucepan. Sprinkle the top with flour; stir gently to combine all the ingredients in the saucepan. Bring to boiling slowly over medium heat, stirring gently, occasionally.
3. Meanwhile, peel, quarter and core the apples. Cut the apples into ½-inch-thick slices.
4. Turn the partially cooked potato mixture into a shallow 2-quart casserole. Push the apple slices between the potato slices as evenly as possible. Drizzle the cream over the casserole. Sprinkle the top with the cheese.
5. Bake the gratin in the preheated slow oven (300°) until the potatoes are tender and the top is browned and bubbly, about 1 hour. Let the gratin stand for 10 minutes before serving.

T·H·E R·E·L·I·S·H T·R·A·Y

Refrigerator Corn Relish

When the corn is really coming out of your ears, make lots of this relish and give to friends.

Makes about 6 cups.

Nutrient Value Per ¼ Cup: 44 calories, 1 g protein, 0 g fat, 10 g carbohydrate, 96 mg sodium, 0 mg cholesterol.

4 cups fresh or frozen whole-kernel corn, cooked (6 cups)
⅔ cup chopped onion (1 medium-size onion)
⅔ cup chopped sweet green pepper
⅔ cup chopped sweet red pepper
1 cup distilled white vinegar
1 cup water
½ cup sugar
1 tablespoon dry mustard
1 teaspoon salt
1 teaspoon pepper
½ teaspoon ground turmeric

1. Combine the corn, onion and green and red pepper in a large heatproof bowl.
2. Combine the vinegar, water, sugar, mustard, salt, pepper and turmeric in a medium-size saucepan. Bring the mixture to boiling, stirring occasionally. Pour the hot mixture over the vegetables in the bowl. Cover the bowl with plastic wrap. Refrigerate the relish overnight, stirring once or twice. The relish is ready to use immediately. It will keep up to 1 month in the refrigerator.

Note: For tips on selecting and freezing corn, see opposite page.

Tangerine-Cranberry Relish

Clementines are a seedless variety of tangerine. Make the relish a day ahead.

Makes 8 servings (2½ cups).

Nutrient Value Per Serving: 78 calories, 1 g protein, 0 g fat, 20 g carbohydrate, 1 mg sodium, 0 mg cholesterol.

½ of 12-ounce package fresh or frozen cranberries (1½ cups)
¼ cup sugar, or more to taste
8 large clementines OR: other small tangerines.

1. Combine the cranberries and sugar in a food processor. Pulse on and off until the cranberries are coarsely chopped. Transfer the cranberry mixture to a large bowl.
2. Cut off one-third of each tangerine from the stem end. Remove the pulp from the cutaway sections and reserve; discard the skin. Cut out the tangerine segments from the remaining two-thirds of each tangerine, leaving the skin as clean as possible to use as cups. Place the cups in a plastic bag and refrigerate.
3. Cut the tangerine segments into ½-inch pieces. If using tangerines other than clementines, remove the seeds. Combine the tangerine pieces with the chopped cranberry mixture in the large bowl. Refrigerate, covered, overnight to blend the flavors.
4. To serve, spoon the relish with a slotted spoon into the tangerine cups.

CORN-Y TIPS

Selecting Corn
● Process and freeze corn the same day you harvest or purchase it.
● Choose corn at the best stage for eating, or even slightly younger.

Scalding or Blanching
Scalding removes dirt and any organisms from the surface of the corn, brightens the color, helps retain the vitamins and reduces the enzyme action that destroys flavor.

Note: For a faster and easier job, work with small quantities of corn.

● Drop 4 ears of husked corn into 3 quarts of boiling water and start counting immediately; keep the heat on high and stir once or twice. Follow the scalding times indicated at right. The boiling water can be reused for more corn, but be sure to keep the water at the proper level and bring to full boil again.
● Underscalding promotes enzyme activity and is worse than no scalding; overscalding causes loss of vitamins, minerals and flavor.

Cooling
● Immediately plunge the corn into a bowl of ice water. Keep the water cold and stir occasionally. The cooling time should be no longer than the scalding time. Drain the corn.

How to Package
● Pack the corn, without seasoning, immediately after cooling and draining.
● Quart or pint plastic freezer bags are suitable for kernel corn and corn on the cob. After placing the corn in the bag, press out as much air as possible. Seal tightly.
● Canning and freezing jars and plastic freezer boxes are good for kernel corn. Pack the kernel corn loosely to fill the container.

Quick Freezing and Storing
● Place the closed containers in the coldest section of the freezer in single layers, leaving 1 inch of space between the packages.
● When completely frozen, the packages may be stacked directly on top of each other.
● Corn can be stored at 0° F for 10 to 12 months.

Thawing and Cooking
● Frozen corn on the cob should be completely thawed before cooking. Kernel corn can be cooked without thawing.
● Cook frozen corn as you would fresh but for a shorter time since the corn has already been partially cooked. Use the smallest amount of water possible.

Scalding Times
● Scald ears 1½ inches in diameter for 6 minutes.
● Scald ears 2 inches in diameter for 8 minutes.

TO FREEZE COBS AND KERNELS
Cob: Cool the ears in ice water, drain the ears and wrap each cob tightly in a moisture-/vapor-proof film. Place the wrapped cobs in freezer bags. Close, label and freeze.

Whole Kernel: Scald the ears. Cool them in ice water. Drain. Cut the kernels from the cobs. Pack the kernels in freezer bags, canning or freezing jars, or freezer boxes. Close, label and freeze.

T·H·E M·A·I·N C·O·U·R·S·E

Nothing but the best: Wine-Glazed Fresh Ham with Gravy (page 85) with Onion "Mums" (page 86).

3

*W*hat's for dinner? It's always the same question — but it doesn't always have to be the same answer. We've put together some main dishes that will help you out whatever the occasion — everyday family meal, a quick bite on-the-go, an orchestrated dinner party or a casual supper with friends.

Let's start with beef: although poultry and fish are gaining in popularity, beef still seems to be the favorite — whether it's crowd-pleasing Tucson Jailhouse Chili *(page 82)* or elegant Rare Roast Ribs of Beef *(page 75)*.

For cold-weather dining, Braised Lamb Shanks *(page 83)* hits the spot. And for something different at holiday time, retire the turkey and feast on Wine-Glazed Baked Fresh Ham with Gravy *(page 85)*.

To your favorite chicken recipes, add some of ours: Honey-Nut Drumsticks *(page 95)* and Chicken with Provençal Vegetables *(page 92)*. And for the pasta-lover in all of us, get out the napkins for rich Linguine with Seafood and Chicken in Cheese Sauce *(page 105)* or Spaghetti with Spinach Pesto *(page 106)*. Of course, there are meatless entrées as well. Try Cheese-topped Spaghetti Squash *(page 111)* and Barley-Lentil Stew *(page 110)*.

For other main-course ideas, flip to the Warm Weather Dining and Smart Eating chapters.

B·E·E·F

London Broil with crispy pan-browned Swiss-Fried Potatoes (page 66).

Rare Roast Ribs Of Beef

Our technique for roasting in this recipe is slightly different than the usual. The roast is taken directly from the refrigerator to a preheated very hot oven, and after roasting, the meat is left in the oven with the door closed for at least 2 hours.

Roast at 500° for time indicated in recipe. Makes 2 servings per rib.

Nutrient Value Per Serving: 565 calories, 65 g protein, 31 g fat, 1 g carbohydrate, 160 mg sodium, 211 mg cholesterol.

**3- or 4-rib roast of beef, without short ribs
    (7 to 12 pounds)
    All-purpose flour
    Salt and black pepper, to taste**

1. Preheat the oven to extremely hot (500°).
2. Remove the roast from the refrigerator. Place in a shallow roasting pan. Sprinkle with a little flour; rub the flour lightly into the fat. Season with salt and pepper to taste. Place a tent of aluminum foil over the meat to protect the oven from fat splatters.
3. Roast the meat in the preheated extremely hot oven (500°) for the following times: for a 3-rib roast, weighing 7 to 9 pounds, roast 40 to 45 minutes; for a 4-rib roast, weighing 10 to 12 pounds, roast 55 to 60 minutes.
4. When the roasting is finished, turn off the oven. Do not open the oven door. Let the roast remain in the oven for at least 2 hours or until the oven is lukewarm. The roast will retain its internal heat for as long as 4 hours.

THE WONDERFUL WORLD OF MUSTARDS

Serve a little dab for dipping with sausages, cold vegetables and cheese twists, spread on broiled lamb chops, flank steak and grilled chicken, and mix with salad dressing, marinades and barbecue sauces. Choose from several varieties.

• Dijon-style mustard — French mustards with a wine flavor and either a smooth or coarse-grained texture.
• Creole or Louisiana mustard — pungent, hot mustards with flecks of spices throughout.
• English, Dusseldorf and German — very hot blends with a deep brown color.
• Herb mustards — mustards flavored with a variety of herbs, such as tarragon, basil and thyme.

London Broil

Makes 6 servings.

Nutrient Value Per Serving: 480 calories, 45 g protein, 31 g fat, 1 g carbohydrate, 155 mg sodium, 153 mg cholesterol.

**3 pound piece top round of beef, 2½ inches
    thick
    Vegetable oil
    Salt and pepper, to taste
¾ cup red wine OR: beef consommé
3 tablespoons butter
    Parsley**

1. Brush the meat generously on both sides with vegetable oil. Sprinkle the meat with salt and pepper.
2. Heat a heavy skillet (large enough to hold the meat) over high heat until hot. Brown the meat for about 5 minutes on each side. Lower the heat to medium. Turn the steak over. Cook another 10 to 15 minutes for rare, turning once or twice.
3. Transfer the steak to a hot serving platter and keep warm. Pour off any excess fat from the skillet. Return the skillet to low heat. Add the wine. Cook for 1 minute, stirring in the brown glaze from the bottom and sides of the skillet with a wooden spoon. Remove the skillet from the heat. Add the butter and swirl the skillet until the butter is melted.
4. Pour the skillet sauce over the meat and garnish with parsley. Carve the meat across the grain into thin slices.

FLAVORED BUTTERS

These butters are easy to prepare and convenient to store in your refrigerator or freezer to have on hand. And the combinations of flavors are limitless. Spread a pat on grilled steak, chicken or fish or toss with cooked vegetables.

Blue Cheese Butter

A tangy butter enhances the flavor of burgers, steaks and poultry. Also spread it on bread as the "secret" ingredient in sandwiches.

Makes ¾ cup.

Nutrient Value Per Teaspoon: 19 calories, 0 g protein, 2 g fat, 0 g carbohydrate, 39 mg sodium, 5 mg cholesterol.

- ½ **cup blue or Roquefort cheese**
- ¼ **cup (½ stick) butter or margarine, softened**
- 2 **tablespoons dry sherry, white wine, brandy or heavy cream**

1. Remove the cheese and the butter or margarine from the refrigerator. Crumble the cheese. Allow both to stand at room temperature for about 1 hour.
2. Mash the cheese with the butter in a small bowl with a fork. Stir in the sherry, wine, brandy or cream and mix to a smooth paste. Turn into a ramekin or small serving bowl. Serve at room temperature to pat on beef of all kinds or chicken breasts.

Almond-Cheese Butter: Add ¼ cup ground almonds. *Nutrient Value Per Teaspoon: 24 calories, 1 g protein, 2 g fat, 0 g carbohydrate, 39 mg sodium, 5 mg cholesterol.*

Green Onion Butter: Add 1 green onion, finely chopped. *Nutrient Value Per Teaspoon: 19 calories, 0 g protein, 2 g fat, 0 g carbohydrate, 39 mg sodium, 5 mg cholesterol.*

Chive Butter

Lemon juice and herbs in butter are a classic topping for grilled meat or fish.

Makes ⅔ cup.

Nutrient Value Per Teaspoon: 25 calories, 0 g protein, 3 g fat, 0 g carbohydrate, 29 mg sodium, 8 mg cholesterol.

- ½ **cup (1 stick) butter or margarine, softened**
- 2 **tablespoons finely chopped chives**
- 2 **tablespoons lemon juice**

1. Blend together the butter or margarine and the chives in a small bowl. Add the lemon juice, a little at a time, and beat well.
2. Turn the butter mixture out onto wax paper and shape into a 2-inch-long stick. Wrap the butter tightly and refrigerate until firm. Cut into slices and serve on meat.

Variations:

Caraway Butter: Omit the chives; add ½ teaspoon caraway seeds, crushed, and 2 tablespoons chopped parsley. *Nutrient Value Per Teaspoon: 25 calories, 0 g protein, 3 g fat, 0 g carbohydrate, 29 mg sodium, 8 mg cholesterol.*

Anchovy Butter: Omit the chives. Add 2 anchovies, rinsed, mashed. *Nutrient Value Per Teaspoon: 25 calories, 0 g protein, 3 g fat, 0 g carbohydrate, 31 mg sodium, 8 mg cholesterol.*

Horseradish Butter: Omit the chives. Add 3 tablespoons prepared horseradish and 2 tablespoons chopped fresh parsley. *Nutrient Value Per Teaspoon: 25 calories, 0 g protein, 3 g fat, 0 g carbohydrate, 30 mg sodium, 8 mg cholesterol.*

Lemon Butter: Add 1 teaspoon grated lemon rind and 2 tablespoons finely chopped parsley. *Nutrient Value Per Teaspoon: 25 calories, 0 g protein, 3 g fat, 0 g carbohydrate, 29 mg sodium, 8 mg cholesterol.*

Mustard Butter: Omit the chives. Add 1 tablespoon prepared mustard. *Nutrient Value Per Teaspoon: 34 calories, 0 g protein, 4 g fat, 0 g carbohydrate, 46 mg sodium, 10 mg cholesterol.*

Food for thought . . .

Tall, thin and grasslike, chives are a member of the onion family. Their mild flavor complements most salads, vegetables, soups and meats.

Béarnaise Sauce

A classic French sauce — the perfect topping for grilled shell or strip steak, or even fancy burgers.

Makes 1 cup.

Nutrient Value Per Tablespoon: 61 calories, 0 g protein, 6 g fat, 1 g carbohydrate, 60 mg sodium, 50 mg cholesterol.

½ **cup dry white wine**
1 **tablespoon tarragon vinegar**
1 **tablespoon finely chopped shallot OR: green onions**
⅓ **teaspoon black pepper**
1 **sprig parsley**
½ **teaspoon leaf tarragon, crumbled**
2 **egg yolks**
½ **cup (1 stick) butter or margarine, melted**
    Pinch ground hot red pepper
1 **teaspoon chopped parsley**

1. Combine the wine, vinegar, shallot or onion, pepper, parsley sprig and tarragon in a small saucepan. Bring to boiling. Lower the heat and then simmer, uncovered, for 8 to 10 minutes or until the liquid measures about ⅓ cup. Strain into a cup.
2. Beat the egg yolks slightly in the top of a double boiler; stir in one-third of the melted butter or margarine. Place the top of the double boiler over simmering, not boiling, water.
3. Beat in the wine liquid, alternately with the remaining melted butter or margarine, with an electric hand mixer on medium. Continue beating, keeping the top over the simmering water until the mixture is fluffy-thick. Remove the top of the double boiler from the water at once. *Do not boil.*
4. Stir in the red pepper and chopped parsley. Serve the sauce warm.

Sauerbraten

Unlike a Pennsylvania Dutch sauerbraten that is thickened and flavored with gingersnaps, this version has a little cornstarch added. Plan to prepare this dish ahead since the meat needs to marinate for 1 to 2 days.

Makes 10 to 12 servings.

Nutrient Value Per Serving: 499 calories, 42 g protein, 33 g fat, 6 g carbohydrate, 469 mg sodium, 134 mg cholesterol.

5 **pounds rolled top eye or bottom round of beef**
½ **cup red wine vinegar**
1½ **cups fruity red wine (such as Beaujolais)**
1 **teaspoon whole peppercorns**
1 **teaspoon salt**
1 **large bay leaf**
6 **whole cloves**
½ **teaspoon ground nutmeg**
2 **cloves garlic, halved**
2 **strips lemon rind**
1 **medium-size onion, halved**
2 **large stalks celery with leaves, coarsely chopped**
2 **carrots, peeled and cut into thin slices**
3 **sprigs parsley**
1 **cup hot water**
1 **can (10½ ounces) beef consommé with gelatin**
2 **tablespoons cornstarch**
¼ **cup cold water**

1. One or 2 days before you plan to serve the dish, place the beef in a large, nonmetallic container. Pour the vinegar and red wine over the meat. Add the peppercorns, salt, bay leaf, cloves, nutmeg, garlic, lemon rind, onion, celery, carrot and parsley. Cover the container and refrigerate for 1 to 2 days, turning the meat occasionally in the marinade.
2. Remove the meat from the marinade. Strain the marinade, reserving the marinade and the vegetables separately. Pat the meat dry with paper toweling.
3. Heat a large kettle or Dutch oven over medium heat. Add the meat, fat-side down. Brown the meat well, turning until all sides are browned, about 30 minutes. Don't rush the browning since you don't want to burn the meat.
4. Meanwhile, pour the reserved marinade into a saucepan. Simmer, adding a little hot water at a time until a total of 1 cup of water has been added. Keep the marinade warm.
5. When the meat is well browned on all sides, reduce the heat to very low. Add the consommé to the kettle. Add the reserved

vegetables from the marinade. Cook, covered, until the meat is tender, about 3½ hours. While the meat is cooking, occasionally baste the meat with some of the hot marinade. Continue basting until all the marinade has been added. Remove the meat to a hot platter; keep warm.

6. Strain the gravy through a sieve or food mill into a saucepan, pressing through as much of the cooked vegetables as possible.

7. Stir together with a fork the cornstarch and the cold water in a small cup until smooth and well blended. Skim the excess fat from the surface of the gravy. Bring the gravy to boiling. Stir in the cornstarch mixture. Cook, stirring constantly, for 2 minutes until the gravy is thickened.

8. Slice the meat. Pour some of the gravy over the slices. Pass the rest of the gravy separately.

Note: For an even more flavorful dish, slice the meat and return to the kettle. Pour the gravy over the meat. Refrigerate, covered, overnight. To serve, gently reheat the meat and gravy in the kettle, covered, in a slow oven or over very low heat on top of the stove.

1. Slice the flank steak thinly across the grain. Reserve.

2. Peel the carrots; cut into thin matchstick pieces. String the snow peas. Plunge the carrots and snow peas into boiling water in a large saucepan for 1 minute. Drain the vegetables in a colander; rinse with cold water; drain. Reserve. Cut the zucchini into thin matchstick pieces. Cut the broccoli into small flowerets; cut the broccoli stalks into thin matchstick pieces. Halve, core and seed the red pepper; cut into thin strips. Reserve the vegetables.

3. Heat 1 tablespoon of the oil in a large skillet. Stir-fry one-half of the meat at a time until browned on both sides. Remove the meat from the skillet. Add the remaining tablespoon oil to the skillet. Stir-fry the carrots and snow peas for 1 minute. Add the zucchini, broccoli and red pepper and stir-fry for 2 minutes. Add the flank steak and ½ cup of the Honey-Tamari Sauce. Heat the mixture to serving temperature and spoon over hot brown rice. Pass the remaining Honey-Tamari Sauce in a small bowl.

Honey-Tamari Sauce: Gradually stir 1¼ cups water into 2 tablespoons cornstarch in a small saucepan until smooth. Add ⅓ cup bottled tamari sauce, ¼ cup honey and ¼ teaspoon crushed red pepper flakes. Cook over medium heat, stirring, until the mixture bubbles, thickens and clears.

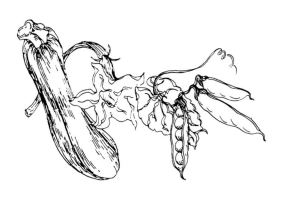

Vegetable and Flank Steak Stir-Fry

Serve this stir-fry with brown rice and complete the dinner with an orange, red onion and pecan salad and bread pudding.

Makes 4 servings.

Nutrient Value Per Serving: 354 calories, 26 g protein, 12 g fat, 38 g carbohydrate, 1,100 mg sodium, 58 mg cholesterol.

12 **ounces flank steak**
3 **carrots**
2 **ounces snow peas**
2 **medium-size zucchini**
1 **small bunch broccoli**
1 **large sweet red pepper**
2 **tablespoons vegetable oil**
   Honey-Tamari Sauce (recipe follows)
   Hot cooked brown rice

WHAT IS TAMARI SAUCE?

A strongly flavored soy sauce with a rich, distinctive taste. You can find it in the Oriental food section in some supermarkets and in health food stores.

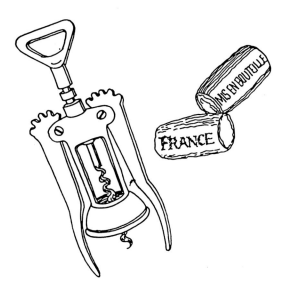

Beef in Burgundy Sauce

A rich beef stew that tastes even better if made the day before.

Bake at 325° for 4 hours.
Makes 8 servings.

Nutrient Value Per Serving: 604 calories, 42 g protein, 42 g fat, 15 g carbohydrate, 492 mg sodium, 139 mg cholesterol.

3   *pounds top round roast, 1½ inches thick*
2   *tablespoons vegetable oil*
2   *tablespoons Cognac OR: brandy*
½ *teaspoon salt*
½ *teaspoon black pepper*
6   *slices bacon, sliced crosswise into*
    small pieces
2   *medium-size onions, chopped*
2   *leeks, trimmed, washed well and thinly*
    sliced, both white and tender
    light green parts
1   *carrot, peeled and chopped*
2   *large cloves garlic, finely chopped*
¼ *cup chopped parsley*
1   *large bay leaf*
½ *teaspoon leaf thyme, crumbled*
1½ *cups dry Burgundy red wine*
    Water
5   *tablespoons butter*
1   *tablespoon all-purpose flour*
1   *pound small white onions (about 1 inch),*
    halved or quartered if large
1   *teaspoon sugar*
2   *tablespoons water*
½ *pound small mushrooms, trimmed*
    Juice of 1 lemon

1. Cut the beef into 1½-inch cubes.
2. Heat the oil in a large, heavy skillet. Working in batches, brown the meat in the skillet; do not overcrowd the pan or the meat will steam rather than brown. The browner the meat, the darker the gravy. Transfer the browned cubes to a 3-quart heavy casserole; keep warm. Add the Cognac, salt and pepper.
3. Preheat the oven to slow (325°).
4. Cook the bacon in the remaining oil in the skillet for 3 to 4 minutes or until the fat begins to render out. Add the onion, leek, carrot, garlic and half the parsley. Cook, stirring, until the vegetables and bacon are browned. Add the contents of the skillet to the casserole with the meat.
5. Add the bay leaf, thyme, wine and enough water to the casserole to just cover the meat and vegetables. Bring the mixture to simmering on top of the stove. Cover.
6. Transfer the casserole to the preheated slow oven (325°) and bake for 2 hours.
7. Mix 1 tablespoon of the butter with the flour and a little hot liquid from the casserole in a small cup until smooth; slowly stir the mixture into the casserole until well blended. Cover the casserole and return to the oven to cook for 2 more hours, adding more liquid if needed.
8. Meanwhile, melt 2 tablespoons of the butter in a small skillet. Add the small onions and sprinkle with the sugar. Cook over medium heat, shaking the pan frequently, until the onions are golden brown. Add the 2 tablespoons water. Cook, covered, over low heat until the onions are tender, 15 to 20 minutes. Reserve.
9. Heat 2 tablespoons of the butter in another skillet. Add the mushrooms, cap-side down; cook until lightly browned. Turn the mushrooms over and sprinkle with half the lemon juice. Cook for 2 minutes longer. Reserve.
10. Skim off the excess fat from the cooking liquid in the casserole. Remove the bay leaf. Taste and correct the seasonings. Stir in the remaining lemon juice. Stir in the onions and mushrooms and sprinkle with the remaining parsley. Serve the stew directly from the casserole.

M·I·N·I - G·U·I·D·E TO M·E·A·T·S

CHOOSING MEATS

Cost: The most accurate way to determine meat cost is to base calculations on price per serving, rather than price per pound. Cuts which contain a lots of bone and fat may not be as economical as higher-priced cuts which contain less waste.

Do not confuse the number of servings with the number of people you can serve. A hearty eater can consume 3 servings at a meal!

To find the cost per serving, divide the price per pound by the number of servings per pound the cut will provide. For example, if a roast costs $1.79 a pound and that cut gives you 2½ servings a pound, your cost per serving would be 71¢.

Cut: Tender cuts come from muscles which are not used in movement and which have the least connective tissue. These muscles are found along the back of the animal and are called rib, loin or sirloin. The remaining muscles are less tender.

Many stores use a standardized meat-labeling system on prepackaged meats. The label tells you the kind of meat (beef, pork, lamb, etc.), the primal or wholesale cut (chuck, rib, loin, round, etc.) which is where the cut comes from on the animal, and the retail cut (blade, arm, short rib, etc.) which tells you from what part of the primal cut the meat comes.

Ground beef, or hamburger, contains not less than 70% lean. Use it for burgers, chili, sloppy joes and casseroles. Lean ground beef, or ground chuck, has not less than 77% lean. Use it for meatloaf, meatballs and steaks. Extra-lean ground beef, or ground round or sirloin, has not less than 85% lean. Use it as you would ground chuck, or when you're watching calorie and fat consumption.

Color: This is an important indication of tenderness. For example, beef can vary from dark pink to dark red. The lighter the color, the younger the animal and more tender the meat.

Caution: Watch out for liquid in a package. The drier the package, the fresher tasting the meat. Liquid also indicates that the meat may have been frozen or is of a lower grade.

DRY-HEAT COOKING METHODS FOR TENDER CUTS

Panbroil: For small, tender pieces cut 1 inch thick or less. Place steak or patty in a heavy frying pan. Don't add fat or water and do not cover the pan. Cook slowly, turning often; pour off any fat as it collects. Brown to the desired degree; season and serve.

Panfry: For very thin, tender cuts or cuts made tender by pounding or cubing. They may be dusted with flour or crumbs. Heat a small amount of fat in a frying pan. Add meat and brown on both sides over high heat, turning occasionally. Stir-frying is a form of panfrying used in Oriental-style cooking. A wok, large pan or electric skillet can be used. Ingredients must be cut into uniform sizes before cooking. Sautéing is the French term for panfrying.

Broil: For tender steaks or patties at least 1 inch thick. Place the meat on a broiler rack over a pan. Broil the meat 2 to 3 inches from the preheated heat source. Broil cuts, thicker than 1 inch, 3 to 5 inches from the heat. Turn the meat with tongs (a fork will pierce the meat, releasing the juices). A charcoal, electric or gas grill can be used for broiling.

Roast: For large, tender roasts. Season with salt, pepper or herbs. Place the meat, fat-side up, on a rack in an open, shallow pan. The fat on top bastes the meat and the rack holds it out of the drippings. Insert a meat thermometer in the center of the largest muscle; do not let it touch bone or rest in fat. Do not add water or cover the meat. Roast in a slow oven (300° to 325° F.). When the thermometer reads 5° F. below the desired degree of doneness, remove the roast from the oven and let stand for 15 minutes for easier carving. Rotisserie cooking is a form of roasting. Use large, uniformly shaped cuts. Insert the rotisserie rod lengthwise through the center of the roast; fasten securely. Place a drip pan underneath to prevent flare-ups.

Microwave: For tender roasts that are compact and uniform in shape. Boneless roasts are ideal. Place the roast on a rack and cover with wax paper. Use a LOW power setting for a longer cooking time to get the most uniform doneness. If a roast is irregular in shape and a portion is cooking too fast, cover that piece with small strips of foil to retard cooking. To assure even cooking, turn the roast or rotate the dish at intervals during the cooking time. To enhance the appearance of meat cooked by microwave, brush the surface with soy sauce, Worcestershire or a browning sauce. Or coat the surface with bread crumbs or a glaze. You can also prebrown the roast in a frying pan or use the browning dish of the microwave. Cooking times will vary, depending on the shape and size of the meat.

Tamale Pie

A delicious make-ahead buffet dish that uses both whole-kernel corn and cornmeal. Serve with a green salad and a cool glass of iced tea.

Bake at 350° for 50 minutes.
Makes 8 servings.

Nutrient Value Per Serving: 511 calories, 28 g protein, 21 g fat, 53 g carbohydrate, 1,086 mg sodium, 80 mg cholesterol.

1½ pounds ground round
¼ pound chorizo (Spanish sausage) OR:
    hot Italian sausage, sliced
1 medium-size onion, chopped (½ cup)
2 teaspoons salt
2 teaspoons hot chili powder
½ teaspoon ground cumin
1 can (14 counces) tomatoes, broken up and
    undrained
1 can (8 ounces) tomato sauce
1 can (4 ounces) green chilies, drained and
    chopped
1½ cups fresh or frozen uncooked whole-
    kernel corn (2 to 3 ears)
⅓ cup ripe pitted black olives, halved
¾ cup shredded sharp Cheddar cheese
    (3 ounces)
8 cups water
3 cups yellow cornmeal

1. Sauté the beef, chorizo and onion in a large skillet over high heat, stirring often, until the meat is browned. Mix in ½ teaspoon of the salt, the chili powder and the cumin. Add the tomatoes, the tomato sauce, two-thirds of the green chilies and the corn. Bring the mixture to boiling. Lower the heat and simmer, uncovered, for 10 minutes. Remove the skillet from the heat. Stir in the olives and ½ cup of the cheese. Reserve the mixture.
2. Combine 5 cups of the water and the remaining 1½ teaspoons salt in a large saucepan. Bring the mixture to boiling.
3. Mix together the cornmeal and the remaining 3 cups water in a medium-size bowl. Slowly pour into the boiling water, stirring constantly. Lower the heat and cook, stirring constantly, until the mush is thickened, about 5 minutes.
4. Preheat the oven to moderate (350°). Coat the inside of a 13 x 9 x 2-inch baking pan with nonstick vegetable cooking spray.
5. Spread half of the cornmeal mush mixture with a wet spoon into an even layer over the bottom of the prepared pan. Spread the meat mixture evenly over the mush. Stir the remaining green chilies into the remaining cornmeal mixture. Spoon evenly over the meat in the baking pan; smooth the top into an even layer with the back of a wet spoon.
6. Bake the pie in the preheated moderate oven (350°) for 35 minutes. Sprinkle the top with the remaining ¼ cup cheese. Bake for 15 minutes longer. Remove the baking pan to a wire rack to cool for 10 minutes before slicing.

Food for thought . . .

Chorizo, a rusty-red Spanish sausage, is made in a variety of lengths, thicknesses and types. The intense paprika and garlic seasoning accounts for its distinctive flavor.

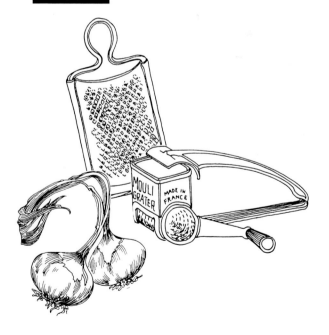

Tucson Jailhouse Chili

One of the most popular dishes served in the Flying V Restaurant at the Ventana Canyon Resort in Tucson, Arizona.

Makes 8 servings.

Nutrient Value Per Serving: 641 calories, 34 g protein, 34 g fat, 52 g carbohydrate, 683 mg sodium, 96 mg cholesterol.

- 1 **onion, diced**
- 1 **tablespoon vegetable oil**
- 6 **cloves garlic, diced**
- 2 **pounds ground beef**
- 1 **can (4 ounces) diced green chilies**
- 1 **can (4 ounces) jalepeño peppers**
- 1 **can (12 ounces) diced tomatoes**
- 1 **can (6 ounces) tomato paste**
- 6 **to 8 tablespoons chili powder**
- 2 **tablespoons brown sugar**
- 1 **tablespoon vinegar**
- 3 **teaspoons ground cumin**
- 1 **pound pinto or kidney beans, cooked following package directions, and drained**
  Salt and pepper, to taste
  Shredded sharp Cheddar cheese for garnish
  Sliced green onions for garnish

1. Sauté the onion in the vegetable oil in a large, heavy pot until softened. Add the garlic and sauté for 30 seconds. Add the ground beef and sauté until lightly browned.
2. Add the green chilies, jalapeño peppers, tomatoes, tomato paste, chili powder, brown sugar, vinegar, cumin and drained pinto or kidney beans.
3. Simmer the chili, *do not boil,* for 1½ to 2 hours. Check the seasoning and add salt and pepper to taste. Garnish with sharp Cheddar cheese and sliced green onions. Serve with corn chips, if you wish.

Classic Tomato Sauce with Meatballs

Prepare the sauce without the meat, if you wish, and add sautéed mushrooms instead.

Makes 5 cups sauce, plus meatballs (8 servings).

Nutrient Value Per Serving: 517 calories, 23 g protein, 41 g fat, 14 g carbohydrate, 494 mg sodium, 166 mg cholesterol.

- 2 **pounds ground beef**
- 2 **eggs**
- 2 **cups soft bread crumbs (4 slices)**
- 2 **tablespoons chopped parsley**
- 2 **tablespoons grated Parmesan cheese**
- 2 **teaspoons leaf basil, crumbled**
- 1 **teaspoon salt, or to taste**
- ¼ **teaspoon pepper**
- ⅓ **cup olive or vegetable oil**
- 1 **large onion, chopped (1 cup)**
- 2 **cloves garlic, finely chopped**
- 1 **large carrot, peeled and chopped**
- 1 **can (2 pounds, 3 ounces) Italian tomatoes, crushed**
- 1 **can (6 ounces) tomato paste**
- ⅓ **cup dry red wine**
- 2 **teaspoons sugar (optional)**
- 2 **teaspoons leaf basil, crumbled**
- 1½ **teaspoons leaf oregano, crumbled**
- 2 **teaspoons salt, or to taste**
- ½ **teaspoon pepper, or to taste**

1. Mix the beef with the eggs, bread crumbs, parsley, Parmesan cheese, 2 teaspoons basil, salt and pepper in a large bowl, just until blended. Shape the beef mixture into small meatballs, about 1 inch in diameter.
2. Heat the oil in a large kettle or saucepan. Add the meatballs one-third at a time, and brown. Remove the meatballs as they brown and reserve.
3. Add the onion, garlic and carrot to the drippings in the kettle; sauté until the onions are soft and transparent. Stir in the tomatoes and their liquid, the tomato paste, wine, sugar, if using, basil, oregano and salt and pepper; break up the tomatoes with a spoon.
4. Return the meatballs to the kettle. Bring the sauce to boiling. Cover the kettle. Lower the heat and simmer, stirring frequently, for 45 minutes or until the sauce thickens and the meatballs are cooked through.

L·A·M·B

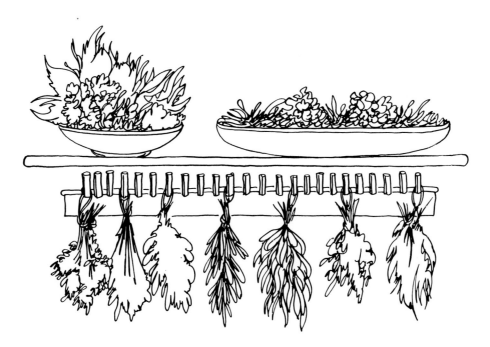

Braised Lamb Shanks

A long-simmering dish guaranteed to warm up a cold winter evening.

Makes 6 servings.

Nutrient Value Per Serving: 442 calories, 24 g protein, 33 g fat, 13 g carbohydrate, 365 mg sodium, 86 mg cholesterol.

3   meaty lamb shanks (about 4 pounds)
⅓   cup olive oil or vegetable oil
3   cloves garlic, finely chopped
1   large onion, sliced
2   carrots, peeled and cut into 2 x ½-inch strips
2   bay leaves, crumbled
½   teaspoon leaf oregano, crumbled
½   teaspoon leaf thyme, crumbled
1   can (16 ounces) stewed tomatoes

1. Brown the lamb shanks in the oil in a large, heavy skillet over medium-high heat for 7 to 10 minutes.
2. While the shanks are browning, lightly oil the bottom of a heavy casserole large enough to hold the shanks in one layer. Sprinkle the bottom of the casserole with the garlic, onion and carrots.
3. Transfer the browned shanks to the bed of vegetables in the casserole. Add the bay leaves, oregano and thyme. Add the tomatoes with their liquid. Cover the casserole.
4. Cook the shanks over low heat for 2½ to 3 hours or until tender, turning the shanks occasionally and checking to make sure the liquid is not boiling rapidly. Add a little water if necessary.
5. With a slotted spoon, transfer the vegetables to a serving platter. Arrange the shanks on top. Keep warm.
6. Skim the fat from the surface of the cooking liquid. Boil the sauce rapidly until reduced to about 1 cup. Serve half a shank per person with some of the sauce spooned over.

LAMB SHANKS

Cut from the front leg of the lamb, the shank is interlaced with stringy connective tissue and yields 1 to 2 servings of full-flavored meat.

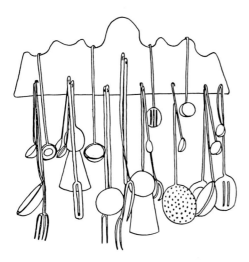

Lamb Stew

Half soup, half stew, this simple dish is made with lamb shoulder.

Makes 8 generous servings.

Nutrient Value Per Serving: 400 calories, 32 g protein, 11 g fat, 43 g carbohydrate, 1,028 mg sodium, 100 mg cholesterol.

- **3 pounds well-trimmed, boneless shoulder of lamb, cut into 1½- to 2-inch pieces**
- **8 cups cold water**
- **2 medium-size onions, chopped**
- **2½ pounds small potatoes, peeled and halved, or quartered if large**
- **4 leeks, trimmed and washed well**
- **4 stalks celery, chopped**
- **2 large cloves garlic, finely chopped**
- **1 tablespoon salt**
- **½ teaspoon whole peppercorns**
- **1 teaspoon leaf marjoram OR: leaf tarragon, crumbled**
- **2 tablespoons tomato paste**
- **12 small white onions, about 1 inch (12 ounces), halved or quartered if large, peeled**
- **6 small white turnips (about 14 ounces), peeled and quartered**
- **6 carrots, peeled and cut into 2 x ½-inch strips**
- **1 tablespoon chopped parsley**

1. Place the lamb in a large soup kettle. Add enough cold water to cover the lamb. Bring to boiling; boil for 5 minutes. Drain through a colander, discarding the water. Rinse the lamb in fresh cold water. Clean the soup kettle. Return the meat to the kettle. Add the 8 cups cold water. Bring slowly to boiling.

2. Add the chopped onion to the stew. Chop 4 of the potatoes and add to the stew. Chop the green part of the leeks and add them to the stew. Reserve the white part. Add the celery, garlic, salt, peppercorns and marjoram. Simmer the stew, covered, for 1½ hours.

3. Remove the meat from the broth with a slotted spoon. Skim the fat from the broth. Strain the broth into a large bowl through a sieve or food mill, pushing through as much of the solids as possible. Return the meat to the kettle. Pour the broth over the meat. Stir in the tomato paste. Add additional salt and pepper, if you wish. Place the white onions, turnip, carrot, remaining potato, reserved white part of leek and the parsley on top. Bring to boiling. Lower the heat; cover the kettle and simmer for 45 minutes or until the vegetables are tender. Skim off any fat from the broth if necessary. Serve the stew in large soup bowls.

MARJORAM AND OREGANO

These two spices are similar in flavor, but marjoram is a bit sweeter and not as assertive as oregano. According to folklore, marjoram was thought to fortify the nerves and prevent apoplexy and other maladies that affect the brain. Use marjoram for seasoning lamb, pork, sausages, chicken and egg dishes.

H·A·M P·O·R·K A·N·D S·A·U·S·A·G·E

Wine-Glazed Baked Fresh Ham with Gravy

Fresh ham is just like roast pork after baking. This spectacular ham, perfect for the holidays or a large family gathering, will give you enough nice slices to serve 16 with small pieces left over for a bonus meal. Use leftovers for a vegetable stir-fry or in stews or casseroles.

Bake at 325° for 5½ hours.
Makes sixteen 5-ounce servings, with leftovers for another meal.

Nutrient Value Per 5-ounce Serving: 458 calories, 39 g protein, 29 g fat, 8 g carbohydrate, 216 mg sodium, 138 mg cholesterol.

1   **fresh ham (leg of pork) weighing about 17 to 18 pounds (give your butcher a few days' notice)**
2   **large carrots, cut into ½-inch-thick slices**
1   **celery stalk, cut into ½-inch-thick slices**
1   **large onion, coarsely chopped**
1¼   **cups dry white wine**
½   **teaspoon leaf thyme, crumbled**
1   **small bay leaf**
¼   **cup apple jelly**
⅓   **cup all-purpose flour**
     Chicken broth
     Salt and pepper, to taste

Garnish:
     Tangerine-Cranberry Relish in Tangerine Cups (see recipe, page 70)
     Onion "Mums" (recipe follows)
     Lemon leaves (optional)

1. With a sharp knife, cut and remove the skin from the fresh ham. Trim the fat, leaving about a ¼-inch-thick layer. Cut 5 or 6 diagonal slashes, about ¼ inch deep and 1½ inches apart, over the fat layer.
2. Preheat the oven to slow (325°).
3. Place the carrots, celery and onion in the center of a large roasting pan. Add 1 cup of the wine, the thyme and bay leaf. Set the ham, fat-side up, over the vegetables. Cover the ham and the pan entirely with heavy-duty aluminum foil.
4. Bake the ham in the preheated slow oven (325°) for 5 hours or until a meat thermometer inserted into the thickest part of the ham, without resting in fat or touching the bone, registers 160°.
5. Meanwhile, to prepare the glaze, heat the remaining ¼ cup white wine and the jelly in a small saucepan until melted.
6. When the ham has reached 160°, remove the foil. Brush the ham with the glaze. Continue to bake the ham, uncovered, for about 30 minutes or until the thermometer registers 170°; brush the ham occasionally with the glaze.
7. Carefully remove the ham from the oven. Transfer to a serving platter; keep warm. Strain the liquid from the roasting pan into a large bowl; discard the vegetables. Let the liquid stand a few minutes for the fat to rise to the top of the juices.
8. To prepare the gravy: Measure ¼ cup fat from the pan liquid into a medium-size saucepan. Skim off and discard any remaining fat from the liquid in the bowl. Heat the fat in the saucepan. Stir in the flour until blended. Cook for 1 minute, stirring. Gradually stir in the meat juices from the bowl and enough chicken broth to make 3½ cups liquid. Cook, stirring constantly, until the gravy thickens and bubbles, about 10 minutes. Taste; season with salt and pepper. Stir in any leftover glaze. Pour the gravy into a warmed gravy boat.
9. To carve the ham: About 6 inches from the end of the shank bone, make a vertical cut down to the bone. About 4 inches from the end of the bone, cut in at a 45° angle to the first cut to loosen a wedge of meat. Remove the wedge and set aside. Beginning with the first vertical cut and moving toward the butt end of the ham, cut vertical slices down to the bone. Make a horizontal cut along the bone to free the slices. Garnish the platter with Tangerine-Cranberry Relish cups, and Onion "Mums" and lemon leaves, if you wish.

Onion "Mums": To make a mum, cut off a 2-inch length from the white part, or root end of a large green onion. Cut off the roots. From the root end, make cuts lengthwise 1 inch deep and ⅛ inch apart, into the onion. Then make cuts at right angles to the first cuts. Drop the onion into a bowl of cold water; let stand until the ends begin to curl. Repeat to make as many mums as you wish. Drain the mums; refrigerate in a plastic bag until ready to use.

Cold Roast Pork with Garlic Mayonnaise

For an enticing buffet presentation, arrange the pork on a platter with a selection of lightly blanched vegetables either chilled or at room temperature. This is also delicious picnic fare.

Preheat oven to 450°; roast pork at 350° for 50 to 60 minutes.
Makes 6 servings.

Nutrient Value Per Serving: 518 calories, 21 g protein, 47 g fat, 1 g carbohydrate, 341 mg sodium, 113 mg cholesterol.

1	**tablespoon vegetable oil**
1	**teaspoon salt**
1	**teaspoon pepper**
2	**teaspoons leaf rosemary, crumbled**
3	**cloves garlic, crushed**
2	**pounds boneless, rolled pork loin roast**

Garlic Mayonnaise:
1	**egg yolk**
1½	**tablespoons lemon juice (1 lemon)**
¾	**cup olive oil**

1. Preheat the oven to very hot (450°).
2. Combine the vegetable oil, salt, pepper, rosemary and 2 cloves of the garlic in a small bowl. Rub the mixture all over the pork loin. Place the pork in a roasting pan.
3. Place the roast in the preheated very hot oven (450°). Immediately lower the oven temperature to moderate (350°). Roast the pork for 50 to 60 minutes or until the internal temperature registers 170° on a meat thermometer. Remove the pork from the oven and let cool.
4. Prepare the Garlic Mayonnaise: Place the remaining clove of garlic, the egg yolk and lemon juice in the work bowl of a food processor or an electric blender. Cover; whirl briefly until the mixture is well blended. With the motor running, add ¼ cup of the olive oil, drop by drop, until the mixture is thickened. Add the remaining oil in a slow, steady stream; the resulting mayonnaise should be thick and smooth. Add salt and pepper, if you wish, and more lemon juice.
5. Serve the pork, thinly sliced, cold or at room temperature with the mayonnaise.

Cold Roast Pork with Garlic Mayonnaise.

Temperature and Time for Roasting Pork

Cut	Approximate Pound Weight	Oven Temperature	Internal Meat Temperature When Done	Minutes Per Pound Roasting Time
Loin				
Center	3 to 5	325° to 350° F.	170° F.	30 to 35
Half	5 to 7	325° to 350° F.	170° F.	35 to 40
Blade Loin or Sirloin	3 to 4	325° to 350° F.	170° F.	40 to 45
Rolled	3 to 5	325° to 350° F.	170° F.	35 to 45
Picnic Shoulder	5 to 8	325° to 350° F.	170° F.	30 to 35
Rolled	3 to 5	325° to 350° F.	170° F.	35 to 40
Cushion Style	3 to 5	325° to 350° F.	170° F.	30 to 35
Boston Shoulder	4 to 6	325° to 350° F.	170° F.	40 to 45
Leg (Fresh ham)				
Whole (Bone in)	12 to 16	325° to 350° F.	170° F.	22 to 26
Whole (Rolled)	10 to 14	325° to 350° F.	170° F.	24 to 28
Half (Bone in)	5 to 8	325° to 350° F.	170° F.	35 to 40
Spareribs	3	325° to 350° F.	Well done	1½ to 2½ hrs. (total)

Temperature and Time for Roasting Cured and Smoked Pork

Cut	Approximate Pound Weight	Oven Temperature	Internal Meat Temperature When Done	Total Roasting Time
Ham (cook before eating)				
Bone in, half	5 to 7 lbs.	325° F.	160° F.	2½ to 3 hours
Ham (fully cooked)				
Bone in, half	5 to 7 lbs.	325° F.	140° F.	1½ to 2¼ hours
Boneless, half	3 to 4 lbs.	325° F.	140° F.	1¼ to 1¾ hours
Arm Picnic Shoulder				
Bone in	5 to 8 lbs.	325° F.	170° F.	2½ to 4 hours
Shoulder				
Boneless roll	2 to 3 lbs.	325° F.	170° F.	1½ to 1¾ hours

Ham and Potato Bake with Cheese

This quick main-dish is made even easier with an assortment of frozen foods. Serve with assorted dinner rolls and tomato slices on a bed of crispy lettuce leaves, drizzled with a vinaigrette dressing.

Bake at 425° for 45 minutes.
Makes 6 servings.

Nutrient Value Per Serving: 733 calories, 32 g protein, 42 g fat, 58 g carbohydrate, 1,610 mg sodium, 102 mg cholesterol.

- 1 **cup chopped onion, fresh or frozen**
- 1 **cup chopped sweet green pepper, fresh or frozen**
- 3 **tablespoons butter**
- 3 **tablespoons all-purpose flour**
- ½ **teaspoon salt**
- ⅛ **teaspoon pepper**
- 3 **cups milk**
- 2 **cups shredded Cheddar cheese (8 ounces)**
- 1 **tablespoon Dijon-style mustard**
- 1 **bag (2 pounds) frozen cottage fry-style potatoes OR: French fry-style potatoes**
- 1 **bag (1 pound) frozen baby carrots**
- 1 **pound canned or vacuum-sealed sliced ham, cut into ½-inch cubes**

1. Preheat the oven to hot (425°). Butter six 2-cup ovenproof casseroles.
2. Sauté the onion and the green pepper in the butter in a Dutch oven over medium heat until soft but not browned, about 5 minutes. Stir in the flour, salt and pepper. Add the milk. Lower the heat and simmer, stirring, until the mixture is thickened, about 2 minutes.
3. Stir in 1 cup of the cheese and the mustard. Cook, stirring, until the cheese is melted. Remove the Dutch oven from the heat. Gently fold in the potatoes, carrots and ham. Spoon the mixture into the prepared casseroles. Cover each with aluminum foil.
4. Bake the casseroles in the preheated hot oven (425°) for 30 minutes. Remove the foil. Sprinkle each casserole with the remaining cheese. Return the casseroles to the oven and bake, uncovered, for 15 minutes or until bubbly.

Ham and Potato Bake with Cheese.

COVERED-DISH SUPPER

For easy transport to a potluck dinner, prepare the Ham and Potato Bake in a 4-quart casserole. Bake, covered, in a preheated hot oven (425°) for 45 minutes. Then bake, uncovered, for 15 minutes.

Mustard-Glazed Pork

Bake at 350° for 1 hour and 30 minutes.
Makes 8 servings.

Nutrient Value Per Serving: 385 calories, 21 g protein, 28 g fat, 13 g carbohydrate, 1,040 mg sodium, 70 mg cholesterol.

- **1 smoked boneless pork butt (2 pounds)**
- **2 large McIntosh apples, halved, cored and cut into wedges**
- **4 medium-size zucchini (1¼ pounds), cut into 1-inch-thick slices**
- **4 medium-size onions, quartered**
- **1 tablespoon currant jelly**
- **2 teaspoons Dijon-style mustard**
- **½ teaspoon pepper**
- **½ teaspoon caraway seeds**

1. Preheat the oven to moderate (350°). Remove the netting from the pork butt.
2. Place the pork on a rack in a roasting pan. Pour water into the pan to a depth of ¼ inch. Cover the pan tightly with a lid or aluminum foil.
3. Bake the pork in the preheated moderate oven (350°) for 1 hour.
4. Drain all but ¼ inch liquid from the pan. Add the apples, zucchini and onion. Cover the pan and cook for 20 minutes.
5. To prepare the glaze, stir together the currant jelly and mustard in a small cup.
6. Uncover the roasting pan. Brush the pork, apples and vegetables with the glaze. Sprinkle the pork with the pepper and caraway seeds.
7. Bake the pork, uncovered, for another 10 minutes.
8. To serve, cut the pork into thin slices and arrange on a serving platter with the vegetables and apples.

Make-Your-Own Sausage

Use ground pork or turkey and adjust the spices to your own taste.

Makes 8 patties.

Nutrient Value Per Patty: 194 calories, 13 g protein, 15 g fat, 0 g carbohydrate, 327 mg sodium, 58 mg cholesterol.

- **1½ pounds ground pork OR: turkey**
- **2 teaspoons leaf sage, crumbled**
- **1 teaspoon paprika**
- **1 teaspoon salt**
- **½ teaspoon ground mace**
- **¼ to ½ teaspoon pepper**
- **2 tablespoons chicken broth OR: water**

1. Combine the pork or turkey, the sage, paprika, salt, mace and pepper in a medium-size bowl until well blended. Stir in the chicken broth or water until the mixture is smooth.
2. Cover the bowl with plastic wrap and refrigerate overnight to blend the flavors.
3. Shape the mixture into 8 equal patties.
4. Preheat the broiler.
5. Broil the sausage patties 4 inches from the heat in the preheated broiler for 10 minutes. Turn and broil 5 minutes longer or until the patties are golden and cooked through. Drain on paper toweling. Keep warm until serving time.

Hungarian Sausage Skillet

Makes 4 servings.

Nutrient Value Per Serving: 472 calories, 19 g protein, 37 g fat, 17 g carbohydrate, 1,184 mg sodium, 79 mg cholesterol.

2 medium-size sweet green peppers
2 medium-size onions (¾ pound)
1 tablespoon vegetable oil
1 tablespoon Hungarian paprika
1 can (16 ounces) whole tomatoes, undrained
⅛ teaspoon pepper
1 pound (25% less sodium) kielbasa, cut into 4 pieces
2 tablespoons chopped parsley

1. Halve and seed the green peppers; cut each pepper into 8 wedges. Halve the onions; cut each onion into 8 wedges.
2. Sauté the green pepper and onion in the oil in a large skillet for 3 minutes, stirring often; be careful not to brown the vegetables. Sprinkle the vegetables with the paprika; cook for 1 minute, stirring the mixture constantly. Add the tomatoes with their liquid and the pepper. Bring the mixture to boiling. Add the kielbasa. Lower the heat, cover the skillet and cook for 10 minutes or until the kielbasa is heated through. Sprinkle the sausage mixture with the parsley. Serve with rye or Italian bread.

Sausages Creole

Take advantage of some of the reduced-fat products in the supermarket.

Makes 4 servings.

Nutrient Value Per Serving: 414 calories, 19 g protein, 29 g fat, 17 g carbohydrate, 1,062 mg sodium, NA mg cholesterol.

1 pound reduced-fat knackwurst
2 tablespoons vegetable oil
1 large sweet green pepper, halved, seeded and finely chopped
2 stalks celery, finely chopped
1 large onion, finely chopped
1 can (15 ounces) tomato sauce (no salt added)
⅛ teaspoon black pepper
⅛ teaspoon ground hot red pepper
Hot cooked rice (optional)

1. Simmer the knackwurst in enough water to cover in a deep skillet for 5 minutes. Drain the water from the skillet. Continue to cook the knackwurst in the skillet until very lightly browned. Cut each knackwurst crosswise into sixths.
2. Heat the oil in a large skillet. Add the green pepper, celery and onion and sauté until the vegetables are tender but not browned, about 5 minutes.
3. Stir in the tomato sauce, black pepper and red pepper. Mix in the knackwurst pieces. Cover the skillet and simmer for 5 minutes or until the mixture is hot. Serve over hot cooked white rice, if you wish.

Sausage Frittata Skillet

A quick dinner prepared with reduced-fat sausage links.

Makes 5 servings.

Nutrient Value Per Serving: 360 calories, 18 g protein, 24 g fat, 21 g carbohydrate, 758 mg sodium, 438 mg cholesterol.

1 package (8 ounces) frozen reduced-fat sausage links, thawed
2 tablespoons vegetable oil
1 small onion, chopped (¼ cup)
⅔ cup chopped sweet green and/or red pepper
2 cups frozen home-fried potatoes
8 eggs
¼ cup chopped parsley
½ teaspoon salt
¼ teaspoon pepper

1. Brown the sausage in a large nonstick skillet. Remove the sausage and reserve.
2. Add the oil to the skillet and heat. Add the onion and pepper and sauté for 2 minutes, stirring often. Add the potatoes, spreading them in an even layer. Cook, stirring occasionally until the potatoes are tender, 8 to 10 minutes.
3. Mix together the eggs, parsley, salt and pepper in a medium-size bowl; pour over the vegetable mixture. Arrange the sausage links over the top of the frittata in a spoke-like manner. Cover the skillet and cook over medium-low heat for 3 minutes. Uncover the skillet. Carefully push the egg mixture in from the sides of the skillet with a spatula, tilting and turning the skillet to let the uncooked portion flow to the bottom. Cover the skillet and cook 2 minutes longer or until the top is as wet or as dry as desired.
4. Cut the frittata into wedges and serve.

P·O·U·L·T·R·Y

Delicious hot or at room temperature: Chicken with Provençal Vegetables (page 92).

Chicken with Provençal Vegetables

Serve this flavorful dish either hot or at room temperature.

Makes 6 servings.

Nutrient Value Per Serving: 242 calories, 29 g protein, 9 g fat, 10 g carbohydrate, 539 mg sodium, 67 mg cholesterol.

1½ **pounds boneless, skinned chicken breasts, cut into ¾-inch strips**
3 **tablespoons olive oil**
1 **medium-size onion, thinly sliced**
3 **cloves garlic, finely chopped**
2 **small zucchini, cut crosswise into ¼-inch-thick rounds**
1 **medium-size sweet green pepper, halved, cored and cut into ¼-inch-wide strips**
1 **medium-size sweet red pepper, halved, cored and cut into ¼-inch-wide strips**
2 **cans (14 ounces each) plum tomatoes, drained**
¼ **cup chicken broth**
2 **tablespoons balsamic vinegar OR: red wine vinegar**
¼ **teaspoon fennel seeds, crushed**
½ **teaspoon salt**
½ **teaspoon pepper**
2 **tablespoons grated Parmesan cheese**

1. Sauté the chicken strips in the oil in a large flameproof casserole or Dutch oven over high heat, stirring, until the chicken is lightly browned, about 4 minutes. Remove the chicken to a plate; set aside and keep warm.
2. Add the onion and garlic to the casserole. Sauté over medium heat, stirring, until the onion is softened, about 2 minutes. Add the zucchini rounds and green and red pepper strips. Cook for 2 minutes more, stirring to coat the vegetables with the oil.
3. Add the drained tomatoes, chicken broth, balsamic or red wine vinegar, fennel seeds, salt and pepper to the casserole. Lower the heat and simmer, covered, stirring frequently, until the vegetables are crisp-tender, about 5 minutes.
4. Return the chicken strips to the casserole and simmer, uncovered, for 2 to 3 minutes longer or until the chicken is cooked through.
5. Sprinkle the mixture with the Parmesan cheese and serve hot.

Food for thought . . .

The anise-flavored root and stalks of fennel, a celerylike vegetable, can be eaten raw as an hors d'oeuvre or braised as a vegetable side dish. The feathery leaves are excellent for flavoring fish dishes and the seeds likewise. Like many other plants, fennel was once thought to have curative powers — it was even considered an antidote for the bite of a mad dog.

Food for thought . . .

Did you know that chicken has been on the menu for 4,000 years! Originally, it was gourmet fare, served for only very special occasions. Chicken Kiev dates back to the czarist days of Russia. Napoleon's chef, Dumand the Younger, created Chicken Marengo in 1800. To honor a popular Italian coloratura soprano, Chicken Tetrazzini was born. And Chicken Divan made Divan Parisien one of the most popular restaurants in New York City.

1. Combine the flour, salt and pepper on a sheet of wax paper. Coat the chicken quarters with the flour mixture.
2. Melt 2 tablespoons of the butter in a large, deep skillet. Add the chicken and sauté over medium heat until the chicken is browned all over. Remove the chicken to a plate.
3. Stir the curry powder into the skillet. Add the onions, mushrooms and garlic. Cook until tender, about 3 minutes, stirring often. Stir in the wine and thyme. Return the chicken to the skillet. Cover the skillet and simmer for 30 minutes.
4. Add the corn. Cover the skillet and simmer for 10 minutes or until the corn is tender.
5. Meanwhile, sauté the sweet pepper in the remaining butter in a small skillet until tender, about 3 minutes. Reserve the pepper.
6. Remove the chicken and corn to a serving platter; keep warm. Stir the cream into the large skillet. Cook over low heat, stirring constantly, until the mixture boils. Lower the heat and simmer a few minutes to thicken the sauce slightly. Pour the sauce over the chicken and corn. Sprinkle with the sautéed pepper.

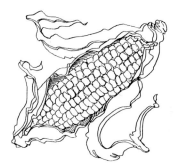

Curried Chicken and Corn (below)
and Tamale Pie (page 81).

Curried Chicken and Corn

Makes 4 servings.

Nutrient Value Per Serving: 917 calories, 49 g protein, 67 g fat, 33 g carbohydrate, 833 mg sodium, 278 mg cholesterol.

- **¼ cup all-purpose flour**
- **1 teaspoon salt**
- **¼ teaspoon pepper**
- **1 broiler-fryer (about 3 pounds), quartered**
- **3 tablespoons butter or margarine**
- **2 teaspoons curry powder**
- **2 medium-size onions, chopped**
- **½ pound mushrooms, sliced**
- **1 clove garlic, crushed**
- **1 cup dry white wine**
- **½ teaspoon leaf thyme, crumbled**
- **4 ears corn, shucked and each cut into 3 or 4 pieces**
- **1 sweet pepper, diced (green, red or a combination)**
- **1 cup heavy cream**

Food for thought . . .

Curry powder is a blend of other spices and can range from fiery to mild. Coriander, cardamom, ground hot red pepper, turmeric, mustard seed, ginger, cinnamon and dried chilies are just some of the ingredients that can be mixed for a curry powder.

BUYING CHICKEN — WHAT TO LOOK FOR

Look for chicken that has moist skin without any dry spots. Avoid packages where blood or juice has accumulated in the bottom — a sign that the chicken has been out for too long, or may have been frozen. Chicken should smell fresh. This can mean no smell at all or a pleasant chicken aroma. If when you open the package at home and smell a slight chicken odor, rinse the chicken under cold water and rub with a lemon half or dip briefly in a mixture of vinegar and water.

Amount to Buy

Chicken for frying: Allow ¾ to 1 pound per serving.

Chicken for roasting: Allow ¾ to 1 pound per serving.

Chicken for broiling or barbecuing: Allow ½ a chicken or 1 pound per serving.

Chicken for stewing: Allow ½ to 1 pound per serving.

Chicken livers: Allow ¼ pound per serving.

Rock Cornish Game Hen: Allow 1 game hen per person.

Storing Chicken

• Refrigerate tray-wrapped chicken from the supermarket for only 2 days from the time of purchase.

• Multiple-bagged chickens should be rinsed, separated into the desired portions and repacked in clean plastic wrap or heavy plastic bags.

• Freeze chickens in moisture-vapor-resistant materials such as heavy-duty aluminum foil, freezer paper or plastic freezer bags. Press air out of package before sealing.

• Small families or single people will find it convenient and economical to wrap and freeze chicken parts in sizes that are just enough for one meal.

• Storage time for home-frozen fresh chicken is 4 to 6 months.

• Cooked chicken can be safely refrigerated for no more than 2 to 3 days in the coldest part of your refrigerator. It can also be frozen and packaged the same way as fresh chicken, but the recommended freezing period is only 2 months.

• Commercially frozen chicken, wrapped and stored under the most favorable conditions, can be safely stored in the freezer for up to 12 months.

• Always refrigerate broth or gravy in separate containers.

• Remove all stuffing from the bird; store separately, in an oven-safe casserole, in the refrigerator. Reheat at 350° for 30 minutes.

Chicken Lasagne

The flavor of the sauce improves if made a day before. Since this rich lasagne contains no ricotta cheese, it is not as creamy as the more traditional version.

Bake at 400° for 1 hour.
Makes 12 servings.

Nutrient Value Per Serving: 572 calories, 30 g protein, 23 g fat, 62 g carbohydrate, 1,109 mg sodium, 82 mg cholesterol.

Chicken Sauce:
- 1 **cup finely chopped onion (1 large)**
- 1 **tablespoon butter**
- 1 **tablespoon olive oil**
- ½ **cup finely chopped carrot (1 carrot)**
- ½ **cup finely chopped celery (1 stalk)**
- 1 **tablespoon finely chopped garlic**
- 2 **pounds uncooked ground chicken OR: uncooked ground turkey**
- 2 **teaspoons salt**
- 2 **cups dry white wine**
- 1 **tablespoon leaf basil, crumbled**
- 2 **teaspoons leaf oregano, crumbled**
- 1 **teaspoon whole fennel seeds**
- ½ **teaspoon leaf rosemary, crumbled**
- 1 **cup milk**
- ¼ **teaspoon ground nutmeg**
- ¼ **teaspoon pepper**
- 1 **can (6 ounces) tomato paste**
- 1 **cup water**
- 1 **can (28 ounces) whole tomatoes, with their liquid**
- 1 **recipe White Sauce (see recipe, at right)**
- 2 **teaspoons olive oil**
- 1½ **pounds lasagne noodles**
- 1 **cup finely chopped parsley**
- 1⅓ **cup grated Parmesan cheese**

1. Prepare Chicken Sauce: Sauté the onion in the butter and olive oil in a large heavy saucepan over medium heat until soft, about 5 minutes. Add the carrot, celery and garlic; sauté 2 to 3 minutes. Crumble in the ground chicken; sprinkle with salt. Cook over low heat, stirring to break up the chicken, until half-cooked, 3 to 4 minutes. Add 1½ cups of the wine, the basil, oregano, fennel and rosemary. Cook over medium-high heat until the wine has evaporated, about 15 minutes. Add the milk, nutmeg and pepper. Cook over medium heat, stirring frequently, until the milk has evaporated, 10 to 15 minutes. Stir in the tomato paste and 1 cup water. Add the tomatoes with their liquid, breaking up with a spoon. Bring to boiling. Lower the heat; simmer, stirring occasionally, 1 hour until thick.

2. Add the remaining ½ cup wine. Simmer for 5 to 10 minutes to blend flavors.
3. Cool the sauce to room temperature (or use right away). Refrigerate, covered, overnight. You'll have 7 cups rich sauce.
4. Prepare the White Sauce and have it hot.
5. Preheat the oven to hot (400°). Lightly grease a deep lasagne pan, about 14 x 10 x 3 inches with 4- to 5-quart capacity, with the 2 teaspoons olive oil.
6. Bring a large pot of lightly salted water to boiling. Add the noodles, one piece at a time. Return to boiling, stirring. Boil just until firm-tender, about 10 minutes. Drain in a colander. Return to the pot and fill with cold water.
7. Spread 1 cup of the Chicken Sauce in the prepared pan. Remove one-quarter of the noodles from cold water; pat dry with paper toweling. Arrange in a layer in the prepared pan, slightly overlapping. Spread with 1½ cups of the Chicken Sauce. Spoon 1 cup of the White Sauce in small spoonfuls evenly spaced over the Chicken Sauce; do not spread out. Sprinkle with ⅓ cup of the parsley and ⅓ cup of the Parmesan. Repeat three more times (there will be no parsley for the top layer). Cover with aluminum foil.
8. Bake in the preheated hot oven (400°) for 45 minutes. Uncover and bake for 15 minutes more or until lightly browned. Let stand 15 minutes before cutting.

White Sauce

Makes 4 cups.

Nutrient Value Per ¼ Cup: 86 calories, 2 g protein, 6 g fat, 6 g carbohydrate, 189 mg sodium, 14 mg cholesterol

1   *quart milk*
3   *tablespoons butter*
2   *tablespoons olive oil*
½   *cup all-purpose flour*
1   *teaspoon salt*
¼   *teaspoon pepper*
¼   *teaspoon grated nutmeg*

1. Heat the milk in a medium-size heavy saucepan over low heat just until bubbles appear around the edge. Remove from the heat.
2. Combine the butter and the olive oil in a clean, heavy medium-size saucepan over medium heat. When the butter has melted, add the flour. Stir until bubbly; cook 1 minute longer. Add the milk all at once, whisking or stirring constantly. Add the salt, pepper and nutmeg. Stir over low heat until thick; simmer for 2 to 3 minutes.

Honey-Nut Drumsticks

Tuck these in the picnic basket or the lunch boxes.

Bake at 350° for 30 minutes.
Makes 4 servings.

Nutrient Value Per Serving: 709 calories, 45 g protein, 43 g fat, 38 g carbohydrate, 1,009 mg sodium, 274 mg cholesterol.

½   *cup milk, at room temperature*
2   *eggs, lightly beaten*
4   *tablespoons honey*
12   *chicken drumsticks (2½ pounds)*
¾   *cup roasted salted peanuts*
¾   *cup unseasoned bread crumbs, packaged or fresh*
1   *teaspoon salt*
2   *teaspoons ground hot red pepper*
3   *tablespoons vegetable oil*

1. Combine the milk, eggs and honey in a small bowl; stir to dissolve the honey. Place the drumsticks in a shallow dish. Pour the mixture over the drumsticks. Refrigerate, covered, for 2 hours, turning the drumsticks frequently.
2. Chop the peanuts in an electric blender or food processor with on-and-off pulses, as fine as possible without turning the peanuts into peanut butter. (For a crunchier coating for the chicken, coarsely grind the peanuts.) Combine the peanuts, bread crumbs, salt and red pepper in a shallow dish.
3. Preheat the oven to moderate (350°).
4. Lift a drumstick from the milk bath; roll in the nut mixture, patting the nut mixture firmly onto the drumstick to coat it. Place the chicken in a large, shallow baking dish. Repeat the coating process with the remaining drumsticks, adding the drumsticks to the baking dish in single layer. Drizzle the chicken with the oil.
5. Bake the chicken in the preheated moderate oven (350°) for about 30 minutes or until the chicken is no longer pink near the bone. Let the chicken cool slightly, then refrigerate if you are planning to serve the chicken later or the next day. Serve at room temperature.

Terrific picnic fare: Honey-Nut Drumsticks (page 95) *with Couscous Salad* (page 142) *and Summer Muffins* (page 16).

THE THRIFTY CHICKEN

● *Whole birds are about 6¢ to 10¢ less per pound than cut-up chicken. It pays to buy a whole bird and cut it up yourself. Turn to page 98 for illustrated easy step-by-step directions. Deboning your own chicken breast, for example, yields tremendous savings, and you have bones and trimming left over for stock.*

● *Buy chicken breast quarters (wings attached) when available. They are less expensive than breast halves, and you can easily remove the wings to freeze until you have enough for a bonus dish. As a main course, allow about four wings per person.*

● *Save the backs, giblets and bones removed during the deboning. Add water and seasoning and simmer for stock.*

● *Keep a container in the freezer for chicken livers. This way you can save them up until you have enough for a meal.*

● *Substitute deboned chicken breasts for veal in your favorite Parmesan and scallopini recipes.*

● *Chicken is a versatile meat that's compatible with many other foods. A little chicken will go a long way when you combine it with economical extenders like rice, pasta, dried beans and sauce for a hearty hot casserole.*

Food for thought . . .

Chicken is well suited to most all dietary needs, providing complete protein at a moderate cost. It is a short-fibered meat, easy to digest, and calorie-conscious consumers concerned with nutrition naturally think of chicken when dieting.

● *Chicken contains fewer calories than most meats. A 3½-ounce serving of broiled chicken (without the skin) has only about 136 calories, but provides 31.2 grams of protein or 52% of the average adult daily requirements, plus vitamin A, thiamine, riboflavin, niacin, iron and phosphorous.*

● *Chicken is lower in fats than most red meats. Three ounces of broiled chicken, even with the skin, yields about 9 grams of fat. That amount is doubled or tripled in an equal portion of other meats. Chicken skin contains about 17% fat, a small amount compared to the flavor it offers, and two-thirds of the fat is unsaturated.*

● *Team chicken with low-calorie vegetables — broccoli, tomatoes, zucchini — instead of starchy fillers.*

● *Cook chicken in low-cal ways — poached in defatted broth, sautéed in a nonstick skillet without oil.*

● *If you are really counting the calories, don't eat the skin. Perk up the flavor with herbs and spices such as rosemary, tarragon, or dill.*

HOW TO CUT AND BONE A CHICKEN

1. Place the chicken breast-side up. Using a sharp knife, make a lengthwise slit through the skin and flesh from the neck to the cavity. Turn the bird over and repeat the cut.

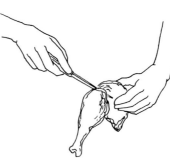

5. The thigh may be left attached to the leg for broiling; but for frying, bend the leg joint. Cut through the joint with a sharp knife, separating the leg from the thigh.

2. Using poultry shears (a) or kitchen shears (b), cut right through the bones (ribs). Cutting to one side of the breastbone is easier than cutting through it.

6. To separate the wing from the breast, bend the joint. Cut through the joint with a sharp knife. The chicken will now be in eight pieces and is ready for frying.

3. Turn the chicken over. Cut through the bones, cutting to one side of the backbone. You may remove the backbone. A small bird is cut this way for serving.

7. If your recipe calls for skinned chicken breasts, use a sharp, small paring knife to start, then slip your fingers between the skin and flesh and peel the skin.

4. To quarter the chicken, continue using the shears. Cut across half the bird, following the natural division just below the rib cage and the breastbone.

8. To bone the chicken breast, use a small paring knife. Cut the meat away from the rib bones with quick little strokes, feeling your way along with your fingers.

LS

Chicken Breasts Milano

Marinating the chicken breasts in an Italian-style liquid before roasting gives them a special flavor.

Bake at 375° for 45 minutes.
Makes 12 servings.

Nutrient Value Per Serving: 353 calories, 32 g protein, 24 g fat, 1 g carbohydrate, 137 mg sodium, 99 mg cholesterol.

---

8   **whole chicken breasts (about 10 ounces each), split**
½   **cup olive or vegetable oil**
½   **cup dry white wine**
2   **cloves garlic, crushed**
1   **tablespoon chopped Italian flat-leaf or curly parsley**
1   **teaspoon leaf oregano, crumbled**
    Salt and pepper, to taste
⅛   **to ¼ teaspoon crushed red pepper flakes**
⅓   **cup grated Parmesan cheese**
    Steamed spinach leaves
    Hot cooked rice
    Red pepper strips

1. Preheat the oven to moderate (375°).
2. Combine the oil, wine, garlic, parsley, oregano, salt and pepper to taste and red pepper flakes in a shallow pan. Add the chicken and turn to coat with the marinade. Cover the pan and refrigerate for several hours or overnight. Remove the chicken from the marinade, reserving the marinade.
3. Place the breast halves, skin-side up, in 1 or 2 roasting pans. Brush the chicken with part of the reserved marinade.
4. Bake the chicken in the preheated moderate oven (375°), basting occasionally with the marinade, for 40 minutes or until the skin is crisp.
5. Sprinkle part of the Parmesan cheese over the chicken. Return the chicken to the oven and bake just until the Parmesan cheese begins to turn golden. Remove from the oven.
6. Line a platter with the spinach, then the rice. Arrange the chicken breast halves on top. Sprinkle with additional Parmesan cheese and garnish with the red pepper strips.

TYPES OF CHICKEN

Poultry is graded by the Government to insure quality. This grading system, U.S. Grade A (or No. 1), U.S. Grade B (or No. 2) and U.S. Grade C (or No. 3), is based on such factors as health, pep, fleshing and feathering. Animals that rate below these grades are rejected.

Here are the types of chickens available today.
Broiler-Fryer is a meaty, tender, all-purpose chicken that tastes good when cooked by any method. Broiler-fryers weigh around 2½ to 3½ pounds and are marketed when they're about 7 to 8 weeks old.
Roaster is a slightly larger and older chicken. It weighs between 4½ to 6 pounds and is best roasted as its name implies.
Stewing Chicken or **Bro-Hen** is a plump, meaty bird, a year or more old. It weighs around 4½ to 6 pounds. Because it is older, this chicken is tougher than either the roaster or broiler-fryer and is best stewed.
Capon is a young male chicken that has been desexed. Capons are fleshy and tender with a high proportion of white meat. They can weigh from 6 to 9 pounds and can be cooked many ways but are superb roasted.
Rock Cornish Game Hen is a special breed developed by crossing a Cornish game cock with a white Rock hen. It is marketed at 4 to 6 weeks old and weighs 1½ pounds or less. It's popular with white-meat lovers.
Chicken in Parts is available in most markets today, making it possible to buy only those parts you prefer — breasts, drumsticks, wings, thighs or combinations of any of the above. Skinned and boned breasts are also available.
New Chicken Products are showing up more and more in the supermarkets. For example, chicken nuggets are available uncooked or fully cooked. Other cooked varieties of chicken range from whole barbecued chickens to chicken frankfurters.

HOW TO DEFROST FROZEN BIRDS

It's best to thaw chicken in the refrigerator. Don't unwrap it, because the skin tends to dry out and toughen when exposed to air. Allow 12 to 16 hours for thawing whole birds under 4 pounds, 4 to 9 hours for thawing chicken parts. For more rapid thawing, place chicken, still wrapped, in cold water. Refreezing chicken is not recommended. Do not refreeze thawed raw chicken. Instead, cook the chicken, then freeze.

CHICKEN SUITS SINGLE HOUSEHOLDS

Single households are an important part of today's lifestyle, and chicken fits their special food needs. It can be brought in small quantities, it's nutritious and easy to prepare, it's economical, and it's versatile.

The National Broiler Council recommends the following cooking times for baking individual chicken servings. Dip the chicken first in melted butter, turn and baste once during cooking. (*Note:* Cooking in a toaster oven will save energy and cleanup.)

Cooking Time for Chicken Parts

Part	Temperature	Time
4 Chicken Wings	350°	25 to 27 minutes
1 Half Breast	350°	25 to 27 minutes
2 Chicken Thighs	375°	22 minutes
1 Leg-Thigh Combination	375°	35 minutes

A new idea for turkey: Cold Roast Turkey with Sweet and Sour Eggplant.

Cold Roast Turkey with Sweet and Sour Eggplant

The turkey breast and the eggplant mixture can be prepared a day or two ahead and refrigerated. Allow both to come to room temperature before serving. Try the eggplant on its own as a condiment with other roast meats and grilled fish.

Roast turkey at 350° for 1½ to 2 hours. Makes 8 servings (4 ounces each) with leftovers.

Nutrient Value Per Serving: 494 calories, 57 g protein, 26 g fat, 6 g carbohydrate, 449 mg sodium, 166 mg cholesterol.

- 1 **uncooked whole turkey breast with bone (about 5 pounds)**
- 1 **eggplant (about ¾ pound), cut into ½-inch-thick slices**
- ¼ **cup olive oil**
- 4 **small cloves garlic, finely chopped**
- 4 **medium-size ripe tomatoes, halved, seeded and diced (2 cups)**
- ½ **cup red wine vinegar**
- ¾ **teaspoon sugar**
- ½ **teaspoon salt**
- ½ **teaspoon pepper**
- ⅓ **cup oil-cured black olives, pitted and halved**
- 2 **tablespoons capers, drained**
- 3 **tablespoons chopped parsley**

1. Preheat the oven to moderate (350°). Place the turkey breast in a medium-size casserole or Dutch oven. Cover the casserole.
2. Roast the turkey in the preheated moderate oven (350°) for 1½ to 2 hours or until the internal temperature of the turkey registers 170° on a meat thermometer. Remove the casserole from the oven and let the turkey cool. Refrigerate the turkey, covered.
3. Meanwhile, turn the oven to broil. Place the eggplant slices on a baking sheet. Brush the eggplant slices with 1 tablespoon of the olive oil. Broil the slices 6 inches from the source of heat for 7 minutes or until the eggplant is lightly browned. Turn the slices over and brush with another tablespoon of the olive oil. Broil for 7 minutes or until the eggplant is soft but not mushy. Set the eggplant aside to cool.
4. Sauté the garlic, stirring, in the remaining 2 tablespoons of oil in a medium-size skillet

over medium heat for 1 minute; do not let the garlic brown. Add the tomatoes and cook, stirring, for 1 minute or until the tomatoes are coated with oil and slightly softened.

5. Cut the cooled eggplant slices into a small dice. Combine the eggplant, tomatoes, vinegar, sugar, salt, pepper, olives and capers in a large bowl. Refrigerate the mixture, covered, at least 1 hour or up to 2 days for the flavors to mellow. Stir the mixture occasionally.

6. Remove the eggplant mixture and the turkey from the refrigerator 1 hour before planning to serve. Thinly slice the turkey. Arrange the slices on a platter with the eggplant mixture. Garnish with the chopped parsley.

Food for thought . . .

Capers are actually the buds of a wild Mediterranean shrub, which are picked and then salted and preserved in vinegar. Use as a condiment or to zip up mayonnaise sauces and seafood and veal dishes.

TYPES OF TURKEY

Roaster, the traditional big bird, comes in sizes that range from about 10 pounds to 30 pounds. Big birds look most festive on the groaning board and are the most economical in cost per serving; however, they take longer to roast, and if you have a family that goes for drumsticks and wings, you might consider substituting with two smaller turkeys, and you'll double the number of drumsticks and wings.

Fryer-Roaster is a small, meaty turkey weighing from 4 to 9 pounds. Perfect for smaller families.

Boneless Turkey Roast is plump roast weighing from 2 to 5 pounds and provides an easy-to-carve combination of white and dark meat. Ideal to slice for sandwiches.

Frozen Prestuffed Turkey can go directly from the freezer to the oven with no thawing. Available in a broad range of sizes.

Frozen Self-Basting Turkey is injected with butter before being frozen and bastes itself as it cooks. Available in a wide range of sizes.

Frozen Boneless Turkey Roll can come raw, fully cooked or smoked, and also as all-dark or all-white meat, or as a combination. Sizes range from 3 to 10 pounds.

Frozen Turkey Steaks are turkey minute steaks that come either plain or breaded.

Turkey Parts — drumsticks, wings, thighs and breasts — are marketed just like chicken parts. Legs and wings offer especially good eating at relatively low cost.

Smoked Turkey is a gourmet item, ready to slice and eat.

How Much To Buy
When buying turkeys under 12 pounds, allow ¾ to 1 pound per serving; when buying birds weighing more than 12 pounds, allow ½ to ¾ pound per serving. Remember, the bigger the bird, the more meat there will be in proportion to bone. Half of a 20-pound bird, for example, will be meatier than a 10-pound bird — and less expensive per serving.

TURKEY TALK

Storing
Fresh turkeys Refrigerate at all times. Cook within 1 to 2 days of purchase.
Frozen whole turkeys Store in its original wrapper for up to 12 months at 0° F. or lower.

Thawing
Conventional (Long) Method
Thawing time: 3 to 4 days, about 24 hours for each 5 pounds of whole frozen turkey.
• Leave the turkey in its original wrapper.
• Place the frozen turkey on a tray in the refrigerator.

Cold Water (Short) Method
Thawing time: about 30 minutes per pound of whole frozen turkey.
• Leave the turkey in its original wrapper.
• Place the turkey in the sink or a large pan.
• Completely cover with cold water.
• Change the water every 30 minutes.
• Keep immersed in cold water at all times.

Note: Never freeze stuffing that is in a cooked or raw bird. Remove all the stuffing from the cooked bird, wrap separately and refrigerate.

COOKING A TURKEY

Cooking that bird may be intimidating, but don't get "turkey trauma.' Today's turkeys are marketed at a young age so they are meaty and tender; it's no longer necessary to cook them to tenderize.

The best way to cook a turkey is in an open pan. Spread butter, margarine, solid shortening or vegetable oil lightly over the skin before roasting to prevent cracking and promote a mouthwatering golden brown color. Once the turkey is brown, cover the breast loosely with a tent of aluminum foil to prevent further browning. Try to use a pan no more than 2″ deep so it doesn't shield the heat from the drumstick area and increase the roasting time.

Timetable for Roasting Turkey (325°)

Bird Weight	Stuffed	Unstuffed
(pounds)	(hours)	(hours)
6 to 8	3 to 3½	2½ to 3½
8 to 12	3½ to 4½	3 to 4
12 to 16	4 to 5	3½ to 4½
16 to 20	4½ to 5½	4 to 5
20 to 24	5 to 6½	4½ to 5½

For Microwave Cooking Chart, see page 269.

Testing for Doneness
• Meat thermometer inserted in the meatiest part of the thigh next to the body but not touching the bone reads 180° F. to 185° F. If the turkey is stuffed, insert the thermometer in the center of the stuffing. It should read 150° to 155° F.
• Turkey juices run clear.
• Drumsticks move up and down easily.

Resting period
Let the turkey stand at room temperature for 20 minutes. This allows the juices to settle and the meat to firm up for easier carving.

Turkey Shepherd's Pie

Bake at 375° for 45 to 50 minutes.
Makes 4 servings.

Nutrient Value Per Serving: 341 calories, 20 g protein, 12 g fat, 41 g carbohydrate, 1,509 mg sodium, 175 mg cholesterol.

1½ **pounds all-purpose potatoes, pared and cut into eighths**
2 **teaspoons vegetable oil**
2 **cups coarsely chopped onion**
2 **cups coarsely chopped sweet green pepper (about 3 medium-size)**
1 **cup finely chopped carrots**
1 **clove garlic, finely chopped**
½ **teaspoon leaf basil, crumbled**
½ **teaspoon leaf oregano, crumbled**
2 **teaspoons salt**
½ **teaspoon pepper**
½ **pound packaged ground turkey, thawed if frozen**
2 **tablespoons all-purpose flour**
1 **cup beef broth, made from bouillon cube**
3 **tablespoons tomato paste**
¼ **cup skim milk**
2 **eggs**

1. Cook the potatoes in enough boiling water to cover them in a large saucepan until tender, 15 minutes. Drain the potatoes. Transfer to a bowl and keep warm.
2. Meanwhile, heat the oil in a large nonstick saucepan over medium-low heat. Stir in the onion, green pepper, carrot and garlic. Sauté the vegetables, stirring, for about 8 minutes. Add a few tablespoons of water, if necessary, to prevent sticking. Stir in the basil, oregano, 1 teaspoon of the salt and the pepper.
3. Crumble the turkey into the saucepan; cook until the turkey is no longer pink. Carefully drain off any excess fat. Stir in the flour until well blended. Add the broth and tomato paste; stir until blended. Cook for 1 minute, stirring, until the mixture thickens slightly. Turn the turkey mixture into an ungreased 8-inch-square baking pan, spreading the mixture evenly.

4. Preheat the oven to moderate (375°).
5. Mash the potatoes with the remaining salt. Beat in the skim milk until very smooth and fluffy. Beat in the eggs, one at a time. Spoon the potato mixture over the meat filling, spreading evenly; make sure the potato touches all sides of the pan. Decorate by drawing the tines of a fork across the top of the potatoes.
6. Bake the pie in the preheated moderate oven (375°) for 45 to 50 minutes or until the top is puffed and golden.

Turkey with Thickened Pan Juices

Bake at 325° for about 2½ hours.
Makes sixteen 3-ounce servings.

Nutrient Value Per Serving: 148 calories, 27 g protein, 3 g fat, 2 g carbohydrate, 298 mg sodium, 59 mg cholesterol.

2 **large carrots, pared and cut into ½-inch-thick slices**
1 **celery stalk, cut into ½-inch-thick slices**
1 **large onion, coarsely chopped**
¾ **cup dry white wine**
½ **cup water**
½ **teaspoon leaf thyme, crumbled**
1 **small bay leaf**
6 **pounds turkey breast on the bone, thawed if frozen**
   Cold chicken broth, about 1 to 3 cups, all fat skimmed off top
2 **to 3 tablespoons all-purpose flour**
½ **teaspoon salt**
¼ **teaspoon pepper**

1. Preheat the oven to slow (325°).
2. Place the carrots, celery and onion in the center of a large roasting pan. Add the wine, water, thyme and bay leaf. Set the turkey, skin-side up, over the vegetables. Cover the turkey and the pan entirely with a large sheet of heavy-duty aluminum foil.

3. Bake the turkey in the preheated slow oven (325°) for 1 hour. Uncover. Bake 1 hour 15 minutes to 1 hour 30 minutes longer or until a meat thermometer inserted into the thickest part of the turkey (without touching the bone) registers an internal temperature of 180°.
4. Carefully remove the turkey from the oven and transfer to a serving platter; keep warm. Strain the liquid from the roasting pan into a 4-cup glass measure; discard the vegetables. Let the liquid stand a few minutes for the fat to rise to the top. Remove all of the top fat layer, using a bulb baster or spoon.
5. To prepare the thickened pan juices: Add enough chicken broth to the pan juices in the glass measure to make 3 cups liquid. Pour into a medium-size saucepan. Stir ½ cup of additional chicken broth with the 2 tablespoons flour (3 tablespoons if thicker pan juices are desired) in a small bowl until smooth. Stir into the saucepan. Bring to boiling, stirring constantly. Cook until the juices thicken slightly, 3 to 5 minutes. Season the juices with the salt and pepper. Pour into a gravy boat.
6. Slice the turkey and pass the gravy boat.

P·A·S·T·A C·H·E·E·S·E A·N·D L·E·G·U·M·E·S

Meatless and wonderful: Peppers Stuffed with Eggplant (page 110).

Linguine with Seafood and Chicken in Cheese Sauce

A fast and easy main dish prepared in the time it takes to boil the water and cook the pasta. Serve with a tossed green salad.

Makes 6 servings.

Nutrient Value Per Serving: 621 calories, 34 g protein, 22 g fat, 73 g carbohydrate, 745 mg sodium, 89 mg cholesterol.

1 **pound linguine**
2 **cloves garlic, lightly smashed**
2 **tablespoons butter**
1 **tablespoon all-purpose flour**
2 **cups half-and-half**
½ **cup milk**
1 **cup shredded Monterey Jack cheese (4 ounces)**
2 **tablespoons grated Parmesan cheese**
⅛ **teaspoon white pepper**
Generous pinch ground hot red pepper
1 **package (10 ounces) frozen peas, thawed**
1 **package (8 ounces) imitation crab meat substitute from the freezer, thawed according to directions**
2 **cans (5 ounces each) chunk white chicken in water, drained**

1. Cook the linguine in a large pot of boiling water, following the package directions.
2. Meanwhile, sauté the garlic in the butter in a medium-size saucepan until golden, about 2 minutes. Remove the saucepan from the heat; discard the garlic.
3. Stir the flour into the butter in the saucepan until smooth. Return the saucepan to the heat. Add the half-and-half and the milk. Bring to boiling, stirring, over medium heat until the mixture is thick and bubbly.
4. Add the Monterey Jack cheese, Parmesan cheese, white pepper and red pepper. Cook over low heat, stirring gently, until the cheese is melted.
5. Stir in the peas, crab meat substitute and chunk chicken. Cook over low heat until the sauce is heated through, about 3 minutes. Toss the sauce with the drained linguine and serve.

CRABMEAT SUBSTITUTE (SURIMI)

Crab meat substitute is usually a combination of pollock, shellfish and other ingredients and can be found in the seafood or frozen food section of your supermarket.

Chicken, Broccoli, Tomato and Shells

Makes 2 servings.

Nutrient Value Per Serving: 563 calories, 32 g protein, 29 g fat, 45 g carbohydrate, 808 mg sodium, 0 mg cholesterol.

3 **ounces small macaroni shells**
½ **pound cooked or raw broccoli flowerets**
1 **can (5 ounces) chunk white chicken packed in water, drained and rinsed**
3 **tablespoons olive oil**
3 **tablespoons red wine vinegar**
2 **teaspoons leaf basil, crumbled**
¾ **teaspoon leaf oregano, crumbled**
½ **teaspoon lemon juice**
¼ **teaspoon ground pepper**
1 **medium-size tomato, diced**
¼ **cup chopped red onion**
2 **ounces sliced, reduced-calorie pasteurized process cheese product, cut in ½-inch-wide strips**

1. Cook the macaroni in boiling salted water to cover in a saucepan, according to the package directions. (If the broccoli is raw, add to the macaroni for the last 2 minutes of cooking time.) Drain the macaroni in a colander.
2. Break the chicken into chunks.
3. Combine the olive oil, vinegar, basil, oregano, lemon juice and pepper in a large bowl. Add the hot macaroni, broccoli, chicken, tomato, onion and cheese. Stir to mix well. Serve immediately.

A switch from basil-based pesto: Spaghetti with Spinach Pesto.

Spaghetti with Spinach Pesto

Try the pesto as a sauce with cold roast chicken or as a dip with raw vegetables.

Makes 4 servings.

Nutrient Value Per Serving: 990 calories, 22 g protein, 71 g fat, 69 g carbohydrate, 633 mg sodium, 14 mg cholesterol.

Spinach Pesto:
½ **cup blanched slivered almonds**
1 **clove garlic**
1 **cup olive oil**
2 **cups firmly packed spinach leaves, coarsely chopped (about ¼ pound spinach)**
¾ **cup firmly packed flat-leaf Italian parsley leaves (1 small bunch)**
½ **cup grated Parmesan cheese (about 2½ ounces) Salt and pepper, to taste**

1 **tablespoon vegetable oil**
½ **teaspoon salt**
¾ **pound spaghetti**

1. Prepare the Spinach Pesto: Place the almonds in the container of an electric blender or food processor. Cover and whirl until the nuts are finely ground; do not overgrind. Add the garlic; whirl until the garlic is finely chopped. Add the olive oil, spinach and parsley; whirl until the mixture is evenly chopped but still slightly chunky. Stir in the Parmesan cheese and the salt and pepper to taste.*

2. Bring a large pot of water to a rolling boil over high heat. Add the vegetable oil and the ½ teaspoon salt. Add the spaghetti. Cook until *al dente*, firm but still tender, 10 to 12 minutes. Drain the spaghetti and toss with the pesto. Transfer the spaghetti to a serving bowl. Pass extra Parmesan cheese.

*Note: The pesto can be made up to 5 days ahead and stored, tightly covered, in the refrigerator.

P•A•S•T•A

Buy pasta in well-wrapped packages and avoid packages with too many broken pieces.

Cooking time varies with the size, shape and type of pasta, as well as its freshness. Be sure to read individual package directions and test after minimum time; *do not* overcook.

How much pasta should you cook and serve? It's a matter of personal preference. One pound of spaghetti is sufficient for 6 to 8 first-course or side-dish servings but makes only 3 to 4 main-dish servings.

Different pasta shapes are interchangeable in most recipes, but if the sizes or thicknesses are different, the amount of pasta needed may have to be adjusted. Dry or uncooked pasta should be substituted by weight, not measurement, because pastas of different shapes will not have the same volume. A cupful of one pasta may differ in weight from a cupful of a differently shaped pasta. Cooked pasta can be substituted cup for cup.

How to Cook Pasta
1. Use a large kettle because the pasta needs plenty of room to bubble if it's to cook without sticking.
2. Do not cook more than 1 pound of pasta at a time in the same kettle. It will clump or stick together.
3. Fill a large kettle with water, leaving about 4 inches at the top (for 1 pound of pasta, you should use at least 12 cups of water). Add a drop of olive or vegetable oil (this helps keep pasta from sticking), set the kettle over high heat and bring to a boil. Salt the water, if you wish.
4. When cooking long macaroni or spaghetti, slowly lower a handful at a time into the rapidly boiling water until it softens enough to fit into the kettle. Stir once or twice to separate strands, if necessary.
5. Boil rapidly, uncovered, until a strand of pasta cut in half shows no raw starch in the center — it

shows up as a white dot — or until the pasta has no raw starch taste, but *does* feel a bit firm between the teeth (*al dente* is the Italian term for this firm tenderness).

6. Drain pasta in a large colander the instant it's *al dente*. But do not rinse in cool water unless the pasta is for a salad.

7. If pasta must stand for a few minutes before being served, toss with a little oil, set the colander over a kettle containing about 1 inch of simmering water and cover.

Beef and Tofu Spaghetti Sauce

High protein tofu is a healthful way to extend beef.

Makes enough for 1 pound spaghetti (6 servings).

Nutrient Value Per Serving of Sauce: 246 calories, 14 g protein, 13 g fat, 22 g carbohydrate, 707 mg sodium, 26 mg cholesterol.

- 2 **large onions, chopped (about 2 cups)**
- 1 **sweet green pepper, halved, seeded and chopped**
- 4 **cloves garlic, finely chopped**
- 1 **tablespoon safflower or olive oil**
- ½ **pound lean ground beef**
- 1 **can (35 ounces) Italian tomatoes, chopped and with their liquid**
- 1 **can (6 ounces) tomato paste**
- ¼ **cup grated carrot**
- 2 **teaspoons leaf basil, crumbled**
- 1 **teaspoon leaf oregano, crumbled**
- ½ **teaspoon salt**
- ¼ **teaspoon ground hot red pepper**
- 1½ **cups boiling water**
- ½ **cup dry red wine**
- 8 **ounces firm tofu, cut into small cubes**

1. Sauté the onion, pepper and garlic in the oil in a large skillet or Dutch oven over medium-low heat until the onions are soft, about 8 minutes.

2. Raise the heat to high. Add the beef, breaking it up with a wooden spoon. Cook until the beef loses its red color, 2 to 3 minutes. Add the tomatoes with their liquid, the tomato paste, carrot, basil, oregano, salt, red pepper, boiling water and wine. Bring the sauce to boiling. Lower the heat and cook gently, stirring occasionally, until the sauce thickens, about 30 minutes. Stir in the tofu. Serve over hot, cooked spaghetti.

Cheese Enchiladas with Bean and Corn Chili

A quick, spur-of-the-moment main dish made easier since you will most likely already have the ingredients in your cupboard or refrigerator.

Bake at 375° for 30 minutes.
Makes 5 servings.

Nutrient Value Per Serving: 533 calories, 26 g protein, 27 g fat, 49 g carbohydrate, 1,067 mg sodium, 54 mg cholesterol.

- 1 **cup chopped onion, fresh or frozen**
- 2 **cloves garlic, finely chopped**
- 3 **tablespoons vegetable oil**
- 1 **can (14 ounces) Italian-style plum tomatoes**
- ¾ **teaspoon ground cumin**
- ¼ **teaspoon salt**
- ⅛ **teaspoon black pepper**
- ⅛ **teaspoon crushed red pepper flakes**
- 1 **can (19 ounces) kidney beans, undrained**
- 1 **can (12 ounces) corn niblets, drained**
- 1 **can (4 ounces) chopped green chilies, drained**
- 1 **container (8 ounces) ricotta cheese**
- 2 **cups shredded Monterey Jack-style cheese (8 ounces)**
- 1 **package (5.3 ounces) 5-inch corn tortillas**

Fast and fabulous Cheese Enchiladas.

1. Sauté the onion and the garlic in 1 tablespoon of the oil in a large skillet until the onion is soft, about 5 minutes.
2. Add the tomatoes. Stir in the cumin, salt, black pepper and red pepper flakes. Bring the mixture to boiling, breaking up the tomatoes with a spoon. Add the beans, corn and half the chilies. Return the mixture to boiling. Lower the heat and simmer, covered, for 15 minutes, stirring occasionally.
3. Lightly grease a 13 x 9 x 2-inch baking pan. Spoon the chili into the pan.
4. Combine the ricotta, 1½ cups of the Monterey Jack-style cheese and the remaining chilies in a small bowl.
5. Heat ½ teaspoon of the oil in a small skillet over medium-high heat. Add 1 tortilla and soften briefly, turning once. Remove the tortilla to a work surface. Spoon 2 tablespoons of the cheese filling down the center of the tortilla. Roll the tortilla up to enclose the filling. Place the tortilla, seam-side down, on the chili. Repeat with the remaining tortillas and filling; you should have about 10 enchiladas. Sprinkle the remaining cheese over the enchiladas.
6. Preheat the oven to moderate (375°).
7. Bake the enchiladas on the chili in the preheated moderate oven (375°) for 30 minutes or until the enchiladas are heated through and the chili is bubbly hot.

C·H·E·E·S·E

There are literally hundreds of different kinds of cheeses in the world, yet all have the same main ingredient — milk. Milk is curdled by the action of heat or rennet (or other bacteria) or both, then the watery part, called whey, is separated from the curd. The curd, and sometimes the whey, is made into cheese.

The origin of cheese-making is lost in antiquity, but it was probably discovered by chance. Records show that cheese was known to the Sumerians in 4000 B.C. and we do know that cheese existed in Biblical times. Roman conquerors probably introduced cheese to England and cheese was made later by monks during the Middle Ages.

The word "cheese" comes from *cese* or *cyse* in Old English. To the French, cheese is *fromage;* Italians call it *fromaggio.*

Cheese is often divided into two categories: *natural cheeses,* and *cheese blends,* in which natural cheeses are used to make new products.

Natural cheeses may be subdivided by texture or consistency and degree or kind of ripening. The amount of whey drained from the curd generally determines the consistency of the cheese. Examples:
• Very hard — Parmesan, Romano
• Semi-soft to hard — Colby, Gouda
• Semi-soft — blue, brick, Muenster, Roquefort
• Soft — Brie, Camembert, cottage cheese, cream cheese, Limburger, Neufchâtel, ricotta.

Cheese blends can be subdivided into three products:
• Pasteurized process cheese is a blend of shredded fresh and aged natural cheese heated with water and an emulsifier to a homogeneous mixture. It is shaped into loaves or wheels. Buy it by the piece, or presliced or cut up and packaged. Popular-priced, it is perfect for cooking or making sandwiches. American cheese is an example.
• Pasteurized process cheese food is made the same way as process cheese, but with nonfat dry milk added. The moisture content is higher so it is softer and spreads more easily. It will melt faster than process cheese. It is packaged as loaves, rolls or links.
• Pasteurized process cheese spread is similar to process cheese food but spreads more easily because it contains more moisture. The milk-fat content is lower. It's packaged in jars, tubes and pressurized cans. Some may be flavored with pimiento, olives or onions. Cheese spreads can be used for appetizers and sandwiches.

Storing Cheese: The softer the cheese, the more perishable it is. The harder the cheese, the longer it will keep. Keep cheese chilled, the same as milk. Use soft cheeses — cottage, cream, ricotta, Brie — within a week. Hard cheeses will keep for weeks if left in their original wrapper or rewrapped tightly with plastic wrap. Should the surface of a hard cheese get moldy, simply cut off the affected area. Cheese mold is harmless and should not affect the cheese's quality. Some pasteurized cheese products do not need refrigeration, but once they are opened, they should be refrigerated if labels direct. Freeze cheese only if you must. Cheese loses flavor and becomes crumbly when frozen.

Cooking Cheese: Cheese is very heat sensitive and can curdle or become rubbery with excessive heat. Cook cheese over low or moderate heat. Since it melts quickly, you really don't need much heat. When making a cheese sauce, add the cheese last and cook just to melt it.

Cheese Nutrition: Cheese is a good source of high quality protein (as that in meat, poultry and eggs). It contains most of the nutrients of milk, including calcium and riboflavin.

POPULAR CHEESES

Kind	Description	Flavor	Uses
American	Process cheese of uniform texture made from domestic Cheddar; in slices and loaves.	Mild. Very popular with children.	A favorite of sandwiches and casseroles.
Bel Paese	Mellow, semi-soft Italian cheese.	Mildly nutty.	Team with fresh fruit as dessert, or with cocktails.
Blue, Gorgonzola, Roquefort	Medium-soft with blue to blue-green veins, crumbles easily.	Mild to tangy, slightly peppery.	These give a gourmet touch to appetizers, salads, dressings, desserts.
Brie, Camembert	Rounds and wedges with an edible gray-white crust; soft inside.	Mild to pungent, depending on age.	Favorites for desserts and appetizers. Serve at room temperature.
Cheddar	Semi-hard, cream to orange color. Sold as wedges, cubes, slices or shredded.	Mild to very sharp, depending on aging — check the package.	America's choice for sandwiches, cooked dishes, salads, snacks, desserts.
Cottage, Ricotta, Cream	Cottage and ricotta are creamy-white curd-like, low-calorie. Cream cheese is smooth and calorie-rich.	All are delicately mild; easily spoonable and spreadable.	Perfect for appetizers, sandwiches, cooked dishes, desserts, cake fillings or frostings.
Edam, Gouda	Creamy orange with red-wax coat. Edam is round; Gouda, flattish.	Mellow, slightly salty, with a nut-like taste.	Excellent for appetizer and dessert trays. Good snack cheeses, too.
Gruyère	Smooth, firm, pale, cream-colored cheese; process Gruyére is often sold in foil-wrapped triangles.	Nut-like, faintly caramel.	An all-purpose cheese, excellent for sauces, toppings. Also good in salads, soufflés and omelets.
Liederkranz, Limberger	Soft, bacteria-ripened cheese.	Strong to overpowering; acquired tastes.	Best eaten out-of hand or on crackers.
Mozzarella	Soft and white with a ball-like shape. Also comes shredded.	Mild and a bit chewy to eat, especially when heated.	Known as the pizza-lasagne cheese. Use in salads or on appetizer platters.
Muenster, Brick	Creamy-yellow to white; semisoft; tiny holes.	Muenster is mild; brick, mild to sharp.	Appetizers, sandwiches, salads, desserts.
Parmesan, Romano, Sapsago	The grating cheeses — very hard. White to light green. Sold in blocks, as well as grated.	Parmesan is pungent, but milder than Romano. Sapsago has herb-like flavor.	Topper for casserole dishes and spaghetti. Also popular for sauces and vegetable seasoners.
Port du Salut	Firm, smooth French cheese, the color of cream.	Fairly sharp.	A good cocktail or dessert cheese.
Provolone	Light brown outside; light yellow inside. Sometimes lined with rope marks.	Mellow to sharp, smoky and salty.	Try it in macaroni, spaghetti dishes, for sandwiches, snacks or appetizer trays.
Swiss	Light to creamy-yellow; large uneven holes. Buy sliced or in cuts.	Mild, with nut-like sweetness. One of our most popular cheeses.	Same as Cheddar, but in cooked dishes it may string somewhat.

Barley-Lentil Stew

Serve this stew with a tossed green salad and whole-grain bread.

Makes 4 servings.

Nutrient Value Per Serving: 374 calories, 18 g protein, 5 g fat, 68 g carbohydrate, 1,060 mg sodium, 2 mg cholesterol.

1   *large onion, chopped (about 1 cup)*
2   *cloves garlic, finely chopped*
1   *tablespoon safflower oil*
1   *cup dried lentils (about 5 ounces)*
⅔   *cup pearl barley*
1   *can (28 ounces) tomatoes, broken up and with their liquid*
3   *vegetable bouillon cubes*

1. Sauté the onion and the garlic in the oil in a medium-size heavy saucepan over medium-low heat, stirring often, until the onion is tender, about 5 minutes.
2. Meanwhile, wash and pick over the lentils and the barley. Add to the saucepan with the tomatoes and the vegetable bouillon cubes. Bring the stew to boiling. Lower the heat. Cover the saucepan and cook the stew gently, stirring occasionally, until the lentils and barley are tender, about 1 hour. Add a little water, if necessary, if the mixture becomes too dry.

Peppers Stuffed with Eggplant

A deliciously satisfying meatless main dish.

Bake at 375° for 30 minutes.
Makes 8 servings.

Nutrient Value Per Serving: 191 calories, 8 g protein, 15 g fat, 8 g carbohydrate, 128 mg sodium, 91 mg cholesterol.

4   *sweet green or red peppers, seeded and cut lengthwise in half*
¼   *cup vegetable oil*
1   *large eggplant, peeled and cut in ½-inch dice*
2   *eggs*
1   *cup diced mozzarella cheese*
1   *tablespoon finely chopped fresh basil Salt and pepper, to taste*
4   *tablespoons bread crumbs*
8   *slices mozzarella cheese*

1. Preheat the oven to moderate (375°).
2. Cook the peppers in salted boiling water in a large saucepan for 10 minutes. Drain the peppers and reserve.
3. Heat the oil in a large skillet and cook the eggplant, covered, until very tender, about 15 minutes.
4. Beat the eggs in a medium-size bowl. Add the eggplant, diced cheese, basil, salt and pepper. Add enough bread crumbs to hold the mixture together.
5. Oil a baking dish large enough to hold the pepper halves. Place the pepper halves in the dish. Fill the pepper halves with the eggplant mixture.
6. Bake the peppers in the preheated moderate oven (375°) for 20 minutes. Top with the cheese slices and bake 10 minutes longer or until the cheese melts.

Note: You can garnish the peppers with sliced pitted ripe olives and serve them with steamed tipped green beans.

GREASELESS EGGPLANT COOKING

Eggplant will absorb a lot of fat if you fry it in a skillet on top of the stove. For greaseless eggplant slices, brush the slices very lightly with olive oil and place on a cookie sheet. Broil 4 to 5 inches from the heat until tender.

Potato-Broccoli Squares

Bake at 425° for 12 minutes; then at 350° for 35 minutes.
Makes 6 servings.

Nutrient Value Per Serving: 199 calories, 11 g protein, 7 g fat, 23 g carbohydrate, 413 mg sodium, 235 mg cholesterol.

2   *large baking potatoes*
1   *tablespoon grated onion*
½   *teaspoon prepared mustard*
¾   *teaspoon salt*
½   *teaspoon pepper*
1   *tablespoon butter or margarine*
¼   *pound mushrooms, sliced OR: 1 can (4 ounces) sliced mushrooms, drained*
1   *package (10 ounces) frozen broccoli spears, cooked and drained*
5   *eggs*
2   *cups skim milk*
⅛   *teaspoon ground nutmeg*

1. Peel the potatoes and cut into quarters. Place the potatoes in a medium-size saucepan. Add cold water to the saucepan to a 1-inch depth. Bring to boiling. Cover the saucepan and lower the heat. Simmer for 25 minutes or until the potatoes are tender. Drain the potatoes and place in a large bowl. Mash or beat the potatoes with an electric mixer until the potatoes are smooth and free of lumps.
2. Preheat the oven to hot (425°).
3. Add the grated onion, mustard, ¼ teaspoon of the salt and ¼ teaspoon of the pepper. Press the potato mixture into a 9-inch-square baking pan. Prick the top all over with a fork.
4. Bake the potato mixture in the preheated hot oven (425°) for 12 minutes. Remove the pan from the oven and cool slightly. Lower the oven temperature to moderate (350°).
5. Melt the butter or margarine in a small skillet. Add the mushrooms and sauté for 3 minutes or until the mushrooms are tender. Spoon the mushrooms over the potatoes.
6. Cut the cooked and drained broccoli into bite-size pieces; arrange the broccoli over the mushrooms.
7. Beat the eggs, milk, remaining ½ teaspoon of salt, the remaining ¼ teaspoon of pepper and the nutmeg in a medium-size bowl with a wire whisk until blended. Pour the egg mixture over the vegetables in the dish.
8. Bake the vegetable mixture in the preheated moderate oven (350°) for 35 minutes or until the custard is set. Cool the dish for 15 minutes. Cut into squares to serve.

SPAGHETTI SQUASH

Oval shaped but with rounded ends, this vegetable is filled with long strands that resemble spaghetti. Some squash are larger than others, so choose one that fits your serving needs; but remember, the larger the squash the larger the noodlelike strands. Select a squash that feels hard, with a uniformly yellow, smooth skin without blemishes. You can store spaghetti squash at room temperature for several weeks. To steam, halve or quarter the squash lengthwise. Remove and discard the seeds. Place in a steamer rack and steam for 15 to 30 minutes, depending on size and age, or until the outer skin is soft. Remove the strands with a fork from the shell. You can also bake the squash, whole or halved, in a preheated moderate oven (350°) until the skin is tender, 45 to 60 minutes. Or boil whole, 25-35 minutes, until fork-tender.

Cheese-Topped Spaghetti Squash

Each serving contains about one-third of the 1,000 milligrams of calcium recommended daily for adults.

Bake at 350° for 45 minutes.
Makes 6 servings.

Nutrient Value Per Serving: 282 calories, 12 g protein, 18 g fat, 20 g carbohydrate, 805 mg sodium, 48 mg cholesterol.

1   **spaghetti squash (approximately 3 pounds)**
1   **medium-size onion, chopped (½ cup)**
½   **cup chopped sweet green pepper**
½   **cup chopped carrot**
½   **cup sliced fresh mushrooms**
3   **tablespoons butter**
1   **can (15 ounces) tomato sauce**
1   **cup water**
1   **teaspoon Italian seasoning**
⅛   **teaspoon garlic powder**
⅛   **teaspoon black pepper**
1   **cup shredded Provolone (4 ounces)**
1   **cup shredded Cheddar cheese (4 ounces)**

1. Preheat the oven to moderate (350°).
2. Cut the squash in half using a sharp knife; remove the seeds. Place the squash, cut-side down, in a shallow baking pan with approximately 1-inch depth of water.
3. Bake the squash, in the preheated moderate oven (350°) for 45 minutes or until the squash is tender.
4. Sauté the onion, green pepper, carrot and mushrooms in the butter in a medium-size saucepan for 10 minutes or until the vegetables are tender. Add the tomato sauce, water, Italian seasoning, garlic powder and pepper. Simmer the sauce, uncovered, for 15 minutes. Stir in the Provolone and Cheddar cheese until melted. Remove the saucepan from the heat.
5. Scoop the pulp from the squash, using a fork. Serve topped with the sauce.

W·A·R·M W·E·A·T·H·E·R D·I·N·I·N·G

Round up the gang for Cheese-Topped French Fries (page 58), *Corn Chip Dogs* (page 126), *Finger Lickin' Ribs* (page 125) *and Peanutty Chicken Legs* (page 133).

4

America loves to eat *al fresco*, in the great outdoors. Whenever the weather permits, barbecue chefs drag out the grill, and picnic afficionados head out to the beach, woods or even the backyard. Casual, easy, make-ahead — that's warm weather dining.

Ever since the discovery of fire, the barbecue has been a popular means of cooking. Grill up the Giant Burgers *(page 115)* or opt for something more unusual, like Fajitas with Tortillas *(page 122)*. Kabobs can be prepared ahead of time, then popped on the grill at the last minute. They come in a wide variety: Seafood *(page 136)*, Chicken *(page 134)* and Vegetable *(page* 137). And if you never thought of grilling fruits and vegetables, take a look at the recipe ideas and tips on page 139.

Warm weather dining also means light — lighter foods and less time in the kitchen. Hearty salads are a marvel to today's busy cook; they're make-ahead, easy and a meal. Case in point: our Classic Layered Salad *(page 141)*. Some can be made spur-of-the-moment, with cupboard ingredients and leftovers. Check out our Curried Rice *(page 142)* or Mexican Salad *(page 146)*.

And what would be warm weather without icy drinks — colorful, frothy and some with a touch of spirit. A Goombay Smash *(page 159)* is the next best thing to sitting on tropical sand, and Mangoade *(page 163)* refreshes after gardening, mowing or a game of tennis.

B·A·R·B·E·C·U·E

Nutty Burgers (page 116), *a change-of-pace crowd pleaser.*

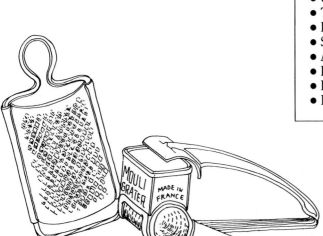

Giant Burgers

These basic burgers are just the start of something big. Top them with a piece of Cheddar cheese and a halved cherry tomato as we did, or try one of the combinations at right.

Grill for 16 to 30 minutes.
Makes 8 servings.

Nutrient Value Per Serving: 595 calories, 40 g protein, 37 g fat, 22 g carbohydrate, 401 mg sodium, 139 mg cholesterol.

4   pounds ground beef
2   tablespoons bottled steak sauce
      Salt and pepper, to taste
2   tablespoons grated onion
1   package (8 buns) hamburger buns
      Cheddar cheese
4   cherry tomatoes, halved

1. Prepare the grill so the coals are medium-hot.
2. Mix the ground beef lightly with the bottled steak sauce, salt, pepper and grated onion in a large bowl. Shape into 8 equal thick patties.
3. Grill the patties 6 inches from the heat for 8 minutes per side for rare, 10 minutes per side for medium or 15 minutes per side for well done, or until the beef is done as you like it.
4. Place the burgers on the bun bottoms, then top each with a pat of Cheddar cheese and half of a cherry tomato, and any of the combinations at right, if you wish.

BURGER TOPPERS

BACON BURGERS — Top with crumbled crisp bacon and ½ cup applesauce.

ITALIAN BURGERS — Combine ¼ cup shredded mozzarella cheese with ¼ cup tomato sauce and ¼ teaspoon leaf oregano, crumbled, blending well.

HAWAIIAN BURGERS — Top with a halved broiled or grilled pineapple slice and toasted coconut. Finely chopped macadamia nuts add a flavorful crunch.

TACO BURGERS — Top with crushed corn chips and mild or hot salsa.

HEALTHFUL BURGERS — Top with a mixture of grated carrot, radish and celery combined with plain yogurt.

WEST COAST BURGERS — Cut slices of avocado in half crosswise; arrange 2 slices on each burger. Top with a dollop of plain yogurt and chopped nuts.

GREEK BURGERS — Place burgers in pita pockets with shredded lettuce, chopped tomato, crumbled feta cheese and cucumber slices.

And don't forget these favorites:
- Grilled sweet pepper rings
- Three-bean salad, drained
- Bottled hot chili sauce
- Sautéed mushroom slices
- Avocado slices and sour cream
- Italian herbs
- Diced pimiento
- Roasted sweet red and green peppers

Nutty Burgers

These hamburgers boast pine nuts as the surprise ingredient.

Grill for 10 minutes.
Makes 6 servings.

Nutrient Value Per Serving: 356 calories, 76 g protein, 77 g fat, 4 g carbohydrate, 170 mg sodium, 163 mg cholesterol.

1½ **pounds ground beef**
1 **medium-size onion, chopped**
1 **clove garlic, finely chopped**
1 **cup dry bread crumbs**
⅓ **cup grated Parmesan cheese**
⅔ **cup pine nuts***
⅓ **cup chopped fresh parsley**
2 **eggs**
1½ **teaspoons salt**
1 **teaspoon pepper**

1. Prepare the grill so the coals are medium-hot.
2. Combine all the ingredients in a large bowl, blending well. Shape the meat mixture into 6 equal thick patties.
3. Place the patties on a grill rack over medium-hot coals. Cover the grill.
4. Grill the burgers for 5 minutes on each side or until desired doneness. Serve the burgers with buttered, grilled French rolls, fresh fruit and a green salad.

Note: Slivered almonds or sunflower seeds may be substituted for the pine nuts.

GROUND MEAT TIPS

• *Buy ground meat the day you plan to use it and if possible, have the butcher grind it fresh for you.*
• *To save ground meat for the next day, wrap in wax paper and keep in the coldest part of your refrigerator.*
• *To freeze ground meat, wrap in plastic wrap, then in aluminum foil or freezer wrap and store in the freezer.*

Spade Ranch Barbecue Sauce

Chili powder makes this hot.

Makes about 4 cups.

Nutrient Value Per ¼ Cup: 65 calories, 1 g protein, 0 g fat, 16 g carbohydrate, 402 mg sodium, 0 mg cholesterol.

3 **cans (8 ounces each) tomato sauce**
⅔ **cup firmly packed brown sugar**
½ **cup catsup**
½ **cup vinegar**
4 **tablespoons prepared mustard**
1 **cup chopped onion**
2 **cloves garlic, chopped**
3 **tablespoons chili powder**

Combine the tomato sauce, brown sugar, catsup, vinegar, mustard, onion, garlic and chili powder in a medium-size saucepan. Simmer for 5 minutes to blend the flavors.

Perfect T-Bone Steak

Grill for 20 to 40 minutes.
Makes 4 servings.

Nutrient Value Per Serving: 309 calories, 29 g protein, 20 g fat, 1 g carbohydrate, 70 mg sodium, 84 mg cholesterol.

1 **T-bone or Porterhouse steak, cut 2 inches thick (about 2 pounds)**
⅓ **cup vegetable oil**
¼ **cup dry red wine**
3 **shallots, chopped OR: 1 small onion, chopped (¼ cup)**
  Butter or margarine
  Salt and ground pepper, to taste

1. Trim any excess fat from the steak and score the remaining fat at the edges at 1-inch intervals. Place the steak in a large shallow glass dish. Combine the oil, red wine and shallots or onion in a 1-cup measure; pour the marinade over the steak. Allow the steak to marinate at room temperature for at least 2 hours. Remove the steak from the marinade.
2. Prepare the grill so the coals are medium-hot.
3. Grill the steak 5 inches from the heat for 10 minutes on each side for rare, 15 minutes

on each side for medium and 20 minutes on each side for well done.

4. Place the steak on a carving board. Spread the steak with a pat of butter or margarine and season with the salt and pepper. Allow the steak to "rest" for 10 minutes. To carve the steak, remove the T-bone and slice across the steak so that each slice will have the back tenderloin and a piece of the loin strip.

Barbecue Sauce

Makes about 7 cups.

Nutrient Value Per ¼ Cup: 72 calories, 1 g protein, 0 g fat, 17 g carbohydrate, 576 mg sodium, 0 mg cholesterol.

- **1 quart (4 cups) catsup**
- **¾ cup bottled chili sauce**
- **1 onion, finely diced**
- **2 cloves garlic, finely chopped**
- **½ cup firmly packed brown sugar**
- **1 tablespoon dry mustard**
- **1 teaspoon black pepper**
- **½ cup red wine vinegar**
-    **Juice of 1 lemon**
- **¼ cup Worcestershire sauce**
- **¼ cup steak sauce**
- **1 tablespoon prepared mustard**
- **4 ounces (½ cup) beer**

Combine all the ingredients in a saucepan and simmer for 30 to 45 minutes. If the sauce is too thin, add a mixture of cornstarch and water, but only a little at a time.

TAKING THE MYSTIQUE OUT OF MESQUITE

Mesquite is one of the wide variety of woods that adds special flavor to outdoor-cooked meals. Long used as a charcoal in Texas where the wood grows profusely, mesquite imparts a pungent taste to roast brisket, poultry, sausage and, for the adventurous cook, goat. Mesquite is available in two forms — charcoal and wood chips. The former is used interchangeably with charcoal briquets. Mesquite charcoal produces a hotter fire than the standard briquets do, so raise the cooking grid accordingly. Mesquite wood chips, on the other hand, burn slowly and should always be used in conjunction with charcoal briquets. Add a handful of chips directly to the coals after they have been soaked in water for at least 30 minutes. Keep children away from the grill, since mesquite charcoal has a tendency to snap and send sparks flying.

GRILLING THE PERFECT STEAK					
Meat	**Thickness**	**Doneness**	**Fire**	**Distance**	**Time****
Beef	1 inch	rare	medium-hot	4 inches	5 min.
		medium	medium-hot		7 min.
		well-done	medium-hot		10 min.
	2 inches	rare	medium	5 inches	15 min.
		medium	medium		20 min.
		well-done	medium		25 min.
Ham	1 inch	medium	medium	5 inches	8 min.
Lamb	¾ inch	rare	medium-hot	6 inches	5 min.
		medium	medium-hot		7 min.
		well-done	medium-hot		9 min.
Pork*	1 inch	well-done	medium	5 inches	14 min.

*All fresh pork must be grilled to well-done. **Per side. All steaks to room temperature.

Steak Au Poivre

Grill for 30 to 50 minutes.
Makes 8 servings.

Nutrient Value Per Serving: 258 calories, 36 g protein, 11 g fat, 1 g carbohydrate, 80 mg sodium, 107 mg cholesterol.

1   sirloin steak, 2 inches thick (about 4 pounds)
4   to 8 tablespoons cracked pepper
     Salt, to taste
¼   cup brandy (optional)

1. Wipe the steak with damp paper toweling. Press half of the pepper into each side of the steak, using your fingers and the heel of your hand. Let the steak stand at room temperature for 1 hour.
2. Prepare the grill so the coals are medium-hot.
3. Grill the steak 5 inches from the heat for 15 minutes per side for rare, 20 minutes per side for medium and 25 minutes per side for well done, or until the steak is done as you like it. Sprinkle the steak with salt.
4. Transfer the steak to a hot sizzle-platter. Very carefully warm the brandy, if using, in a small metal saucepan with a flameproof handle over the grill. Pour the brandy over the steak. Carefully ignite, using long fireplace matches. Serve.

Grilled Sirloin Steak

Grill for 30 to 50 minutes.
Makes 8 servings.

Nutrient Value Per Serving: 336 calories, 37 g protein, 20 g fat, 0 g carbohydrate, 80 mg sodium, 107 mg cholesterol.

1   sirloin steak, cut 2 inches thick (about 4 pounds)
⅔   cup olive or vegetable oil
⅓   cup wine or cider vinegar
1   teaspoon salt
1   teaspoon leaf thyme, crumbled
¼   teaspoon pepper

1. Remove the steak from the refrigerator 2 hours before cooking. Trim off any excess fat, then score the remaining fat edge at 1-inch intervals so the meat will lie flat on the grill. Place the steak in a shallow 13x9x2-inch glass dish.

2. Mix the oil, vinegar, salt, thyme and pepper in a small bowl. Pour over the steak. Cover the dish with plastic wrap and let stand at room temperature for 2 hours.
3. Prepare the grill so the coals are medium-hot.
4. Grill the steak 5 inches from the heat, brushing the steak several times with the marinade from the pan, for 15 minutes on each side for rare, 20 minutes on each side for medium and 25 minutes on each side for well done, or until the steak is done as you like it.
5. Remove the steak to a cutting board or a large platter. Let the steak "rest" for 15 minutes before slicing. Slice the steak ¼ inch thick.

Rosemary Steak

Rosemary is a delicious herb to team with beef on the barbecue.

Grill for 30 to 50 minutes.
Makes 8 servings.

Nutrient Value Per Serving: 353 calories, 42 g protein, 19 g fat, 1 g carbohydrate, 113 mg sodium, 135 mg cholesterol.

1   chuck steak, cut 2 inches thick (about 4 pounds)
     Vegetable oil
2   tablespoons leaf rosemary, crumbled
2   tablespoons butter or margarine
2   tablespoons chopped chives

1. Remove the steak from the refrigerator 1 hour before grilling. Trim off any excess fat, then score the remaining fat edge at 1-inch intervals so the meat will lie flat on the grill.
2. Brush the steak all over with the vegetable oil; pat the rosemary onto both sides of the steak. Let the steak stand at room temperature for 1 hour.
3. Prepare the grill so the coals are medium-hot.
4. Grill the steak 5 inches from the heat for 15 minutes per side for rare, 20 minutes per side for medium, 25 minutes per side for well done, or until the steak is done as you like it.
5. Remove the steak to a cutting board or a large platter. Dot the steak with butter or margarine and let melt into the steak. Sprinkle the steak with the chives. Slice the steak ¼ inch thick.

What a feast! Grilled London Broil with Chive Butter.

Grilled London Broil with Chive Butter

Top round offers a London broil-type cut that is less expensive than flank steak.

Grill for 30 to 50 minutes.
Makes 8 servings.

Nutrient Value Per Serving (without butter): 264 calories, 38 g protein, 11 g fat, 0 g carbohydrate, 141 mg sodium, 100 mg cholesterol.

1 **top round steak, cut 2 inches thick (3 pounds)**
¼ **cup vegetable oil**
1 **tablespoon lemon juice**
1 **clove garlic, finely chopped**
½ **teaspoon salt**
¼ **teaspoon pepper**
   Chive Butter (see recipe, page 76)

1. Place the steak in a plastic bag or in a shallow glass dish.
2. Combine the oil, lemon juice, garlic, salt and pepper in a cup. Pour the marinade over the flank steak. Close the bag securely or cover the dish with plastic wrap, and refrigerate for 4 to 6 hours or overnight, turning the meat occasionally. Let the steak stand at room temperature to marinate for 1 hour before grilling. Pour off and reserve the marinade.
3. Prepare the grill so the coals are medium-hot.
4. Grill the steak on one side 5 inches from the heat for 15 minutes for rare, 20 minutes for medium and 25 minutes for well done. Brush the steak with the marinade. Turn the steak over. Grill for 15 minutes for rare, 20 minutes for medium and 25 minutes for well done.
5. Place the steak on a wooden carving board and top with the heated remaining marinade and pats of Chive Butter.

LS

Strip Steak with Béarnaise Sauce

The flavor of New York strip or shell steak is enhanced by a simple red wine marinade/baste.

Grill for 10 to 30 minutes.
Makes 4 servings.

Nutrient Value Per Serving (without sauce): 367 calories, 44 g protein, 20 g fat, 1 g carbohydrate, 108 mg sodium, 124 mg cholesterol.

> 4 **New York strip or shell steaks (about 10 ounces each)**
> 1/3 **cup vegetable oil**
> 1/4 **cup dry red wine**
> 3 **shallots, chopped OR: 1 small onion, chopped (1/4 cup)**
>   **Salt and pepper, to taste**
>   **Béarnaise Sauce (see recipe, page 77)**

1. Trim any excess fat from the steaks and score the remaining fat around the edge at 1-inch intervals so the meat will lie flat. Place the steaks in a large shallow glass dish. Combine the oil, wine and shallots or onion in a 1-cup measure. Pour the marinade over the steaks and cover. Allow the steaks to marinate at room temperature for at least 2 hours. Remove the steaks from the marinade. Reserve the marinade.
2. Prepare the grill so the coals are medium-hot.
3. Grill the steaks 4 inches from the heat, brushing with the marinade, for 5 minutes on each side for rare, 10 minutes on each side for medium and 15 minutes on each side for well done, or until the steaks are done as you like.
4. Place the steaks on a carving board and season with the salt and pepper. Allow the steaks to "rest" for 10 minutes. Serve with the Béarnaise Sauce.

Garlic-Grilled Steak with Blue Cheese Butter

Rib-eye steak is a flavorful individual steak for barbecuing.

Grill for 15 to 35 minutes.
Makes 3 servings.

Nutrient Value Per Serving (without butter): 1,130 calories, 83 g protein, 86 g fat, .3g carbohydrate, 210 mg sodium, 272 mg cholesterol.

> 1/4 **cup vegetable oil**
> 1 **clove garlic, halved**
> 3 **rib eye steaks, cut 2 inches thick (about 1 pound each)**
>   **Blue Cheese Butter (see recipe, page 76)**
>   **Salt and pepper, to taste**

1. Combine the oil and garlic in a cup and let stand until the coals are ready.
2. Prepare the grill so the coals are medium-hot.
3. Trim the excess fat from the steaks and score the remaining fat at 1-inch intervals so the meat will lie flat on the grill.
4. Coat the steak generously with the garlic oil on both sides.
5. Grill the steak 6 inches from the heat for 10 minutes for rare, 15 minutes for medium and 20 minutes for well done. Turn the steaks over and grill 5 minutes for rare, 10 minutes for medium and 15 minutes for well done.
6. Remove the steak to a sizzle platter. Top with the Blue Cheese Butter. Sprinkle with the salt and pepper.

HOW TO GRILL THE PERFECT STEAK

Below are the best four cuts of beef steak plus pork and lamb suggestions — all great grilled outdoors.

1. Bone-in Chuck Steak is a delicious way to serve the family steak often and keep within the budget. Be sure to treat with instant meat tenderizer or marinate for up to 24 hours before grilling to assure that the beef is fork-tender.

2. Strip or **New York-Cut Steak** is the most deluxe individual-size steak. Perfect when you want to grill each guest's steak to desired doneness. Look for supermarket specials that offer a whole shell of beef on sale and have it cut to order.

3. T-Bone Steak is the perfect choice when you want a steak to serve two. This very tender cut of beef should be at least 1½ to 2 inches thick for a well-charred surface with rare beef on the inside.

4. Sirloin Steak is the tender, juicy answer when you wish to serve four to six guests. Unless it is cut from prime meat, treat with instant meat tenderizer or marinate.

5. Cured Ham Steak is an ideal change of pace on the barbecue. Since the meat is already cooked, it just needs basting and heating. Buy half a ham and ask the butcher to cut a 1½-inch-thick center slice — you will still have a Sunday roast for a little more than the cost of a precut ham steak.

6. Fresh Pork Steak is a cut that you might not have considered before. It too is cut from the center half of a fresh ham. However, since the pork is uncooked, it requires longer, slower grilling.

7. Lamb Steak is one of the most delicious steaks you can offer guests. It is also cut from the center half of a leg of lamb. Cook it just to rare. You can always return it to the grill, if desired.

BARBECUE SAFETY

Preparing For A Barbecue
• Read the manufacturer's instructions for your grill and follow them carefully.
• Check previously used equipment to ensure it is in proper working order, i.e., vents free from foreign material. On gas models, check to see there are no leaking connections.
• Situate the barbecue grill so that the operator's back is to the wind.
• Place the grill on a level, non-combustible surface and allow at least an 18-inch clearance on all sides to maintain sufficient supply and circulation of air.
• Keep a fire extinguisher handy in case of accidents.
• Cut all excess fat from meats to eliminate the risk of flare-ups.

Lighting The Barbecue
• Use only the manufacturer's recommended starter fuel. Gasoline and other highly volatile fuels are extremely dangerous.
• After use, reseal starter fluid and place it at a safe distance from the grill and all flames.
• Do not lean over the grill when lighting the coals or cooking.
• When lighting a gas model, be sure the cover remains open until the burner is burning smoothly.
• Never add liquid starter after coals are lighted.

Using Your Barbecue
• Never wear loose clothing when working with a barbecue. Loose clothing can present a potential fire hazard.
• Wear barbecue mitts when adjusting hot vents and, of course, whenever using the grill.
• Use long-handled tongs or spatula when turning food on the grill.
• If flare-ups do occur, remove the food to the side of the grill until the flames have died down.
• Keep young children and all animals away from the hot grill.

The End Of A Successful Barbecue
• If you absolutely must move a hot grill, exercise extreme caution.
• Do not dispose of coals until they have cooled completely.
• Make sure all burner control valves are switched off and, if applicable, gas supplies discontinued.
• Clean the barbecue grill once it has cooled down and store in a dry place.

▓ LS

Herb-Basted Steak

Tie a bunch of washed fresh parsley, rosemary or tarragon and use instead of a brush to baste flank steak — fun and flavorful.

Grill for 10 to 18 minutes.
Makes 8 servings.

Nutrient Value Per Serving: 251 calories, 21 g protein, 17 g fat, 1 g carbohydrate, 72 mg sodium, 60 mg cholesterol.

    1   cup dry red wine
    ¼   cup sliced green onion
    ¼   cup chopped sweet green pepper
    ¼   cup chopped celery
    ¼   cup olive or vegetable oil
    1   clove garlic, finely chopped
    1   teaspoon salt
    1   flank steak (about 2 pounds)
    1   bunch parsley, rosemary or tarragon

1. Combine the wine, green onion, green pepper, celery, olive oil, garlic and salt in a small saucepan. Bring to boiling; reduce the heat and cover. Simmer for 15 minutes. Cool completely.
2. Place the flank steak in a shallow glass dish. Pour the cooled marinade over the meat. Marinate the meat for at least 1 hour at room temperature.
3. Prepare the grill so the coals are medium-hot.
4. Tie a large bunch of washed parsley, rosemary or tarragon with a string. Pour the marinade from the steak into a bowl.
5. Grill the steak 4 inches from the heat, basting with the reserved marinade, using the parsley, rosemary or tarragon bunch as a basting brush, for 5 minutes per side for rare, 7 minutes per side for medium and 9 minutes per side for well done, or until the steak is done as you like it.
6. Carve the steak on the diagonal into thin slices and serve with garlic bread, if you wish.

LS

Fajitas

Grilled morsels of marinated skirt steak are the Southwest's fastest growing dish.

Grill for 10 to 18 minutes.
Makes 8 servings.

Nutrient Value Per Serving: 427 calories, 29 g protein, 18 g fat, 37 g carbohydrate, 81 mg sodium, 66 mg cholesterol.

    2   to 2½ pounds skirt steak*
    2   cans beer
        Juice of 1 lime
        Juice of 1 lemon
    ½   onion, sliced
    1   teaspoon chopped garlic
    ½   teaspoon whole thyme spikes
    ½   teaspoon ground cumin
    3   bay leaves
   16   flour tortillas

1. Trim all the fat and membrane from the steak. Place the meat in a pan large enough to hold the meat and the marinade. Combine the beer, lime and lemon juices, onion, garlic, thyme, cumin and bay leaves in a medium-size bowl. Add the marinade to the beef; cover the pan with plastic wrap. Refrigerate and marinate for at least 5 hours.
2. Barbecue the meat over charcoal with mesquite or hickory wood until desired doneness.
3. Soften the flour tortillas in an ungreased skillet over medium heat for 10 to 15 seconds. Slice the grilled meat into strips and roll up in the tortillas. Serve with guacamole and salsa, if you wish.

Note: You can substitute flank steak, round steak or boneless chuck for the skirt steak.

FAJITAS

Fajitas, a staple snack in Southern Texas for years, originated in the land bordered by Mexico to the south and west, the Nueces River to the north and the King Ranch to the east. It is a beef dish that developed out of necessity.

Back in the 1930s the cattle in South Texas ate brush, weeds and sparse grasses and often had to travel 12 to 15 miles a day just to find food. The result was lean, lanky steers with tough, stringy meat that was best suited to ground beef.

However, the Mexicans of the area had a much better way of serving what many Texans saw as a very low grade of beef. They took the fajita (or skin) steak, which has a skin on both sides, and threw it onto a fire made with wood from the mesquite trees. After a few quick turns the meat was taken off the fire and the skin peeled off. The skin kept in the juices of the meat and when the meat was wrapped in flour tortillas it became "Taco de Fajitas." To make fajitas on your own grill, use skirt steak, flank steak or a boneless chuck steak, cut into strips.

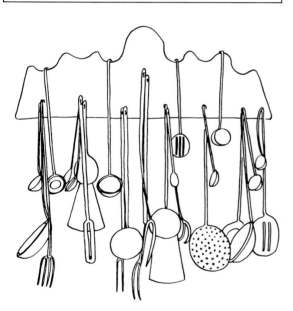

They're out of this world! Valley of the Moon Kabobs.

Valley of the Moon Kabobs

Cubes of beef soak up a soy-based marinade, then are grilled with pineapple chunks.

Grill 6 to 10 minutes.
Makes 12 servings.

Nutrient Value Per Serving: 211 calories, 22 g protein, 11 g fat, 5 g carbohydrate, 733 mg sodium, 61 mg cholesterol.

- 3 **pounds New York strip steaks**
- 1 **cup soy sauce**
- ½ **cup peanut or vegetable oil**
- 3 **tablespoons sugar**
- 4 **teaspoons dry mustard**
- 4 **teaspoons ground ginger**
- 10 **to 12 cloves garlic, sliced**
- 4 **green onions, sliced**
- ½ **teaspoon ground hot red pepper**
  Juice of 1 orange
- 1 **fresh pineapple**
  Romaine lettuce leaves
  Orange slices
  Parsley

1. Prepare the grill so the coals are medium-hot.
2. Trim any excess fat from the steaks. Cut into 1-inch cubes.
3. Mix the soy sauce, peanut oil, sugar, dry mustard, ginger, garlic, green onion, red pepper and orange juice in a glass bowl. Cover and let the marinade stand at room temperature for 1 hour.
4. Add the beef cubes to the marinade and let stand for 15 minutes.
5. Cut the pineapple in half lengthwise; reserve one half. Peel the other half; core and cut into cubes. On bamboo skewers soaked in water, alternate the beef and pineapple cubes.
6. Place the kabobs on a grill rack over medium-hot coals. Cover the grill.
7. Grill the kabobs for 6 to 10 minutes or until done as you like beef. Turn the kabobs frequently and brush each side once with the marinade.
8. To serve, line a large platter with lettuce leaves. Center the remaining pineapple half on the platter. Poke the bamboo skewers into the pineapple in a fan shape. Garnish with the orange slices and parsley. Serve immediately.

Tropical Barbecue

Peaches and oranges alternate with robust chunks of beef in a sweet-sour glaze.

Grill for 10 to 16 minutes.
Makes 12 skewers.

Nutrient Value Per Skewer: 205 calories, 20 g protein, 7 g fat, 16 g carbohydrate, 57 mg sodium, 53 mg cholesterol.

  3   pounds top sirloin OR: chuck steak
  2   teaspoons salt
  1   cup peach jam
  ½   cup lemon juice
  1   tablespoon Worcestershire sauce
  2   large eating oranges
  2   fresh peaches

1. Trim the beef and cut into 1½-inch cubes. Sprinkle with the salt. Place in a large glass or ceramic dish.
2. Combine the peach jam, lemon juice and Worcestershire sauce in a bowl until smooth. Pour the marinade over the beef. Cover the dish with plastic wrap. Refrigerate for 2 hours.
3. Drain the marinade from the beef and reserve. Cut the oranges and peaches into wedges. Alternate the beef and orange and peach wedges on 12 long skewers.

4. Prepare the grill so the coals are medium-hot.
5. Grill the kabobs 4 inches from the heat, basting and turning the kabobs several times, for 10 minutes for rare, 13 minutes for medium and 16 minutes for well done beef.

Beef and Veggie Kabobs

Zucchini, eggplant and artichoke hearts are grilled with tender pieces of beef in a robust, oregano-flavored marinade.

Grill for 10 to 15 minutes.
Makes 6 servings.

Nutrient Value Per Serving: 508 calories, 30 g protein, 38 g fat, 13 g carbohydrate, 229 mg sodium, 95 mg cholesterol.

  2   pounds beef sirloin tip, cut into cubes
  1   cup bottled Italian salad dressing
  1   teaspoon leaf oregano, crumbled
  1   small eggplant, cut into cubes
  2   medium-size zucchini, cut into slices
  2   large yellow squash, cut into slices

1. Place the beef in a shallow glass dish with the Italian dressing and oregano; toss well to coat the meat. Cover the dish with plastic wrap.
2. Refrigerate the beef for at least 2 hours. Then let stand at room temperature for 1 hour.
3. Place the eggplant, zucchini and yellow squash in separate piles in a large skillet. Pour in boiling water to a depth of 1 inch. Bring to boiling; lower the heat and simmer for 5 minutes. Drain the vegetables.
4. Prepare the grill so the coals are medium-hot.
5. Remove the beef from the dish; reserve the marinade. Thread the meat alternately with the vegetables on 6 long skewers. Brush the kabobs with the marinade.
6. Grill them 4 inches from the heat, turning and basting the kabobs with the marinade, for 10 minutes for rare, 12 minutes for medium and 15 minutes for well done.

Finger Lickin' Ribs

Cook the ribs the day ahead, then grill at party time.

Bake at 325° for 1 hour and 30 minutes; grill for 20 minutes.
Makes 8 servings.

Nutrient Value Per Serving: 436 calories, 26 g protein, 28 g fat, 20 g carbohydrate, 868 mg sodium, 107 mg cholesterol.

4   pounds spareribs
1   can (12 ounces) ginger ale
1   large onion, sliced
1   bottle (16 ounces) barbecue sauce

1. Preheat the oven to slow (325°).
2. Arrange the spareribs in a baking pan. Pour the ginger ale over the ribs and sprinkle with the onion rings. Cover the pan with heavy-duty aluminum foil.

3. Bake the ribs in the preheated slow oven (325°) for 1 hour and 30 minutes or until the ribs are tender. Cool completely. Cut between the ribs so each rib is separated. Wrap the ribs and refrigerate.
4. One hour before serving, remove the ribs from the refrigerator and let come to room temperature. Brush the ribs with some of the barbecue sauce.
5. Prepare the grill so the coals are medium-hot.
6. Grill the ribs 4 inches from the heat for 10 minutes. Brush the ribs with the barbecue sauce and turn. Grill for 10 minutes longer or until the ribs are well glazed. Pile the ribs into a basket and serve with plenty of paper napkins.

Hearty Sausage and Peppers (page 126).

Sausage and Peppers

This sauce is also wonderful teamed with grilled Italian hero rolls.

Grill for 30 minutes.
Makes 12 servings.

Nutrient Value Per Serving: 237 calories, 12 g protein, 19 g fat, 5 g carbohydrate, 512 mg sodium, 43 mg cholesterol.

- 2 **pounds hot and/or sweet Italian sausage**
- 2 **large onions, cut into thick rings**
- ¼ **cup olive oil**
- 2 **sweet red peppers, halved, seeded and cut into 1-inch pieces**
- 2 **sweet green peppers, halved, seeded and cut into 1-inch pieces**
- 2 **sweet yellow peppers, halved, seeded and cut into 1-inch pieces**
- ½ **teaspoon leaf oregano, crumbled**
  Chopped cilantro (coriander)

1. Prepare the grill so the coals are medium-hot.
2. Prick the sausages with a fork all over.
3. Grill the sausages, turning often, for 15 minutes. Remove the sausages from the grill to a plate. Halve the sausages, crosswise.
4. Sauté the onion in the oil in a very large skillet with a flameproof handle on the grill until very soft. Push the onions to one side. Add the pepper pieces. Sauté until the pieces are soft.
5. Add the sausages to the skillet; sprinkle with the oregano.
6. Push the skillet to the side of the grill. Cook, stirring the sausage and peppers together gently, until the sausages are cooked through and the onions and peppers are tender. Sprinkle with the cilantro.

Grilled Sausage Ring

Be sure the sausage is thoroughly cooked.

Grill for 20 minutes.
Makes 8 servings.

Nutrient Value Per Serving: 288 calories, 16 g protein, 16 g fat, 20 g carbohydrate, 767 mg sodium, 43 mg cholesterol.

- 1 **ring sausage (1 to 1½ pounds)**
- 6 **tortillas**
- 1 **can (1 pound) refried beans, heated**
- 1 **cup shredded Cheddar cheese (4 ounces)**
  Chopped green onion
  Shredded iceberg lettuce

1. Prepare the grill so the coals are hot.
2. Score the ring sausage about ½ inch deep. Secure the sausage with 2 long wooden skewers at right angles.
3. Grill the sausage 6 inches from the heat, turning the sausage several times, for 20 minutes or until well cooked.
4. Heat the tortillas on the grill, turning with tongs, while the sausage cooks.
5. Cut the sausage into 6 equal pieces. Place a piece of sausage on each tortilla. Top with the refried beans, shredded cheese, green onion and lettuce. Roll up the tortilla and serve hot.

Corn Chip Dogs

Team two of your kids' favorites — hot dogs and corn chips — for an easy yet special barbecue treat.

Grill for 7 minutes.
Makes 8 servings.

Nutrient Value Per Serving: 426 calories, 11 g protein, 77 g fat, 34 g carbohydrate, 1,012 mg sodium, 31 mg cholesterol.

- 1 **package (1 pound) frankfurters**
  Prepared mustard
- 2 **cups corn chips, crushed**
  Hot dog rolls, toasted

1. Prepare the grill so the coals are medium-hot.
2. Coat the frankfurters well with the mustard. Spread the corn chips on a sheet of wax paper. Roll the coated frankfurters in the corn chips.
3. Grill the frankfurters 4 inches from the heat for 4 minutes on each or until well glazed. Pile the frankfurters into a basket. Serve on toasted rolls.

HOT DOG TOPPERS

Try one of these additions the next time you grill up franks.

Red & Green Dogs — *Top hot dogs with a slaw made with both red and green cabbage; sprinkle raisins on top.*

Potato & Cheese Dogs — *Spoon hot mashed potatoes over hot dogs and top with shredded American cheese.*

Chili Dogs — *Heat chili; spoon over hot dogs; top with dairy sour cream.*

Corn Dogs — *Top hot dogs with bottled corn relish.*

Apple Dogs — *Arrange apple slices with a hot dog in a toasted bun; cover with pancake syrup.*

Bacon-Wrapped Franks

Everybody will want seconds!

Grill for 10 minutes.
Makes 16 franks.

Nutrient Value Per Frank: 358 calories, 12 g protein, 22 g fat, 26 g carbohydrate, 1,012 mg sodium, 36 mg cholesterol.

2 **packages (1 pound each) frankfurters**
1 **package (1 pound or 16 slices) bacon**
   Zippy Tomato Sauce (recipe follows)
2 **packages (8 buns each) hot dog buns, toasted**

1. Prepare the grill so the coals are very hot.
2. Score the frankfurters about ¾ inch deep. Wrap 1 strip of bacon around each frankfurter; secure the bacon with wooden picks. Brush each frankfurter with the Zippy Tomato Sauce to coat well.
3. Grill the frankfurters 6 inches from the heat, turning and brushing once or twice with more sauce, for 10 minutes or until the franks are puffed and richly glazed. Serve the franks in toasted buns and top with hot dog relish, if you wish.

Zippy Tomato Sauce: Combine ⅓ cup light molasses, ⅓ cup prepared mustard and ⅓ cup cider vinegar in a large jar with a screw top; shake the sauce well. Add ½ cup tomato juice and ½ teaspoon ground pepper; shake the sauce again to blend well. Makes 1½ cups. *Nutrient Value Per Tablespoon: 15 calories, 0 g protein, 0 g fat, 3 g carbohydrate, 62 mg sodium, 0 mg cholesterol.*

Quick-Grilled Pork Chops

Thin pork chops or lamb chops are a special treat for brunch.

Grill for 20 minutes.
Makes 8 servings.

Nutrient Value Per Serving: 230 calories, 18 g protein, 17 g fat, 0 g carbohydrate, 46 mg sodium, 63 mg cholesterol.

3 **tablespoons vegetable oil**
2 **teaspoons grated orange rind**
1 **teaspoon salt**
¼ **teaspoon pepper**
8 **thin pork chops (about 2 pounds), at room temperature**

1. Prepare the grill so the coals are medium-hot.
2. Combine the vegetable oil, orange rind, and salt and pepper in a cup. Brush the baste over the pork chops.
3. Grill the chops 4 inches from the heat for 10 minutes on each side or until the chops are golden and cooked through.

Orange Sauce For Pork

A spicy accompaniment to fresh or smoked ham or spare ribs.

Makes about 1½ cups.

Nutrient Value Per Tablespoon: 17 calories, 0 g protein, 0 g fat, 4 g carbohydrate, 23 mg sodium, 0 mg cholesterol.

3 **oranges**
3 **small green chilies, seeded and finely chopped**
¼ **cup water OR: white wine**
3 **tablespoons vinegar**
3 **tablespoons sugar**
¼ **teaspoon salt**
⅛ **teaspoon leaf oregano, crumbled**

Squeeze the juice from the oranges into a small bowl; use a sharp-edged spoon to remove the pulp and add to the juice. Add the chilies, water or wine, vinegar, sugar, salt and oregano, blending well. Let the sauce stand for 1 hour. Serve with pork.

Temperature Guide for Grilling

Testing by Thermometer

Low: about 300°

Medium: about 350°

Hot: about 400°

Testing by Hand*

Low: 4 to 5 seconds

Medium: 3 to 4 seconds

Hot: less than 3 seconds

*The length of time you can hold your hand over the coals before you have to remove it determines the distance your grill should be from the coals.

Grilling Tips

• Store the charcoal in its tightly closed package in a cool, dry place. Charcoal is difficult to light if it gets wet or absorbs a lot of moisture from the air.

• For easy cleanup, line the fire pan with heavy-duty aluminum foil.

• Heap the charcoal in the center of the grill or around the drip pan (if you're using one) and set aflame.

• To start the fire, use charcoal starter or an electric starter. Chemical charcoal starters may cause "off" flavors in foods, but the electric starter imparts no odor. If using liquid starter, wait for 2 minutes for the starter to soak in before igniting.

• Start a charcoal fire at least 30 to 40 minutes before you start to cook, to allow the coals to burn and become covered with a gray ash. The heat will be radiant and will cook the food gradually without burning.

• When the coals are hot, separate them into an even layer on the bottom of the grill. To add coals, start them burning in another pan and transfer them to the grill when they are gray.

• Spinkle the charcoal with fresh herbs such as marjoram, rosemary, thyme or mint, or dried herbs such as bay leaf or fennel, soaked in water, to give the grilled meat a subtle flavor. Additional flavorings such as hickory, apple, cherry, alder and mesquite may be obtained in the form of soaked aromatic wood chips. Sprinkle the chips over the glowing coals before grilling.

• Brush the grill with fat or oil or use vegetable cooking spray just before cooking to prevent food from sticking.

• When grilling fatty foods, make a drip pan of foil (see page 129) and place it directly under the food to prevent fat flare-ups.

• To maintain an even temperature, place the grill in a sheltered place away from drafts. On a windy day, cover the grill with a hood or a tent of foil.

• When grilling foods that need slow cooking, set the grill rack at its highest position and lower it during cooking as the coals get cooler.

• When you use a gas grill, the same principles apply. Preheat the grill to allow the ceramic element to become radiantly hot. Use marinades and barbecue sauces that contain as little sugar as possible. If you have a favorite sweet sauce, keep the grill rack as high as possible and turn foods every 5 minutes. Brush with the sauce every time the food is turned. Use tongs for turning to prevent piercing the food and releasing the juices.

• If any marinade or basting sauce remains, heat it in a saucepan on the grill rack and serve it.

• The last glowing embers can be used to keep coffee hot, toast marshmallows or pound cake, heat fudge or butter-pecan sauce for ice cream, warm cookies, rolls, apple pie, or grill orange or pineapple slices.

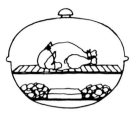

Kettle Roasting

This technique can be used to cook large cuts of meats such as pork shoulder, beef eye round roast or leg of lamb, or turkey, large chickens or ducklings. Also use this method to cook or heat casseroles.

To Grill Meat: Arrange gray coals around a drip pan; place the meat, fat side up, directly on the grill, directly over the drip pan. *(See the drawing above.)* Cover the kettle and arrange the vents, following the manufacturer's directions; follow the individual recipe directions for cooking times.

To Cook Casseroles: Arrange gray coals in a ring around the edge of the barbecue. Place the casserole inside the ring on the grill. Cover the kettle and arrange the vents, following the manufacturer's directions; follow the individual recipes for cooking times.

To Make A Grill Cover or Dome for a Barbecue Grill

When the recipe calls for a covered grill, an open-style grill may be used by constructing your own dome from a wire coat hanger frame and covering it with aluminum foil. Snip the hooks off of several hangers and open them out into straight pieces. With pliers, twist together the ends of 2 or 3 hanger pieces to make a ring the size of your grill. Use 5 or 6 more to fashion a dome. Twist the ends of the hangers, forming the dome around the ring base *(left).* Then cover the dome with several sheets of overlapping aluminum foil, gathering the foil at the top of the dome and twisting it together to form a topknot for a handle. Cut several flaps for vents near the top *(right).*

PICNIC PREPARATION & PACKING TIPS

- *Wash your hands before handling the food—both at home and at the picnic.*
- *After cooking the food at home, refrigerate it. Avoid letting the food sit at room temperature.*
- *Keep hot foods hot, cold foods cold.*
- *Pack all the perishable picnic foods in insulated bags or chests with frozen ice packs to keep well chilled and prevent spoilage.*
- *Pack the picnic items in a carry-all in the reverse order in which they will be set out; for example, place the food on the bottom, then the serving utensils, tableware, etc.*
- *Be sure to take a bag for garbage.*

How To Make a Drip Pan

Fat flare-ups will be a problem of the past when you place a custom-size, make-it-yourself drip pan under the meat you are kettle-grilling or roasting on the rotisserie. Tear off three 24-inch pieces of 18-inch-wide heavy-duty aluminum foil. Fold the pieces in half to make a double thickness (Fig. 1). Turn up the edges 2 inches on each side and press the edges firmly together to form mitered corners (Fig. 2). Press the mitered corners inwards, towards the pan sides, to make a firm pan (Fig. 3). *(Note:* This will give you an 8 x 14-inch drip pan. If this is not the right side for your needs, begin with the size pan you will need, add 4 inches to both the length and the width and then double the measurement of the width.)

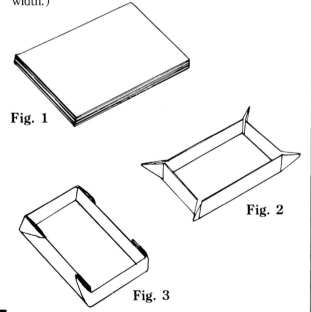

Fig. 1

Fig. 2

Fig. 3

Grilled Lamb Steaks

Ask your butcher to cut steaks from a leg of lamb, or use thick shoulder chops.

Grill for 20 minutes.
Makes 4 servings.

Nutrient Value Per Serving: 298 calories, 30 g protein, 19 g fat, 0 g carbohydrate, 191 mg sodium, 213 mg cholesterol.

```
4   lamb steaks, cut 1 inch thick
      (about 2 pounds)
      Salt and pepper, to taste
¼   cup (½ stick) butter or margarine,
      softened
2   tablespoons chopped fresh mint
```

1. Trim any excess fat from the lamb, and score the remaining fat around the edge of the steaks to prevent curling. Let the steaks stand at room temperature for 1 hour before grilling.
2. Prepare the grill so the coals are medium-hot.
3. Grill the lamb 5 inches from the heat for 10 minutes. Turn and grill the steaks for 10 minutes longer. Sprinkle the salt and pepper over the steaks and place them on a heated platter.
4. Combine the butter or margarine and mint in a small bowl. Spread the butter over the steaks and serve very hot.

Marinade for Lamb

Extra flavorful, this marinade doubles as a baste during grilling.

Makes 2 cups.

Nutrient Value Per ¼ Cup: 126 calories, 0 g protein, 14 g fat, 2 g carbohydrate, 5 mg sodium, 0 mg cholesterol.

```
1   cup dry red wine
½   cup olive oil
2   tablespoons finely chopped parsley
2   tablespoons chopped chives
2   cloves garlic, crushed
½   teaspoon Worcestershire sauce
¼   teaspoon pepper
      Pinch each leaf marjoram, rosemary and
        thyme, crumbled
```

Combine the wine, olive oil, parsley, chives, garlic, Worcestershire sauce, pepper, marjoram, rosemary and thyme in a small bowl. Blend well.

Best-Ever Barbecued Cornish Hens

Grill for 40 minutes.
Makes 4 to 6 servings.

Nutrient Value Per Serving: 389 calories, 37 g protein, 18 g fat, 17 g carbohydrate, 699 mg sodium, 117 mg cholesterol.

```
1   cup catsup
2   tablespoons brown sugar
2   tablespoons cider vinegar
1   tablespoon Worcestershire sauce
1   teaspoon prepared mustard
¼   teaspoon garlic salt
2   tablespoons grated onion
1   small clove garlic, finely chopped
      Salt and pepper, to taste
4   Cornish game hens
```

1. Prepare the grill so the coals are medium-hot.
2. Combine all the ingredients, except the Cornish hens, in a small saucepan. Simmer for 5 minutes, stirring frequently.
3. Halve the Cornish hens and remove the backbones. Season with the salt and pepper.
4. Arrange the hens, cut-side down, on a greased grill, 3 to 5 inches from the coals. Turn and brush the hens with the prepared sauce every 5 minutes until the hens are done, about 20 minutes per side.

Note: You can also spit-roast the Cornish game hens whole for 1 hour; baste often during the last 30 minutes of cooking.

MARINADE MAXIMS

A marinade imparts flavor to meat and can also tenderize or moisturize tougher cuts of meat.

Dry rub: *To tenderize as well as flavor, season meats with spices and herbs.*

Oil-based sauce: *While cooking, slow-roasted meats need moisture. Olive oil is best, but any oil-based sauce will help to retain internal juices by sealing the surface of the meat quickly.*

Acidic mixture: *Wine-, vinegar- or citrus juice-based marinades act as a tenderizer by breaking down the tough fibers of meat. Marinate large cuts overnight, small cuts for about 1 hour.*

Light up the grill for Best-Ever Barbecued Cornish Hens.

Turkey Meats At-A-Glance

Turkey Meat	Grilling Time	Suggested Preparation	Suggested Serving
Turkey Bratwurst • Precooked • Low fat • Grill like traditional bratwurst.	Grill 4-6 inches over a solid bed of medium-glowing coals. Cook, turning often, for about 10 minutes until heated through.	• Make slash down middle and stuff with Muenster cheese just before done. Continue to cook until cheese is melted. • Plump first by boiling in beer before placing on grill.	• Serve on toasted rye buns. • Serve with sauerkraut, chopped onions. • Serve as part of a mixed grill of other sausages.
Turkey Sausages • Precooked • Low in cholesterol • Lowfat alternate to pork sausage.	Grill 4-6 inches over a solid bed of medium-glowing coals. Cook, turning often, for about 10 minutes or until done to your liking and heated through.	• Make slash down middle and stuff with complementary cheese: — Italian/mozzarella — Polish/Swiss — Smoked/Cheddar. • Cut into chunks and make kabobs.	• Serve on onion rolls, French bread, deli rye. • Toast rolls with melted cheese before serving.
Fresh Ground Turkey • Lowfat alternate to hamburgers • Grill with pineapple slices.	Cook burgers (½ inch thick) 4-6" over hot coals for about 4 minutes per side.	• Stuff with cheese and then glaze with compatible sauce: — Cheddar/barbecue — Monterey Jack/salsa sauce — American/barbecue. • Wrap with 2 strips of bacon prior to grilling.	• Serve on whole-wheat buns, crusty French buns. • Make smaller patties and serve on biscuits with spicy mustard. • Serve with horseradish sauce, curry sauce, salsa, relishes.
Turkey Breast Meat • Comes in 2 to 3 pound boneless roasts.	Grill over medium-hot coals 6-8 inches from heat, covered, until meat springs back when touched and interior is no longer pink, for 1 hour and 30 minutes.	• Marinate or rub meat with spices. • Glaze 15 minutes before removing from grill. • Cut into cubes for kabobs.	• Serve roast with potatoes roasted on grill. • Serve kabobs on rice, wild rice, pilaf.
Turkey Hot Dogs • Precooked • Low-calorie • Lowfat	Grill 4-6 inches over a solid bed of medium-glowing coals. Cook, turning often, for about 5 minutes.	• Make slash down middle and stuff with Cheddar cheese *or*, wrap with slice of American cheese just before placing on bun.	• Serve wrapped in warm flour tortilla. • Serve with spicy mustard, horseradish, sliced onions, guacamole.
Turkey Italian Sausage (Ground) • Grill like traditional hamburgers. Top with cranberry sauce.	Grill 4-6 inches over a solid bed of glowing coals. Cook, turning once, for 4-5 minutes per side.	• Stuff with mozzarella, Parmesan or Romano cheese. • Brush with marinara sauce and sprinkle with grated cheese 15 minutes before removing from grill.	• Serve on crusty Italian rolls. • Serve with slices of tomato and chopped onion.
Breast Tenderloins • Alternative to chicken breasts. • Substitute for veal.	Grill 6 inches over a solid bed of hot coals. Cook for 10 minutes per side.	• Marinate in wine or lemon juice. • Cut pockets in side and fill with cheese or favorite dressing. • Wrap with bacon before grilling. • Cut into cubes for kabobs.	• Serve with cold pasta salad. • Serve extra stuffing on side. • Serve kabobs with rice.
Drumstick Steaks • Boneless • Skinless	Grill 6 inches over a solid bed of hot coals, for 6 minutes per side.	• Slice or cut into cubes and skewer for kabobs. • Brush with barbecue sauce before removing from grill.	• Serve steaks on crusty rolls. • Serve kabobs with pilaf or plain rice. • Grill corn along with kabobs.

Sweet and Sour Chicken Legs

This pineapple-based glaze tastes good with short ribs or chops.

Grill for 50 minutes.
Makes 8 servings.

Nutrient Value Per Serving: 224 calories, 22 g protein, 11 g fat, 7 g carbohydrate, 424 mg sodium, 77 mg cholesterol.

1   **can (8 ounces) pineapple juice**
¼ **cup honey**
¼ **cup lemon juice**
1   **tablespoon soy sauce**
1   **tablespoon Worcestershire sauce**
1   **clove garlic, finely chopped**
2   **teaspoons salt**
1   **teaspoon leaf basil, crumbled**
1   **teaspoon dry mustard**
¼ **teaspoon liquid red-pepper seasoning**
8   **broiler-fryer legs or quarters (about 3 pounds)**

1. Combine the pineapple juice, honey, lemon juice, soy sauce, Worcestershire sauce, garlic, salt, basil, mustard and red-pepper seasoning in a large jar with a screw top. Shake to blend well. Refrigerate the glaze for at least 2 hours to blend the flavors.
2. Prepare the grill until the coals are medium-hot.
3. Grill the chicken pieces, skin-side down, 6 inches from the heat, turning the pieces with tongs several times, for 30 minutes.
4. Brush the chicken with the glaze. Grill, turning and basting several times, 20 minutes longer or until the chicken is tender and well glazed.

Food for thought . . .

A commercially prepared table condiment and recipe ingredient, Worcestershire is an aged blend of soy, vinegar, tamarind, molasses, sugar, anchovies, garlic, shallots and a variety of other spices and flavorings. Based on an Indian recipe, the sauce was originally created in a shop in Worcester, England, belonging to Lea and Perrins.

Lemon Barbecue Sauce

Use this lively lemon-based sauce to perk up chicken and Cornish hens.

Makes ¾ cup.

Nutrient Value Per Tablespoon: 43 calories, 0 g protein, 5 g fat, 1 g carbohydrate, 186 mg sodium, 0 mg cholesterol.

½ **cup lemon juice**
¼ **cup vegetable oil**
1   **large clove garlic**
1   **teaspoon salt**
½ **teaspoon celery seed**
½ **teaspoon leaf thyme, crumbled**

Combine the lemon juice and oil in a small bowl. Mash the garlic in the salt in a cup and add to the lemon juice mixture along with the celery seed and thyme, blending well. Let the sauce stand at room temperature overnight. Brush or pour over chicken or Cornish hens.

Peanutty Chicken Legs

Drumsticks are perfect finger foods for kids. Chopped peanuts add crunch.

Grill for 40 minutes.
Makes 8 servings.

Nutrient Value Per Serving: 416 calories, 34 g protein, 30 g fat, 3 g carbohydrate, 159 mg sodium, 119 mg cholesterol.

8   **chicken legs**
¼ **cup (½ stick) butter or margarine, melted Salt and pepper, to taste Honey**
1   **cup chopped peanuts**

1. Prepare the grill so the coals are medium-hot.
2. Brush the chicken legs with the melted butter or margarine and season with the salt and pepper.
3. Grill the legs 6 inches from the heat, turning the legs for 30 minutes or until they are almost tender.
4. Brush the chicken legs with honey and roll in the peanuts spread out on wax paper.
5. Return the legs to the grill and grill for 10 minutes longer or until the legs are richly glazed. Pile the legs in a basket and serve with plenty of paper napkins.

Chicken Kabobs

Boneless, skinned breast meat is the lowest in calories of all chicken pieces. Since it's low in fat, be sure not to overcook it.

Grill for 10 minutes.
Makes 6 servings.

Nutrient Value Per Serving: 251 calories, 37 g protein, 7 g fat, 10 g carbohydrate, 107 mg sodium, 88 mg cholesterol.

2   **pounds boneless, skinned chicken breasts, cut into 1-inch-wide strips**
2   **tablespoons olive or vegetable oil**
2   **tablespoons white wine vinegar**
2   **tablespoons chopped parsley**
1   **tablespoon chopped fresh basil OR: 1 teaspoon leaf basil, crumbled**
1   **large zucchini, trimmed and sliced**
2   **ears corn on the cob, cut into 1-inch chunks, boiled 5 minutes**
1   **sweet red pepper, halved, seeded and cut into chunks**
12 **mushrooms**

1. Combine the chicken with the oil, vinegar, parsley and basil in a medium-size bowl. Marinate the chicken for 1 hour at room temperature, or cover the bowl and refrigerate overnight. Drain the chicken, reserving the marinade.
2. Prepare the grill so the coals are medium-hot.
3. Thread the chicken with the zucchini, corn, red pepper and mushrooms on 12 long metal skewers. Brush with the reserved marinade.
4. Grill the kabobs 6 inches from the heat for 5 minutes on each side, brushing with the marinade, or until the chicken is cooked through and the vegetables are tender.

Mexican Turkey Patties

Use ground turkey, rather than beef for these South-of-the-Border burgers.

Grill for 10 minutes.
Makes 4 servings.

Nutrient Value Per Serving: 236 calories, 24 g protein, 14 g fat, 2 g carbohydrate, 551 mg sodium, 84 mg cholesterol.

1   **pound ground turkey**
1/2 **cup shredded Monterey Jack cheese**
1/4 **cup medium taco sauce**
1/4 **cup chopped cilantro**
1/2 **teaspoon salt**
1/4 **teaspoon chili powder**
1/8 **teaspoon garlic powder**
     Additional taco sauce (optional)

1. Prepare the grill so the coals are medium-hot.
2. Combine all the ingredients in a medium-size bowl and shape the mixture into 4 equal patties.
3. Grill the patties for 10 to 12 minutes, turning once. Serve on your favorite bun with additional taco sauce, if you wish.

Kabob it! From left: Seafood Kabobs (page 136) and Chicken Kabobs over brown rice pilaf.

Seafood Kabobs

Thread scallops and shrimp with squash and cherry tomatoes, for a quick-to-cook entrée.

Grill for 10 minutes.
Makes 6 servings.

Nutrient Value Per Serving (2 skewers): 189 calories, 23 g protein, 6 g fat, 10 g carbohydrate, 289 mg sodium, 101 mg cholesterol.

 2 tablespoons olive or vegetable oil
 2 tablespoons fresh lime juice
 1 tablespoon Dijon-style mustard
 2 dozen sea scallops
 2 dozen shrimp, shelled and deveined
 2 medium-size yellow squash, trimmed and sliced
 1 lime, cut into thin wedges
 1 pint cherry tomatoes, stemmed

1. Combine the oil, lime juice and mustard in a large bowl. Add the scallops and shrimp and marinate for 1 hour at room temperature. Drain the seafood, reserving the marinade.
2. Prepare the grill so the coals are medium-hot.
3. Thread the seafood with the squash slices, lime wedges and tomatoes on 12 long metal skewers. Brush with the marinade.
4. Grill the kabobs 6 inches from the heat, brushing with the marinade, for 10 minutes on each side or until the seafood is cooked.

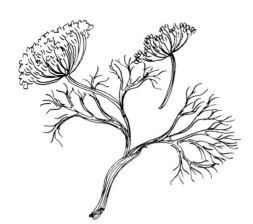

 LS

Dilled Swordfish

Thick swordfish or salmon steaks are bathed in a lemon and dill marinade.

Grill for 20 minutes.
Makes 8 servings.

Nutrient Value Per Serving: 155 calories, 20 g protein, 8 g fat, 0 g carbohydrate, 56 mg sodium, 57 mg cholesterol.

 4 swordfish OR: salmon steaks, cut 1 inch thick (about 2 pounds)
 ¼ cup vegetable oil
 2 tablespoons lemon juice
 1 tablespoon chopped fresh dill OR: 1 teaspoon dillweed
 1 tablespoon paprika
 1 teaspoon salt
 ¼ teaspoon pepper

1. Place the swordfish or salmon in a single layer in a large shallow glass dish.
2. Combine the oil, lemon juice, dill, paprika, and salt and pepper in a cup. Pour the marinade over the steaks. Cover the dish with plastic wrap. Let stand at room temperature for 1 hour.
3. Prepare the grill so the coals are medium-hot.
4. Grill the fish 4 inches from the heat, basting the fish with the marinade and turning once, for 20 minutes or until the fish flakes easily when tested with a fork. Serve the fish with parslied boiled potatoes and buttered peas, if desired.

Baste for Fish Steaks

This tangy marinade will enhance the taste of any firm-fleshed fish.

Makes 1 cup.

Nutrient Value Per Tablespoon: 66 calories, 1 g protein, 7 g fat, 1 g carbohydrate, 359 mg sodium, 0 mg cholesterol.

 ½ cup vegetable oil
 ⅓ cup soy sauce
 ¼ cup lemon juice
 2 teaspoons Dijon-style mustard
 1 teaspoon grated lemon rind
 1 clove garlic, finely chopped

Combine the oil, soy sauce, lemon juice, mustard, grated lemon rind and garlic in a small bowl, blending well. Pour the baste over fish steaks in a glass baking dish. Cover the dish and marinate in the refrigerator for 3 hours before grilling.

Mustard Grilled Salmon

Grill for 10 minutes.
Makes 8 servings.

Nutrient Value Per Serving: 374 calories, 35 g protein, 74 g fat, 1 g carbohydrate, 199 mg sodium, 60 mg cholesterol.

6   salmon steaks (8 ounces each)
¼   cup vegetable oil
¼   cup dry white wine
¼   cup lemon juice
3   tablespoons Dijon-style mustard
1   small onion, chopped (¼ cup)
2   cloves garlic, finely chopped
     Salt and pepper, to taste

1. Place the salmon steaks in a single layer in a large shallow glass dish.
2. Combine the oil with the wine, lemon juice, mustard, chopped onion, garlic, and salt and pepper in a small bowl; mix to blend well. Pour the marinade over the salmon; turn the steaks in the mustard mixture to coat well. Refrigerate the salmon, covered, for 3 hours, turning once.
3. Prepare the grill so the coals are very hot.
4. Drain the salmon, reserving the marinade. Place the salmon on the grill. Brush with the reserved marinade.
5. Grill the salmon 4 inches from the heat for 5 minutes. Turn the salmon; brush with the marinade. Grill for 5 minutes longer or until the fish flakes when tested with a fork.

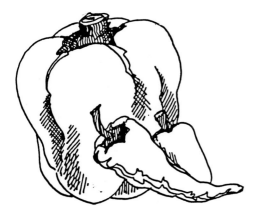

Vegetable Kabobs

Garden-fresh vegetables cook to perfection over the coals. Try parboiled small new potatoes or large fresh mushrooms, too.

Grill for 15 minutes.
Makes 6 servings.

Nutrient Value Per Serving: 142 calories, 4 g protein, 8 g fat, 16 g carbohydrate, 493 mg sodium, 21 mg cholesterol.

1   pound small white onions
2   medium-size zucchini, trimmed and cut into chunks
2   medium-size yellow squash, trimmed and cut into chunks
1   pint cherry tomatoes, halved
2   large sweet green peppers, seeded and cut into squares
¼   cup (½ stick) butter or margarine
2   teaspoons chopped chives
1   teaspoon dillweed
1   teaspoon salt
¼   teaspoon lemon pepper

1. Prepare the grill so the coals are medium.
2. Parboil the onions, zucchini and yellow squash in enough boiling salted water to cover in a small saucepan for 5 minutes. Drain the vegetables and cool. Peel and halve the onions.
3. Thread 6 long skewers with the onion and cherry tomatoes, alternately with the green pepper squares and chunks of the zucchini and yellow squash.
4. Melt the butter or margarine in a small saucepan with a flameproof handle on the grill.. Stir in the chives, dillweed, salt and lemon pepper.
5. Grill the kabobs 4 inches from the heat, turning and brushing the kabobs several times with the butter mixture, for 15 minutes or until the vegetables are crisp-tender.

Sweet Potato Boats

Turn your barbecue into a festive dinner by serving a vegetable once reserved for holiday meals.

Grill for 1 hour.
Makes 6 servings.

Nutrient Value Per Serving: 188 calories, 2 g protein, 8 g fat, 28 g carbohydrate, 459 mg sodium, 21 mg cholesterol.

6   **small sweet potatoes**
¼   **cup (½ stick) butter or margarine**
2   **tablespoons brown sugar**
1   **teaspoon salt**
½   **teaspoon ground nutmeg**

1. Prepare the grill so the coals are very hot.
2. Scrub the sweet potatoes and prick with a fork to allow the steam to escape. Wrap each potato in aluminum foil. Place on the side of the grill.
3. Grill the potatoes 6 inches from the heat, turning several times, for 1 hour or until the sweet potatoes are tender when pierced with a two-tined fork.
4. Remove the potatoes from the grill. Remove the aluminum foil. Scoop out the sweet potatoes, leaving a ¼-inch shell. Place the potato insides in a medium-size bowl. Beat in the butter or margarine, brown sugar, salt and nutmeg until well blended. Spoon the mixture into the hollowed-out shells, dividing evenly. Sprinkle the tops with additional nutmeg, if you wish. Keep the potatoes warm on the side of the grill. Serve the potatoes hot.

PEELING TOMATOES

Add tomatoes, a few at a time, to a large pot of boiling water. When the water returns to boiling, boil 10 seconds for very ripe tomatoes and 20 seconds for firmer tomatoes. Remove with a slotted spoon and rinse under cold water to stop the cooking. (If the skin splits while cooking, remove the tomato immediately.) Working from the bottom to the stem end, peel off the skin with a paring knife.

COOL, NOT COLD, TOMATOES

Never refrigerate tomatoes, under any circumstances. The cold spoils their delicate flavor. Ideally, store tomatoes in a dark place between 50° and 70°.

Anchovy-Stuffed Tomatoes

There's always room on the grill for a special vegetable dish.

Grill for 20 minutes.
Makes 6 servings.

Nutrient Value Per Serving: 254 calories, 16 g protein, 8 g fat, 30 g carbohydrate, 1,312 mg sodium, 26 mg cholesterol.

6   **large firm tomatoes**
   Salt and pepper, to taste
1   **can (about 7 ounces) tuna, drained and flaked**
2   **cups Italian-flavor dry bread crumbs**
1   **can (2 ounces) anchovy fillets, drained and chopped**
¼   **cup chopped parsley**
2   **tablespoons olive or vegetable oil**
¼   **cup grated Parmesan cheese**

1. Cut a ½-inch slice from the tops of the tomatoes; scoop out the insides and reserve the insides for soups or sauces. Season the tomato shells with the salt and pepper; turn the shells upside down on paper toweling. Drain the shells for 10 minutes.
2. Combine the tuna, crumbs, anchovies and parsley in a medium-size bowl. Divide the mixture among the tomato shells.
3. Arrange the tomatoes in a heavy metal baking pan. Drizzle the tops with the oil and sprinkle with the grated Parmesan cheese. Cover the pan with heavy-duty aluminum foil.
4. Cook the tomatoes on the back of the grill for 20 minutes or until the tomatoes are tender.

Grilling Fruits And Vegetables

Simple fresh vegetable and fruit side dishes add flavor and variety to an outdoor dinner. Grilled eggplant, tomato, mushroom and pepper kabobs, honey-roasted pineapple and caramel peaches are easy to prepare, fresh and naturally delicious.

These tips will help you take advantage of a good barbecue fire. Remember that you have less control over the heat than cooking on an indoor stove. Be watchful, particularly of delicate vegetables or fruit cooked with sugar; all can burn easily.

Foil-Wrapped Vegetables

This is a simple, easy way to prepare vegetables for grilling. They may be cooked alone or in combination. Wash the vegetables, but do not dry. The excess moisture helps steam-cook most vegetables. Place up to 4 servings of the vegetables on a sheet of heavy-duty aluminum foil. Dot with butter, margarine or olive oil (allow 2 tablespoons for every four servings) and season. Try the different fresh seasonal herbs: fresh basil with zucchini and carrots; fresh tarragon with mushrooms; fresh thyme with green beans. Experiment. Wrap the vegetables tightly in foil and place 4 to 6 inches above a solid bed of medium-glowing coals. Shift the packets occasionally so the vegetables cook evenly. Most vegetables are done if tender when pierced with a two-tined fork.

Cooking times for foil-wrapped vegetables will vary depending on the size of the packets and the size of the vegetables. Asparagus will take about 15 minutes, while winter squash (cut in quarters) may require 30 to 45 minutes, and a whole baked potato will need 1 hour.

When cooking vegetables in combination, try to keep their sizes uniform.

Vegetable Kabobs

Cooking the vegetables on separate skewers makes for a tastier kabob. The vegetables will not be overcooked nor the meat underdone. Vegetable kabobs may also be cooked alongside pieces of meat or chicken on the grill.

Wash and cut vegetables into 1-inch lengths (i.e., zucchini, eggplant, onions, summer squash) if necessary. Alternately thread vegetables that have about the same cooking times, on metal or wooden skewers. Place the grill rack 4 to 6 inches above a solid bed of low-glowing coals. Cook, turning often, and baste with melted butter or margarine or a basting sauce for 10 to 15 minutes, or until done.

Roasting Vegetables On The Grill

Corn on-the-cob, potatoes, yams and onions may be grilled in their own natural wrapping.

Corn: Pull the husks back, remove the silk, then brush the corn generously with melted butter or margarine. Replace the husks and secure with wooden picks or wires, and place 4 to 6 inches above a solid bed of medium-glowing coals for 15 to 20 minutes, turning occasionally. Remember to remove wire or wooden picks before serving.

Potatoes and Yams: Wash, then prick with a two-tined fork to allow steam to escape. Place 4 to 6 inches above a solid bed of medium-glowing coals and cook, shifting several times, for about 1 hour or until the potatoes are soft when squeezed. The skins will become brown and crunchy.

Onions: Prick large mild yellow onions with a two-tined fork. Do not peel. Place the onions, wrapped in heavy-duty aluminum foil, 4 to 6 inches above a solid bed of medium-glowing coals and grill, shifting several times, about 35 to 45 minutes or until the onions are soft when squeezed. Before serving, remove the skins; brush with olive oil and basil.

Direct Grilling

Potatoes, eggplant and zucchini become crispy and flavorful when grilled on a sheet of heavy-duty aluminum foil placed directly over the rack of your grill.

Cut the vegetables lengthwise, approximately ¼-inch thick; brush both sides with butter, margarine or oil, sprinkle with salt and pepper to taste (add chopped fresh herbs for extra flavor) and place on greased heavy-duty aluminum foil. Place the foil-wrapped package on the grill rack 4 to 6 inches above a solid bed of medium-glowing coals. Cook, turning as needed to brown both sides, for 15 to 30 minutes or until the vegetables are cooked to desired doneness.

Foil-Wrapped Fruit

An unusual side-dish accompaniment to grilled meat, poultry or seafood or as a light dessert, foil-wrapped fruit is deliciously easy to cook over the open fire. Simply cut fruit, place on a sheet of heavy-duty aluminum foil and dot with butter. If desired, sweeten with granulated sugar, brown sugar or honey. Add ground cinnamon, ginger or nutmeg (or a combination) and add a splash of lemon juice for extra flavor, if desired.

Seal and place the foil-wrapped package on the grill rack 4 to 6 inches above a solid bed of medium coals. Cook, shifting the packet often, for 5 to 15 minutes, depending on the fruit, or until heated through.

Fruits best suited to foil cooking are apples, bananas, peaches, nectarines, pears, pineapples, grapefruit, oranges and rhubarb.

The Drugstore Wrap

This is a great way to wrap and seal packets of food for the barbecue (or meats for the freezer). It is essential that the seal be tight, so that the juices of the cooking food won't spill over into the fire (and the air won't get into the meat and cause freezer-burn). Start by placing the item to be wrapped in the center of a piece of heavy-duty aluminum foil that is large enough to go around the food and allow for folding at the top and sides. Bring the two long sides up and over the food and fold them over about 1 inch (FIG. 1). Make a crease the entire length; make one more tight fold to bring the wrapping down to the level of the food surface. Press out the air toward the ends (FIG. 2). Fold the ends up and over, pressing out the air and shaping to the contours of the food (FIG. 3).

DOUBLE-DUTY SALAD DRESSINGS

Put your prepared or homemade salad dressings to work at the barbecue: they make quick seasonings for marinades, basting sauces and for fish and vegetables grilled in aluminum-foil packets. Test your favorite combinations with regular and low-cal dressings.

WINTER BARBECUING

Grilling vegetables needn't be limited to the summer months. For those longing for the taste of summer in February and willing to brave the weather, several winter vegetables make good candidates for the grill. Turnips, parsnips and beets, cooked in aluminum foil for 25 to 30 minutes, help summertime chefs span the season.

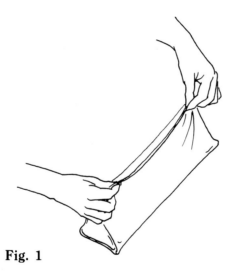

Fig. 1

Fig. 2

Fig. 3

M·A·I·N-D·I·S·H
S·A·L·A·D·S

Classic Layered Salad

Present this beautiful salad to your guests, and little will they know you did it all the day before.

Makes 8 servings.

Nutrient Value Per Serving: 222 calories, 9 g protein, 16 g fat, 10 g carbohydrate, 324 mg sodium, 28 mg cholesterol.

Creamy Parsley Dressing:

- 1   cup mayonnaise
- ⅓   cup plain yogurt
- ¼   cup loosely packed parsley leaves, chopped
- 1   tablespoon snipped fresh or freeze-dried chives
- ¼   teaspoon ground pepper

Salad:

- 1   head iceberg lettuce, quartered, cored and shredded (about 8 cups)
- 1   large sweet red pepper, halved, seeded and cut lengthwise into ¼-inch-wide strips
- 2   large carrots, peeled and cut diagonally into thin slices (about 1 cup)
- ⅔   cup finely chopped green onions (about 1 bunch)
- 1   package (10 ounces) frozen peas, thawed
- ½   pound sliced bacon, crisply fried, drained and crumbled
- 4   ounces sharp Cheddar cheese, shredded (1 cup)

1. Prepare the Creamy Parsley Dressing: Combine the mayonnaise, yogurt, parsley, chives and pepper in a small bowl until well blended. Taste the dressing and adjust the seasonings, if necessary.
2. Assemble the Salad: Place the lettuce in a 4-quart glass or crystal bowl. Arrange the red pepper and carrots vertically against the side of the bowl. Arrange the green onions and peas around the outer edges of the bowl. Spread the dressing over the top. Arrange the bacon and the cheese over the dressing. Cover the bowl with plastic wrap and refrigerate the salad until serving time, up to 1 day.
3. To serve: Present the salad to the diners. Transfer the salad to a large, clean dish pan or roasting pan. Gently toss the salad so all the ingredients are well coated with the dressing.

THE SALAD DAYS OF SUMMER

These salads are ideal for summer buffet tables. The layers are assembled the night before or early in the day and the dressing is gently drizzled or spread over the top. After the salad is presented, all is tossed.

Food for thought . . .

Couscous is a classic meal in Northern Africa. The meat and vegetable ingredients will vary, but one ingredient that always remains the same is the cereal, a fine-grained semolina which is cooked to a light and fluffy stage.

Couscous Salad with Eggs and Vegetables

Makes 4 servings.

Nutrient Value Per Serving: 458 calories, 15 g protein, 19 g fat, 46 g carbohydrate, 764 mg sodium, 206 mg cholesterol.

- 1½ **cups chicken broth**
- 1 **carrot, peeled and cut into ½-inch dice**
- 1¼ **cups couscous**
- 4 **tablespoons olive oil**
- 1½ **tablespoons fresh lemon juice**
- 1 **teaspoon ground cumin**
- ¾ **teaspoon salt**
- ½ **teaspoon pepper**
- 1 **medium-size zucchini**
- 3 **hard-cooked eggs, cut lengthwise into 8 wedges**
- ¾ **cup seedless grapes, halved**
- ½ **sweet red pepper, cored, seeded and thinly sliced lengthwise**

1. Bring the chicken broth to boiling in a small saucepan over high heat. Add the carrot; lower the heat and simmer for 6 minutes or until the carrot is tender-crisp.
2. Add the couscous; stir. Cover the saucepan; remove from heat. Let stand for 5 minutes.
3. Meanwhile, whisk together the oil, lemon juice, cumin, salt and pepper in a medium-size bowl. Turn the couscous into the bowl with the dressing. Fluff the couscous with a fork to separate the grains.
4. Bring 2 cups of water to boiling in a saucepan. Add the zucchini; boil for 8 minutes or until the zucchini is crisp-tender. Drain the zucchini and cool. Trim ends; half the zucchini lengthwise. Cut crosswise into ¼-inch-thick slices.
5. Add the zucchini, egg wedges, grapes and red pepper to the couscous; toss to blend well. Serve the salad at room temperature. Refrigerated, this salad will keep 2 to 3 days.

Monterey Jack and Tomato Salad

Makes 4 servings.

Nutrient Value Per Serving: 291 calories, 15 g protein, 24 g fat, 5 g carbohydrate, 710 mg sodium, 50 mg cholesterol.

- ½ **pound Monterey Jack cheese, cut into 1½ x ½ x ½-inch pieces (about 1½ cups)**
- 2 **medium-size ripe tomatoes, halved, seeded and each half cut into 6 wedges**
- 1 **to 2 pickled jalapeño peppers, stemmed, seeded and thinly sliced**
- 2 **tablespoons chopped fresh coriander* OR: parsley (preferably flat-leaf Italian)**
- 2 **tablespoons olive oil**
- ½ **clove garlic, finely chopped** **Salt, to taste**

Combine all the ingredients in a medium-size bowl. Toss to mix well. Cover the bowl with plastic wrap and refrigerate for at least 2 hours. Bring the salad to room temperature before serving.

Curried Rice Salad

A delicious way to use leftover chicken or turkey.

Makes 6 servings.

Nutrient Value Per Serving: 455 calories, 24 g protein, 23 g fat, 36 g carbohydrate, 312 mg sodium, 65 mg cholesterol.

- 4 **cups hot cooked rice**
- ¼ **cup bottled oil and vinegar salad dressing**
- 1 **to 3 teaspoons curry powder**
- 1 **large sweet green pepper, halved, seeded and chopped**
- 1 **medium-size onion, chopped (½ cup)**
- 3 **cups cooked turkey or chicken**
- ½ **cup mayonnaise or salad dressing** **Salt and pepper, to taste** **Crisp salad greens** **Tomato wedges for garnish**

1. Toss the hot rice with the bottled oil and vinegar salad dressing and curry powder in a large bowl until well blended. Let the rice mixture stand at room temperature for 15 minutes to blend the flavors.

2. Add the green pepper, onion, turkey or chicken and mayonnaise or salad dressing to the rice mixture. Toss to combine well. Taste and season with salt and pepper. Cover the bowl with plastic wrap and refrigerate for 1 hour.

3. Line a large salad bowl with the salad greens. Spoon the rice mixture on the top. Garnish with the tomato wedges.

Food for thought . . .

Counting calories? Tuna packed in water contains about 100 fewer calories per serving than tuna packed in oil.

Southern Fried Chicken Salad

Chicken breasts cut into bite-size pieces and batter-fried make a deliciously different main-dish salad.

Makes 6 servings.

Nutrient Value Per Serving: 350 calories, 24 g protein, 15 g fat, 30 g carbohydrate, 333 mg sodium, 98 mg cholesterol.

> 1 **pound boneless, skinned chicken breasts**
>   **Vegetable oil for frying**
> 1½ **cups all-purpose flour**
> ½ **teaspoon salt**
> ½ **teaspoon garlic powder**
>   **Pinch ground hot red pepper**
> 1 **egg**
> ½ **cup milk**
> 4 **cups shredded red cabbage**
> 1 **small head leaf lettuce, shredded**
>   **Tomato wedges**
> ¼ **cup Green Onion Dressing (recipe follows)**

1. Cut the chicken breasts into bite-size pieces.
2. Pour the oil into a large skillet or deep fryer to a depth of 1 inch. Heat the oil slowly to 375° or until a cube of white bread turns golden brown in 30 seconds.
3. Combine the flour, salt, garlic powder and red pepper in a pie plate. Beat the egg in a small bowl; stir in the milk.
4. Dip the chicken first into the flour mixture, then into the egg-milk mixture, then again into the flour mixture to coat completely. Let dry on a sheet of wax paper.
5. Fry the chicken, part at a time, in the hot oil until golden; do not crowd the pan. Remove the chicken with a slotted spoon and drain on paper toweling.
6. Place the shredded red cabbage, then the lettuce in a salad bowl. Top with the warm fried chicken. Arrange the tomato wedges around the edge of the salad bowl. Top with the Green Onion Dressing and toss.

Green Onion Dressing

Makes about 1½ cups.

Nutrient Value Per Tablespoon: 100 calories, 0 g protein, 11 g fat, 1 g carbohydrate, 106 mg sodium, 8 mg cholesterol.

> 1½ **cups mayonnaise or salad dressing**
> 1 **to 2 tablespoons Dijon-style or sharp-**
>   **flavored mustard**
> ½ **cup finely chopped green onion**

Combine the mayonnaise or salad dressing, mustard and green onion in the container of a food processor or electric blender. Cover and process on high speed for 1 minute or until blended.

FOR A CURRIED TUNA SALAD

Substitute 2 cans (7 ounces each) tuna, drained and flaked, for the 3 cups cooked turkey or chicken, and add 2 cups halved grapes, if you wish.

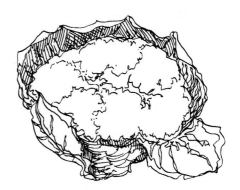

Cool and tasty Rice Salad with Tuna and Shrimp.

Rice Salad with Tuna and Shrimp

Makes 4 servings.

Nutrient Value Per Serving: 447 calories, 25 g protein, 19 g fat, 44 g carbohydrate, 600 mg sodium, 83 mg cholesterol.

1   cup uncooked long-grain white rice
3   tablespoons olive oil
½   pound medium-size shrimp with shells
½   medium-size cucumber (cut lengthwise), peeled, seeded and cut crosswise into thin slices
1   can (6½ ounces) tuna packed in oil, broken into chunks
1½   tablespoons capers, drained
¼   cup lemon juice (2 lemons)
3   canned flat anchovy fillets, finely chopped
1   clove garlic, finely chopped
⅓   cup firmly packed fresh basil leaves, coarsely chopped OR: 1 tablespoon leaf basil, crumbled
    Salt and pepper, to taste
10   oil-cured black olives, pitted
10   cherry tomatoes

1. Cook the rice according to the package directions. Mix in 1 tablespoon of the olive oil. Set the rice aside and let cool completely.
2. Steam the shrimp over boiling water in a tightly covered saucepan or steamer until the shrimp are pink and firm, 4 to 5 minutes. When the shrimp are cool enough to handle, remove the shells and devein.
3. Combine the rice, shrimp, cucumber, tuna and capers in a serving bowl.
4. Mix together the lemon juice, anchovies, garlic and the remaining 2 tablespoons of the oil in a small bowl. Add the dressing to the rice mixture along with the basil and salt and pepper. Toss to mix the salad well.
5. Garnish the salad with the black olives and cherry tomatoes. Serve the salad cold or at room temperature.

Fish and Fruit Salad

Serve as a luncheon dish or first course.

Bake fish at 450° for 30 minutes for frozen, 10 minutes for fresh.
Makes 6 servings.

Nutrient Value Per Serving: 207 calories, 15 g protein, 9 g fat, 17 g carbohydrate, 233 mg sodium, 50 mg cholesterol.

1   pound frozen or fresh cod fillets
5   teaspoons lemon juice
1   tablespoon butter
¼   teaspoon salt
1   can (17 ounces) fruit cocktail, drained
¾   cup diced celery
3   tablespoons mayonnaise
3   tablespoons dairy sour cream
1   tablespoon thinly sliced green onion
1   small head iceberg lettuce, separated for lettuce cups

1. If using frozen fish, unwrap the fish fillets and let stand at room temperature for 20 minutes.
2. Preheat the oven to very hot (450°).
3. Place the frozen or fresh fish on a sheet of greased aluminum foil large enough to enclose the fish fillets. Sprinkle the fish with 2 teaspoons of the lemon juice; dot the fillets with the butter. Fold the foil over the fish, folding the edges together to form a tightly sealed package.
4. Bake the fish in the preheated very hot oven (450°) for about 30 minutes for the frozen fillets, 10 minutes for the fresh fillets, or until the fish flakes easily when pierced with a fork.
5. Carefully unwrap the fish. Separate into bite-size pieces and remove any bones. Season the fish with the salt. Place the fish on a plate; cover and refrigerate until chilled.

6. Combine the fruit cocktail and the celery in a medium-size bowl. Add the fish to the bowl; mix together lightly. Combine the mayonnaise, sour cream, the remaining 3 teaspoons lemon juice and the green onion in a small bowl. Gently fold the dressing into the fish mixture. Serve the salad in the lettuce cups.

Oriental Salad

This shrimp-flavored salad can be assembled a day ahead.

Makes 6 servings.

Nutrient Value Per Serving: 327 calories, 11 g protein, 25 g fat, 19 g carbohydrate, 406 mg sodium, 63 mg cholesterol.

Creamy Sesame Dressing:
¾ **cup mayonnaise**
¼ **cup plain yogurt**
1½ **teaspoons grated fresh gingerroot**
½ **teaspoon finely chopped garlic**
2 **green onions, finely chopped**
2 **teaspoons soy sauce**
1½ **teaspoons Oriental sesame oil**
1½ **teaspoons honey**
⅛ **teaspoon ground hot red pepper**

Salad:
4 **cups shredded Chinese cabbage (about 1 pound)**
2 **cups shredded red cabbage (about ½ pound)**
1 **cup thinly sliced celery (about 2 medium-size stalks)**
½ **pound medium-size shrimp, cooked, shelled, deveined and halved lengthwise**
1 **small head broccoli, cut into flowerets and steamed until crisp-tender (reserve steamed stems)**
1 **can (8 ounces) water chestnuts, drained and slivered**
¼ **pound snow peas, trimmed and cooked until crisp-tender**
1 **tablespoon sesame seeds, toasted**

1. Prepare the Creamy Sesame Dressing: Combine the mayonnaise, yogurt, gingerroot, garlic, green onion, soy sauce, sesame oil, honey and red pepper in a small bowl until well blended.

2. Assemble the Salad: Layer the shredded Chinese cabbage, then the red cabbage in a 4-quart glass or crystal bowl. Top with the celery. Arrange the halved shrimp in a decorative pattern around the side of the bowl. Slice the reserved broccoli stems into ½-inch pieces. Arrange the flowerets

around the edge of the bowl; fill the center with the stem pieces. Top with the water chestnuts. Spread the dressing over the top of the salad. Arrange the snow peas over the dressing. Sprinkle the top with the sesame seeds. Cover the bowl with plastic wrap. Refrigerate the salad until serving time, up to 1 day ahead.

3. To serve: Present the salad to the diners. Transfer the salad to a large, clean dish pan or roasting pan. Gently toss the salad so all the ingredients are well coated with the dressing.

Food for thought . . .

The water chestnut, a crunchy, white vegetable used often in Chinese cooking, is a tuber, or corm, of a tropical plant. The marsh plant produces the tubers in the mud several inches under water. A freshwater chestnut has a chestnut-brown skin with a disklike shape that tapers to a point at one of its flat sides. It's about 1½ inches in diameter. When peeled with a knife, it can be eaten raw or cooked. Commercially canned water chestnuts have lost all their sweet, starchy flavor, but still retain their crunchiness.
Availability of fresh *— Available in Chinese markets of major cities from July to September. Refrigerate in a brown paper bag or unsealed plastic bag for up to several weeks.*

Mexican Salad

A chicken salad gone Mexican! And even better, the salad can be assembled the day before the fiesta.

Makes 6 servings.

Nutrient Value Per Serving: 637 calories, 31 g protein, 42 g fat, 38 g carbohydrate, 1,178 mg sodium, 84 mg cholesterol.

Creamy Avocado Dressing:
- 1 large clove garlic
- 2 green onions, trimmed and quartered
- 2 ripe avocados
- ¼ cup mayonnaise
- ¼ cup dairy sour cream
- ¼ cup fresh lime juice
- 1 tablespoon bottled chili sauce
- 1 teaspoon salt
- ½ teaspoon crushed red pepper flakes
- ⅛ teaspoon black pepper

Salad:
- ½ head romaine lettuce, shredded (about 4 cups)
- 1 can (8 ounces) whole-kernel corn, drained
- ½ head iceberg lettuce, quartered, cored and shredded (about 4 cups)
- 1 sweet green pepper, halved, seeded and chopped (about 1 cup)
- 1 can (16 ounces) chick-peas, drained
- 2 cups cooked shredded chicken or turkey (about ½ pound)
- 1 jar (3 ounces) pimiento-stuffed olives, drained and sliced
- ½ pound Monterey Jack cheese, shredded (2 cups)
- ½ of 7½-ounce package taco-flavored tortilla chips, broken

1. Prepare the Creamy Avocado Dressing: Drop the garlic through the feed tube of a food processor with the motor running; process the garlic until finely chopped. Turn the motor off. Add the green onions; process until the green onions are finely chopped.
2. Halve and pit the avocados. Spoon the flesh into the processor bowl. Add the mayonnaise, sour cream, lime juice, chili sauce, salt, red pepper flakes and black pepper. Process the dressing with on-and-off pulses until the mixture is smooth and well blended.
3. Assemble the Salad: Place the romaine in the bottom of a 4-quart glass or crystal bowl. Add a layer of corn. Top with the iceberg lettuce. Add layers of green pepper, chick-peas, chicken and olives. Spread the dressing over the top of the salad. Sprinkle with the cheese.

Cover the bowl with plastic wrap and refrigerate until serving time, up to 1 day ahead.
4. To serve: Sprinkle the tortilla chips over the top of the salad. Present the salad to the diners. Transfer the salad to a large, clean dish pan or roasting pan. Gently toss to coat all the ingredients well.

Food for thought . . .

The avocado, or alligator pear, was originally found in Mexico and Central America. This fruit has a buttery-textured, nutty-tasting flesh. The California Fuerte variety, available from October to May, is green, thin-skinned and weighs 8 to 16 ounces. The Hass variety, sold from May to October, has a dark pebbly skin. Florida varieties are generally larger than those from California. Sold from July to January, they are smooth and light green.

AVOCADO SMARTS

To select: *Hold an avocado in your hands and gently press the ends. If it yields to gentle pressure, it's ripe and ready. (Most avocados, however, are not allowed to mature on the tree and will consequently be hard.) It's best to plan ahead and buy several underripe avocados and let them stand at room temperature to ripen. Enclosing them in a brown paper bag will hasten the ripening.*

Nutrition: *Avocados have a high fat content, most of which is unsaturated. Half of an 8-ounce avocado has 150 calories and provides vitamin C, riboflavin, magnesium and potassium. When the flesh of the avocado is cut, it discolors rapidly. Brush the cut surfaces with citrus juice, diluted vinegar or an ascorbic-acid mixture to reduce the discoloration. If you have half an avocado left over, keep unpeeled, with the pit still in, wrap in aluminum foil and refrigerate.*

Appealing and colorful Salade Niçoise (page 148).

Salade Niçoise

Makes 4 servings.

Nutrient Value Per Serving: 741 calories, 29 g protein, 57 g fat, 32 g carbohydrate, 1,024 mg sodium, 157 mg cholesterol.

Dressing:
- ¾ **cup olive oil**
- 2 **tablespoons white wine**
- 2 **tablespoons lemon juice (1 lemon)**
- 2 **cloves garlic, finely chopped**
- 2 **tablespoons finely chopped fresh basil OR:**
  - **1½ teaspoons leaf basil, crumbled**
- ½ **teaspoon dry mustard**
- ½ **teaspoon salt**
- ¼ **teaspoon white pepper**

Salad:
- 4 **small red-skinned potatoes**
- ½ **pound green beans, ends removed**
- 1 **small sweet yellow pepper, cored and seeded**
- 1 **small sweet red pepper, cored and seeded**
- 1 **medium-size red onion, peeled**
- 1 **medium-size tomato, cored**
- 1 **large head green leaf lettuce**
- 2 **hard-cooked eggs, thinly sliced**
- 2 **cans (6½ ounces each) tuna, drained**
- ⅓ **cup (about 16) oil-cured olives**

1. **Prepare the Dressing:** Whisk together the olive oil, white wine, lemon juice, garlic, basil, mustard, salt and white pepper in a medium-size bowl. Cover the bowl with plastic wrap and set aside.
2. **Prepare the Salad:** Cook the potatoes in enough boiling water to cover the potatoes in a medium-size pot until the potatoes are fork-tender, about 15 minutes. Remove the potatoes from the water with a slotted spoon and plunge into a bowl of ice water to stop the cooking. Remove the potatoes from the water and drain on paper toweling. Thinly slice the potatoes, keeping the slices of each potato together in the original potato shape.
3. Drop the green beans into a medium-size saucepan of enough boiling water to cover the beans. Cook the beans until tender-crisp, 2 to 3 minutes. Drain the beans and plunge them into a bowl of ice water to stop the cooking. Drain the beans again and dry on paper toweling.
4. Slice the yellow and red peppers lengthwise into ¼-inch-wide slices. Slice the red onion into six ⅛-inch-thick slices. Cut the tomato into 6 equal wedges.
5. Reserve 2 or 3 large lettuce leaves; tear the remainder into bite-size pieces. Arrange the pieces in a large shallow serving bowl.
6. Fan the sliced potatoes slightly; arrange the potatoes, spoke-fashion from the outside edge of the bowl, dividing the salad into 4 sections. Arrange half of the red and yellow peppers and the green beans in one section. Arrange remaining half in the section directly opposite.
7. Arrange the onion, egg slices and tomato wedges in the remaining two sections.
8. Place the reserved whole lettuce leaves in the center of the salad to form a cup. Arrange the tuna in the lettuce cup. Scatter the olives over the salad.
9. Pour the dressing over the salad and serve.

Food for thought . . .

The 3 main olives imported from France are salt or brine cured, and have a stronger flavor than oil-cured:

Niçoise — *a small olive with a large pit in proportion to the meat; salt-brine cured and often packed with herbs; brown to brown-green-black.*

Nyons — *somewhat bitter tasting; dry-salt cured and rubbed with oil; black in color with a green cast.*

Picholine — *mild, subtle flavor but slightly salty; salt-brine cured; medium green with a smooth skin.*

The name says it all: Overnight Delight (page 150).

Overnight Delight

Prepare this salad the night before, and it's ready to go! No cooking in the heat of the day.

Makes 8 servings.

Nutrient Value Per Serving: 209 calories, 15 g protein, 10 g fat, 17 g carbohydrate, 750 mg sodium, 10 mg cholesterol.

- ½ **cup red wine vinegar**
- ¼ **cup Italian dressing**
- 1 **tablespoon Dijon-style mustard**
- 1 **clove garlic, chopped**
  Salt and pepper, to taste
- 1 **large onion, chopped**
- ½ **cup chopped pimiento-stuffed green olives**
- 1 **can (8 ounces) mushrooms, drained**
- 2 **packages (16 ounces each) frozen broccoli, thawed**
- 2 **cans (6½ ounces each) tuna fish**
- 3 **medium-size tomatoes, cut into wedges**
- 1 **can (10½ ounces) mexicorn, drained**
  Romaine lettuce leaves

1. Blend together in a medium-size bowl the vinegar, Italian dressing, mustard, garlic and salt and pepper to taste. Add the chopped onion, olives and mushrooms. Toss well to blend. Cover and refrigerate overnight.
2. The following day add the broccoli, tuna fish, tomato and corn to the olive mixture; toss well to mix. Line a salad bowl with romaine leaves. Spoon in the salad. Garnish with raw onion rings and grated cheese, if you wish. Serve at room temperature.

CANNED TUNA GUIDE

Light meat tuna — *from the yellowfin, skipjack or small bluefin tuna.*

White meat tuna — *from the albacore tuna. Use the light meat in mayonnaise-dressed salads, casseroles or any other dish where appearance is not important. The more expensive white tuna is more attractively suited for antipasto platters and vinaigrette salads.*

Three styles of canned tuna — *solid-packed has large pieces of tuna; chunk tuna has about 3 chunks, filled in with small bits; and flake tuna is entirely small bits or fragments.*

Nutrition — *Tuna packed in water has about half the calories of tuna packed in oil. But even packed-in-oil tuna has only 200 to 300 calories per ½ ounce serving, while providing ⅓ to ½ of the suggested daily protein requirement. Also available are some reduced-sodium brands which have 60% less sodium.*

Salami Wedges with Cream Cheese

Here's something different for the hors d'oeuvres tray.

Makes 8 servings.

Nutrient Value Per Serving: 100 calories, 3 g protein, 9 g fat, 2 g carbohydrate, 182 mg sodium, 27 mg cholesterol.

- 1 **package (3 ounces) cream cheese, softened**
- 6 **slices lower-salt salami**
- 8 **thin slices of cucumber**
- 4 **slices of red onion**

1. Spread the cream cheese evenly on 4 slices of the salami. Place 4 of the cucumber slices on each of 2 of the salami slices that have been spread with the cream cheese. Top the other 2 salami slices spread with the cream cheese with the sliced red onion. Stack the salami slices on top of each other, alternating the cucumber and onion slices. Top the stack with the remaining salami slices. Refrigerate for 2 hours.
2. At serving time, cut the salami into 8 wedges. Garnish with cream cheese and parsley, if you wish.

When it's party time, try this deli platter: Salami Wedges with Cream Cheese; Hot Dog "Stars" (page 152); Bologna "Roses" (page 152); luncheon meats wrapped around cheese sticks, garnished with cucumber slices, red pepper rings and an artichoke.

Hot Dog Stars

Microwave on Full Power for 1 to 1¼ minutes;
then broil for 1 to 2 minutes.
Makes 3 servings.

Nutrient Value Per Star: 217 calories, 11 g protein, 14 g fat,
12 g carbohydrate, 358 mg sodium, 40 mg cholesterol.

1 **lower-salt jumbo hot dog**
1 **bagel, uncut, flavor of your choice**
3 **ounces lower-salt Monterey Jack OR:**
     Cheddar cheese, shredded

1. Cut the hot dog crosswise into thirds. Cut one
   end of each hot dog piece into fourths, cutting
   about 1 inch deep. Be careful not to cut all the
   way through the hot dog. Place the hot dogs in a
   shallow microwave-safe dish.
2. Microwave the hot dogs on Full Power for 1 to
   1¼ minutes or until each hot dog piece curls into
   a star.
3. Slice the bagel horizontally into thirds. Place a
   hot dog star in the center of each bagel slice.
   Sprinkle with the cheese.
4. Broil the bagels with the hot dogs for 1 to
   2 minutes or until the cheese melts and the hot
   dogs bubble.

Note: Hot Dog Stars can be made by baking the hot
dog pieces in a preheated moderate oven (350°) for
6 to 8 minutes.

Bologna "Rose"

Make this decorative "flower" the centerpiece of any hors
d'oeuvre platter.

Makes 1 "rose."

Nutrient Value Per "Rose": 91 calories, 3 g protein, 8 g fat,
1 g carbohydrate, 191 mg sodium, 15 mg cholesterol.

1 **slice lower-salt bologna OR: lower-salt**
     salami
1 **slice carrot, about ¼-inch thick**
     Celery leaves

1. Starting at the outside edge of the bologna slice,
   cut one continuous, ¾-inch strip out of the
   bologna, cutting towards the center in a spiral.
   Be careful not to break the strip. Form the rose
   center by tightly rolling one end of the bologna
   strip. Roll the rest of the strip loosely around the
   center to make the petals. Secure with wooden
   picks.

2. With a small cookie cutter or sharp knife, cut a
   flower shape out of the carrot slice. Place the
   cutout in the center of the rose. Use the celery
   leaves around the base of the rose for greenery.

Easy-to-do Bologna "Roses".

Italian Rice Salad

Add seasonings to hot rice for a really flavorful salad.

Makes 8 servings.

Nutrient Value Per Serving: 443 calories, 16 g protein, 29 g fat,
30 g carbohydrate, 1,491 mg sodium, 37 mg cholesterol.

2   **cups water**
¼   **cup bottled Italian dressing**
1   **teaspoon salt**
1   **cup uncooked long-grain rice**
2   **cups thinly sliced zucchini**
1   **can (14 ounces) artichoke hearts, drained**
        and halved
1½   **cups sliced carrots**
1   **cup chopped sweet green pepper**
¾   **cup ripe olives, sliced**
½   **cup sliced radishes**
½   **cup chopped green onion**
¾   **cup bottled Italian dressing**
⅓   **cup mayonnaise OR: salad dressing**
3   **cups diced cooked ham**
        Anchovies
        Tomato wedges

1. Combine the water, the ¼ cup Italian dressing
   and the salt in a medium-size saucepan. Bring to
   boiling; add the rice. Cook the rice mixture

for 10 minutes or until tender yet firm. Spoon the rice into a large glass or ceramic bowl.

2. Add the zucchini, artichoke hearts, carrots, green pepper, sliced olives, radishes, green onion and the ¾ cup Italian dressing to the rice; toss until well blended. Let the rice mixture stand at room temperature for at least 2 hours.

3. Add the mayonnaise or salad dressing and the ham to the rice mixture and toss until well blended. Spoon the salad onto a serving platter. Garnish with the anchovies and tomato wedges.

Imperial Salad Bowl

Crisp, fresh salad greens combine to create the best of all summer main-dish salads.

Makes 8 servings.

Nutrient Value Per Serving: 469 calories, 16 g protein, 41 g fat, 9 g carbohydrate, 994 mg sodium, 63 mg cholesterol.

- **4 cups shredded red cabbage**
- **8 cups broken iceberg lettuce**
  Limestone or red-tipped leaf lettuce, broken
- **½ pound thinly sliced salami, quartered**
- **½ pound Provolone, cut into thin sticks**
- **1 red onion, sliced**
  Ripe olives
  Pimiento strips
  Creamy Italian Dressing (recipe follows)
  Herb-flavored croutons
  Freshly ground pepper

1. Layer the cabbage in the bottom of a large salad bowl. Layer the iceberg lettuce over the cabbage; arrange the leaf lettuce over the iceberg as the next layer.

2. Pile the salami pieces in the center of the bowl. Arrange the Provolone, spoke-style, around the salami. Garnish the salad with the red onion rings, ripe olives and pimiento strips. Cover the bowl with plastic wrap and refrigerate until serving time.

3. To serve, add the Creamy Italian Dressing and toss to coat the salad evenly with the dressing. Sprinkle the top with the herb-flavored croutons and freshly ground pepper. Serve on chilled salad plates or in soup bowls, with bread sticks, if you wish.

Creamy Italian Dressing: Combine 1 container (8 ounces) dairy sour cream, ½ cup mayonnaise or salad dressing and ½ cup bottled Italian dressing in a medium-size bowl. Wrap the bowl with plastic wrap and chill until serving time. Makes about 2 cups. *Nutrient Value Per Tablespoon: 57 calories, 0 g protein, 6 g fat, 1 g carbohydrate, 52 mg sodium, 5 mg cholesterol.*

Note: You may add ½ cup crumbled Gorgonzola, Roquefort or blue cheese to the above recipe.

Cassoulet Salad

The classic French dish becomes a hearty main-dish salad. Perfect with French bread.

Makes 12 servings.

Nutrient Value Per Serving: 407 calories, 18 g protein, 27 g fat, 25 g carbohydrate, 1,108 mg sodium, 41 mg cholesterol.

- **1 can (16 ounces) chick-peas, drained**
- **2 cans (16 ounces each) red kidney beans, drained**
- **1 can (16 ounces) pinto beans, drained**
- **½ cup thinly sliced green onion**
- **½ cup chopped pimiento**
- **¾ cup vegetable oil**
- **⅓ cup wine vinegar**
- **1 teaspoon leaf oregano, crumbled**
- **½ teaspoon leaf basil, crumbled**
- **½ teaspoon salt**
- **½ teaspoon pepper**
  Few drops liquid red-pepper seasoning
- **1 pound sliced smoked sausages**
  Romaine lettuce
- **½ pound thinly sliced salami, halved**

1. Combine the chick-peas, kidney beans, pinto beans, green onion and pimiento in a large glass or ceramic bowl until well blended.

2. Combine the oil, vinegar, oregano, basil, salt, pepper and red-pepper seasoning in a jar with a screw top; shake well to blend the dressing. Pour over the vegetable mixture; toss well to blend. Cover the bowl with plastic wrap and refrigerate for at least 3 hours.

3. At serving time, toss the smoked sausage with the bean mixture. Line a large salad bowl with the romaine leaves. Drain the bean and sausage mixture and place in the salad bowl. Garnish with salami slices placed around the edge of the bowl.

Pasta Stuffed Tomatoes

Summer is the best time to serve salads in their own tomato cups.

Makes 6 servings.

Nutrient Value Per Serving: 438 calories, 16 g protein, 28 g fat, 32 g carbohydrate, 1,055 mg sodium, 42 mg cholesterol.

- 6   **large ripe tomatoes**
      Salt
- 6   **slices salami**
- 6   **slices Provolone**
- 1   **package (7 ounces) ready-cut elbow macaroni, cooked and drained**
- 1/3 **cup chopped sweet green pepper**
- 1/3 **cup chopped sweet red pepper**
- 1/2 **cup mayonnaise OR: salad dressing**
- 2   **tablespoons vinegar**
- 2   **teaspoons prepared mustard**
- 1/2 **teaspoon salt**
      Parsley
      Deviled eggs (optional)

1. Cut the tops from the stem ends of the tomatoes in a zigzag fashion. Gently hollow out the tomatoes with a spoon, leaving a ½-inch shell. Save the insides for another use. Sprinkle the insides of the tomatoes with salt; invert the shells onto paper toweling and let drain for 20 minutes.
2. Finely chop the salami and the Provolone. Place in a large bowl. Add the drained macaroni and chopped green and red peppers; toss gently to combine.
3. Mix together the mayonnaise or salad dressing, vinegar, mustard and salt in a small bowl. Stir the dressing into the chopped salad mixture. Spoon the salad into the tomato cups, dividing evenly. Place the tomatoes on a serving platter lined with parsley. Garnish with deviled eggs, if you wish.

Pasta Salad Italiano

Make this savory salad the night before and dinner's ready when you get home.

Makes 6 servings.

Nutrient Value Per Serving: 548 calories, 10 g protein, 42 g fat, 34 g carbohydrate, 721 mg sodium, 11 mg cholesterol.

- 1   **package (7 ounces) enriched macaroni**
- 6   **slices salami, cut in wedges**
- 1   **package (10 ounces) frozen peas, thawed**
      Italian Vinaigrette (recipe follows)
- 1   **bunch radishes, sliced**
      Fresh coriander OR: parsley sprigs
      Lettuce leaves

1. Cook the elbow macaroni in boiling salted water in a saucepan until *al dente*, firm but tender, following the package directions. Immediately rinse the macaroni in cold water. Drain well.
2. Place the drained macaroni in a large bowl. Add the salami wedges and peas. Pour the Italian Vinaigrette over the macaroni. Toss to combine well. Cover the bowl and refrigerate for at least 4 hours or overnight.
3. Before serving, add the radishes and the coriander or parsley sprigs to the salad; toss to blend. (If the radishes are added too far in advance, they'll lose their color.) Spoon the salad into a lettuce-lined salad bowl.

Italian Vinaigrette: Combine 1 cup olive or vegetable oil, ½ cup garlic-flavored red wine vinegar, 2 tablespoons dry red wine, 1 teaspoon Dijon-style mustard, 1 teaspoon Worcestershire sauce, 1 teaspoon salt, ½ teaspoon leaf oregano, crumbled, and ½ teaspoon sugar in a 2-cup jar with a screw-top. Cover and shake vigorously until the dressing is well blended. Makes about 1¾ cups. *Nutrient Value Per Tablespoon: 70 calories, 0 g protein, 8 g fat, 0 g carbohydrate, 86 mg sodium, 0 mg cholesterol.*

Apple and Sausage Salad

A light luncheon dish for four.

Makes 4 servings.

Nutrient Value Per Serving: 375 calories, 16 g protein, 27 g fat, 18 g carbohydrate, 1,081 mg sodium, 84 mg cholesterol.

1 **large tart firm apple, Golden Delicious or Granny Smith**
1 **or 2 boiling potatoes (8 ounces), cooked, cooled and peeled**
1 **piece pepperoni (2 ounces)**
1 **piece (4 ounces) hot pepper cheese OR: mild Monterey Jack cheese**
2 **ounces thinly sliced prosciutto**

Creamy Mustard Dressing:
½ **cup heavy cream**
1 **tablespoon wine vinegar**
1 **teaspoon Dijon-style mustard**
1 **large green onion (both white and green parts), finely chopped**
¾ **teaspoon salt**
¼ **teaspoon pepper**

½ **head romaine or red leaf lettuce, shredded**
¼ **teaspoon slivered almonds, toasted**

1. Halve and core the apple; leave the skin on. Cut the apple into ½-inch-thick slices; cut the slices into matchsticks, 1 inch long. Do the same with the potatoes, cutting into matchsticks. Cut the pepperoni and cheese into the same-size pieces. Shred the prosciutto. Combine the apple, potato, pepperoni, prosciutto and cheese in a large bowl.
2. Prepare the Creamy Mustard Dressing: Whisk the cream in a small bowl until it begins to thicken. Add the vinegar, mustard, green onion, salt and pepper; whisk to combine well.
3. Add the dressing to the salad ingredients in the bowl; toss to coat well.
4. Arrange the shredded lettuce on a serving platter. Mound the salad on top. Sprinkle the salad with the toasted almonds. Serve.

OOPS! FORGOT TO SOAK DRIED BEANS OVERNIGHT?

Use the following quick method in a pinch: Cover the beans in a saucepan with cold water. Bring to boiling and simmer for 2 minutes. Remove the saucepan from the heat and tightly cover the pan. Let stand for 1 hour.

ROAST YOUR OWN SWEET RED PEPPERS

Broil sweet red or yellow peppers, turning occasionally, until charred on all sides, for about 20 minutes. Place while still hot in a brown paper bag and close. Let the peppers steam until they are cool, for 15 to 20 minutes. Remove from the bag to a cutting board. Halve, core and seed. Remove the blackened skin. Marinate the peppers in a vinaigrette and serve as part of an antipasto plate.

Lentil Salad with Kielbasa and Peppers

Makes 4 servings.

Nutrient Value Per Serving: 399 calories, 16 g protein, 28 g fat, 24 g carbohydrate, 1,304 mg sodium, 18 mg cholesterol.

⅔ **cup dried lentils**
1 **teaspoon salt**
1 **sweet green pepper, cut into ¼-inch dice (about 1 cup)**
2 **tablespoons thinly sliced green onion**
½ **pound fully cooked kielbasa, skin removed and meat cut into ½-inch dice (about 1½ cups)**
½ **cup bottled roasted red peppers, cut into ½-inch dice**
2 **tablespoons Dijon-style mustard**
1 **teaspoon cider vinegar**
3 **tablespoons olive oil**
   Salt and pepper, to taste

1. Cover the lentils with 3 cups of water in a bowl; let the lentils soak overnight.
2. Drain the lentils. Rinse under cold running water.
3. Place the lentils in a small saucepan. Cover with water. Add the 1 teaspoon salt. Bring to boiling over medium heat. Lower the heat and simmer until the lentils are tender but not falling apart, about 20 minutes. Drain the lentils. Place in a medium-size bowl and let cool.
4. Combine the green pepper, green onion, kielbasa and roasted peppers with the lentils. Mix together the mustard, vinegar and oil in a small cup. Add the dressing to the lentil mixture. Season with salt and pepper. Toss the salad well. Cover the bowl with plastic wrap and let stand for at least 1 hour.
5. Serve the salad at room temperature. This salad will keep up to 3 days, refrigerated.

Oils and vinegars! From left: French white wine vinegar with herbs and cloves; Italian vintage extra-virgin olive oil; French champagne vinegar; Italian olive oil; Italian olive oil with chili peppers, herbs and garlic; American red wine vinegar with mixed herbs; French almond and hazelnut oils.

OIL & VINEGAR: NOT JUST FOR SALADS

Deluxe oils and vinegars are available in most specialty shops.

As a general rule, it's best to pair highly flavored oils with simple vinegars, elaborately spiced vinegars with plainer oils.

The following combinations highlight the versatility of these special oils and vinegars in dishes.

- *Marinate chicken breasts in herb vinegar and virgin olive oil. Then barbecue the breast brushing with additional vinegar and oil.*
- *Toss blueberries and raspberries with honey and raspberry vinegar. Chill until very cold. Serve in melon rings.*
- *Prepare mayonnaise with hazelnut or walnut oil. Use on a salad of blanched string beans, onion rings and toasted walnuts or blanched hazelnuts.*
- *Add Spanish Sherry vinegar to gazpacho or garbanzo beans and sausage.*
- *Italian Bread Salad: Toss toasted bread cubes with lettuce, tomato, red onion, cucumber and Niçoise olives. Dress with a vinaigrette of olive oil and garlic-flavored vinegar. Refrigerate.*
- *Marinate poached fish fillets or steaks in a vinaigrette made with lemon and tarragon vinegar. Serve as a cold entrée or appetizer.*
- *Pan-grill thin steaks in a skillet. Remove the steaks from the skillet and keep warm. Deglaze pan with champagne vinegar; add finely chopped shallots, beef stock and fresh rosemary; reduce the liquid until thickened, then swirl in some butter. Pour the sauce over steaks and serve.*
- *Prepare a salad of spinach leaves, toasted almond slivers and peeled orange sections. Dress the salad with a vinaigrette made with almond oil.*
- *Marinate fish before grilling or broiling with Provence-flavored oil. Serve with chopped tomatoes dressed with the oil and red wine vinegar.*
- *Sauté calves' liver in a skillet. Serve with very well-cooked sautéed onions flavored with raspberry vinegar.*
- *Prepare aluminum-foil pouches containing a variety of chopped fresh vegetables. Dot with butter and sprinkle with tarragon vinegar. Seal the pouches and barbecue on the grill.*
- *Brush slices of Italian bread with olive oil flavored with garlic and herbs. Grill on the barbecue. Top with sliced fresh tomatoes, mozzarella cheese and freshly ground pepper. Drizzle with additional oil, just before serving.*

MAKE YOUR OWN FLAVORED VINEGARS AND OILS

First, add the flavorings (herbs, chilies, garlic, etc.) to a clean bottle or jar. Pour the oil or vinegar into the bottle with the flavoring. Vinegar should first be slightly heated in a nonaluminum saucepan. Let stand for about 2 weeks, shaking every 2 or 3 days. Strain the oil or vinegar into a decorative container and add fresh herbs or other flavoring ingredients.

Oils and vinegars

Italian Salad

A hearty salad made with deli roast beef, and it can be layered the day before.

Makes 8 servings.

Nutrient Value Per Serving: 221 calories, 12 g protein, 16 g fat, 8 g carbohydrate, 272 mg sodium, 34 mg cholesterol.

Creamy Herb Dressing Parmesan:
- 1 clove garlic
- ¼ cup mayonnaise
- ½ cup plain yogurt
- ¼ cup grated Parmesan cheese
- 1 tablespoon capers, drained
- 1 tablespoon reserved marinade from artichoke hearts (see Salad, right)
- ½ teaspoon mixed Italian herbs, crumbled

Salad:
- 1 medium-size head romaine lettuce, shredded (10 cups)
- 1 can (6 ounces) marinated artichoke hearts, drained (reserve 1 tablespoon marinade) and each heart cut into thirds
- 6 cherry tomatoes, sliced
- 3 ounces (½ of 6-ounce can) pitted ripe black olives
- ½ medium-size red onion, thinly sliced (about ¾ cup)
- 1 bunch watercress, stems removed
- ½ pound cooked deli roast beef, sliced and cut into thin strips
- ½ pound Provolone, cut into ½-inch cubes
- 4 sesame breadsticks, broken up

1. Prepare the Creamy Herb Dressing Parmesan: Drop the garlic through the feed tube of a food processor with the motor running; process until the garlic is finely chopped. Turn off the motor. Add the mayonnaise, yogurt, Parmesan cheese, capers, reserved marinade and Italian herbs; process the dressing with on-and-off pulses until smooth and creamy. Taste and adjust the seasonings, if necessary.
2. Assemble the Salad: Place the shredded romaine in a 4-quart glass or crystal bowl. Top with layers of the artichoke hearts, tomatoes, olives and red onion. Layer half of the watercress, the roast beef and then the remaining watercress. Spread the dressing over the top of the salad. Sprinkle the top with the Provolone. Cover the bowl with plastic wrap and refrigerate the salad until serving time, up to 1 day.
3. To serve: Just before serving, sprinkle the broken breadsticks over the top of the salad. Present the salad to the diners. Transfer the salad to a large, clean dish pan or roasting pan. Gently toss the salad so all the ingredients are well coated with the dressing.

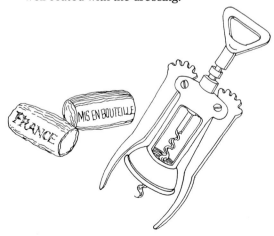

C·O·O·L·I·N·G D·R·I·N·K·S

Planter's Punch

There are as many Planter's Punch recipes as there are islands in the Caribbean. This Bahamian version is delicious made with or without the rum.

Makes 1 serving.

Nutrient Value Per Serving (without rum): 54 calories, 1 g protein, 0 g fat, 13 g carbohydrate, 3 mg sodium, 0 mg cholesterol.

- ¼ **cup orange juice**
- 2 **tablespoons unsweetened pineapple juice**
- 1 **tablespoon lime juice**
- ½ **teaspoon grenadine syrup**
- 1 **ounce (2 tablespoons) dark rum (optional)**
- ½ **orange slice for garnish (optional)**
  Club soda (optional)

Combine the orange, pineapple and lime juices, the grenadine and rum in a glass measure. Stir well and pour over ice cubes in an on-the-rocks glass. Garnish with ½ orange slice, if you wish. For a tall drink, pour the mixture over ice in a highball glass, add a splash of club soda and stir lightly.

Goombay Smash

Coconut rum gives this Bahamian drink its creamy smoothness.

Makes 1 serving.

Nutrient Value Per Serving: 188 calories, 1 g protein, 7 g fat, 15 g carbohydrate, 23 mg sodium, 0 mg cholesterol.

- ⅓ **cup pineapple juice**
- 1 **tablespoon lemon juice**
- 1 **ounce (2 tablespoons) light rum**
- 1 **ounce (2 tablespoons) coconut rum (canned cream of coconut may be substituted)**
  Pineapple wedge and strawberry for garnish (optional)

Shake together the pineapple juice, lemon juice, light rum and coconut rum with several ice cubes in a bar shaker, or other airtight glass or plastic container. Strain the drink over several ice cubes in an on-the-rocks glass. Garnish with a pineapple wedge and strawberry, if you wish.

Cremasse

This sweet cordial idea comes from Haiti. Be careful; it goes down very smoothly.

Makes 4 servings.

Nutrient Value Per Serving: 97 calories, 2 g protein, 2 g fat, 10 g carbohydrate, 24 mg sodium, 7 mg cholesterol.

- ¼ **cup sweetened condensed milk**
- ¼ **cup dark rum**

Combine the sweetened condensed milk and rum in a 1-cup liquid measure. Divide the mixture among 4 cordial glasses.

Note: This drink is also delicious served over crushed ice in a cocktail glass.

Tropical Breeze

A cooling pineapple drink from Puerto Rico.

Makes 2 servings.

Nutrient Value Per Serving: 179 calories, 0 g protein, 0 g fat, 18 g carbohydrate, 3 mg sodium, 0 mg cholesterol.

- 1 **can (6 ounces) unsweetened pineapple juice**
- 3 **ounces (6 tablespoons) light rum**
- 1 **tablespoon lemon juice**
- 1 **cup crushed ice**
- 1 **tablespoon superfine sugar**
  Fresh mint sprigs

1. Add the pineapple juice, rum, lemon juice and ice to the container of an electric blender.
2. Place the sugar in a small bowl. Add 1 sprig of mint and crush the mint with a wooden spoon to flavor the sugar. Discard the crushed mint and add the sugar to the blender. Cover; whirl until the ice is dissolved and the mixture is frothy, about 1 minute. Pour the drink into 2 balloon wine glasses and garnish with the mint sprigs.

Pineapple Quencher

There's a refreshing taste of the Islands in every sip.

Makes 8 servings.

Nutrient Value Per Serving: 97 calories, 1 g protein, 0 g fat, 24 g carbohydrate, 18 mg sodium, 0 mg cholesterol.

2 **cans (6 ounces each) frozen concentrate for pineapple juice, thawed**
1 **tablespoon bottled lemon juice**
   Ice cubes
2 **cans (12 ounces each) club soda**
¾ **cup light rum (optional)**
   Maraschino cherries, drained
   Wedges of lime

1. Combine the frozen concentrate for the pineapple juice, lemon juice and 3 juice-cans of cold water in a large bottle; seal and shake until well blended. Refrigerate the mixture until serving time.
2. To serve, pour the juice mixture into a large pitcher with ice cubes. Add the club soda and rum, if using. Stir until blended.
3. Garnish with maraschino cherries and wedges of lime threaded on a long skewer.

THROWING A PARTY?

To make a fruited ice mold, pour ½-inch depth of water into a 4-cup ring mold that will fit into the punch bowl. Freeze for about 20 minutes. Arrange the cut-up fresh fruits of your choice in a pretty pattern. Pour ¾ cup very cold water over the fruit. Freeze for 15 minutes or until frozen. Continue adding the water gradually until the mold is filled. Freeze for 8 hours. To unmold, dip the mold in and out of a pan of hot water or allow to stand at room temperature for 5 minutes. Then invert the ring onto a cookie sheet. Slide the ring into a punch bowl no more than one-third full of punch.

Orange Refresher

Two kinds of citrus — lemon and orange — are the basis of this dog-day thirst quencher.

Makes 8 servings.

Nutrient Value Per Serving: 178 calories, 1 g protein, 0 g fat, 33 g carbohydrate, 3 mg sodium, 0 mg cholesterol.

1 **cup sugar**
1 **cup water**
   Rind of 1 lemon and 1 orange, cut in strips and bitter white part removed
3 **cups water**
2 **cups orange juice**
¾ **cup vodka OR: club soda**
¼ **cup bottled lemon juice**
   Ice cubes
   Red seedless grapes

1. Combine the sugar, the 1 cup water and the lemon and orange rinds in a small saucepan. Bring to boiling and boil for 8 to 10 minutes or until the sugar dissolves and the mixture is syrupy. Remove and discard the rinds. Cool the syrup to room temperature.
2. Pour the cooled syrup into a large pitcher. Stir in the 3 cups water, orange juice, vodka or club soda and bottled lemon juice; blend well. Add ice cubes to chill.
3. To serve, pour the mixture into stemmed glasses. Garnish with small clusters of red seedless grapes or other fresh fruit, cut up in small pieces, if you wish.

The thirst-busters, from left: Pineapple Quencher (page 160); Orange Refresher (page 160); Cherry Punch and Lemon/Lime Sparkler (both, below).

Cherry Punch

A couple of effervescent ingredients add a new dimension to canned tropical fruit punch.

Makes 8 servings.

Nutrient Value Per Serving: 187 calories, 0 g protein, 0 g fat, 46 g carbohydrate, 12 mg sodium, 0 mg cholesterol.

   Lemon Ice Cubes (recipe follows)
4 **cups (from a 46-ounce can) cherry-flavored tropical fruit punch**
1 **can (12 ounces) lemon-lime soda**
¾ **cup white wine OR: ginger ale**
¼ **cup light corn syrup**
2 **nectarines, halved, pitted and cut into wedges**

1. Empty 1 tray of Lemon Ice Cubes into a large pitcher. Stir in the cherry-flavor tropical fruit punch, lemon-lime soda, white wine or ginger ale and corn syrup; blend well.
2. Thread a long skewer with the nectarine wedges; place in the pitcher and use as a stirrer. Garnish with chunks of cantaloupe, if you wish.

Lemon Ice Cubes: Prepare 1 can (6 ounces) frozen concentrate for lemonade (or any fruit-flavored concentrate) following the label directions. Pour into 2 ice cube trays and freeze.

Lemon/Lime Sparkler

Kids of all ages will love this soft drink mix inspired beverage.

Makes 8 servings.

Nutrient Value Per Serving: 119 calories, 0 g protein, 0 g fat, 30 g carbohydrate, 17 mg sodium, 0 mg cholesterol.

1 **envelope lemon/lime-flavored soft drink mix**
½ **cup water**
2 **bottles (28 ounces each) ginger ale, chilled**
¾ **cup white wine (optional)**
   Ice cubes
   Strawberries
   Wedges of lemon and lime

1. Combine the soft drink mix and the water in a large pitcher. Stir in the ginger ale and the wine, if using.
2. Add the ice cubes. Garnish with whole strawberries and wedges of lemon and lime threaded on a long skewer.

Easy Lemonade Punch

Ginger ale adds a new dimension to a lemonade drink.

Makes 8 servings.

Nutrient Value Per Serving: 136 calories, 1 g protein, 1 g fat, 32 g carbohydrate, 22 mg sodium, 3 mg cholesterol.

- 1 **envelope lemonade-flavor unsweetened soft drink mix**
- ½ **cup water**
- 2 **bottles (28 ounces each) ginger ale, chilled**
- 1 **pint lemon sherbet**

1. Combine the soft drink mix and the water in a small punch bowl. Stir in the ginger ale.
2. Just before serving, drop small scoops of the sherbet into the punch. Garnish with slices of lime, if you wish.

Florida Orange Punch

This easy punch recipe is versatile too; try it with different soft drink mix flavors.

Makes 8 servings.

Nutrient Value Per Serving: 1 calorie, 0 g protein, 0 g fat, 0 g carbohydrate, 38 mg sodium, 0 mg cholesterol.

- 1 **envelope orange-flavor unsweetened soft drink mix**
- ½ **cup water**
- 2 **bottles (28 ounces each) club soda, chilled**
  Fruited Ice Cubes (recipe follows)

1. Combine the soft drink mix and water in a small punch bowl. Stir in the club soda.
2. Just before serving, add the Fruited Ice Cubes.

Fruited Ice Cubes: Fill an ice cube tray with cold water. In each compartment, place a single piece of fruit, such as a maraschino cherry, raspberry, blueberry or strawberry. Freeze.

Orange Blossom

Gin or vodka blend so well with orange juice in an early day cocktail.

Makes 8 servings.

Nutrient Value Per Serving: 195 calories, 1 g protein, 0 g fat, 18 g carbohydrate, 10 mg sodium, 0 mg cholesterol.

- 1 **quart orange juice, chilled**
- 1½ **cups gin or vodka**
- ½ **cup triple sec**
- 1 **can (12 ounces) club soda**
  Ice cubes

Combine the orange juice and gin or vodka, triple sec and club soda in a large pitcher. Add the ice cubes and pour into stemmed glasses. Serve the drink at once.

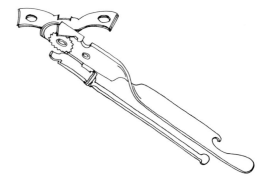

Mimosa

Champagne and orange juice team in a sprightly brunch beverage.

Makes 8 servings.

Nutrient Value Per Serving: 134 calories, 1 g protein, 0 g fat, 17 g carbohydrate, 6 mg sodium, 0 mg cholesterol.

- 1 **quart orange juice, chilled**
- 1 **bottle (750 ml) champagne, chilled**
  Ice cubes

Combine the orange juice and champagne in a large pitcher. Add the ice cubes and pour into stemmed glasses.

Sangria Tea-Light

Lemon-flavored sugar-free iced tea mix adds flavor, not calories, to a refreshing beverage.

Makes 6 servings.

Nutrient Value Per Serving: 88 calories, 1 g protein, 0 g fat, 12 g carbohydrate, 15 mg sodium, 0 mg cholesterol.

1   **bottle (4/5 quart) light rosé wine**
¼   **cup lemon-flavored sugar-free iced tea mix**
1   **cup sliced strawberries**
1   **medium-size orange, sliced**
2   **cups club soda, chilled**

1. Combine the wine, iced tea mix, strawberries and sliced orange in a large pitcher; stir until well blended.
2. At serving time, add the chilled club soda to the pitcher. Pour the wine mixture over ice cubes in 6 tall glasses.

Wake-Up Whirl

Tea for breakfast? Try this slushy version made with yogurt, orange juice and ice cubes.

Makes 6 servings.

Nutrient Value Per Serving: 106 calories, 4 g protein, 1 g fat, 20 g carbohydrate, 51 mg sodium, 4 mg cholesterol.

¼   **cup lemon-flavored sugar-free iced tea mix**
2   **containers (8 ounces each) vanilla yogurt**
2   **cups orange juice**
2   **cups ice cubes (12 to 16)**

1. Combine 2 tablespoons of the iced tea mix, 1 container of the yogurt and 1 cup of the orange juice in the container of an electric blender; whirl at high speed until blended.
2. Add 1 cup of the ice cubes, one at a time; whirl at high speed until blended. Repeat with the remaining ingredients.

Mangoade

For a pleasing change-of-pace, treat yourself or the kids to this non-alcoholic mango drink from Jamaica.

Makes 4 servings.

Nutrient Value Per Serving: 82 calories, 1 g protein, 0 g fat, 21 g carbohydrate, 17 mg sodium, 21 mg cholesterol.

1   **can (12 ounces) mango nectar**
1   **cup orange juice, preferably freshly squeezed**
3   **tablespoons lime juice (1½ limes)**
2   **teaspoons lemon juice**
1   **bottle (7 ounces) club soda**
    Lemon and lime slices for garnish (optional)

Combine the mango nectar, orange juice, lime and lemon juices in a 1½-quart pitcher with ice. Add the club soda. Stir lightly and garnish with lemon and lime slices, if you wish. Serve immediately.

O·U·R F·A·V·O·R·I·T·E
D·E·S·S·E·R·T·S

This is our idea of a terrific dessert buffet: Cranberry-Apple Tart (page 167); Individual Open-Faced Pear Tarts with Red Wine Sauce (page 173); Mini Ricotta-Fruit Tartlets (page 178); Cassis Sherbet Ring with Gingered Fruit (page 210).

5

Whether you are looking for a "knock-the-socks-off-them" finale, easy make-aheads, cooling desserts or sweets that will double as gifts, you'll find it among our favorites in this chapter. If you are really watching calories, limit desserts to one or two a week, keep the portions small and take a look at "Sweets" in Chapter 6.

As American as apple pie — our pie selection is just that, from New England Apple Pie *(page 168)* to the unusual Cranberry-Apple Tart *(page 167)*. If America loves pies, then it's crazy about cheesecake, and there's no better than our rich Oreo Cheesecake *(page 181),* except maybe the Creamy Cranraspberry-Glazed Cheesecake *(page 188).*

When it comes to cookies, homemade still ranks #1. Make them as elaborate as Eight-Layer Shortbread Slices *(page 194),* or as simple and homey as Lemon Snowflake Cookies with Lemon Icing *(page 199).*

Cold desserts conjure up summertime, but something cool is scrumptious after a warm, wintery meal. At holiday time, try mincemeat in a different guise, Brandied Mincemeat Ice Cream Ring with Custard Sauce *(page 211).* Or end with the unexpected: a Pumpkin Ice Cream Cake *(page 209)* or Cassis Sherbet Ring with Gingered Fruit *(page 210).*

Or try this idea: Make several desserts, invite the gang, and serve a dessert buffet!

T·A·R·T·S A·N·D P·I·E·S

Scrumptious Cranberry-Apple Tart

Cranberry-Apple Tart

An apple adds just a touch of sweetness to the cranberry filling.

Bake the tart shell at 375° for 12 to 15 minutes; bake the meringue at 400° for 3 to 6 minutes. Makes 8 servings.

Nutrient Value Per Serving: 485 calories, 6 g protein, 19 g fat, 75 g carbohydrate, 150 mg sodium, 99 mg cholesterol.

Cranberry Filling:
- ¼ **cup water**
- ¾ **cup sugar**
- ½ **cup red currant jelly**
- 3 **cups fresh or frozen cranberries (12-ounce package)**
- 1 **apple, preferably Yellow Delicious, peeled, cored and chopped (1 cup)**

Tart Shell:
- ½ **cup (1 stick) butter**
- 1¼ **cups all-purpose flour**
- ¼ **cup sugar**
- ⅔ **cup finely chopped or ground walnuts**
- ½ **teaspoon ground cinnamon**
- 2 **egg yolks**

Meringue:
- 4 **egg whites**
- ⅛ **teaspoon cream of tartar**
- ½ **cup sugar**

1. Prepare the Cranberry Filling: Combine the water, sugar and jelly in a medium-size saucepan. Heat to melt the jelly and dissolve the sugar. Bring the mixture to boiling; add the cranberries and the apple. Cook, uncovered, over medium heat until the cranberries pop and the mixture thickens slightly, for 10 to 15 minutes. Cool completely.
2. Prepare the Tart Shell: Cut the butter into the flour in a medium-size bowl with a pastry blender until crumbly. Mix in the sugar, nuts and cinnamon. Add the egg yolks; mix lightly with a fork just until the pastry holds together and cleans the side of the bowl. Press the dough over the bottom and up the side of a 9-inch tart pan with a removable bottom. Prick the bottom all over with a fork. Refrigerate the tart shell for 30 minutes.
3. Preheat the oven to moderate (375°).
4. Bake the tart shell in the preheated moderate oven (375°) for 12 to 15 minutes or until golden. Cool the tart shell completely.
5. Spoon the cooled Cranberry Filling into the cooled pastry shell.
6. Preheat the oven to hot (400°).
7. Prepare the Meringue: Beat the egg whites with the cream of tartar in a medium-size bowl until soft peaks form. Gradually beat in the ½ cup sugar until stiff, but not dry, peaks form. Spread half the meringue over the top of the tart. Pipe the remaining meringue in a lattice pattern over the top.
8. Place the tart in the preheated hot oven (400°) for 3 to 6 minutes or until the meringue is golden brown. Decorate the top with additional cranberries, if you wish.

Food for thought . . .

Cranberries really are an American tradition. The early settlers of New England witnessed Indians eating cranberries, both raw and cooked. The tart flavor of the cranberry was probably appealing to the Pilgrims since they had no sugar from the West Indies at that point and were used to many foods in their diet with sharp flavor. A good source of vitamin C, cranberries were packed in barrels and taken on colonial ships during long voyages to prevent scurvy and rickets. In the early 1800s, cranberries were exported to Europe as a delicacy. The word cranberry itself may come from a German or Dutch word meaning an area where cranes and other waterfowl feed — a bog or marsh.

New England Apple Pie

Bake at 400° for 50 to 60 minutes.
Makes 8 servings.

Nutrient Value Per Serving: 555 calories, 5 g protein, 27 g fat, 75 g carbohydrate, 520 mg sodium, 3 mg cholesterol.

> 3 **cups unbleached all-purpose flour**
> 2 **teaspoons baking powder**
> 1½ **teaspoons salt**
> 6 **tablespoons ice water**
> 1 **cup vegetable shortening**
> 2½ **pounds tart apples (about 5 large), such as Baldwin or Granny Smith**
> ⅔ **to 1 cup sugar, to taste**
> ¼ **teaspoon ground cinnamon**
> ¼ **teaspoon ground nutmeg**
> 1 **tablespoon heavy cream**

1. Combine the flour, baking powder and salt in a medium-size bowl; stir to mix the dry ingredients well. Remove ½ cup of the mixture to a small bowl; mix with the ice water until smooth. Cut the shortening into the remaining flour mixture in a medium-size bowl until the mixture resembles coarse meal; mix in the flour-water mixture until well blended. Shape the dough into a ball. Wrap the dough in wax paper. Refrigerate the dough while preparing the apple filling.
2. Quarter the apples. Core, peel and slice the apples into a large bowl. Reserve.
3. Combine the sugar, cinnamon and nutmeg in a small bowl.
4. Preheat the oven to hot (400°).
5. Divide the pastry in half. Roll out each half between 2 pieces of wax paper into 11-inch circles. Fit one circle into a 9-inch pie plate. Add half the apples; sprinkle the apples with the sugar mixture. Top with the remaining apple slices. Moisten the edge of the pastry with water. Cover the top of the pie with the second pastry circle. Press the edges together. Trim the pastry and shape the edge as desired. Prick the top crust with the tines of a fork. Brush the top with the cream.
6. Bake the pie in the preheated hot oven (400°) for 50 to 60 minutes or until the apples are tender. Cool the pie on a wire rack. Serve the pie warm or cold.

Note: If the top browns too quickly, cover the top loosely with a sheet of aluminum foil.

GIVE YOUR PIES A PERFECT EDGING

Scalloped Edge: Place your left thumb and forefinger on the outside of the rim. With a teaspoon, press the inside of the rim between your fingers, forming a large, rounded scallop. Repeat about every inch around the pastry rim.

Rope Edge: Press the pie rim firmly between the thumb and forefinger of your right hand, pressing down, toward the right, with your thumb. Continue pressing, turning the pie clockwise as you do, until the entire rim is finished.

Note: Lefthanded people should reverse hands.

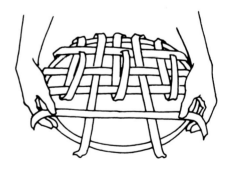

Lattice Top: Roll the remaining half of the Flaky Pastry dough or other dough being used to a 12 x 8-inch rectangle. Cut lengthwise into ½-inch strips. Weave into a lattice over the pie filling. Trim the overhang even with the bottom crust. Pinch to seal the edge. Turn the sealed edge *under*. Pinch again to make a stand-up edge; flute. **Note:** You may find it easier to weave the lattice on a piece of wax paper or heavy-duty aluminum foil, then flop it over the filling. Also, a pastry wheel will make pretty, unusually shaped lattice strips.

Cool and creamy Mint Mist Pie. (It's a cinch to make!)

Mint Mist Pie

Makes 6 servings.

Nutrient Value Per Serving: 655 calories, 12 g protein, 37 g fat, 73 g carbohydrate, 423 mg sodium, 75 mg cholesterol.

---

1 **package (8 ounces) cream cheese, softened**
1 **can (14 ounces) sweetened condensed milk**
1 **teaspoon mint extract**
    Few drops green food coloring (optional)
1 **container (8 ounces) nondairy whipped topping**
²⁄₃ **cup miniature chocolate pieces**
1 **packaged ready-to-use (no-bake) 8-inch pie crumb crust**

1. Beat the cream cheese in a medium-size bowl until light and fluffy. Gradually beat in the condensed milk, mint extract and food coloring, if using. Beat the mixture until smooth.
2. Gently fold in the whipped topping with a rubber spatula. Fold in the chocolate pieces. Spoon the filling into the piecrust. Place the pie in the freezer until hardened, for at least 8 hours or overnight.
3. Remove the pie from the freezer 5 minutes before serving. Garnish the pie with chocolate pieces and mint leaves, if you wish.

PREVENT OVERBROWNING

If the pastry of a pie edge is browning too quickly,
cover it with strips of aluminum foil.

Caramel Cashew Cream Pie

Toast cashews at 400° for 12 to 15 minutes;
bake pie at 400° for 25 minutes.
Makes 8 servings.

Nutrient Value Per Serving: 670 calories, 10 g protein, 52 g fat,
46 g carbohydrate, 184 mg sodium, 127 mg cholesterol.

2	**cups whole raw cashews* (about two 5-ounce packages)**
¾	**cup sugar**
3	**tablespoons butter**
1	**cup heavy cream**
1	**egg**
1	**teaspoon vanilla**
½	**of 11-ounce package piecrust mix, made into 9-inch pie shell and partially baked following label directions**

Topping:
1 **cup heavy cream**
1 **teaspoon vanilla**
2 **tablespoons sugar**

1. Toast the cashews on a cookie sheet in a preheated hot oven (400°) for 12 to 15 minutes, stirring occasionally so the nuts brown evenly. Reserve the nuts; leave the oven at 400°.
2. Combine ½ cup of the sugar and the butter in a heavy-bottomed 2-quart saucepan. Place the saucepan over medium-high heat, stirring occasionally with a metal spoon, until the mixture turns golden and caramelizes, for 3 to 4 minutes; do not let the mixture burn. Remove the saucepan from the heat.
3. Stir in 1½ cups of the toasted cashews and ½ cup of the cream. Stir over low heat until the caramel has dissolved into the cream and the mixture is smooth, for about 1 minute. Remove from the heat again. Measure out ½ cup of the caramel-cashew mixture; reserve for the garnish.
4. Place the remaining ½ cup of the toasted cashews and the ¼ cup sugar in the container of an electric blender or a food processor. Cover; whirl until the mixture is ground very fine. Add the egg, the remaining ½ cup cream and the vanilla. Blend to combine. Briefly stir the custard mixture into the caramel-cashew mixture in the saucepan to create a slightly marbled effect. Pour the mixture into the pie shell.
5. Bake the pie in the preheated hot oven (400°) for 25 minutes or until the custard is set. Cool the pie on a wire rack for 30 minutes.
6. Mound the reserved ½ cup caramel-cashew mixture onto the center of the pie. If the mixture is too thick to mound, warm briefly in the top of a double boiler over hot water, then mound on the pie. Refrigerate the pie for several hours.
7. When the pie is thoroughly chilled, prepare the Topping: Beat together the cream, vanilla and sugar in a small bowl until stiff. Decorate the pie with the Topping, using a pastry bag fitted with a large star tip or by spreading with a metal spatula, around the cashew garnish in the center. Refrigerate the pie until ready to serve.

Note: Raw cashews can be found in health food stores or specialty food shops.

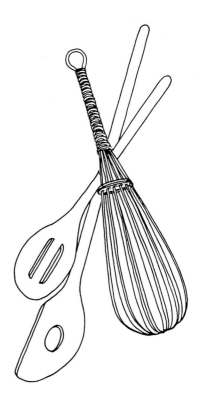

Food for thought . . .

Vanilla flavoring has been around for a long time. A physician to King Philip II of Spain in the 16th century described the spicing of drinks with vanilla fruit and the vanilla pod that came from New Spain. He believed vanilla had properties as a brain tonic and an antidote against poisonous bites. The vanilla bean is the fruit of a pale yellow orchid native to Mexico, but now also grown in Madagascar, Island of Reunion and Comores, Tahiti and Java. The fruit, when harvested, resembles a green bean. It is then dried and covered to induce fermentation. The process is repeated until the bean turns dark brown. The whole curing and drying process takes about 6 months. Vanilla extract is extracted or percolated from the bean with alcohol and water.

Favorite Fruit Pie

An easy, make-ahead frozen pie.

Makes 6 servings.

Nutrient Value Per Serving: 327 calories, 6 g protein, 9 g fat, 58 g carbohydrate, 268 mg sodium, 10 mg cholesterol.

  1 **can (11 ounces) mandarin oranges, drained**
  1 **can (16 ounces) pitted tart red cherries, drained**
  1 **ripe banana, peeled and diced**
  ¼ **cup flaked coconut**
  1 **large container (16 ounces) vanilla yogurt**
  1 **packaged ready-to-use (no-bake) 8-inch pie crust**

1. Gently fold together the oranges, cherries, banana, coconut and yogurt in a large bowl. Pour the filling into the piecrust. Place the pie in the freezer until hardened, for at least 8 hours or overnight.
2. Remove the pie from the freezer to soften 1 hour before serving.

Heavenly Pineapple Pie

Makes 6 servings.

Nutrient Value Per Serving: 528 calories, 5 g protein, 35 g fat, 50 g carbohydrate, 570 mg sodium, 103 mg cholesterol.

  1 **cup heavy cream**
  1 **can (20 ounces) crushed pineapple in heavy syrup**
  1 **package (8 ounces) cream cheese, softened**
  1 **package (3¾ ounces or 4-serving size) instant vanilla pudding and pie filling**
  1 **packaged ready-to-use (no-bake) 8-inch pie crumb crust**

1. Whip the cream in a small bowl until stiff. Refrigerate.
2. Drain the pineapple, reserving the juice.
3. Beat together the cream cheese, the reserved pineapple juice and the vanilla pudding in a medium-size bowl until smooth.
4. Gently fold the crushed pineapple and the whipped cream into the pudding mixture. Spoon the filling into the piecrust. Place the pie in the freezer until hardened, for at least 8 hours or overnight.
5. Remove the pie from the freezer to soften 1 hour before serving.

Mocha Pie

Makes 6 servings.

Nutrient Value Per Serving: 317 calories, 6 g protein, 12 g fat, 48 g carbohydrate, 379 mg sodium, 7 mg cholesterol.

- 1   **package (3¼ ounces) butterscotch pudding and pie filling**
- ¼   **cup sugar**
- 1   **teaspoon instant coffee granules**
- 1½ **cups (13-ounce can) evaporated milk**
- 2   **tablespoons orange juice**
- 1   **packaged ready-to-use (no-bake) 8-inch pie crumb crust**

1. Mix together the pudding, sugar and coffee granules in a small saucepan. Add ½ cup of the evaporated milk. Bring the mixture to boiling, stirring constantly, over medium heat. Cook for 1 minute. Pour the mixture into a medium-size bowl. Cover the surface of the pudding mixture with wax paper or plastic wrap to prevent a skin from forming. Set the pudding mixture aside in the refrigerator to cool, for about 30 minutes.
2. Meanwhile, pour the remaining 1 cup of evaporated milk into a shallow dish. Place the dish in the freezer until soft ice crystals form around the edge, for about 20 to 30 minutes. Transfer the mixture to a small bowl and beat until soft peaks form. Add the 2 tablespoons orange juice. Beat until stiff peaks form.
3. Gently fold about 1 cup of the whipped evaporated milk mixture into the pudding; fold in the remaining whipped evaporated milk mixture. Spoon the filling into the piecrust. Place the pie in the freezer until hardened, for at least 8 hours or overnight.
4. Remove the pie from the freezer about 5 minutes before serving.

Special Strawberry Pie

Makes 6 servings.

Nutrient Value Per Serving: 511 calories, 6 g protein, 28 g fat, 62 g carbohydrate, 337 mg sodium, 65 mg cholesterol.

- 1   **package (8 ounces) cream cheese, softened**
- ½   **cup sugar**
- 1   **cup dairy sour cream**
- 2   **packages (10 ounces each) quick-thaw strawberries, thawed and drained**
- 1   **packaged ready-to-use (no-bake) 8-inch pie crumb crust**

1. Beat together the cream cheese and the sugar in a medium-size bowl until light and fluffy. Gently fold in the sour cream and the strawberries. Pour the mixture into the piecrust. Place the pie in the freezer until hardened, for at least 8 hours or overnight.
2. Remove the pie from the freezer to soften 1 hour before serving.

Luscious Lemon Pie

Makes 6 servings.

Nutrient Value Per Serving: 286 calories, 6 g protein, 10 g fat, 45 g carbohydrate, 291 mg sodium, 7 mg cholesterol.

- 1   **package (3 ounces) lemon-flavored gelatin**
- ¼   **cup sugar**
- ½   **cup boiling water**
- 4   **tablespoons fresh lemon juice**
- 1   **cup evaporated milk**
- 1   **tablespoon grated lemon rind**
- 1   **packaged ready-to-use (no-bake) 8-inch pie crumb crust**

1. Add the gelatin and sugar to the boiling water in a small bowl. Stir until the sugar and gelatin are completely dissolved. Add 2 tablespoons of the lemon juice. Set the gelatin mixture aside in the refrigerator until chilled and thickened to the consistency of unbeaten egg whites, for about 45 to 60 minutes.
2. Meanwhile, pour the evaporated milk into a shallow dish. Place the dish in the freezer until soft ice crystals form around the edge, for about 20 to 30 minutes. Transfer the mixture to a medium-size mixer bowl and beat until soft peaks form. Add the remaining 2 tablespoons of lemon juice to the evaporated milk and beat until stiff peaks form.

3. Gently fold the gelatin mixture and the lemon rind into the whipped evaporated milk mixture. Spoon the filling into the piecrust. Place the pie in the freezer until hardened, for at least 8 hours or overnight.
4. Remove the pie from the freezer to soften 1 hour before serving.

Clever Chocolate Pie

Chocolate and chocolate chip ice creams are layered with a rich chocolate sauce.

Makes 6 servings.

Nutrient Value Per Serving: 536 calories, 6 g protein, 34 g fat, 57 g carbohydrate, 287 mg sodium, 74 mg cholesterol.

½ **cup heavy cream**
1 **package (6 ounces) semisweet chocolate pieces**
1 **teaspoon vanilla**
1 **pint chocolate ice cream, slightly softened**
1 **packaged ready-to-use (no-bake) 8-inch pie crumb crust**
1 **pint chocolate chip ice cream, slightly softened**

1. Heat the cream in a small saucepan until bubbles appear around the edge of the saucepan. Remove the saucepan from the heat. Add the chocolate pieces; stir until the chocolate is melted and the mixture is smooth. Stir in the vanilla. Set the chocolate sauce aside in the refrigerator to cool and thicken, for about 15 to 20 minutes.
2. Spoon the chocolate ice cream evenly into the piecrust. Place in the freezer for about 20 minutes to harden. Spoon about two-thirds of the chocolate sauce over the top. Place in the freezer for about 20 minutes to harden.
3. Spoon the chocolate chip ice cream over the top of the sauce. Place in the freezer for about 20 minutes to harden. Drizzle the remaining chocolate sauce over the top of the pie. Freeze the pie until hardened, for at least 8 hours or overnight.
4. Remove the pie from the freezer to soften 30 minutes before serving.

Pear Tarts with Red Wine Sauce

Individual Open-Faced Pear Tarts with Red Wine Sauce

Poach the pears and prepare the sauce ahead of time, then assemble and bake the tarts just before serving.

Bake at 425° for 10 to 15 minutes.
Makes 6 servings.

Nutrient Value Per Serving: 382 calories, 3 g protein, 11 g fat, 72 g carbohydrate, 182 mg sodium, 0 mg cholesterol.

2 **cups hearty red wine, such as a California Zinfandel**
1 **cup sugar**
½ **lemon, quartered**
1 **cinnamon stick**
1 **cup water, approximately**
6 **firm-ripe Bosc or Bartlett pears, with stems attached (2½ to 3 pounds)**
8 **ounces frozen puff pastry (½ of 17¼-ounce package)**

1. In a non-aluminum saucepan just large enough to hold the pears, combine the wine, sugar, lemon, cinnamon stick and water. Bring the mixture slowly to boiling, stirring to dissolve the sugar.
2. Peel the pears, leaving the stems on. Add to the wine mixture. Add water, if necessary, so the pears are covered by the liquid. Simmer the pears, covered, for 20 to 30 minutes or until the pears are just tender. Transfer the pears with a slotted spoon to a shallow bowl. Cool the pears. Discard the lemon and the cinnamon stick.
3. Cook the remaining syrup in the saucepan over high heat, uncovered, until the syrup is reduced to ¾ to 1 cup. Refrigerate the pears and the syrup, separately, covered, until ready to bake.

4. When ready to bake, thaw and unfold the pastry, following the package directions.
5. Preheat the oven to hot (425°).
6. Roll the pastry out to a 12-inch square. Using the pear as a guide, cut out 6 pear-shapes from the pastry, each about ½ inch larger than the pear. Place the pastry cutouts 2 inches apart on a large ungreased cookie sheet. Cut 2x¼-inch strips from the scraps for stems. Attach the stems to the tops of the pear cutouts with a little water. Cut leaf shapes from the remaining scraps, if you wish.
7. Trim about one-third of each pear, lengthwise along the side. Remove the cores. Place the pears flat on a cutting board. Starting about ¾ inch below the stem, make 8 evenly spaced lengthwise cuts through each pear. Fan out the slices gently. Place one pear on each pastry cutout.
8. Bake the tarts in the preheated hot oven (425°) along with the leaf cutouts, if making, for 10 to 15 minutes or until the pastry is puffed and golden. Place the tarts on dessert plates. Brush the pears with some of the reserved wine sauce. Serve the tarts warm with the remaining sauce.

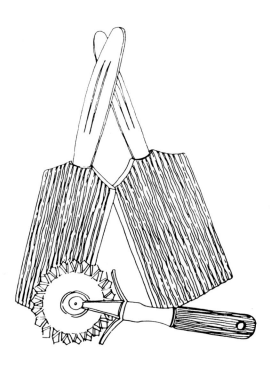

Sinfully good Pecan Tartlets.

Pecan Tartlets

These tartlets are addictive. They are especially easy to serve for dessert after an elaborate dinner, since they can be prepared several days ahead.

Bake at 350° for 25 to 30 minutes.
Makes 24 tartlets.

Nutrient Value Per Tartlet: 128 calories, 1 g protein, 9 g fat, 10 g carbohydrate, 47 mg sodium, 28 mg cholesterol.

Cream Cheese Pastry:
1 **cup unsifted all-purpose flour**
½ **cup (1 stick) unsalted butter, slightly softened**
1 **package (3 ounces) cream cheese, softened**
¼ **teaspoon salt**

Pecan Filling:
1 **egg, slightly beaten**
½ **cup Lyle's Golden Syrup OR: dark corn syrup**
⅓ **cup firmly packed dark brown sugar**
2 **tablespoons unsalted butter, melted**
1 **teaspoon vanilla**
   Pinch salt
1 **cup coarsely broken pecans (4 ounces)**
   Chocolate Topping (optional; recipe follows)

1. Preheat the oven to moderate (350°).
2. Prepare the Cream Cheese Pastry: Blend together the flour, butter, cream cheese and salt in a large bowl with a mixer or your fingertips until well blended and the dough forms a ball. Divide the dough into 24 equal pieces. Roll each piece into a ball. Press the pieces into small brioche pans or mini-muffin tins. If the dough gets too soft, chill briefly. Use floured fingers to press the dough up against the sides of the tins. Be careful not to let the tin show since the filling will stick.
3. Prepare the Pecan Filling: Combine the egg, syrup, sugar, butter, vanilla and salt in a medium-size bowl; stir together until well blended. Stir in the pecans. Spoon the filling into the pastry-lined tins. The filling should come almost to the top of the tins, but not touch any of the exposed area.
4. Bake the tartlets in the preheated moderate oven (350°) for 25 to 30 minutes or until the filling is set but the center is still soft. Cool the tartlets in the tins on wire racks. Loosen the sides with the tip of a knife, if necessary. Carefully unmold the tartlets.
5. Decorate the tartlets with drizzles of the Chocolate Topping, if you wish. Store in an airtight container at room temperature.

Chocolate Topping: Melt together 2 squares (1 ounce each) of semisweet chocolate and 2 teaspoons of flavorless oil in the top of a double boiler over hot, not simmering, water, stirring constantly, until the chocolate is melted. Use a parchment paper cone or a spoon to drizzle the chocolate over the top of the tartlets.

Apple Tart With Cranberries

Bake at 425° for 20 minutes; then at 400° for 15 minutes.
Makes 8 servings.

Nutrient Value Per Serving: 440 calories, 3 g protein, 22 g fat, 59 g carbohydrate, 341 mg sodium, 52 mg cholesterol.

- ¼ cup water
- 1 cup firmly packed light brown sugar
- 2 tablespoons butter
- 1 tablespoon quick-cooking tapioca
- 1 teaspoon ground ginger
- ½ teaspoon grated orange rind
- 2 cups cranberries
- 2 large Golden Delicious apples (about ¾ pound)
- 1 package (11 ounces) piecrust mix
- 1 tablespoon butter, softened
- 1 tablespoon sugar
- ½ teaspoon lemon juice
- 1 egg yolk combined with 1 tablespoon water

1. Combine the water, brown sugar, the 2 tablespoons butter, the tapioca, ginger and orange rind in a medium-size heavy saucepan. Bring the mixture to boiling; lower the heat and simmer, stirring frequently, until the sugar is dissolved, for 3 to 4 minutes. Add ½ cup of the cranberries; simmer until the berries pop, for 3 to 4 minutes. Remove the cranberries with a slotted spoon to a bowl; reserve.
2. Meanwhile, peel, core and finely chop one of the apples. Add with the remaining 1½ cups cranberries to the simmering mixture in the saucepan. Simmer until thickened, for about 15 minutes. Remove to a bowl. Cool.
3. Prepare the piecrust mix, following the directions for a double-crust 9-inch pie. Roll one-half of the dough into a 10-inch circle. Fit into the bottom of a 9-inch tart pan with a removable bottom.
4. Peel, halve, core and slice the remaining apple lengthwise into ¼-inch-thick slices.
5. Fill the tart shell with the cranberry-apple mixture. Arrange the apple slices, slightly overlapping, in concentric circles over the top of the tart. Arrange the reserved popped cranberries between the apple slices.
6. To glaze the apples, combine the softened butter, sugar and lemon juice in a small bowl. Brush the glaze over the apple slices.
7. Preheat the oven to hot (425°). Place the oven rack in the bottom third of the oven.

8. Roll out the second half of the dough into a 9-inch circle. Cut the circle into eight ½-inch-wide strips and three ¾-inch-wide strips. Brush the top edge of the pan with water. Weave the ½-inch strips in a lattice design over the top. Place the ¾-inch strips around the edge of the pan, trimming to fit but with the ends slightly overlapping. Brush the egg yolk glaze over the pastry.

9. Bake the tart in the bottom third of the preheated hot oven (425°) for 20 minutes. Lower the oven temperature to 400°. Bake for 15 minutes or until the apples are tender. If the pastry browns too quickly, cover the sides loosely with aluminum foil. Cool the tart on a wire rack. Remove the side of the pan to serve.

Apple Tart with Cranberries (page 175).

Apple-Nut Tortes

Bake at 350° for 25 to 30 minutes.
Makes 8 servings.

Nutrient Value Per Serving: 259 calories, 5 g protein, 11 g fat, 37 g carbohydrate, 89 mg sodium, 69 mg cholesterol.

2   **large cooking apples (¾ to 1 pound), such as Cortland, Golden Delicious, Jonathan**
⅔   **cup plus 1½ tablespoons sugar**
¼   **teaspoon ground cinnamon**
2   **eggs**
1   **teaspoon vanilla**
¾   **cup unsifted all-purpose flour**
1   **teaspoon baking powder**
    Pinch salt
1   **cup chopped walnuts (4 ounces), lightly toasted**
    Whipped cream

1. Preheat the oven to moderate (350°). Grease and lightly flour eight 6-ounce custard cups.
2. Peel, core and cut the apples into ½-inch dice; you should have about 2 cups.
3. Combine the 1½ tablespoons sugar and the cinnamon with the apples in a medium-size bowl; toss to mix.
4. Combine the eggs, the ⅔ cup sugar and the vanilla in a large bowl. Beat with an electric mixer at low speed until the ingredients are combined. Then beat at high speed until the mixture is very thick and pale, for about 5 minutes.
5. Sift together the flour, baking powder and salt onto a piece of wax paper. Sift the ingredients together again. Fold lightly into the egg mixture.
6. Fold the apple mixture and the chopped nuts into the batter. Turn the batter into the prepared custard cups. Place the cups on a baking sheet.
7. Bake the tortes in the preheated moderate oven (350°) for 25 to 30 minutes or until the tops are crispy. Serve the tortes with a dollop of the whipped cream.

Apple-Nut Torte

WHIPPING HEAVY CREAM

Whipping cream is very straightforward, unless the weather is very warm or the cream has been allowed to reach room temperature. For the best results, place the bowl and the electric beaters in the freezer for 30 minutes before whipping the cream. If it is very warm, also place the cream in the freezer until cold, but not frozen. Beat the cream at medium speed with an electric mixer. If sweetening the cream with sugar, add the sugar after the cream has thickened slightly.

A must with coffee: Mini Ricotta-Fruit Tartlets.

Mini Ricotta-Fruit Tartlets

The tartlet shells and the filling can be prepared ahead of time, and then assembled just before serving.

Bake at 400° for 10 to 12 minutes.
Makes about 24 tartlets.

Nutrient Value Per Tartlet: 101 calories, 2 g protein, 4 g fat, 14 g carbohydrate, 44 mg sodium, 21 mg cholesterol.

6   **tablespoons butter**
3   **tablespoons sugar**
1   **egg yolk**
1   **teaspoon grated lemon rind**
1   **cup unsifted all-purpose flour**
Ricotta Filling:
¾   **cup ricotta cheese**
¼   **cup 10X (confectioners') sugar**
2   **tablespoons finely chopped mixed candied fruits**
¼   **square (1 ounce square) semisweet chocolate, chopped**
1   **tablespoon Grand Marnier OR: other orange-flavored liqueur**
    Assorted fresh fruit such as strawberries, blueberries, raspberries, banana, kiwi, orange
½   **cup apricot preserves, warmed and strained**
3   **tablespoons chopped pistachio nuts**

1. Beat together the butter, sugar and the egg yolk in a small bowl until the mixture is light and fluffy. Stir in the lemon rind. Stir in the flour, blending well to make a soft dough. Wrap the dough and refrigerate for 1 hour.
2. When ready to bake, preheat the oven to hot (400°).
3. Press 1 to 2 teaspoons of the dough into 1½- to 2-inch tartlet pans. Place the pans on cookie sheets.
4. Bake the tartlet shells in the preheated hot oven (400°) for 10 to 12 minutes or until golden. Cool the tartlet shells in the pans for 5 minutes. Gently loosen the tartlets from the pans with the tip of a knife. Remove the shells to wire racks to cool completely. The tartlet shells can be prepared several days ahead and stored at room temperature in a tightly covered container.
5. Prepare the Ricotta Filling: Combine the ricotta cheese, 10X sugar, candied fruit, chocolate and Grand Marnier in a small bowl; mix until well blended. Refrigerate the filling, covered, until ready to use.
6. To serve, fill each tartlet shell with 1 to 2 teaspoons of the ricotta filling. Arrange whole or cut-up fruits on top of the filling. Brush the tops with apricot preserves. Sprinkle the edges of the tartlet shells with the nuts.

BAKING PIE PASTRY BLIND

The crust for a pie or tart is sometimes partially or completely baked before the filling is added. To bake the crust blind, line the pie or tart pan with the dough. Prick the dough all over with a fork to prevent bubbling or blistering. Line the pastry with parchment paper or wax paper. Fill with dried beans or rice to weigh down the dough. Bake the dough until it no longer has a raw, shiny appearance. Remove the paper and the beans and return the shell to the oven to dry further. For a shell that needs to be completely baked, bake longer until a golden brown.

LEMON JUICE

1 medium-size lemon = 2 tablespoons lemon juice
1 medium-size lemon = 2 teaspoons grated lemon rind

Pure heaven: Pear Tarte Elegante.

Pear Tarte Elegante

Bake crust at 375° for 10 minutes; then tarte at 375° for 25 to 35 minutes more.
Makes 8 servings.

Nutrient Value Per Serving: 328 calories, 6 g protein, 20 g fat, 34 g carbohydrate, 157 mg sodium, 115 mg cholesterol.

Pastry:
- ¼ **cup (½ stick) butter or margarine, softened**
- 2 **tablespoons sugar**
- ½ **teaspoon grated lemon rind**
- ½ **teaspoon vanilla**
- 1 **egg yolk**
- ¾ **cup unsifted all-purpose flour**
- ¼ **cup finely ground blanched almonds**

Cream Cheese Filling:
- 1 **package (8 ounces) cream cheese, softened**
- 3 **tablespoons sugar**
- ½ **teaspoon grated lemon rind**
- ½ **teaspoon almond extract**
- 1 **egg**

- 5 **canned pear halves, well drained**
- 1 **cup strawberries, halved**
- ¼ **cup red currant jelly**

1. Preheat the oven to moderate (375°).
2. Prepare the Pastry: Combine the butter, sugar, lemon rind, vanilla and egg yolk in a small bowl; beat until well mixed. Add the flour and almonds; stir to mix well. Press the mixture into an even layer over the bottom and up the sides of a 9- or 10-inch quiche pan with a removable bottom.
3. Bake the tarte crust in the preheated moderate oven (375°) for 10 minutes. Remove the crust from the oven to a wire rack. Leave the oven on.
4. Prepare the Cream Cheese Filling: Combine the cream cheese, sugar, lemon rind, almond extract and egg in a small bowl; beat until smooth. Pour the filling into the pastry crust. Arrange the pears, cut-side down, over the filling.
5. Bake the tarte in the moderate oven (375°) for 25 to 35 minutes until the center of the filling is set. Remove the tarte to the wire rack to cool to room temperature. Refrigerate the tarte to chill.
6. Arrange the strawberries over the filling. Melt the jelly in a small saucepan. Spoon the jelly over the tarte. Remove the tarte from the pan.

C·A·K·E·S

Divine decadence: Oreo Cheesecake.

Oreo Cheesecake

Bake at 350° for 1 hour; let stand in turned-off oven for 1 hour.
Makes 12 servings.

Nutrient Value Per Serving: 492 calories, 7 g protein, 35 g fat, 36 g carbohydrate, 327 mg sodium, 194 mg cholesterol.

18 to 20 Oreo cookies
4 packages (8 ounces each) cream cheese, softened
1⅓ cups sugar
1½ teaspoons vanilla
2 teaspoons cornstarch
4 eggs
½ cup heavy cream

1. Preheat the oven to moderate (350°). Butter a 8 x 3-inch springform pan.
2. Trim one-third from each of 12 cookies; reserve the trimmings. Stand the 12 cookies, rounded-side up, around the inside of the pan. Cut the remaining cookies into quarters; combine with the reserved trimmings. Set aside.
3. Beat the cream cheese in the large bowl of an electric mixer at medium speed until smooth. Gradually beat in the sugar, vanilla and cornstarch, scraping down the side of the bowl frequently. Add the eggs, one at a time, beating well after each addition. Stir in the heavy cream.
4. Spoon about one-fourth of the cheese mixture into the prepared pan. Sprinkle one-third of the cookies over the mixture. Alternate layers of the cheese mixture and the cookies, ending with the cheese mixture. Wrap the bottom and the sides of the pan with a double layer of heavy-duty aluminum foil to prevent any leaking when the pan is placed in a water bath.
5. Set the cake pan in a large pan. Place the pan on the oven rack. Add hot water to the large pan to a depth of 1½ inches.
6. Bake the cake in the preheated moderate oven (350°) for 1 hour. Turn off the oven and leave the cake in the oven with the door closed, for 1 more hour.
7. Remove the cheesecake from the water bath to a wire rack to cool completely. Refrigerate, covered, for several hours or overnight.
8. To serve, remove the side of the pan. Decorate the cheesecake with whipped cream and additional cookie pieces, if you wish.

Food for thought . . .

Cheesecake is not a 20th century phenomenon invented in New York City. Greek philosophers and historians wrote much about cheesecake, and the Roman philosopher Cato even wrote down his favorite recipe for cheesecake. Ancient Sicily had its version of cheesecake, an affair similar to what we know as a cassata.

Wai-Aniwa Carrot Cake

Bake at 375° for 45 minutes; then at 350° for 30 minutes.
Makes 16 servings.

Nutrient Value Per Serving: 493 calories, 6 g protein, 27 g fat, 60 g carbohydrate, 278 mg sodium, 74 mg cholesterol.

1 pound carrots, peeled, cut into chunks
3 cups unsifted all-purpose flour
2 cups sugar
1 tablespoon baking soda
1½ teaspoons ground cinnamon
½ teaspoon salt
½ teaspoon ground cloves
½ teaspoon grated nutmeg
4 eggs
1¼ cups vegetable oil
¼ cup dark rum
2 teaspoons vanilla
1 cup walnuts, chopped
1 cup shredded coconut
½ cup golden raisins
1 can (8 ounces) crushed pineapple in pineapple juice, drained and juice reserved for glaze
Cream Cheese Glaze (recipe follows)

1. Steam the carrots in a medium-size saucepan until very tender. Cool the carrots to room temperature. Purée the carrots in a food processor; you should have about 1½ cups of purée. Set aside.
2. Place the oven rack in the lower third of the oven. Preheat the oven to moderate (375°). Grease and flour a 9- or 10-inch (12 cup) Bundt® pan.

3. Stir together the flour, sugar, baking soda, cinnamon, salt, cloves and nutmeg in a large bowl until well mixed.
4. Beat the eggs in a small bowl. Stir in the oil, rum, vanilla and carrots.
5. Pour the liquid ingredients into the flour mixture. Blend at low speed with an electric mixer until well mixed; then beat the batter at medium speed for 3 minutes, scraping down the side of the bowl occasionally. Stir in the walnuts, coconut, raisins and pineapple. Pour the batter into the prepared pan.
6. Bake the cake in the lower third of the preheated moderate oven (375°) for 45 minutes. Lower the oven temperature to 350°. Bake the cake for 30 minutes longer. Cool the cake in the pan on a wire rack for 15 minutes. Remove the cake from the pan; cool the cake on the wire rack to room temperature.
7. Prepare the Cream Cheese Glaze.
8. Place the cake on a serving plate. Spoon the glaze over the cake. Garnish the cake with pineapple and walnuts, if you wish.

Cream Cheese Glaze: Stir together 1 package (3 ounces) softened cream cheese and ⅔ cup *sifted* 10X sugar in a small bowl until smooth. Mix in 1 to 1½ tablespoons of the reserved pineapple juice until the cream cheese mixture is a good glazing consistency.

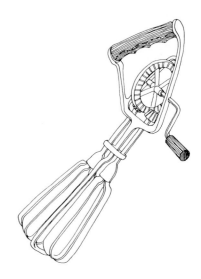

Wai-Aniwa Carrot Cake (page 181), packed with walnuts, coconut and raisins.

Food for thought . . .

Rum is a spirit distilled from molasses, a by-product from sugar refining. The first recorded mention of rum occurs in the early 1600s, in the West Indies, and it was a popular drink among both British and colonial sailors. Rum can be light colored, light bodied and very dry, or darker, amber-colored, with a full-bodied, rich flavor.

DOES YOUR BAKED CAKE HAVE AN UNEVEN TOP?

Using a long, sharp serrated knife, trim the top of the cake so it is even and straight. Then proceed with the frosting and decorating. (Save the scraps for munching or for making cake crumbs to be used in other desserts.)

Something special: Genoise á L'Orange.

Genoise A L'Orange

A light sponge cake flecked with orange rind and glazed with dark chocolate.

Bake at 350° for 30 minutes.
Makes 8 servings.

Nutrient Value Per Serving: 422 calories, 5 g protein, 24 g fat, 48 g carbohydrate, 43 mg sodium, 177 mg cholesterol.

Orange Sponge Cake:
 4 **eggs**
 ½ **cup sugar**
 ½ **cup sifted cake flour**
 ½ **cup sifted cornstarch**
 3 **tablespoons clarified brown butter***
 1 **tablespoon finely grated orange rind**
 1 **teaspoon vanilla**

Grand Marnier Syrup:
 ½ **cup water**
 ¼ **cup sugar**
 2 **to 3 tablespoons Grand Marnier OR: other orange-flavored liqueur**

Orange-Chocolate Glaze:
 7 **squares (1 ounce each) semisweet chocolate**
 ⅔ **cup heavy cream**
 1 **tablespoon plus 1 teaspoon Grand Marnier OR: other orange-flavored liqueur**
 ⅓ **cup toasted sliced almonds (optional)**

1. Preheat the oven to moderate (350°). Grease and flour a 9-inch springform pan; tap out the excess flour.
2. Prepare the Orange Sponge Cake: Combine the eggs and sugar in a large mixing bowl. Place the bowl in the top of a saucepan of simmering water; make sure the bottom of the bowl doesn't touch the water. Heat the mixture, stirring constantly with a whisk, just until lukewarm. Remove the bowl from the saucepan. Beat the egg mixture with an electric mixer on high speed until tripled in volume, for about 5 minutes.
3. Sift together the flour and cornstarch onto a piece of wax paper. Heat the clarified butter in a saucepan until warm. Add the orange rind and the vanilla to the butter.
4. Remove 1 cup of the beaten egg mixture to a small bowl. Whisk in the melted butter mixture. Set aside.
5. Lightly sprinkle the flour mixture over the beaten egg mixture in the large mixing bowl. Gently but rapidly fold in the flour just until the flour has disappeared. Fold in the reserved butter mixture just until incorporated. Pour the batter immediately into the prepared pan.
6. Bake the cake in the preheated moderate oven (350°) for 30 minutes or until the cake is golden brown and starts to shrink slightly from the side of the pan. Do not open the oven door during the baking as the cake could fall. Toward the end of the baking time, open the oven door slightly, and if at a quick glance it does not appear done, close the door at once, gently. Check again in 5 minutes. A wooden pick inserted in the center should come out clean.
7. When the cake is done, remove from the oven. Run a spatula around the side of the cake. Remove the side of the springform pan and remove the cake to a greased wire rack to cool. Wrap the cooled cake in plastic wrap and store at room temperature.
8. Prepare the Grand Marnier Syrup: Combine the water and sugar in a small saucepan. Bring to a full, rolling boil, stirring to dissolve the sugar. Cover the saucepan at once and remove from the heat. Keep the saucepan covered until cool. Pour the syrup into a glass measuring cup. Add enough Grand Marnier to equal ¾ cup. The syrup can be refrigerated in a tightly covered jar for up to 1 month.
9. Prepare the Orange-Chocolate Glaze: Chop the chocolate in a food processor, electric blender or by hand with a knife until very fine. Heat the cream in a small saucepan until bubbles appear around the edge. Remove the saucepan from the heat. Add the chocolate. Cover the saucepan and let stand for 5 minutes. Stir gently in a figure-8 motion until the chocolate is fully melted and the mixture is smooth. If necessary, heat slightly to help melt the chocolate. Be careful not to incorporate air bubbles into the mixture. Let cool to lukewarm. Gently stir in the Grand Marnier. At lukewarm, a small amount of glaze should mound just a tiny bit when dropped from a spoon back into the glaze,

before disappearing smoothly into the mixture. If the glaze is too thick and the mound remains on the surface of the glaze, add warm water or liqueur by the teaspoonful, testing the consistency of the glaze until correct. If the glaze is too thin, stir in more finely grated chocolate and heat just until melted.

10. Meanwhile, remove the top and bottom crusts from the cake with a serrated knife. Brush the cake evenly with the syrup.

11. Place the cake on a cardboard-round the same size as the cake. Place the cake on a wire rack placed in a shallow pan to catch the dripping glaze.

12. Pour the glaze all at once on the center of the cake, allowing it to cascade over the sides. Run a long metal spatula lightly across the top so the glaze will not be too thick. Work quickly before the glaze sets. Tap the rack lightly to level the surface of the glaze, if necessary. Prick any air bubbles in the glaze with a needle.

13. Allow the glaze to set undisturbed. It will take a few hours at room temperature. If time does not permit, place the cake in the refrigerator until the glaze is set, for about 30 minutes. Any leftover glaze can be refrigerated for up to 3 weeks or frozen for up to 6 months.

14. Decorate the sides and the top of the cake with almonds, if you wish.

*Note: To make 3 tablespoons of clarified brown butter, place ¼ cup (½ stick) unsalted butter in a small, heavy saucepan. Melt and simmer over very low heat until the butter solids drop to the bottom of the saucepan and begin to turn golden brown. Strain the butter mixture through a fine strainer or cheesecloth into a small bowl.

WHAT IS ZEST?

The outermost colored peel or rind of a citrus fruit is the zest. Full of flavorful citrus oil, a little provides a lot of flavor accent when added to soups, salad dressings, sautéed dishes or any other dish needing a little perking up. Use a swivel-bladed vegetable peeler to shave off the zest, making sure not to include any of the bitter-tasting white pith. Slice the zest into very thin strips or chop fine. For a more decorative touch, there is a kitchen tool called a zester. Scraped along the surface of the rind, it peels off very thin, curly strips.

Golden Sangria Cake

Packaged mixes make this cake effortless, and our special touches make it delicious.

Bake at 350° for 50 minutes.
Makes 12 servings (one 9- or 10-inch cake).

Nutrient Value Per Serving: 304 calories, 4 g protein, 13 g fat, 43 g carbohydrate, 370 mg sodium, 91 mg cholesterol.

1 **package (18 ounces) yellow cake mix***
1 **package (3½ ounces) vanilla-flavored instant pudding and pie filling**
⅓ **cup light olive oil**
1 **cup fruity white wine**
4 **eggs**
1 **tablespoon grated orange rind**
   10X (confectioners') sugar

1. Preheat the oven to moderate (350°). Grease and flour a 9-inch fancy tube pan (12 cup) or a 10-inch Bundt® pan.

2. Combine the cake mix and the pudding mix in the large bowl of an electric mixer. Add the oil, wine, eggs and orange rind. Blend the mixture on low speed for 30 seconds. Scrape down the side of the bowl. Beat on medium speed for 2 minutes. Pour the batter into the prepared pan.

3. Bake the cake in the preheated moderate oven (350°) for 50 minutes or until a cake tester inserted near the center comes out clean. Cool the cake in the pan on a wire rack for 15 minutes. Turn the cake out onto the wire rack to cool completely. Wrap the cake lightly and refrigerate overnight to mellow.

4. Serve the cake at room temperature. Sprinkle the cake with 10X sugar. Garnish with orange slices, grapes and mint, if you wish.

*Note: If you are using a cake mix with the pudding mix already added, prepare the cake mix following the package directions, but substitute olive oil for the vegetable oil and white wine for the water. Use the eggs as called for in the package directions and add 1 tablespoon grated orange rind. Omit the pudding mix called for in the above recipe. Bake and finish the cake as in Steps 3 and 4 above.

ORANGE JUICE

2 to 4 medium-size oranges = 1 cup orange juice
1 medium-size orange = 4 teaspoons grated orange rind

What more can we say: The Best American Chocolate Layer Cake.

The Best American Chocolate Layer Cake

Bake at 350° for 20 to 30 minutes.
Makes 12 servings (one 9-inch three-layer cake).

Nutrient Value Per Serving: 795 calories, 9 g protein, 53 g fat, 82 g carbohydrate, 531 mg sodium, 187 mg cholesterol.

1⅓ **cups boiling water**
¾ **cup Dutch-processed unsweetened cocoa powder**
4 **eggs, at room temperature**
1½ **teaspoons vanilla**
3¼ **cups sifted *cake flour***
2 **cups sugar**
2 **tablespoons baking powder**
1½ **teaspoons salt**
1 **cup (2 sticks) unsalted butter, softened**

Fudge Frosting:
1 **pound semisweet chocolate**
2 **cups heavy cream**
1 **cup coarsely chopped walnuts**

1. Preheat the oven to moderate (350°). Grease three 9-inch round layer-cake pans. Line the bottoms with wax paper rounds. Grease the paper. Flour the pans.
2. Whisk together the boiling water and the cocoa in a small bowl until smooth. Cool the mixture to room temperature.
3. Combine the eggs and the vanilla in a second small bowl. Lightly whisk in one-quarter of the cooled cocoa mixture.
4. Combine the cake flour, sugar, baking powder and salt in a large mixing bowl. Mix on low speed for 1 minute or until blended.
5. Add the remaining three-quarters cocoa mixture and the butter to the dry ingredients. Beat at medium-speed for 1½ minutes, scraping down the side of the bowl with a rubber spatula. Add the egg-cocoa mixture in thirds, beating at medium-high speed for 20 seconds after each addition. Pour the batter into the prepared pans.
6. Bake the cakes in the preheated moderate oven (350°) for 20 to 30 minutes or until a wooden pick inserted near the centers comes out clean; the cakes should not shrink from the pan sides. Cool the cakes in the pans on wire racks for 10 minutes. Loosen the sides of the cakes gently with a spatula. Invert the cakes onto lightly greased wire racks to finish cooling. Remove the wax paper.
7. Prepare the Fudge Frosting: Chop the chocolate very fine in a food processor.* Heat the cream in a saucepan until bubbles appear around the edge. With the processor motor running, add the hot cream to the chocolate in a steady stream. Process until the mixture is smooth. Transfer the mixture to a bowl. Let cool at room temperature until the frosting is a good spreading consistency. Do not stir the frosting while it is cooling.
8. To assemble the cake: Spread the frosting between the 3 layers, sprinkling each layer with ¼ cup of the chopped nuts. Frost the top and the sides of the cake. Decorate with the remaining nuts.

*__Note:__ If not using a processor, chop or grate the chocolate by hand. Add to the hot cream in the saucepan. Cover the saucepan for 3 minutes; stir the mixture until smooth.

DIVIDING CAKE BATTER EVENLY AMONG BAKING PANS

Use a ladle or a large spoon to divide the batter. Be sure to keep count of the number of ladles used for each pan!

CAKE STORAGE

A piece gone: Cover the cut surface of the cake with plastic wrap and place the cake in a cake keeper or invert a large bowl over the cake plate and store for 2 to 3 days. If the cake has a cream filling or frosting, refrigerate.

Freezing: Unfrosted cakes are the best candidates for freezing. Wrap in aluminum foil, plastic wrap or large plastic bags and freeze for up to 4 months. Thaw at room temperature for about 1 hour.

SIFTING FLOUR

If a recipe calls for a cup measurement of sifted flour, sift the flour onto a piece of wax paper, spoon into a measuring cup and level off the top with a knife or metal spatula. Be sure to use a dry measure cup as opposed to a liquid measure. If the recipe doesn't specify sifted flour, it is best to stir the flour lightly to aerate it, and then spoon it into a dry measuring cup and level the top.

Chocolate Dump Cake with Sugar Glaze

Bake at 350° for 55 to 60 minutes.
Makes 12 servings.

Nutrient Value Per Serving: 310 calories, 3 g protein, 13 g fat, 46 g carbohydrate, 169 mg sodium, 46 mg cholesterol.

1¾ **cups** sifted **cake flour**
1½ **cups sugar**
⅓ **cup unsweetened cocoa powder**
1¼ **teaspoons baking powder**
½ **teaspoon salt**
½ **cup plus 3 tablespoons vegetable shortening**
1 **cup 99% fat-free buttermilk**
2 **eggs**
1 **teaspoon vanilla**
⅓ **cup low-calorie jam, stirred well**
½ **cup** unsifted **10X (confectioners') sugar**
2 **to 3 teaspoons water**

1. Preheat the oven to moderate (350°). Grease and flour one 9 x 9 x 2-inch square baking pan. Set aside.
2. Sift together the flour, sugar, cocoa, baking powder and salt into a large bowl. Add the shortening; mix in with your hands.
3. Add the buttermilk; beat for 2 minutes. Add the eggs; beat for 2 minutes more. Add the vanilla. Pour the batter into the prepared pan.
4. Bake the cake in the preheated moderate oven (350°) for 55 to 60 minutes or until the cake top springs back when lightly touched with your fingertip and the sides begin to pull away from the pan. Transfer the cake to a wire rack to cool completely.
5. Split the cake horizontally into 2 even layers. Spread the jam over the bottom layer. Place the second layer on top. Refrigerate the cake while preparing the glaze.
6. Place the 10X sugar in a bowl. Stir in enough of the water to make a good drizzling consistency. Pour the glaze over the top of the cake, smoothing with a metal spatula. Allow any excess glaze to drip down the sides of the cake. Refrigerate the cake for 15 to 20 minutes or until the glaze is set.

WHEN TO USE CAKE FLOUR IN A RECIPE

When a recipe calls for cake flour, you should use it. In general, cakes with a high proportion of sugar to flour, such as pound cakes, work well with cake flour. A combination of cake flour and all-purpose flour is ideal for a pastry such as puff pastry which needs some strength but where too much would produce a tough product. TIP: If you want to substitute all-purpose flour for cake flour in a recipe, measure the flour called for in the recipe, then remove 2 tablespoons of flour for each cup.

SPLITTING A BAKED CAKE LAYER

Using a long, sharp serrated knife, draw a line around the side of the cake at the point where it needs to be cut. Continue to cut deeper into the cake, revolving the cake against the knife and keeping the knife parallel to the work surface.

Kid-pleasers: Korn On The Kob, Hot Diggidy Dog and Merry Chef (both, page 188).

Korn On The Kob

A great dessert for your next special barbecue.

Makes 1 serving.

Nutrient Value Per Cake: 1,432 calories, 1 g protein, 52 g fat, 218 g carbohydrate, 809 mg sodium, NA cholesterol.

**1 cream-filled snack cake
Ready-to-spread vanilla frosting
Yellow and green food colorings**

1. Trim the end of the snack cake to give it a tapered look.

2. Tint some of the frosting bright yellow. Fill a pastry bag fitted with a #7 tip with the bright yellow frosting. Starting at the bottom of the tapered end of the cake, squeeze out enough frosting to resemble a kernel of corn. Repeat until the snack cake is covered with kernels.

3. Tint some of the vanilla frosting a medium green. Fill a pastry bag fitted with a #67 tip with the green frosting. Squeeze out the husk from the nontapered end to approximately halfway down the cob. Place the snack cake on a piece of aluminum foil or plate. Let the frosting set before serving.

Hot Digiddy Dog

This will be a hit at any birthday party for kids of all ages.

Makes 1 serving.

Nutrient Value Per Cake: 1,110 calories, 1 g protein, 40 g fat, 170 g carbohydrate, 643 mg sodium, NA cholesterol.

1 cream-filled snack cake
Ready-to-spread vanilla frosting
Red, green and yellow food colorings

1. Cut the snack cake in half lengthwise.
2. Tint ½ cup of the frosting a hot dog shade by adding red and green food colorings to reach the desired shade.
3. Fill a pastry bag fitted with a #7 tip with the tinted frosting. Squeeze out a "hot dog" from left to right on the bottom half of the snack cake, using medium pressure. Place the top half of the snack cake over the "hot dog."
4. Fill a pastry bag fitted with a #16 tip with frosting that has been tinted yellow. Pipe stars around the bottom and top halves to cover the snack cake completely for the bun.
5. Fill a pastry bag fitted with a #2 tip with yellow frosting. Pipe on the "mustard" as shown in the photo . Repeat to add "catsup" by using frosting tinted with red food coloring. Let the frosting set.

Merry Chef

A must for a barbecue on Father's Day.

Makes 1 serving.

Nutrient Value Per Cake: 795 calories, 1 g protein, 29 g fat, 123 g carbohydrate, 480 mg sodium, NA cholesterol.

1 cream-filled snack cake
Ready-to-spread vanilla frosting
Red and green food colorings

1. Tint some of the vanilla frosting flesh color with the red and green food colorings. Fill a pastry bag fitted with a #48 tip with the flesh-colored frosting. Pipe the frosting out over one end of the snack cake. Using the same tip, fill the pastry bag with frosting that has been tinted brown with more red and green food colorings. Pipe the frosting out to cover the rest of the snack cake.
2. Fill a pastry bag fitted with a #2 tip with brown frosting. Squeeze out the brown frosting on the flesh-colored end to draw the face and hair.
3. Fill a pastry bag fitted with a #7 tip with vanilla frosting . Pipe on an apron, then smooth out the apron with a spatula.

4. Tint some of the vanilla frosting red. Fill a pastry bag fitted with a #2 tip with the red frosting. Pipe out a bow tie and outline the apron.
5. Using a #2 tip, write on the apron in brown lettering; add a collar.
6. Using a #7 tip, squeeze vanilla frosting out to make the chef's hat, starting at the top of the head and increasing pressure as you get to the top of the hat.
7. Using a #7 tip, add the arms using flesh-colored frosting. Squeeze out the ears. Let the frosting set before serving.

Creamy Cranraspberry-Glazed Cheesecake

A dense and very moist lemon cheesecake with an almond sponge cake base.

Bake sponge cake at 450° for 7 to 8 minutes; bake cheesecake at 350° for 1 hour and 5 minutes; leave in turned-off oven for 1 hour. Makes 12 servings.

Nutrient Value Per Serving: 613 calories, 12 g protein, 42 g fat, 50 g carbohydrate, 301 mg sodium, 301 mg cholesterol.

Almond Sponge Cake Base:
3 egg yolks
2 whole eggs
½ cup sugar plus 1 tablespoon sugar
⅓ cup finely ground blanched almonds
¾ teaspoon vanilla
3 tablespoons cake flour
2 egg whites
¼ teaspoon cream of tartar
Cream Cheese-Lemon Filling:
3 packages (8 ounces each) cream cheese, softened
1⅓ cups sugar
1 tablespoon cornstarch
4 eggs
¼ cup fresh lemon juice (2 lemons)
2 teaspoons vanilla
¼ teaspoon salt
2 containers (16 ounces each) dairy sour cream

Rich, dense, wonderful: Creamy Cranraspberry-Glazed Cheesecake.

Cranraspberry Glaze:
4 teaspoons cornstarch
¾ cup cranberry-raspberry juice concentrate, thawed and undiluted
1 tablespoon Chambord OR: cranberry liqueur (optional)

1. Prepare the Almond Sponge Cake Base: Preheat the oven to very hot (450°). Grease a 15½x10½x1-inch jelly-roll pan. Line the pan with wax paper; grease and flour the paper.
2. Beat together the 3 yolks, 2 whole eggs, the ½ cup sugar and the almonds in a large bowl until tripled in volume and almost white, for about 5 minutes. Stir in the vanilla.
3. Sift the cake flour over the beaten egg mixture. Fold the flour in gently with a whisk or a rubber spatula just until no dry particles remain.
4. Beat the 2 egg whites with the cream of tartar in a small bowl until soft peaks form. Gradually add the 1 tablespoon sugar and beat until the whites are almost stiff. Fold the whites into the egg batter. Pour the batter into the prepared pan and spread evenly with a spatula.
5. Bake the sponge cake in the preheated very hot oven (450°) for 7 to 8 minutes or until lightly browned and springy to the touch. Invert the sponge cake onto a wire rack. Remove the wax paper. Cool the cake completely.
6. Cut out a 9-inch round from the sponge cake for the base of the cheesecake. Using cookie cutters, make stars, snowflakes or other decorative shapes for the top of the cake. Keep the cutouts wrapped to prevent drying out.

7. Prepare the Cream Cheese-Lemon Filling: Preheat the oven to moderate (350°). Grease a 9x3-inch springform pan. Wrap the outside in a sheet of 18-inch-wide aluminum foil or a double layer of regular-width foil to prevent water seepage when the cheesecake is baked in a water bath. Line the bottom of the springform pan with the sponge cake round.
8. Beat together the cream cheese and the sugar in a large bowl until the mixture is smooth. Beat in the 1 tablespoon cornstarch. Add the eggs, one at a time, beating well after each addition. Add the lemon juice, vanilla, salt and sour cream. Beat until smooth.
9. Pour the filling into the prepared springform pan. Set the pan in a roasting pan. Pour in hot water to a depth of 1 inch.
10. Bake the cheesecake in the preheated moderate oven (350°) for 1 hour and 5 minutes. Turn the oven off and leave the cake in the oven with the door closed for 1 hour. Remove the cake from the water bath and cool on a wire rack for 1 hour or until the cake is room temperature. Run a spatula around the side of the cake to prevent cracking as the cake shrinks and cools. Cover the pan with plastic wrap and refrigerate overnight.
11. Run a spatula or knife around the side of the cake. Remove the springform pan side. Smooth the side of the cake with a spatula.
12. Prepare the Cranraspberry Glaze: Dissolve 4 teaspoons cornstarch in the cranberry-raspberry juice concentrate in a small saucepan. Bring to boiling, stirring constantly. Lower the heat and simmer for 1 minute. Remove the saucepan from the heat and stir in the liqueur, if using. Spoon the glaze on top of the cake. Spread evenly over the top and sides of the cake with a spatula. Refrigerate the cake until the glaze sets.
13. To serve, place the sponge cake cutouts on the top and sides of the cake.

BEATING EGG WHITES

Ideally whites should be at room temperature for maximum volume when beating. To warm refrigerator-cold whites, place in a bowl and set in a larger bowl of warm water. Stir the whites briefly to remove the chill. Add a pinch of salt to help the whites liquefy to a point where they will begin absorbing air. Then start beating the whites, slowly. If using an electric mixer, set on medium speed. Continue beating until the whites are very white and opaque. Then increase the speed to high and beat until the whites are the desired consistency, soft peaks or firm. If you are adding sugar, add in a very slow, thin stream when you increase the mixer speed.

Be careful not to overbeat the whites or they will separate and become granular.

Apricot Brandy Buttercream

Makes enough to frost and decorate one 13x9x2-inch cake.

Nutrient Value Per Portion: 332 calories, 0 g protein, 12 g fat, 58 g carbohydrate, 127 mg sodium, 31 mg cholesterol.

1 **cup (2 sticks) butter or margarine**
2 **packages (1 pound each) 10X (confectioners') sugar, sifted**
   Pinch salt
3 **tablespoons milk**
¼ **cup apricot brandy**

1. Beat the butter or margarine in a large bowl with an electric mixer at medium speed until soft.
2. Beat in the 10X sugar, part at a time, and the salt until the mixture is crumbly and all of the sugar has been added.
3. Add the milk and the brandy. Beat until the mixture is smooth and spreadable, adding additional milk, if necessary. Keep the bowl covered with dampened paper toweling while frosting the cake.

SEPARATING EGGS

Eggs separate most easily when cold since the whites hold together better. After separating the whites from the yolks, however, the whites should be brought to room temperature for maximum volume when beating. (Avoid getting any of the yolk mixed with the whites since the fat from the yolk will decrease the volume of the beaten whites.)

Celebration Cake

Vary the top decoration to suit the occasion.

Bake at 325° for 45 to 50 minutes.
Makes 16 servings (13x9-inch cake).

Nutrient Value Per Serving: 810 calories, 7 g protein, 38 g fat, 111 g carbohydrate, 432 mg sodium, 265 mg cholesterol.

2 **cups (4 sticks) butter, at room temperature**
2 **cups sugar**
10 **eggs**
4½ **cups cake flour (not self-rising)**
1 **teaspoon baking powder**
4 **teaspoons vanilla**
¼ **cup apricot brandy**
   Apricot Brandy Buttercream (recipe at left)

1. Preheat the oven to slow (325°). Grease and flour a 13x9x2-inch baking pan.
2. Beat the butter and sugar in a large bowl with an electric mixer at high speed until the mixture is fluffy, scraping down the side of the bowl as necessary.
3. Add the eggs, 2 at a time, beating well after each addition.
4. Sift together the flour and baking powder over the bowl; stir in the flour with a wire whisk. Stir in the vanilla until well blended.
5. Pour the batter into the prepared baking pan.
6. Bake the cake in the preheated slow oven (325°) for 45 to 50 minutes or until a wooden pick inserted in the center comes out clean.
7. Cool the cake in the pan on a wire rack for 20 minutes. Loosen the cake around the sides of the pan with a sharp knife. Invert the cake onto the rack; cool the cake completely. Brush the top and the sides of the cake with the brandy to settle the crumbs.
8. Prepare the Apricot Brandy Buttercream.
9. Place the cake on a piece of cardboard cut slightly smaller than the cake. Spread the sides, then the top, with some of the Apricot Brandy Buttercream, swirling the buttercream in an attractive fashion. Place the cake on a serving platter.
10. With a pastry bag fitted with a large star tip, pipe a border of frosting rosettes around the bottom edge of the cake. With a pastry bag fitted with a small shell tip, pipe a border of overlapping shells along the top edge of the cake.

For a shower, anniversary or christening: Celebration Cake.

Harvest Apple Strudel

A strudel made easier with phyllo dough.

Bake at 375° for 35 minutes.
Makes 8 servings.

Nutrient Value Per Serving: 468 calories, 6 g protein, 21 g fat, 66 g carbohydrate, 249 mg sodium, 47 mg cholesterol.

- **⅓ cup granulated sugar**
- **2 tablespoons cornstarch**
- **½ cup apple juice**
- **5 cups sliced tart apples such as Granny Smith or Cortland (about 2 pounds)**
- **⅓ cup firmly packed light brown sugar**
- **1 teaspoon ground cinnamon**
- **¼ teaspoon ground nutmeg**
- **⅓ cup raisins**
- **⅓ cup chopped walnuts**
- **12 phyllo pastry sheets from 1 pound package (16x12-inch size), thawed (about 8 ounces)**
- **¾ cup (1½ sticks) butter or margarine, melted**
- **10 tablespoons dry bread crumbs**

1. Combine the granulated sugar, cornstarch and juice in a small saucepan. Cook over medium heat, stirring constantly, until the mixture thickens and boils.
2. Toss the apples with the brown sugar, cinnamon and nutmeg in a medium-size bowl. Mix in the juice mixture until the apples are coated. Fold in the raisins and nuts.
3. Unfold the phyllo dough and cover with a damp towel to prevent the dough from drying out. Place a clean towel on a flat surface. Spray the towel with cold water to dampen lightly. Place one sheet of phyllo on the towel, long side toward you. Place another sheet, overlapping 4 inches at the top, to make a 20x16-inch rectangle. Brush the dough with the butter; sprinkle with 2 tablespoons of the crumbs. Repeat with the remaining phyllo, butter and crumbs. Do not sprinkle any crumbs on the top layer. Spoon the apple mixture in an even row across the side of the pastry near you, 2 inches in from the edge.

Using the towel as an aid, roll the dough over the filling; fold the ends in to enclose the filling completely. Roll up like a jelly roll, using the towel to aid in the rolling; do not roll the towel up in the cake.

4. Preheat the oven to moderate (375°). Line a large cookie sheet with a sheet of heavy-duty aluminum foil.
5. Ease the roll onto the cookie sheet, seam-side down. Brush the roll with some of the butter. Turn the foil up ½ inch all around the edge to catch any spills.
6. Bake the roll in the preheated moderate oven (375°) for 35 minutes or until the pastry is crisp and golden. Let the roll cool for 20 minutes. Slide the roll onto a board. Sprinkle with 10X sugar, if you wish.

Food for thought . . .

Phyllo is a paper-thin pastry made from flour and water and is frequently used in Turkish and Greek cooking for both sweet and savory dishes. Phyllo leaves can be found in 1-pound packages, frozen, in your supermarket or fresh in some ethnic specialty shops.

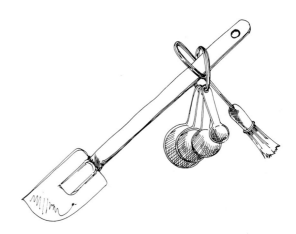

C·O·O·K·I·E·S &
T·O·P·P·I·N·G·S

Cookie Madness! From bottom, clockwise: Eight-Layer Shortbread Slices (page 194)*; Jam Pin-Wheel Butter Cookies* (page 194)*; Tiny Fudge Brownie Cups* (page 195)*; Apricot-Almond Bar Cookies* (page 196)*; Biscotti* (page 197).

Eight-Layer Shortbread Slices

Bake at 375° for 10 minutes.
Makes 3 to 3½ dozen cookies.

Nutrient Value Per Cookie: 94 calories, 1 g protein, 6 g fat, 10 g carbohydrate, 56 mg sodium, 14 mg cholesterol.

2¼ **cups unsifted all-purpose flour**
½ **cup cornstarch**
1 **cup plus 2 tablespoons (2¼ sticks) butter or margarine, at room temperature**
1 **cup 10X (confectioners') sugar**
2 **teaspoons vanilla**
¼ **cup unsweetened cocoa powder**
1 **egg white**

1. Sift together the flour and cornstarch onto a piece of wax paper. Set aside.
2. Beat the butter and sugar together in a medium-size bowl until blended. Stir in the vanilla. Gradually beat in the flour mixture to make a soft dough. Divide the dough in half.
3. Knead the cocoa powder into one-half of the dough in a bowl. Flatten both the doughs and wrap separately in plastic wrap or wax paper. Chill for 1 hour or until the dough is easy to handle.
4. Roll each batch of dough between 2 pieces of wax paper into a 10-inch square. Push the sides in to make absolutely even, using a ruler or long-bladed knife. If the dough becomes too soft or sticky, refrigerate the dough on a cookie sheet.
5. Remove the top piece of wax paper from the nonchocolate dough. Brush the top with some of the egg white. Remove the wax paper from the top of the chocolate dough; invert the chocolate dough onto the nonchocolate dough, matching the sides up exactly. Peel off the remaining piece of wax paper. Cut the dough into 4 equal strips, each 10 x 2⅓ inches. Brush the strips lightly with the egg white. Stack the dough strips neatly to make 8 alternating layers. Wrap the stack in plastic wrap. Chill for several hours or overnight. The dough can be refrigerated for up to 1 week.
6. Preheat the oven to moderate (375°).
7. Cut the dough crosswise into slices slightly less than ¼ inch thick. Place the slices on ungreased cookie sheets, 1 inch apart.
8. Bake the cookies in the preheated moderate oven (375°) for 10 minutes or until the edges begin to brown. Transfer the cookies to wire racks to cool completely. Store the cookies in tightly covered containers in a cool, dry place.

Jam Pin-Wheel Butter Cookies

A delicious butter cookie made especially rich with sour cream.

Bake at 375° for 12 to 14 minutes.
Makes 2 dozen cookies.

Nutrient Value Per Cookie: 105 calories, 1 g protein, 6 g fat, 11 g carbohydrate, 63 mg sodium, 17 mg cholesterol.

1½ **cups unsifted all-purpose flour**
2 **tablespoons granulated sugar**
¾ **cup (1½ sticks) butter or margarine**
¼ **cup dairy sour cream**
1 **to 2 egg whites**
¼ **to ⅓ cup pearl sugar* OR: coarsely ground sugar cubes**
About 3 tablespoons raspberry, apricot or black currant jam

1. Combine the flour and the granulated sugar in a medium-size bowl. Cut in the butter with a pastry blender or 2 knives held scissors-fashion until the mixture is crumbly. Add the sour cream and stir with a fork until the dough holds together. Wrap the dough and chill for several hours or overnight.
2. Divide the dough in half. Work with one-half at a time, leaving the other half refrigerated. Roll the dough out on a floured surface to a 10 x 7-inch rectangle. Cut the dough with a pastry wheel or knife into twelve 2½-inch squares. Transfer the squares to an ungreased cookie sheet, placing the squares 1 inch apart.
3. Make a cut 1¼ inches long from each corner of a square toward the center. Fold every other tip to the center to make a pin-wheel shape. Press the center down gently. Repeat with the remaining squares. Refrigerate the cookies on the cookie sheet for 15 minutes.
4. Preheat the oven to moderate (375°).
5. Brush each cookie with a little egg white. Sprinkle each cookie with about ½ teaspoon of pearl sugar. Place ¼ teaspoon of jam in the center of each cookie.
6. Bake the cookies in the preheated moderate oven (375°) for 12 to 14 minutes or until golden brown and slightly puffed. Transfer the cookies to a wire rack to cool completely. Store the cookies in a tightly covered container.

*Note: Pearl sugar is available in some supermarkets and in specialty food shops that carry decorative baking supplies.

Tiny Fudge Brownie Cups

These are delicious, European-style, not-too-sweet brownies.

Bake at 350° for 10 to 12 minutes.
Makes 2 dozen.

Nutrient Value Per Brownie Cup: 68 calories, 1 g protein, 4 g fat, 8 g carbohydrate, 23 mg sodium, 17 mg cholesterol.

4 tablespoons (½ stick) butter or margarine
3 squares (1 ounce each) semisweet chocolate
⅓ cup firmly packed light brown sugar
½ teaspoon vanilla
1 egg
5 tablespoons unsifted all-purpose flour
2 ounces milk chocolate
   Chopped pistachio nuts

1. Preheat the oven to moderate (350°). Lightly butter 24 miniature muffin tins, about 1½ x ¾ inch.
2. Melt together the butter, semisweet chocolate and sugar in a small saucepan over low heat, stirring constantly, until the mixture is smooth. Remove the saucepan from the heat.
3. Beat in the vanilla; then add the egg, stirring until incorporated. Fold in the flour until blended. Spoon a slightly rounded teaspoonful of the chocolate mixture into each tin; the tin should be about half full.
4. Bake the brownie cups in the preheated moderate oven (350°) for 10 to 12 minutes or until the centers of the brownies spring back when lightly touched with your fingertip. Cool the brownies in the pans on a wire rack for 10 minutes. Remove the brownie cups from the pans and cool completely on the wire rack. Store the brownie cups, unfrosted and wrapped airtight, in the refrigerator.
5. To frost, melt the milk chocolate in a bowl set over hot, not boiling, water in a saucepan; stir the chocolate until smooth. Spread a little chocolate on top of each brownie cup with a small spatula. Sprinkle the brownies with the chopped pistachio nuts.

Food for thought . . .

Chocolate is a product of the New World. As early as the 16th century, Mexicans were already enjoying a frothy chocolate drink and the Spanish invaders under Cortez took the dark brown mystery product back to Europe. Hot chocolate in particular became an instant favorite. It wasn't long before there were chocolate shops galore where people went to enjoy a cup of the brew.

Chocolate is produced from cacao beans. Cacao beans are the seeds of a large, oval fruit. The fruit grows directly on the main branches of the cacao tree. Each fruit contains about 25 to 40 olive-size seeds or beans. The seeds are removed from the pulp and dried. Then they are roasted and ground until the fat in them liquefies. The rich, dark liquid is unsweetened chocolate. Cacao beans are also called cocoa beans.

In Colonial America, chocolate was imported from Europe until the first chocolate factory in Massachusetts started production in 1765.

MELTING CHOCOLATE

• *Chocolate scorches easily, so melt it over hot, not boiling water. A double boiler is best, but you can improvise by using a cup or bowl in a small saucepan. Either way, keep the water just below simmering. If steam gets into melting chocolate it will thicken the mixture and make it difficult to mix with the other ingredients. However, if this happens, simply soften the chocolate by adding 1 to 2 tablespoons of vegetable shortening (not butter) and stir vigorously.*
• *If there is liquid in a chocolate recipe, such as milk, water or spirits, melt the chocolate in the liquid in a small saucepan over direct heat. There should be at least ¼ cup of liquid for every 6 ounces of chocolate.*
• *You can also melt chocolate with the fat in the recipe directly over very low heat. Use a heavy saucepan and watch the mixture carefully.*

STORING CHOCOLATE

When chocolate is stored in a too warm place, or during hot weather, it often develops a whitish film known as "bloom." This is caused by the cocoa butter rising to the surface. It will not affect the eating quality. Chocolate keeps best stored at a temperature between 60° F and 70° F, with a low humidity factor.

STORING COCOA

Store cocoa in a tightly covered container at a moderate temperature and humidity level to keep it from forming lumps or hardening.

DECORATING WITH CHOCOLATE

Cakes, pies, cookies, candies, puddings and ice-cream desserts take on a professional look with a garnish of grated chocolate or chocolate curls.

To grate: *Start with cold chocolate, a dry, cold grater and cold hands. Rub the square up and down over the grating surface, working quickly and handling the chocolate as little as possible.*

To make curls: *Warm a square of chocolate slightly at room temperature. For little curls, shave thin strips with a vegetable parer from the narrow side; for large ones, from the bottom. Pick up the curls with a wooden pick (otherwise they shatter) and chill until firm before arranging them on food.*

Apricot-Almond Bar Cookies

Bake at 325° for 45 to 50 minutes.
Makes 15 to 18 cookies.

Nutrient Value Per Cookie: 122 calories, 1 g protein, 6 g fat, 16 g carbohydrate, 51 mg sodium, 21 mg cholesterol.

    Apricot Filling (recipe follows)
¾ ***cup plus 2 tablespoons* unsifted all-purpose flour**
¼ ***cup finely ground blanched almonds***
7 ***tablespoons butter or margarine, at room temperature***
½ ***cup granulated sugar***
½ ***egg (lightly beat 1 egg and divide)***
½ ***teaspoon almond extract***
    10X (confectioners') sugar
    Sliced blanched almonds (optional)
    Glacé cherries (optional)

1. Prepare the Apricot Filling.
2. Combine the flour and the ground almonds in a small bowl.
3. Beat together the butter, sugar, egg and almond extract in a medium-size bowl until the mixture is fluffy. Fold in the flour mixture. The dough will be soft. Divide the dough in half; flatten each half into a round. Wrap each half of the dough in wax paper or plastic wrap. Refrigerate the dough for 2 hours.
4. Preheat the oven to slow (325°). Lightly butter a 8 x 8 x 2-inch square baking pan. Line the bottom with parchment paper or wax paper. Set aside.
5. Roll one piece of dough between 2 pieces of wax paper into a 8-inch square to fit the baking pan. Peel off the wax paper from one side of the dough; invert the dough into the prepared pan. Press to fit the dough into the pan. Spread the Apricot Filling over the dough, leaving a ¼-inch border all around the edge. Roll the remaining dough into an 8-inch square between 2 pieces of wax paper. Repeat as above, inverting the dough onto the filling. Peel off the remaining piece of wax paper. Press the dough down gently to seal.
6. Bake the cookie dough in the preheated slow oven (325°) for 45 to 50 minutes or until golden and firm to the touch. Cool the cookies in the pan on a wire rack.
7. Loosen the cookies around the edge of the pan with a metal spatula. Invert onto a wire rack and remove the pan. Invert the cookies again. Sprinkle with the 10X (confectioners') sugar. Cut the cookies into 1½-inch-wide strips. Then cut into diamond-shapes for a total of 15 to 18 cookies.
8. Decorate the cookies with the sliced almonds and glacé cherries, if you wish.

Apricot Filling: Combine ½ cup of chopped dried apricots* and ½ cup of water in a small saucepan. Bring to boiling. Lower the heat; simmer the apricots, covered, for 15 minutes. Turn off the heat and let the apricots stand, covered, for 30 minutes. The water should be absorbed and the apricots very soft. If the water remains, heat the apricots gently to evaporate the water. Stir in ¼ cup of sugar. The mixture should be quite smooth, so there is no need to purée the apricots. Cool the apricot mixture completely. Makes about ½ cup.

*Note: If Turkish apricots are used, the cooking time will increase since they are drier and firmer.

COOKIE STORAGE

- *Store soft cookies in an airtight container, with a slice of apple on a piece of wax paper to keep the cookies soft and moist.*
- *Store crisp cookies in a container with a loose fitting lid. If the cookies begin to soften, place them in a slow oven (300°) for a few minutes to make them crisp again.*

Biscotti

Crispy, anise-flavored biscuits that are delicious with coffee or tea. And you're allowed to dunk.

Toast the hazelnuts at 350° for 12 minutes; bake the biscuits at 350° for 18 to 20 minutes; crisp at 350° for 10 to 15 minutes.
Makes 3 dozen.

Nutrient Value Per Biscuit: 101 calories, 2 g protein, 4 g fat, 13 g carbohydrate, 58 mg sodium, 30 mg cholesterol.

½ **cup hazelnuts (about 2½ ounces)**
2¾ **cups unsifted all-purpose flour**
2 **teaspoons baking powder**
½ **cup (1 stick) butter, at room temperature**
⅔ **cup sugar**
3 **eggs**
3 **tablespoons anisette liqueur (licorice-flavored liqueur)**
1 **teaspoon anise seeds, lightly crushed with a mortar and pestle or in a blender**
1 **teaspoon vanilla**
¼ **cup halved red glacé cherries**
2 **tablespoons coarsely chopped candied citron**

1. Preheat the oven to moderate (350°). Grease a large cookie sheet. Set aside.
2. Spread the hazelnuts in a single layer in a baking pan.
3. Toast the hazelnuts in the preheated moderate oven (350°) until the nuts are pale golden under their skins, for about 12 minutes. Leave the oven temperature at 350°. Rub the nuts vigorously in a coarse kitchen towel to remove as much skin as possible. Cool the nuts. Halve or coarsely chop the nuts. Set aside.
4. Sift together the flour and baking powder on a piece of wax paper.
5. Beat together the butter, sugar and eggs in a large bowl until smooth and well blended. Beat in the anisette, anise seeds and vanilla. Stir in the flour mixture, nuts, cherries and citron. Divide

the dough in half. Shape each half into a 12-inch-long log. Place the logs 3 inches apart on the prepared cookie sheet. Flatten the logs so that they are 2½ inches across.

6. Bake the logs in the preheated moderate oven (350°) for 18 to 20 minutes or until pale golden. Leave the oven temperature at 350°. Cool the logs on the cookie sheet until cool enough to handle. Then cut the logs crosswise into ½- to ¾-inch-thick slices. Lay each slice flat on the cookie sheet.
7. Bake the slices in the preheated moderate oven (350°) for 10 to 15 minutes or until lightly browned. Remove the biscuits to a wire rack and cool completely. Store the biscuits in an airtight container.

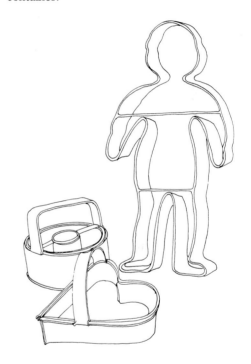

Food for thought . . .

Anise is an herb plant native to southwest Asia, northern Africa and southeast Europe. Both the leaves and the seeds of the plant are used to impart a slightly sweet licorice flavor to vegetable, chicken and fish dishes and many fruit preparations.

*Lemon Snowflake Cookies with Lemon Icing,
Swiss Honey Cakes, Fruit 'n' Nut Florentines.*

Swiss Honey Cakes

***Make the dough for these cakes at least one day before you
plan on baking.***

Bake at 350° for 20 minutes.
Makes about 3 dozen.

---

*Nutrient Value Per Cake: 116 calories, 2 g protein, 2 g fat,
24 g carbohydrate, 34 mg sodium, 8 mg cholesterol.*

---

  1 **cup honey**
 ¹/₂ **cup firmly packed dark brown sugar**
  1 **teaspoon baking soda**
  2 **tablespoons rum or brandy**
 ³/₄ **cup chopped blanched almonds**
 ¹/₃ **cup chopped candied citron**
 ¹/₄ **cup candied orange peel**
  1 **egg**
  1 **tablespoon grated fresh orange rind**
  1 **teaspoon ground cinnamon**
  1 **teaspoon ground cloves**
 ¹/₄ **teaspoon ground nutmeg**
  3 **cups unsifted all-purpose flour**

Glaze:
 ¹/₃ **cup granulated sugar**
  2 **tablespoons water**
     Red glacé cherries (optional)
     Chopped citron (optional)

1. Combine the honey and the sugar in a small
   saucepan. Heat the mixture, stirring to dissolve
   the sugar, until almost boiling, but do not boil.
   Cool the mixture to lukewarm, for about 20
   minutes. Transfer to a medium-size bowl.
2. Dissolve the baking soda in the rum or brandy in
   a small bowl.

3. Stir the almonds, citron, candied orange peel,
   egg, fresh orange rind, baking soda-rum mixture,
   cinnamon, cloves and nutmeg into the honey
   mixture. Gradually add the flour to make a soft,
   sticky dough. Cover the dough in the bowl with
   plastic wrap. Refrigerate the dough overnight or
   for several days.
4. Preheat the oven to moderate (350°).
5. Roll the dough out on a lightly floured board into
   a 12 x 10-inch rectangle. Slide a large cookie
   sheet under the dough.
6. Bake the dough in the preheated moderate oven
   (350°) for 20 minutes or until the cake is slightly
   browned and the center springs back when
   lightly pressed with your fingertip.
7. Meanwhile, prepare the Glaze: Combine the
   sugar and water in a small saucepan. Heat,
   stirring to dissolve the sugar. Simmer the glaze
   for 4 minutes.
8. Brush the hot glaze over the hot cake on the
   cookie sheet. With a sharp, wet knife, cut the
   cake into squares or rectangles; do not separate
   until the cake is completely cool.
9. Decorate the pieces of cake with the glacé
   cherries and citron, if you wish. Store the cakes
   for a few days to mellow, in a tightly covered
   container with wax paper between the layers of
   cakes.

Food for thought . . .

*Confectioners' sugar, also known as
powdered sugar, is granulated sugar that
has been crushed and screened. The
degree of fineness is indicated by the
number of X's — 4X is fine, 6X is very
fine and 10X is ultra fine. 10X sugar is
mixed with a little cornstarch to prevent it
from caking.*

Fruit 'n' Nut Florentines

These lace cookies are delicious but very fragile. Be very careful when you remove the cookies from the cookie sheets.

Bake at 350° for 8 to 10 minutes.
Makes about 2 dozen double cookies.

Nutrient Value Per Florentine: 120 calories, 2 g protein, 8 g fat, 13 g carbohydrate, 37 mg sodium, 9 mg cholesterol.

- ¼ **cup (½ stick) butter**
- ¼ **cup sugar**
- ¼ **cup heavy cream**
- 2 **tablespoons honey**
- ½ **cup chopped mixed candied fruits**
- 1 **cup sliced blanched almonds**
- ¼ **cup unsifted all-purpose flour**
- 4 **squares (1 ounce each) semisweet chocolate**

1. Preheat the oven to moderate (350°). Grease 2 cookie sheets.
2. Combine the butter, sugar, heavy cream and honey in a small saucepan. Heat the mixture slowly over low heat, stirring constantly, until bubbly. Remove the saucepan from the heat.
3. Toss the fruits and the nuts in the flour in a medium-size bowl. Add the fruits and nuts to the butter mixture; stir to combine.
4. Drop the batter by rounded measuring teaspoonfuls, 3 inches apart, onto the prepared cookie sheets. Spread the cookies slightly with the back of a spoon to 1½ inches in diameter.
5. Bake the cookies in the preheated moderate oven (350°) for 8 to 10 minutes or until the cookies are a deep golden color. The cookies will spread to 2 to 2½ inches. Cool the cookies on the cookie sheets for 1 minute or until firm. Carefully lift the cookies with a spatula to a wire rack to cool.
6. Melt the chocolate in a small bowl set in hot, not boiling, water in a saucepan; stir the chocolate until smooth. Spread or brush the chocolate onto the flat side of one cookie. Top with a second cookie to make a sandwich. Repeat with the remaining cookies and chocolate. Store the cookies, refrigerated, in an airtight container with wax paper between the layers of cookies.

Lemon Snowflake Cookies with Lemon Icing

Bake at 375° for 10 to 12 minutes.
Makes about 3½ dozen.

Nutrient Value Per Cookie: 57 calories, 0 g protein, 3 g fat, 6 g carbohydrate, 34 mg sodium, 9 mg cholesterol.

- ¾ **cup (1½ sticks) butter or margarine, at room temperature**
- ½ **cup 10X (confectioners') sugar**
- 1 **tablespoon grated lemon rind**
- 1 **cup unsifted all-purpose flour**
- ½ **cup cornstarch**
  Lemon Icing (recipe follows)
  Granulated sugar (optional)
  Multicolored sprinkles (optional)

1. Beat the butter and 10X sugar in a medium-size bowl until blended. Beat in the lemon rind.
2. Mix together the flour and the cornstarch in a small bowl. Stir the flour mixture into the butter mixture until well blended and smooth. Wrap the dough in plastic wrap and chill for 1 to 2 hours or until firm enough to handle.
3. Form the dough into a log 11 inches long and about 1¾ inches in diameter. Roll the log in a mixture of equal parts of sprinkles and granulated sugar, if you wish. Wrap the log in wax paper. To keep the round shape, cut a tube from a paper towel roll; open the tube lengthwise. Place the wrapped log in the tube. Chill the log for at least 4 hours or overnight.
4. Preheat the oven to moderate (375°).
5. Cut the dough into ¼-inch-thick slices. Place the slices, 1 inch apart, on an ungreased cookie sheet. Use as much dough as you wish. Rewrap and refrigerate the remaining dough.
6. Bake the cookies in the preheated moderate oven (375°) for 10 to 12 minutes or until the edges of the cookies are golden. Transfer the cookies to a wire rack to cool completely.
7. Prepare the Lemon Icing.
8. Pipe or drizzle the Lemon Icing in 3 or 4 concentric circles on one cookie. Working quickly, draw a wet wooden pick from the center to the outer edge in several places, dragging the icing along to make a snowflake effect. Repeat with the remaining cookies and icing.

Lemon Icing: Place ½ cup *un*sifted 10X (confectioners') sugar in a small bowl. Gradually stir in 2 teaspoons of lemon juice to make a smooth, fairly thick icing. Makes enough icing to decorate about half the cookies.

Cherry Squares

Bake at 375° for 15 minutes.
Makes 12 squares.

Nutrient Value Per Square: 218 calories, 5 g protein, 9 g fat, 31 g carbohydrate, 116 mg sodium, 153 mg cholesterol.

1 **cup unsifted all-purpose flour**
1 **teaspoon baking powder**
6 **tablespoons (¾ stick) unsalted butter**
6 **eggs, separated**
1 **cup sugar**
  Grated rind of ½ lemon
1 **teaspoon vanilla**
¼ **teaspoon salt**
1 **pound cherries, stemmed and pitted OR: 1 can (16 ounces) sweet, pitted cherries, well drained**

1. Preheat the oven to moderate (375°). Grease and flour a 15 x 10 x 1-inch jelly-roll pan.
2. Sift together the flour and baking powder onto a piece of wax paper. Set aside.
3. Melt the butter in a small saucepan.
4. Beat the egg yolks, sugar, lemon rind and vanilla in a large bowl with an electric mixer until the yolks are light and cream colored, for 4 to 5 minutes. Mix in the melted butter.
5. Beat the egg whites with the salt in a large bowl with an electric mixer with clean beaters until stiff peaks form.
6. Carefully fold the flour mixture into the egg yolk mixture. Stir in one-third of the beaten whites. Fold in the remaining whites; do not overmix. Spread the batter evenly in the prepared pan; the batter should be about ½ inch thick. Drop the cherries onto the batter, distributing them evenly.
7. Bake the square in the preheated moderate oven (375°) for 15 minutes or until golden brown and the top springs back when lightly touched with your fingertip. Cool the pan on a wire rack. Cut into 12 equal squares.

Food for thought . . .

The citron fruit, a variety of lemon, originated in the Himalayas and is now grown in Mediterranean countries and on islands in the West Indies. The peel of the fruit is candied and used in a variety of confections.

Lemon-Ginger Curd

Serve with toast in the A.M., scones in the P.M. Use as a quick filling for precooked tart shells or as a center filling for cake.

Makes 2½ cups.

Nutrient Value Per Tablespoon: 59 calories, 1 g protein, 4 g fat, 5 g carbohydrate, 40 mg sodium, 68 mg cholesterol.

9 **egg yolks**
1 **cup sugar**
2 **tablespoons grated lemon rind (1 lemon)**
¾ **cup lemon juice (6 lemons)**
½ **cup (1 stick) butter, cut into 8 pieces**
1½ **teaspoons grated, peeled, fresh gingerroot**

1. Combine the yolks and sugar in the top of a double boiler over simmering water. Whisk until the mixture is smooth. Add the lemon rind and lemon juice, butter and gingerroot. Cook, stirring constantly with a rubber spatula, until the curd is thickened, about 15 to 20 minutes. Do not let the curd boil. Pour the curd into sterilized jars with screw-top lids. Cover the tops of the jars with wax paper. Chill the jars in the refrigerator.
2. Cap the jars after they are completely chilled. The curd can be refrigerated for up to 3 weeks.

Hazelnut Chocolate Chip Cookies with Orange

Bake at 350° for 10 minutes.
Makes about 3 dozen cookies.

Nutrient Value Per Cookie: 79 calories, 1 g protein, 4 g fat, 9 g carbohydrate, 57 mg sodium, 11 mg cholesterol.

- 1/4 **cup (1/2 stick) unsalted butter**
- 1/2 **cup firmly packed light brown sugar**
- 1/4 **cup granulated sugar**
- 1 **egg**
- 1/2 **teaspoon vanilla**
- 1 **cup unsifted all-purpose flour**
- 2 **teaspoons baking powder**
- 1/2 **teaspoon salt**
- 3/4 **cup miniature semisweet chocolate pieces**
- 3/4 **cup hazelnuts with skins on, coarsely chopped**
- 1 1/2 **teaspoons grated orange rind**

1. Preheat the oven to moderate (350°). Lightly grease 2 cookie sheets.
2. Beat together the butter and the sugars in a medium-size bowl with an electric mixer until light and fluffy. Add the egg and vanilla and beat until smooth.
3. Sift together the flour, baking powder and salt onto a piece of wax paper. Stir the flour mixture into the butter mixture. Add the chocolate pieces, nuts and orange rind. Mix well.
4. Drop the dough by tablespoonfuls, 1 1/2 inches apart, onto the cookie sheets.
5. Bake the cookies in the preheated moderate oven (350°) for 10 minutes or until the cookies are lightly browned around the edges. Remove the cookie sheets to wire racks. Let the cookies cool slightly before removing them from the cookie sheets.

Note: The dough may be made several days in advance and refrigerated.

Homemade Fudge Sauce

Serve with ice cream or pound cake.

Makes 3 cups.

Nutrient Value Per Tablespoon: 64 calories, 0 g protein, 4 g fat, 7 g carbohydrate, 23 mg sodium, 12 mg cholesterol.

- 1 1/4 **cups sugar**
- 1 **cup Dutch-processed unsweetened cocoa powder**
- 1/2 **teaspoon ground cinnamon**
- 1 **cup heavy cream**
- 1/2 **cup milk**
- 1/4 **cup hazelnut liqueur OR: other nut-flavored liqueur**
- 1/2 **cup (1 stick) unsalted butter, cut into 8 pieces**
- 2 **teaspoons vanilla**

1. Mix together the sugar, cocoa powder and cinnamon in a large, heavy-bottomed saucepan until no lumps remain. Add the cream, milk and liqueur, stirring until smooth.
2. Bring the mixture to boiling; boil for 2 minutes, stirring constantly. Remove the saucepan from the heat. Cool for 15 minutes. Stir in the butter until melted. (Do not place the saucepan back on the heat.) Stir in the vanilla. Cool the sauce to room temperature. Store the sauce, covered, in the refrigerator for up to 1 month. Stir the sauce just before using.

Food for thought . . .

Cocoa powder is made from dry cocoa cakes, ground up, which still contain anywhere from 10% to 24% fat. The Dutch-style or processed cocoa powder contains a small amount of added alkali which neutralizes some of the acid in the chocolate. Instant cocoa powder, most familiar in breakfast drinks, contains a high percentage of sugar and additives to help it to more quickly dissolve in hot water or milk.

Vanilla-Pear Butter

Try this fresh-tasting sauce spooned over biscuits, muffins, pancakes or ice cream.

Makes 4 cups.

Nutrient Value Per Tablespoon: 33 calories, 0 g protein, 2 g fat, 5 g carbohydrate, 15 mg sodium, 4 mg cholesterol.

3½ pounds firm-ripe Bartlett pears, peeled, cored and quartered
½ cup sugar
¼ cup lemon juice (2 lemons)
½ cup (1 stick) butter, cut into 8 pieces
2½ teaspoons vanilla

1. Combine the pears, sugar and lemon juice in a large, heavy Dutch oven or casserole. Bring the mixture to boiling over medium heat. Cook, covered, for 15 minutes or until the pears are very tender and mushy.
2. Drain the pears well over a small, heavy-bottomed saucepan, reserving the juices. Bring the juices to boiling. Reduce the heat to medium and cook, stirring frequently, until the liquid is reduced to ¼ cup. Be careful not to let the mixture burn.
3. Place the pears in the work bowl of a food processor or, working in batches, in a blender container. Process the pears until well blended. Pour into a large bowl. Add the hot reduced liquid. Add the butter and stir until melted. Stir in the vanilla. The fruit butter can be stored in jars in the refrigerator for up to 4 weeks.

Chocolate Truffles

Makes about 5 dozen truffles.

Nutrient Value Per Truffle: 59 calories, 0 g protein, 5 g fat, 5 g carbohydrate, 24 mg sodium, 9 mg cholesterol.

½ cup heavy cream
½ cup sugar
¼ cup raspberry-flavored liqueur OR: orange-flavored liqueur
6 squares (1 ounce each) semisweet chocolate
2 squares (1 ounce each) unsweetened chocolate
¾ cup (1½ sticks) butter, cut into small pieces

Coating:
½ cup unsweetened cocoa powder
¼ cup 10X (confectioners') sugar
Finely ground blanched almonds (optional)

1. Combine the cream, sugar and liqueur in a large, heavy-bottomed saucepan. Bring to boiling; boil for 1 minute, stirring to dissolve the sugar. Remove the saucepan from the heat. Add both chocolates; stir until the chocolates are completely melted and smooth. Let the chocolate mixture stand for 10 minutes or until just warm to the touch. Add the butter and stir until melted. Pour the truffle mixture into a non-aluminum shallow baking dish, about 9 x 9 x 2 inches. Cover the dish and refrigerate until the truffle mixture is completely chilled.
2. Scoop out truffle balls about 1 inch in diameter with a melon baller. Roll the truffles quickly between your palms to form smooth balls. The heat of your hands will melt the truffles, so work quickly. If the mixture melts too much, chill for 5 minutes in the refrigerator.
3. To coat the truffles: Sift together the cocoa powder and 10X sugar onto a piece of wax paper. Place the ground almonds, if using, on a second sheet of wax paper. Roll the truffles in the cocoa mixture, or the almonds, to coat. Place the truffles in individual candy wrappers. The truffles can be stored in the refrigerator for up to 3 weeks.

Peanut Butter Kisses

These are addictive! Since they are so easy to prepare, kids can enjoy making them too.

Bake at 300° for 20 minutes.
Makes about 4 dozen.

Nutrient Value Per Kiss: 51 calories, 2 g protein, 3 g fat, 5 g carbohydrate, 28 mg sodium, 6 mg cholesterol.

1 cup smooth peanut butter
¾ cup firmly packed light brown sugar
1 egg
1 teaspoon vanilla
¼ cup semisweet chocolate pieces

1. Preheat the oven to slow (300°).
2. Combine the peanut butter, brown sugar, egg and vanilla in a large bowl; stir until smooth. Roll the dough into small balls, about ¾ inch in diameter. Place the balls, about 1 inch apart, on an ungreased cookie sheet. Flatten each slightly. Press 1 chocolate piece in the center of each cookie.
3. Bake the cookies in the preheated slow oven (300°) for 20 minutes or until light brown. The kisses can be stored in airtight containers for several days.

C·O·L·D T·H·I·N·G·S

Sweet, refreshing, tingly-cold — that's Kiwi Ice (page 207).

French Vanilla Ice Cream Ring

Fill the center of this rich ice cream ring with an assortment of our fruit-flavored ices.

Makes 16 servings.

Nutrient Value Per Serving: 370 calories, 5 g protein, 27 g fat, 28 g carbohydrate, 52 mg sodium, 258 mg cholesterol.

2   **recipes French Vanilla Ice Cream (recipe follows)**
1   **pint assorted fruit-flavored ices (see recipes, pages 205-207)**
     Whipped cream, sliced almonds, strawberries, blueberries and raspberries for garnish (optional)

1. Prepare the 2 recipes French Vanilla Ice Cream. Transfer the ice cream from the ice cream maker to an 8-cup ring mold. Freeze the ice cream until solid.
2. Prepare the fruit-flavored ices.
3. To serve the ring: Dip the mold briefly in warm water. Invert a chilled serving plate on the mold. Turn the mold and plate right-side up. Lift off the mold. Return the ring briefly to the freezer. Fill the center of the ring with scoops of the ices. Garnish the ring with whipped cream, almonds and berries, if you wish.

French Vanilla Ice Cream

Makes about 2½ pints.

Nutrient Value Per ½ Cup: 280 calories, 4 g protein, 22 g fat, 18 g carbohydrate, 40 mg sodium, 207 mg cholesterol.

1½ **cups milk**
2   **cups heavy cream**
½   **vanilla bean OR: 1 tablespoon vanilla extract**
5   **egg yolks**
¾   **cup sugar**

1. Combine the milk and the cream in a medium-size saucepan. Halve the vanilla bean lengthwise and scrape out the little seeds with the tip of a knife. Add the seeds and the pod to the cream mixture. (If using the vanilla extract, add later in Step 3.) Heat the cream mixture just until bubbles appear around the edge.
2. Beat the egg yolks slightly in a large bowl with an electric mixer. Gradually beat in the sugar; continue beating the yolk mixture until fluffy-thick and a ribbon forms when the beaters are lifted. Stir a little hot cream mixture into the

yolks; stir the yolk mixture into the saucepan.
3. Cook the cream-yolk mixture, stirring constantly, over low heat until the mixture thickens slightly and coats the back of a metal spoon, for about 20 minutes; do not boil the mixture. Strain the mixture into a bowl; discard the vanilla pod. (If using the vanilla extract, stir into the custard at this point.)
4. Cool the custard completely, stirring occasionally. Refrigerate the custard, covered, for at least 1 hour or overnight.
5. Freeze the custard in an ice cream maker according to the manufacturer's instructions.
6. Freeze the ice cream, tightly covered, for several hours to mellow. If the ice cream becomes frozen solid, soften slightly in the refrigerator before serving.

French Chocolate Ice Cream: Chop 5 squares (1 ounce each) of semisweet chocolate; place in a large bowl. In Step 3 in the above recipe, strain the hot custard mixture over the chocolate in the bowl. Stir until the chocolate melts. Proceed with the rest of the recipe. Makes 2½ pints. *Nutrient Value Per ½ Cup: 352 calories, 4 g protein, 27 g fat, 26 g carbohydrate, 41 mg sodium, 207 mg cholesterol.*

Food for thought . . .

Where did ice cream originate? Marco Polo may have brought back from the Far East tales of exotic-looking people eating flavored ices. In the late 1500s, an Italian cook prepared ice cream for Catherine De' Medici, and she took it to the French, as she did many other foods. During his travels through France, Thomas Jefferson wrote down several recipes for ice cream. But it is Dolly Madison who is traditionally credited with introducing ice cream to this country in 1808 at a White House dinner.

LS

Blueberry-Yogurt Sherbet

Makes about 2½ pints.

Nutrient Value Per ½ Cup: 111 calories, 2 g protein, 1 g fat, 26 g carbohydrate, 27 mg sodium, 2 mg cholesterol.

> **3 cups fresh or frozen blueberries**
> **1 cup water**
> **½ cup sugar**
> **Strip lemon peel, 3 x 1 inch**
> **1 tablespoon lemon juice**
> **¼ cup honey**
> **1½ cups plain yogurt**
> **⅛ teaspoon ground nutmeg**

1. Combine the blueberries, water, sugar, lemon peel and juice in a medium-size saucepan. Bring to boiling, stirring, until the sugar dissolves. Cook the mixture until the blueberries are tender, for 8 to 10 minutes. Cool the mixture.
2. Press the blueberry mixture through a sieve or food mill into a large bowl. Cool completely. Stir in the honey, yogurt and nutmeg. Refrigerate until chilled.
3. Pour the mixture into a 9-inch square metal pan. Freeze the purée until almost frozen solid, for 2 to 4 hours; stir several times around the edges so the sherbet freezes evenly.
4. Transfer the mixture to a food processor or a large chilled bowl. Quickly process or beat with an electric mixer until the sherbet is smooth and fluffy. Return the sherbet to the pan. Freeze for 30 minutes. Process or beat the sherbet again until smooth and fluffy.
5. Freeze the sherbet, tightly covered, until almost firm, for 1 to 2 hours. If the sherbet freezes solid, soften it in the refrigerator for 30 minutes before serving.

LS

Pineapple-Orange Ice

Makes about 2½ pints.

Nutrient Value Per ½ Cup: 75 calories, 0 g protein, 0 g fat, 16 g carbohydrate, 1 mg sodium, 0 mg cholesterol.

> **1 ripe pineapple, peeled, quartered, cored and cut into 1-inch chunks (about 4 cups)**
> **½ cup 10X (confectioners') sugar**
> **1 cup orange juice**
> **2 to 4 tablespoons white rum**

1. Working in batches if necessary, combine the pineapple, sugar and orange juice in a food processor. Cover; whirl until puréed. Add the rum.
2. Pour the mixture into an 8-inch square metal pan. Freeze the ice until almost frozen solid, for 2 to 4 hours; stir the ice several times, especially around the edges, so the ice freezes evenly.
3. Transfer the ice mixture to the food processor or a large chilled bowl. Quickly process or beat the ice with an electric mixer until the ice is smooth and fluffy. Return the ice to the pan. Freeze the ice for 30 minutes. Process or beat the ice again until smooth and fluffy.
4. Freeze the ice, tightly covered, until almost firm, for 1 to 2 hours. If the ice freezes solid, soften in the refrigerator for 30 minutes before serving.

Food for thought . . .

Roman emperors had ice brought from the Alps to Rome to make flavored ices. It is written that Nero particularly liked snow flavored with honey.

Honeydew Melon Ice

Makes about 2½ pints.

Nutrient Value Per ½ Cup: 72 calories, 1 g protein, 0 g fat, 19 g carbohydrate, 14 mg sodium, 0 mg cholesterol.

½ cup water
⅓ cup sugar
1 medium-size honeydew melon
4 to 5 tablespoons lime juice

1. Combine the water and the sugar in a small saucepan. Heat to boiling, stirring until the sugar dissolves. Simmer the syrup, uncovered, for 3 minutes. Cool the syrup completely.
2. Cut the melon into quarters; remove and discard the seeds and the rind. Cut the melon into 1-inch chunks. Working in batches if necessary, purée the melon in a food processor until moderately smooth. Transfer the purée to a bowl. Stir in the cooled sugar syrup and the lime juice.
3. Pour the melon purée into a 9-inch square metal pan. Freeze the purée until almost frozen, for 2 to 4 hours; stir the ice several times, especially around the edges, so the ice freezes evenly.
4. Transfer the ice to the food processor or a large chilled bowl. Quickly process or beat the ice with an electric mixer until it is smooth and fluffy. Return the ice to the pan; freeze for 30 minutes. Process or beat again until smooth and fluffy.
5. Freeze the ice, tightly covered, until almost firm, for 1 to 2 hours. If the ice freezes solid, soften in the refrigerator for 30 minutes before serving.

Peach Marsala Ice

Makes about 2½ pints.

Nutrient Value Per ½ Cup: 63 calories, 0 g protein, 0 g fat, 15 g carbohydrate, 1 mg sodium, 0 mg cholesterol.

½ cup water
⅓ cup sugar
2½ pounds ripe peaches, peeled, pitted and diced (about 4 cups)
1 tablespoon lemon juice
¼ cup Marsala wine

1. Combine the water and the sugar in a small saucepan. Heat to boiling, stirring until the sugar dissolves. Simmer the syrup, uncovered, for 3 minutes. Cool the syrup completely.
2. Working in batches if necessary, place the peaches, lemon juice and the syrup in a food processor. Cover; whirl until the mixture is smooth. Stir in the Marsala.
3. Pour the fruit purée mixture into an 8-inch square metal pan. Freeze the purée until almost frozen, for 2 to 4 hours; stir it several times, especially around the edges, so it freezes evenly.
4. Transfer the ice to the food processor or a large chilled bowl. Quickly process or beat the ice with an electric mixer until the ice is smooth and fluffy. Return the ice to the pan. Freeze the ice for 30 minutes. Process or beat the ice again until smooth and fluffy.
5. Freeze the ice, tightly covered, until almost firm, for 1 to 2 hours. If the ice freezes solid, soften in the refrigerator for 30 minutes before serving.

Food for thought . . .

Marsala is a fortified wine, similar to sherry and port. After the usual fermentation process of a wine has ended, if it's the right type of wine more alcohol can be added to make a sweeter wine; with marsala, brandy is added. This is the process called fortification. The percentage of alcohol in fortified wines (20%) is much higher than in non-fortified wines (11-13%). Marsala can range from very sweet to dry; it is meant to be drunk before or after a meal, and probably not during one.

Food for thought . . .

The kiwifruit, grown primarily in New Zealand and California, is shaped like a large egg and has a brown, fuzzy outer skin and a green pulp with small, edible black seeds. The flavor is both tart and sweet. The fruit is delicious by itself, chilled and sliced, or paired with chicken or fish. Kiwi sorbets are very popular in some restaurants.

Strawberry-Wine Ice

Makes about 2 pints.

Nutrient Value Per ½ Cup: 107 calories, 0 g protein, 0 g fat, 23 g carbohydrate, 2 mg sodium, 0 mg cholesterol.

¾ **cup water**
⅔ **cup sugar**
2 **boxes (1 pint each) ripe strawberries, halved**
¾ **cup fruity white wine, such as California Riesling**
1 **tablespoon lemon juice**

1. Combine the water and the sugar in a small saucepan. Bring to boiling, stirring until the sugar dissolves. Simmer the syrup, uncovered, for 3 minutes. Cool the syrup completely.
2. Purée the strawberries in a food processor. Combine the syrup and purée in a bowl; let stand for 30 minutes.
3. Add the wine and lemon juice to the strawberry mixture. Pour the fruit purée mixture into an 8-inch square metal pan. Freeze the purée until almost frozen, for 2 to 4 hours; stir the ice several times, especially around the edges, so the ice freezes evenly.
4. Transfer the ice to the food processor or a large chilled bowl. Quickly process or beat the ice with an electric mixer until the ice is smooth and fluffy. Return to the pan. Freeze the ice for 30 minutes. Process or beat the ice again until smooth and fluffy.
5. Freeze the ice, tightly covered, until almost firm, for 1 to 2 hours. If the ice freezes solid, soften in the refrigerator for 30 minutes before serving.

Kiwi Ice

Makes about 2 pints.

Nutrient Value Per ½ cup: 70 calories, 1 g protein, 0 g fat, 17 g carbohydrate, 5 mg sodium, 0 mg cholesterol.

1 **envelope unflavored gelatin**
½ **cup sugar**
½ **cup water**
10 **large ripe kiwi fruit**
¼ **cup lemon juice (2 lemons)***

1. Combine the gelatin and the sugar in a small heavy saucepan. Stir in the water. Cook the mixture over low heat, stirring constantly, until the gelatin and sugar dissolve. Remove the saucepan from the heat; cool to room temperature.
2. Peel the kiwi fruit; pull out the hard core at the stem end by twisting and pulling. Slice or dice the fruit (you should have about 4 cups).
3. Place half of the kiwi and half of the lemon juice in the container of a food processor or blender. Cover; whirl until the kiwi is puréed. Strain the purée through a sieve into the cooled gelatin-sugar syrup in the saucepan. Purée the remaining kiwi with the lemon juice. Stir the purée, without straining, into the kiwi mixture in the saucepan. Pour the kiwi ice mixture into a shallow metal pan. Cover the pan and freeze until the ice is firm but not solid, for about 1 hour.
4. Spoon the ice into a medium-size bowl. Beat the ice with an electric mixer until light and fluffy; do not overbeat. Return the ice to the pan and freeze until the ice is firm enough to scoop, for at least 3 hours or overnight.
5. To serve the ice, let stand at room temperature to soften slightly, for about 15 minutes. Scoop the ice into stemmed glasses. Garnish with half slices of kiwi and thin strips of lemon rind, if you wish.

***Note:** If the kiwi fruit are firm and not very sweet, use less lemon juice.*

THE DIFFERENCE BETWEEN SWEETENED CONDENSED MILK AND EVAPORATED MILK

Sweetened condensed milk has about half of its water content removed and sugar added. A 14-ounce can contains the equivalent of 2½ cups milk and 8 tablespoons sugar. Evaporated milk is canned whole milk with about 60% of its moisture content removed. To substitute for 1 cup of whole milk, combine ½ cup water with ½ cup of the evaporated milk.

LS

Amaretto-Apricot Ice Cream

You can choose a different liqueur and use peaches or nectarines, if you wish.

Makes 2 quarts.

Nutrient Value Per ½ Cup: 222 calories, 1 g protein, 17 g fat, 17 g carbohydrate, 17 mg sodium, 62 mg cholesterol.

8 **apricots, peeled, pitted and diced (about 2 cups)**
¼ **cup amaretto liqueur**
3 **cups heavy cream**
1 **cup sugar**

1. Toss the apricots with the amaretto in a large bowl; mash the apricots lightly.
2. Combine 1 cup of the cream and the sugar in a small saucepan. Heat slowly, stirring constantly, until the sugar dissolves. Pour the cream mixture over the apricot mixture; stir in the remaining 2 cups cream. Cover the bowl and refrigerate for at least 1 hour or until well chilled.
3. Pour the mixture into the 8-cup can of an electric or handcranked ice-cream freezer; freeze, following the manufacturer's directions.
4. Pack the ice cream into an 8-cup plastic freezer container; cover the container tightly and freeze until serving time.

Nutty Banana Ice Cream

Sweetened condensed milk is the backbone of this velvety-smooth frozen dessert made with an electric mixer.

Makes about 2 quarts.

Nutrient Value Per ½ Cup: 253 calories, 6 g protein, 19 g fat, 18 g carbohydrate, 64 mg sodium, 100 mg cholesterol.

3 **egg yolks**
1 **can (14 ounces) sweetened condensed milk (not evaporated milk)**
1 **ripe medium banana, mashed (about ½ cup)**
¼ **cup smooth peanut butter**
1 **tablespoon vanilla**
2 **cups (1 pint) heavy cream, whipped**
½ **cup chopped peanuts**

1. Beat the egg yolks in a large bowl with an electric mixer until smooth. Beat in the sweetened condensed milk, mashed banana, smooth peanut butter and vanilla until well blended. Fold in the whipped cream and the peanuts until no streaks of white remain.
2. Pour the mixture into a 9 x 5-inch loaf pan or other 2-quart container; cover. Freeze for 6 hours or until firm. Return any leftovers to the freezer.

Pumpkin Ice Cream Cake.

Pumpkin Ice Cream Cake

Pumpkin-chiffon cake layers are sandwiched with almond ice cream, frozen, and then frosted to make 2 cakes. Be sure to use cake flour.

Bake cakes at 325° for 45 to 55 minutes.
Makes 16 servings (2 loaves).

Nutrient Value Per Serving: 394 calories, 5 g protein, 24 g fat, 42 g carbohydrate, 286 mg sodium, 158 mg cholesterol.

Pumpkin Chiffon Cakes:
- 2 **cups** sifted cake *flour*
- 1½ **cups sugar**
- 1 **tablespoon baking powder**
- 1 **teaspoon salt**
- 1 **teaspoon ground cinnamon**
- ½ **teaspoon ground cloves**
- ½ **teaspoon ground nutmeg**
- 6 **eggs, separated, at room temperature**
- ¾ **cup canned pumpkin purée (from 16-ounce can)**
- ½ **cup vegetable oil**
- ½ **cup water**
- ½ **teaspoon cream of tartar**

Ice Cream Layer:
- 1 **quart butter almond ice cream**
- 2 **tablespoons chopped crystallized ginger**

Frosting:
- 2 **cups (1 pint) heavy cream**
- 2 **tablespoons sugar**

1. Preheat the oven to slow (325°).
2. Prepare the Pumpkin Chiffon Cakes: Sift together the cake flour, 1 cup of the sugar, the baking powder, salt, cinnamon, cloves and nutmeg into a large bowl. Add the egg yolks, pumpkin, oil and water; beat the mixture with a wire whisk until smooth. Set aside.
3. Beat the egg whites with the cream of tartar in a large bowl with an electric mixer until foamy. Gradually beat in the remaining ½ cup sugar. Continue to beat the whites until stiff, but not dry, peaks form. Fold the beaten whites into the pumpkin batter. Turn the batter into two ungreased 9 x 5 x 3-inch loaf pans.
4. Bake the cakes in the preheated slow oven (325°) for 45 to 55 minutes or until the cakes spring back when lightly touched with your fingertip and a wooden pick inserted in the center comes out clean. Cool the cakes in the pans on wire racks.
5. When the cakes are completely cooled, loosen them from the sides of the pans. Remove the cakes from the pans. Using a long serrated knife, split each cake in half horizontally. Place the layers in the freezer to chill while preparing the filling.
6. Wash and dry the loaf pans. Line the pans with heavy-duty aluminum foil cut to cover the bottom and the two long sides, leaving a small overhang to grasp.
7. Prepare the Ice Cream Layer: Soften the ice cream slightly in a bowl. Fold in the ginger.
8. Place the bottom layer of one cake, cut-side up, in one of the foil-lined pans. Spread the cake evenly with half of the ice cream mixture. Cover the ice cream with the top cake layer, cut-side down. Freeze the cake until firm, for about 3 hours. Repeat to make the second cake.
9. When the cakes are firm, lift each cake out of the pan, grasping the foil. Invert the cakes onto serving plates; remove the foil. Return the cakes to the freezer.
10. Prepare the Frosting: Beat together the cream and sugar in a large bowl until stiff. Spoon some of the whipped cream into a pastry bag fitted with a small star tip. Frost the tops and the sides of the cakes with the remaining whipped cream. Pipe cream onto the cakes to decorate. Return the cakes to the freezer until serving time. If not serving the cakes the same day they're frosted, cover the cakes with plastic wrap when the frosting is frozen solid.
11. If cakes are frozen, let them stand for 20 to 30 minutes at room temperature, to soften slightly. Just before serving the cakes, sprinkle the tops lightly with ground ginger, if you wish. Garnish with kumquats, red grapes and green leaves or additional crystallized ginger.

Vanilla Cream Mold

A light summer dessert that's low in calories.

Makes 8 servings.

Nutrient Value Per Serving: 155 calories, 7 g protein, 3 g fat, 25 g carbohydrate, 77 mg sodium, 14 mg cholesterol.

2½ **cups whole milk**
½ **cup sugar**
1 **teaspoon lemon juice**
2 **envelopes unflavored gelatin**
2 **containers (8 ounces each) vanilla yogurt, liquid drained from top, at room temperature**
½ **pint strawberries, sliced**

1. Combine the milk, sugar and lemon juice in a medium-size saucepan. Sprinkle the gelatin over the milk mixture; let stand for the gelatin to soften, for about 3 minutes. Cook the gelatin mixture over low heat, stirring occasionally, until the sugar and gelatin are dissolved; do not let the mixture boil. Remove the saucepan from the heat. Cool to lukewarm.
2. Stir the yogurt in a small bowl until smooth. Very gradually stir in some of the hot mixture until the yogurt is pourable; stir the yogurt mixture back into the saucepan.
3. Ladle the yogurt-gelatin mixture into 8 small decorative molds, 6 ounces each. Refrigerate for 1 to 2 hours or until the cream is firm. Run a sharp knife around the outer edge of each mold; dip the bottom of each mold into warm water. Unmold each cream onto an individual dessert plate. Serve each mold with sliced strawberries on the side.

Food for thought . . .

Cassis is a liqueur made from black currants. One part of cassis mixed with 3 parts of a chilled dry white wine makes a festive summer drink. Crème de cassis is a sweeter version of cassis.

Cassis Sherbet Ring with Gingered Fruit.

Cassis Sherbet Ring with Gingered Fruit

A refreshing dessert garnished with cut-up fresh fruit flavored with a ginger syrup.

Makes 8 servings.

Nutrient Value Per Serving: 345 calories, 2 g protein, 2 g fat, 75 g carbohydrate, 53 mg sodium, 7 mg cholesterol.

1 **quart lemon sherbet**
½ **cup crème de cassis liqueur**
 Red food coloring (optional)
1 **can (8 ounces) sliced pineapple packed in its own juice**
2 **large grapefruits**
 Water
⅓ **to ½ cup sugar, to taste**
¼ **cup corn syrup**
2 **to 3 tablespoons thinly slivered peeled, fresh gingerroot**
½ **cup fresh or frozen cranberries**
1 **red apple**
1 **ripe pear**
2 **cups mixed green and red grapes**

1. Beat the sherbet in a large bowl with an electric mixer until the sherbet is smooth, but not melted. Beat in the crème de cassis and 1 to 2 drops of red food coloring, if you wish.
2. Spoon the sherbet mixture into a 5-cup ring mold. Freeze the mold until firm, for 6 hours or overnight.
3. Drain the juice from the sliced pineapple into a 1-cup glass measure. Cut the pineapple slices into thirds and place in a large bowl.
4. Peel and section the grapefruit with a sharp knife, holding the fruit over a clean bowl to catch the juices. Add the sections to the pineapple in the large bowl. Add the grapefruit juice to the

pineapple juice in the measure. Add water to the juices to make ¾ cup.

5. Combine the juices, sugar and corn syrup in a small saucepan. Bring the mixture to boiling, stirring until the sugar dissolves. Add the gingerroot. Lower the heat and simmer for 5 minutes. Add the cranberries and simmer for 1 minute. Remove the saucepan from the heat and let the syrup cool for 5 minutes. Add the syrup to the pineapple-grapefruit mixture in the large bowl.

6. Quarter and core the apple and the pear. Cut into bite-size pieces. Add to the bowl with the other fruit. Add the grapes. Refrigerate the fruit until chilled, basting the fruit several times with the syrup.

7. To unmold the sherbet ring, dip the mold in hot water for a minute or so. Invert a chilled serving plate with a low rim over the mold. Carefully turn the plate and the mold right-side up. Remove the mold. Place the ring in the freezer to firm. Just before serving, spoon the fruit with the syrup into the center of the ring and around the outside edge of the ring.

Celebrate the season with Brandied Mincemeat Ice Cream Ring with Custard Sauce.

Food for thought . . .

The first reported recipes for mincemeat from the late 1400s contained a variety of gamebirds, strongly seasoned and spiced. Two centuries later the English began to develop their mincemeat, and now we in this country have a version which is usually meatless.

Brandied Mincemeat Ice Cream Ring with Custard Sauce

The brandied mincemeat is folded into softened vanilla ice cream and molded into a ring for a wonderful holiday dessert.

Makes 8 servings.

Nutrient Value Per Serving: 355 calories, 5 g protein, 18 g fat, 41 g carbohydrate, 189 mg sodium, 164 mg cholesterol.

1 quart good-quality vanilla ice cream, softened
1 cup prepared mincemeat with brandy and rum
Custard Sauce:
¼ cup sugar
 Pinch salt
3 egg yolks
¾ cup heavy cream
¼ cup milk
2 tablespoons cognac OR: brandy
½ teaspoon vanilla

1. Chill a 5-cup ring mold. Line the mold evenly with plastic wrap.
2. Stir together the softened ice cream and the mincemeat in a large bowl until well blended, but not melted. Spoon the ice cream mixture into the mold. Cover the mold with aluminum foil or plastic wrap. Place the mold in the freezer for at least 24 hours.
3. Prepare the Custard Sauce: Whisk together the sugar, salt and yolks in a small, heavy non-aluminum saucepan.
4. Heat together the cream and milk in a second clean, heavy saucepan until bubbles appear around the edge of the liquid. Gradually whisk the hot liquid into the yolk mixture, whisking constantly and vigorously.
5. Cook the custard over very low heat, stirring constantly, just until it almost reaches boiling; do not boil the custard. Steam will begin to appear and the custard will be slightly thicker than heavy cream. Strain at once into a clean bowl. Cool.
6. Stir in the cognac or brandy and the vanilla. The sauce can be stored in the refrigerator, covered, for up to 5 days. The sauce will thicken slightly in the refrigerator.
7. To serve, unmold the ice cream ring onto a serving plate. Remove the plastic wrap. Spoon the sauce around the ice cream ring. Garnish the top of the ring with glacé fruit, if you wish.

Rainbow Frozen Mousse

Festive enough for a party, easy enough so you won't mind making it on a hot day.

Makes 12 servings.

Nutrient Value Per Serving: 318 calories, 5 g protein, 14 g fat, 44 g carbohydrate, 149 mg sodium, 40 mg cholesterol.

1   **package (3 ounces) strawberry-flavored gelatin**
    Boiling water
1   **package (½ gallon) vanilla ice cream**
1   **package (3 ounces) lemon-flavored gelatin**
1   **package (3 ounces) lime-flavored gelatin**
1   **container (8 ounces) frozen non-dairy whipped topping, thawed**
    Strawberries

1. Prepare a collar for a 4-cup soufflé dish by tearing a 24-inch piece of aluminum foil from a box and folding in half, lengthwise. Wrap the foil around the dish and secure with paper clips.
2. Dissolve the strawberry-flavored gelatin in 1 cup of boiling water in a medium-size bowl. Stir in one-third of the ice cream, a scoop at a time, until the ice cream melts. Pour into the prepared soufflé dish and freeze for 30 minutes or until firm.
3. Prepare a lemon layer and a lime layer in the soufflé dish, following the directions in Step 2. Freeze each layer until firm. Cover the mousse with plastic wrap and return to the freezer. One hour before serving, remove the mousse to the refrigerator.
4. To serve: Decorate the top of the mousse with a swirl of non-dairy whipped topping and a strawberry.

LS

Layered Fruit Salad

A colorful, festive dessert or salad.

Makes 8 servings.

Nutrient Value Per Serving: 268 calories, 5 g protein, 12 g fat, 39 g carbohydrate, 40 mg sodium, 14 mg cholesterol.

Sour Cream Dressing:
1   **container (8 ounces) plain yogurt**
1   **container (8 ounces) dairy sour cream**
3   **tablespoons sugar**
1   **tablespoon cassis or blackberry liqueur**
    Grated rind of ½ orange (about 1 teaspoon)
⅛   **teaspoon almond extract**

Salad:
1   **large pineapple, quartered, peeled, cored and cut into chunks**
1   **pint strawberries, hulled and halved lengthwise**
2   **ripe kiwi, peeled and sliced**
1   **navel orange, peeled and sectioned**
1   **ripe papaya, halved, pitted, peeled and cut into thick slices**
½   **pound seedless red grapes, stems removed**
½   **cup sliced almonds, toasted**

1. Prepare the Sour Cream Dressing: Combine the yogurt, sour cream, sugar, liqueur, orange rind and almond extract in a small bowl.
2. Assemble the Salad: Place the pineapple chunks in a 2-quart glass or crystal bowl. Arrange the strawberry halves, cut-side out, around the edge of the bowl. Arrange the kiwi slices over the strawberries around the edge of the bowl. Top with the orange sections, papaya slices and red grapes. Pour the dressing evenly over the top. Cover the bowl with plastic wrap. Refrigerate the salad until ready to serve, for up to 1 day.
3. To serve the salad: Just before serving, sprinkle the almonds over the dressing. Present the salad to the diners. Transfer the salad to a large, clean dish pan or roasting pan. Gently toss the salad so all the ingredients are evenly coated with the dressing.

Pumpkin Mousse

Makes 8 servings.

Nutrient Value Per Serving: 303 calories, 5 g protein, 14 g fat, 38 g carbohydrate, 57 mg sodium, 146 mg cholesterol.

- 1 **envelope unflavored gelatin**
- ¾ **cup firmly packed light brown sugar**
- ½ **teaspoon ground cinnamon**
- 1 **can (16 ounces) pumpkin purée**
- ½ **cup milk**
- 3 **eggs, separated**
- 2 **tablespoons finely chopped candied ginger**
- 1 **teaspoon grated orange rind**
- ¼ **cup bourbon**
- ⅓ **cup granulated sugar**
- 1 **cup heavy cream, whipped**

1. Combine the gelatin, brown sugar and cinnamon in a medium-size saucepan. Blend in the pumpkin purée and the milk. Cook the mixture over medium heat, stirring constantly, until the gelatin and sugar are dissolved and the mixture just comes to boiling; do not boil.
2. Beat the 3 egg yolks in a small bowl. Blend in about ½ cup of the hot pumpkin mixture; then stir the yolk mixture back into the saucepan. Heat the saucepan over medium heat, stirring constantly, for 1 minute longer. Do not boil. Pour the mousse mixture into a large bowl. Stir in the ginger, orange rind and bourbon.
3. Place the bowl in a pan of ice and water. Chill in the refrigerator, stirring occasionally, until the mixture mounds slightly when spooned.
4. Beat the egg whites in a medium-size bowl until soft peaks form. Gradually beat in the granulated sugar until the meringue forms stiff, but not dry, peaks.
5. Fold the meringue, then the whipped cream into the pumpkin mixture. Pour the mousse into a 6-cup glass serving bowl or soufflé dish. Chill the mousse, covered, for up to 4 hours. Garnish the mousse with additional whipped cream and candied ginger, if you wish.

Food for thought . . .

Gingerroot is the root or tuber of a sweet plant that resembles a tall iris. Native to China, India, south Asia and the West Indies, the root has a light brown skin and a firm, pungent flesh. The ancient Greeks, Romans and Arabs used ginger extensively and the Chinese boiled ginger with honey — a foreshadowing of our crystallized ginger. Preserved, candied and crystallized ginger are used frequently in cakes, cookies and other confections.

Honey Whole-Wheat Bread Pudding

Bake at 350° for 30 minutes.
Makes 6 servings.

Nutrient Value Per Serving: 193 calories, 7 g protein, 2 g fat, 38 g carbohydrate, 199 mg sodium, 93 mg cholesterol.

- 2½ **cups day-old, small, whole-wheat bread cubes**
- ¼ **cup golden raisins**
- ¼ **cup finely chopped dried apricots**
- 1 **can (5½ ounces) apricot nectar Water**
- ¾ **cup instant nonfat dry milk**
- ⅓ **cup honey**
- 2 **eggs, slightly beaten**
- ¼ **teaspoon ground cinnamon**
- ⅛ **teaspoon salt**

1. Coat the inside of a 1½-quart baking dish with nonstick vegetable cooking spray. Combine the bread cubes, raisins and apricots in the prepared baking dish.
2. Pour the apricot nectar into a 4-cup measure. Add enough water to make 2¼ cups of liquid. Mix in the dry milk, honey, eggs, cinnamon and salt. Pour the liquid over the bread cubes. Let the pudding mixture stand for 15 minutes.
3. Preheat the oven to moderate (350°).
4. Bake the pudding in the preheated moderate oven (350°) for 30 minutes or until the pudding is set in the center. Serve the pudding warm or chilled.

S·M·A·R·T E·A·T·I·N·G

Zesty sauce gives Ocean Perch Creole (page 231) its terrific flavor.

6

*W*e're eating smarter these days — watching our fat, cholesterol and sodium intake. This national trend was confirmed when fast-food restaurants began featuring salad bars. Healthful eating is vital to a healthier, longer life, and we're devoting a full chapter to it, from main courses to desserts.

When you think healthy, you think fish so of course there's a whole catch of fish recipes, from Flounder with Watercress Mayonnaise *(page 229)* to Ocean Perch Creole *(page 231)*. But we also show how you can make other main course dishes healthier too. Sample Parmesan "Fried" Chicken *(page 217)* and Marinated Flank Steak *(page 223)*. There's even a collection of nutritious nibbles for snackers *(page 243)*.

In addition to trying new recipes, sit down and examine your dietary habits: Do you eat foods that provide plenty of complex carbohydrates, such as whole grains, fruits and vegetables? Do you use low-fat milk products and eat breads made with whole-grain flour? Have you curbed your intake of sweet and salty snacks?

Smart eating *is* a way of life — and it's never too soon to start!

GENERAL DIETING GUIDELINES

Caloric intake should equal the calories you expend to maintain your current weight. And 3,500 calories equal 1 pound of fatty tissue. Keep that all-important formula in mind if you're trying to maintain your weight.

Calories do count: Most women will lose weight eating 1,200 to 1,700 calories per day. Eating less may actually impede weight loss by lowering the body's basal metabolic rate. Most men will lose weight by eating 1,600 to 2,000 calories per day. However, any attempt to lose weight should be discussed with a doctor beforehand.

Water: Drink at least 8 glasses of water per day. It cleanses the system, helps to digest food properly, and helps create the feeling of being full.

Carbohydrates: Pasta, whole-wheat breads, rice, beans, potatoes, fresh fruits . . . complex carbohydrates are not fattening! This food group should make up more than ½ of the total calories consumed in one day (60% to 65%). If you eat the right amount of complex carbohydrates, it will help avoid that starved feeling and food cravings.

Protein: Protein is important, but should not be the main source of calories in your diet. Forget the "high-protein, quick weight-loss" diets. Only 20% of the daily calorie total should come from protein.

Fat: Fattening. Don't consume more than 17% of total calories in fat.

Fiber: Fresh fruit, vegetables, oatmeal, brown rice, lentils, beans . . . fiber may help reduce cholesterol, decrease the risk of cancer and prevent a variety of diseases. Plus, fiber gives that "full" feeling.

Fad diets have one big drawback: They don't teach you how to change your eating habits permanently. When the diet ends, so does your ability to control your weight.

Junk food — candy bars, sugary drinks, chips, cookies — are okay as an occasional treat. But avoid a steady diet of "empty calories."

Metabolism is one of the key factors in weight control. Active people burn more calories *all of the time*, not just while exercising.

Nutrient-rich foods pay off — in clear skin, shiny hair, strong teeth. Be sure to get your daily quota of vitamins and minerals.

Osteoporosis — "brittle bones" — is eight times more common in women than in men. Recent studies indicate that regular exercise and a calcium-rich diet can help keep bones strong.

Vitamins are vital for optimal health. Get them by eating a well-balanced diet — fresh fruits and vegetables, lean meats, fish, poultry, whole grains and dairy products.

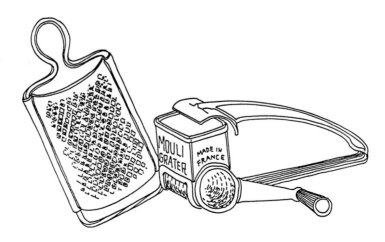

P·O·U·L·T·R·Y A·N·D O·T·H·E·R M·E·A·T·S

Parmesan "Fried" Chicken with shoe-string potatoes and 3-bean salad.

Parmesan "Fried" Chicken

Bake at 400° for 35 to 40 minutes.
Makes 4 servings.

Nutrient Value Per Serving: 268 calories, 35 g protein, 8 g fat, 12 g carbohydrate, 444 mg sodium, 171 mg cholesterol.

4   slices fresh white bread, torn into pieces
1   egg, slightly beaten
2   tablespoons water
5   tablespoons grated Parmesan cheese
¼   teaspoon grated lemon rind
¼   teaspoon salt
⅛   to ¼ teaspoon pepper
**1   small broiler-fryer (2½ pounds), cut into
        eighths, skin and fat removed**

1. Place the bread in the container of a food processor or electric blender. Cover and whirl until the bread is medium-coarse crumbs.
2. Stir together the egg and the water in a 9-inch pie plate. Combine the bread crumbs, cheese, lemon rind, salt and pepper on a piece of wax paper.
3. Dip the chicken pieces first into the egg mixture, then into the seasoned bread crumbs, pressing the coating on the chicken firmly. Arrange the chicken pieces in a shallow baking pan lined with aluminum foil. Refrigerate the chicken, uncovered, for at least 1 hour to set the coating.
4. Preheat the oven to hot (400°).
5. Bake the chicken in the foil-lined pan in the preheated hot oven (400°) for 35 to 40 minutes or until the chicken is no longer pink near the bone.

Food for thought . . .

The average healthy adult woman needs about 2,000 calories daily, and man, 2,700 calories daily. About 8% to 12% of those calories should come from protein in the diet, no more than 30% should come from fat, and the remaining calories should come from complex carbohydrates found in such foods as whole grains, fresh fruits and vegetables and pasta.

One-Pot Tangy Chicken

Makes 4 servings.

Nutrient Value Per Serving: 216 calories, 28 g protein, 3 g fat, 18 g carbohydrate, 544 mg sodium, 64 mg cholesterol.

2   **whole chicken breasts (about 12 ounces each), split in half**
3   **teaspoons reduced-calorie margarine**
2   **medium-size potatoes, peeled and cut into 2-inch chunks**
2   **medium-size carrots, peeled and cut into 1-inch pieces**
2   **stalks celery, sliced into 1-inch pieces**
1   **medium-size onion, coarsely chopped (½ cup)**
2   **cloves garlic, chopped**
⅔   **cup canned chicken broth (from a 13¾-ounce can), refrigerated and fat skimmed off**
3   **tablespoons fresh lemon juice**
½   **to ¾ teaspoon fennel seeds**
½   **teaspoon salt**
½   **teaspoon pepper**
    Chopped parsley (optional)

1. Remove and discard all the skin and visible fat from the chicken. Brown the chicken in 1 teaspoon of the margarine in a large nonstick saucepan or Dutch oven until lightly golden. Transfer the chicken to paper toweling to drain. Wipe the bottom of the saucepan clean with another sheet of paper toweling.
2. Sauté the potatoes, carrot, celery, onion and garlic in the remaining margarine in the saucepan over very low heat for 2 to 3 minutes or until the onion softens.
3. Arrange the chicken, breast-side up, over the vegetables in the saucepan. Stir together the broth, lemon juice, fennel, salt and pepper in a 1-cup glass measure. Pour the liquid over the chicken and vegetables in the saucepan.
4. Bring the mixture to boiling; lower the heat and simmer, covered, for 20 to 25 minutes or until the chicken is no longer pink next to the bone. Sprinkle the chicken with the parsley, if you wish, and ladle the chicken and the liquid with the vegetables into soup bowls.

Chicken Breast in Lime with Hot Ginger Dressing

Marinate the chicken first in the zesty lime mixture, then brush on the hot ginger dressing before cooking.

Bake at 350° for 10 minutes.
Makes 4 servings.

Nutrient Value Per Serving: 210 calories, 28 g protein, 7 g fat, 7 g carbohydrate, 164 mg sodium, 66 mg cholesterol.

- 4 chicken boneless, skinned breast halves (4 ounces each)
- 1 tablespoon lime juice
- 1 tablespoon grated lime rind
- 1 teaspoon reduced-sodium soy sauce
  Liquid red-pepper seasoning
  Whole-wheat flour
- 2 teaspoons safflower oil
- 2 tablespoons Hot Ginger Dressing (recipe follows)
- 1 cup sliced mushrooms
- ¼ cup chicken broth
- 1 tablespoon chopped green onion

1. Place the chicken breasts in a shallow baking dish. Combine the lime juice and rind, the soy sauce and a few drops of the red-pepper seasoning in a cup, mixing well. Pour the marinade over the chicken; turn the chicken to coat well. Cover the dish with plastic wrap and marinate in the refrigerator for 2 to 4 hours.
2. Preheat the oven to moderate (350°).
3. Drain the marinade. Pat the chicken dry with paper toweling. Lightly dust the chicken with whole-wheat flour.
4. Heat the oil in a large skillet and add the chicken. Cook until the chicken is lightly browned on both sides.
5. Brush the browned chicken lightly with the Hot Ginger Dressing. Place the chicken in a shallow baking dish. Cover.
6. Bake the chicken in the preheated moderate oven (350°) for 10 minutes or until the chicken is tender. Remove the chicken to 4 warm serving plates and keep warm.
7. Add the mushrooms to the same skillet and brown slightly. Add the chicken broth and simmer for a few minutes or until the mushrooms are heated through. Stir in the chopped green onion. Pour the mushroom sauce over the chicken, dividing equally.

Hot Ginger Dressing

Try this flavorful dressing on a large mixed green salad. The dressing may also be brushed over chicken, swordfish or shrimp while grilling.

Makes 1 cup.

Nutrient Value Per Tablespoon: 64 calories, 0 g protein, 7 g fat, 1 g carbohydrate, 26 mg sodium, 0 mg cholesterol.

- 1 clove garlic, peeled
- 1½ tablespoons coarsely chopped peeled, fresh gingerroot
- 1½ tablespoons rice vinegar
- 2 teaspoons reduced-sodium soy sauce
- 1 tablespoon water
- 2 teaspoons honey
- 1 teaspoon leaf basil, crumbled
- ½ cup peanut oil

Combine the garlic, gingerroot, rice vinegar, soy sauce, water, honey and basil in the container of an electric blender. Cover. Process on high speed for 30 seconds. Remove the center cap and gradually add the peanut oil until well blended. Refrigerate for up to 1 week in a glass jar with a screw top.

LIME JUICE

1 medium-size lime = 2 tablespoons lime juice
1 medium-size lime = 2 teaspoons grated lime rind

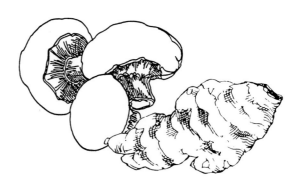

Curried Chicken Stew

Make sure each diner has a soup spoon for the broth.

Bake at 375° for 50 to 55 minutes.
Makes 4 servings.

Nutrient Value Per Serving: 220 calories, 36 g protein, 5 g fat, 5 g carbohydrate, 596 mg sodium, 114 mg cholesterol.

- **1 broiler-fryer (3 pounds), cut into serving pieces**
- **1 medium-size onion, finely chopped (½ cup)**
- **1 clove garlic, finely chopped**
- **1 medium-size sweet green pepper, halved, cored, seeded and coarsely chopped**
- **1 medium-size tomato, chopped**
- **1½ teaspoons ground curry powder**
- **1½ teaspoons ground coriander**
- **½ teaspoon salt**
- **½ teaspoon pepper**
- **½ teaspoon ground cumin**
- **½ teaspoon ground turmeric**
- **½ cup chicken broth, made from a bouillon cube**
- **1 teaspoon fresh lemon juice**

1. Preheat the oven to moderate (375°). Remove and discard all the skin and the excess fat from the chicken pieces.
2. Arrange the chicken in a single layer, meaty-side up, in a 13½ x 8½ x 2-inch glass baking dish. Sprinkle the chicken with the onion, garlic, green pepper, tomato, curry, coriander, salt, pepper, cumin and turmeric. Add the chicken broth and the lemon juice.
3. Bake the chicken, uncovered, in the preheated moderate oven (375°), turning the chicken pieces occasionally, for 50 to 55 minutes or until the chicken is no longer pink next to the bone.

Food for thought . . .

Protein is made up of amino acids. It is a component of all body cells, antibodies and enzymes, and is essential for the growth, repair and maintenance of cells. Proteins from most animal sources are usually complete, having all the amino acids needed for the diet, while proteins from plant sources are usually incomplete and need to be paired with other complementary plant proteins to provide all the necessary amino acids. The National Academy of Sciences recommends a daily intake of 44 grams of protein for the average healthy female and 56 grams for the male.

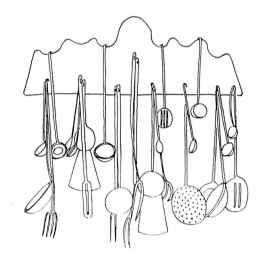

Lemon Turkey Scaloppine with escarole and vermicelli with tomato sauce.

Lemon Turkey Scaloppine

Makes 4 servings.

Nutrient Value Per Serving: 201 calories, 28 g protein, 6 g fat, 7 g carbohydrate, 370 mg sodium, 76 mg cholesterol.

1	**pound turkey cutlets, all visible fat removed**
¼	**cup all-purpose flour**
½	**teaspoon salt**
¼	**teaspoon pepper**
2	**teaspoons butter**
2	**teaspoons vegetable oil**
3	**tablespoons dry white wine**
2	**tablespoons fresh lemon juice**
¼	**cup chopped green onion**

1. Place the turkey cutlets between 2 sheets of wax paper; flatten the cutlets with a meat mallet or rolling pin to ⅛-inch thickness. Cut the meat into 3-inch-wide pieces.
2. Shake the turkey with the flour, salt and pepper in a plastic bag until the turkey is coated on both sides.
3. Spray a 12-inch nonstick skillet with nonstick vegetable cooking spray. Heat 1 teaspoon each of the butter and the oil in the prepared skillet. Panfry half the turkey in the hot fat for about 1 minute on each side. Transfer the cutlets to a serving platter; keep the cutlets warm.
4. Wipe the skillet clean with paper toweling. Respray the skillet with nonstick vegetable cooking spray. Heat the remaining butter and oil in the skillet. Panfry the remaining turkey in the skillet and transfer to the serving platter.
5. Add the wine, lemon juice and green onion to the skillet; boil until the sauce is slightly reduced, for about 1 minute. Pour the sauce over the turkey scaloppine and serve.

HOW TO GET EXCESS SODIUM OUT OF YOUR DIET

- *One-third of the average daily sodium intake comes from salt added at the table or during cooking, so you can control it.*
- *Don't add salt to pasta, vegetables, rice, soups and cereals while cooking.*
- *Use less and reduced-sodium versions of such condiments as soy sauce, chili and barbecue sauces, catsup, mustard, Worcestershire, pickles, relishes, seasoned salts, bouillon and meat tenderizers.*
- *Season with herbs and spices and homemade spice blends instead of salt.*
- *If using canned vegetables or canned beans, drain and rinse well to eliminate some excess sodium.*
- *Introduce some of the new reduced-sodium products into your meal planning — canned tomatoes, tuna fish, broths and soups.*

Food for thought . . .

Sodium is a mineral that in small quantities is necessary for normal blood, muscle and nerve function, but excess sodium in the diet may be harmful to those with high blood pressure. Sodium is most commonly found in table salt, but is also present in: canned products such as soups, vegetables, meats and poultry; frozen vegetables and frozen meat entrées that are heavily sauced; bottled salad dressings; cured, smoked, canned or dried fish, chicken and meats; cheese and processed cheese foods and spreads; dried soup and stew mixes; food preservatives with suffixes of "ate" such as monosodium glutamate; baking powder, baking soda and some medications such as antacids. The United States Department of Agriculture recommends the amount of sodium intake daily for the average healthy adult male and female be between 1,100 and 3,300 milligrams.

Individual Ham-Vegetable Custards

Bake at 350° for 35 to 40 minutes.
Makes 4 servings.

Nutrient Value Per Serving: 141 calories, 12 g protein, 7 g fat, 8 g carbohydrate, 647 mg sodium, 207 mg cholesterol.

½ **cup coarsely chopped celery (⅛ to ¼-inch)**
⅓ **cup coarsely chopped sweet green pepper (⅛ to ¼ inch)**
¼ **cup coarsely chopped onion (⅛ to ¼ inch)**
1 **medium-size zucchini, coarsely chopped (⅛ to ¼ inch)**
1 **tablespoon reduced-calorie margarine**
1 **cup coarsely chopped mushrooms**
2 **to 4 tablespoons water**
3 **slices (1 ounce each) turkey-ham (92%-95% fat-free), finely chopped**
½ **teaspoon leaf thyme, crumbled**
½ **teaspoon salt**
⅛ **teaspoon pepper**
⅛ **teaspoon anise seed, crushed**
1 **cup skim milk**
3 **eggs**
1½ **teaspoons tomato paste**

1. Preheat the oven to moderate (350°).
2. Sauté the celery, green pepper, onion and zucchini in the margarine in a medium-size nonstick saucepan for 2 to 3 minutes. Stir in the mushrooms. Add the water, as necessary, to prevent the vegetables from sticking and cook until the vegetables are very tender, about 7 minutes. Pat the vegetables dry with paper toweling.
3. Transfer the vegetables to a large bowl. Stir in the ham, thyme, salt, pepper and anise.
4. Beat the milk, eggs and tomato paste together in a 2-cup glass measure. Stir into the vegetable mixture.
5. Spray four 6-ounce custard cups with nonstick vegetable cooking spray. Divide the vegetable mixture among the custard cups; do not fill all the way to the top.
6. Place the custard cups in a 9-inch square baking pan and set the baking pan on an oven rack. Pour boiling water into the pan until it comes about two-thirds up the sides of the custard cups.

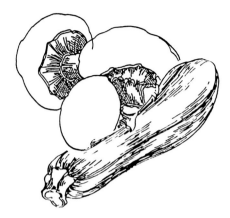

Marinated Flank Steak

For beef-eaters, but still low in calories.

Broil 2 minutes on each side.
Makes 4 servings.

Nutrient Value Per Serving: 184 calories, 24 g protein, 7 g fat, 4 g carbohydrate, 321 mg sodium, 71 mg cholesterol.

½ **cup fresh orange juice**
1 **tablespoon peanut oil**
3 **tablespoons white wine vinegar**
3 **tablespoons tamari OR: soy sauce**
1 **tablespoon honey**
⅛ **teaspoon ground pepper**
1 **pound flank steak, trimmed**

1. Combine the orange juice, oil, vinegar, tamari or soy sauce, honey and pepper in a small bowl until well mixed. Pour the marinade into a 13½ x 8½ x 2-inch glass baking dish.
2. Diagonally score one side of the flank steak with a sharp knife. Place the steak, cut-side down, in the marinade. Cover the dish and refrigerate overnight; turn the meat occasionally.
3. Preheat the broiler.
4. Remove the steak from the marinade. Broil the steak for 2 minutes on each side for medium-rare, basting with the marinade several times. Let the steak stand for 5 minutes. Slice the steak across the grain into thin slices. Spoon 1 tablespoon of the marinade over each serving.

7. Bake the custards in the preheated moderate oven (350°) for 35 to 40 minutes or until a knife inserted into the centers of the custards comes out clean.
8. Remove the custard cups from the water bath. Let the custards stand for 15 minutes. To unmold, run a sharp knife around the edge of the custards; invert the custards onto a serving plate.

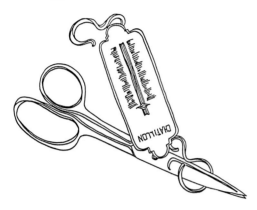

Herbed Pork Loin Chops

Herbs lend an aromatic quality to the marinade. If possible, use fresh tarragon or rosemary so a more assertive flavor will develop.

Broil for 15 to 30 minutes.
Makes 4 servings.

Nutrient Value Per Serving: 267 calories, 22 g protein, 19 g fat, 0 g carbohydrate, 56 mg sodium, 77 mg cholesterol.

 4   **boneless pork loin chops, cut 1-inch thick (approximately 1 pound)**
 1   **tablespoon chopped fresh tarragon or rosemary OR: 1 teaspoon leaf tarragon or rosemary, crumbled**
 1   **tablespoon olive oil**
 1   **clove garlic, finely chopped**
 ¼   **teaspoon cracked black pepper**
     Salt, to taste (optional)

1. Place the chops in a shallow glass dish. Combine the tarragon or rosemary, oil, garlic and pepper in a small bowl. Brush the herb mixture evenly over both sides of the chops. Cover and marinate the chops for 30 minutes.
2. Preheat the broiler.
3. Place the chops on a rack in a broiler pan so the surface of the meat is 4 to 5 inches from the heat.
4. Broil the chops, turning once, for 15 to 30 minutes or until a meat thermometer registers 170° F. Season with salt, if you wish.

Mexican Pork Strips

Great as an appetizer, or serve as a hearty main dish, if you wish.

Broil for 6 minutes.
Makes 4 to 6 main-dish servings.

Nutrient Value Per Serving: 218 calories, 25 g protein, 11 g fat, 4 g carbohydrate, 285 mg sodium, 76 mg cholesterol.

 1¼ **pounds boneless pork loin roast (single loin)**
 2   **tablespoons fresh lime juice**
 2   **tablespoons vegetable oil**
 2   **cloves garlic, finely chopped**

   Salsa:
 2   **tomatoes, seeded and finely chopped**
 3   **tablespoons chopped green chilies**
 2   **tablespoons chopped fresh cilantro**
 1   **green onion, thinly sliced**
 ¾   **teaspoon ground cumin**
 ½   **teaspoon salt**

1. Trim any surface fat from the pork loin; discard. Partially freeze the pork to firm. Slice the pork across the grain into ⅛- to ¼-inch slices; cut each slice in half lengthwise.
2. Combine the lime juice, oil and garlic in a cup. Place the pork in a plastic bag; add the marinade and turn to coat the pork. Close the bag securely and marinate the pork in the refrigerator for 30 minutes, turning occasionally.
3. Soak four 9-inch bamboo skewers in water for 10 minutes.
4. Meanwhile, prepare the Salsa: Combine the chopped tomatoes, chilies, cilantro, sliced green onion, cumin and salt in a medium-size bowl; cover the bowl with plastic wrap and refrigerate until serving time.
5. Remove the pork from the marinade. Thread the strips of pork (weaving back and forth) on the bamboo skewers. Place the kabobs on a rack in a broiler pan so the surface of the meat is 3 inches from the heat.
6. Broil the kabobs for 6 minutes, turning several times. Serve the kabobs immediately with the Salsa.

Veal Cutlets and Apples

By flaming the apple brandy in the sauce you cook away the calories but the delightful taste remains.

Makes 6 servings.

Nutrient Value Per Serving: 218 calories, 23 g protein, 9 g fat, 9 g carbohydrate, 177 mg sodium, 81 mg cholesterol.

Nonstick vegetable cooking spray
1½ pounds veal cutlets
1 tablespoon all-purpose flour
Salt and pepper, to taste
3 tablespoons apple brandy
1 teaspoon finely chopped, peeled fresh gingerroot
1 Red Delicious apple, peeled, cored and thinly sliced
1½ teaspoons sugar
¾ cup dry white wine
¾ cup chicken broth

1. Spray a large skillet with the nonstick vegetable cooking spray. Dredge the veal in the flour; shake off the excess and season with the salt and pepper to taste.
2. Cook the veal in the prepared skillet for 3 minutes on each side or until golden. Remove the veal from the skillet.
3. Add the apple brandy to the skillet. Carefully light the mixture with a long kitchen match. When the flames subside, add the ginger, sliced apple, sugar, wine and broth.
4. Cook the mixture over hight heat for 10 minutes or until the apples are tender and the sauce thickens slightly. Return the veal to the skillet. Cover and cook until the veal is heated through.

NUTRITIOUS NIBBLES

Vegetables and fruits make crisp and healthy, yet relatively low-calorie, additions to the hors d'oeuvres platter. Try the following — you could even keep some bagged in plastic in the refrigerator, ready for munching.

- Leeks, peeled, split and trimmed
- Sweet green pepper, cut into squares
- Radishes, halved
- Cherry tomatoes, halved
- Carrots, peeled and cut in slices or sticks
- Cauliflower, separated into flowerets
- Pineapple, cut into thin slices
- Apples, cut into wedges
- Zucchini, cut into spears
- Turnip, cut into slices
- Celery, cut into 1-inch pieces
- Kiwi, peeled, cut into slices
- Peas, raw
- Endive, separated into leaves
- Small whole cooked beets, cut into sticks
- Mushroom caps, cooked or raw
- Chinese snow peas
- Sweet red pepper, cut into squares
- Sugar snap peas, blanched
- Broccoli, separated into flowerets
- Orange slices, whole or halved

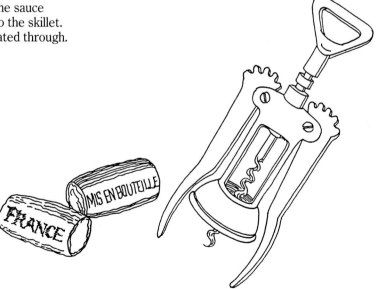

S·E·A·F·O·O·D

Crustless Tuna Quiche

The filling contains so much taste and texture that your guests will never miss the pastry!

Bake at 350° for 45 minutes.
Makes 6 servings.

Nutrient Value Per Serving: 257 calories, 21 g protein, 16 g fat, 8 g carbohydrate, 471 mg sodium, 234 mg cholesterol.

- ⅓ cup sliced green onion
- ¼ cup chopped sweet red pepper
- 1 tablespoon butter
- 4 eggs
- 3 tablespoons all-purpose flour
- ¼ teaspoon salt
- ¼ teaspoon dry mustard
- ⅛ teaspoon pepper
- 1½ cups skim milk
- 1½ cups shredded Cheddar cheese (6 ounces)
- 1 can (6½ ounces) tuna packed in water, drained and flaked
- 1 large ripe tomato, cut into 6 wedges
  Sprigs of fresh cilantro (optional)

1. Preheat the oven to moderate (350°). Spray a 9-inch pie plate or quiche dish with nonstick vegetable cooking spray.
2. Sauté the onion and red pepper in the butter in a small skillet for 3 minutes or until tender.
3. Combine the eggs, flour, salt, dry mustard and pepper in a medium-size bowl; beat until well blended. Stir in the milk; add the shredded Cheddar cheese, tuna and sautéed vegetables, mixing well. Pour the mixture into the prepared dish.
4. Bake the quiche in the preheated moderate oven (350°) for 45 minutes or until a knife inserted near the center comes out clean. Let the quiche cool for 10 minutes before cutting into wedges.
5. Garnish each serving with a tomato wedge and a sprig of cilantro, if you wish.

Oriental-Style Fish

Bake at 450° for 25 to 30 minutes for frozen fish, or 10 to 12 minutes for fresh.
Makes 4 servings.

Nutrient Value Per Serving: 222 calories, 22 g protein, 7 g fat, 17 g carbohydrate, 383 mg sodium, 57 mg cholesterol.

- 1 pound fresh or frozen cod fillets
- ½ cup orange juice
- 1 tablespoon soy sauce
- 1 teaspoon hoisin sauce*
- ¼ cup chopped onion
- ¼ teaspoon ground ginger
- ¼ teaspoon salt
- 1 sweet red pepper, cut in julienne strips (2½ x ¼-inch)
- 2 carrots, peeled and cut in julienne strips (2½ x ¼-inch)
- 1 cup snow peas, trimmed
- 2 tablespoons vegetable oil
- ½ cup drained, canned pineapple cubes
- 2 teaspoons cornstarch
- 2 tablespoons water

1. Preheat the oven to very hot (450°). If using frozen fish, unwrap and let the fish stand at room temperature for 20 minutes.
2. Line a 9-inch square baking pan with enough aluminum foil to fold over the fish. Place the fish on the foil in the pan.
3. Combine the orange juice, soy sauce, hoisin sauce, onion, ginger and salt in a small bowl. Pour the mixture over the fish. Fold the foil over the top of the fish and fold the ends of the foil together to seal.
4. Bake the fish in the preheated very hot oven (450°) for 25 to 30 minutes for frozen fish, 10 to 12 minutes for fresh fish, or until the fish flakes when tested with a fork.
5. Meanwhile, stir-fry the sweet red pepper,

carrots and snow peas in the oil in a large skillet over medium heat until crisp-tender, for 2 minutes. Add the pineapple.

6. When the fish is cooked, open the foil packet and drain the juice into the skillet. Keep the fish warm.** Stir together the cornstarch and the water in a small bowl. Stir the cornstarch mixture into the skillet and cook until thickened, for 2 minutes.

7. Serve the fish with the vegetables and with the sauce spooned over the fish.

Notes: *Bottled hoisin sauce can be found in the Oriental section of some supermarkets.
**The fish may contain bones, so be sure to remove them before serving.

THE MAGIC 10-MINUTE COOKING RULE

1. Measure the fish at its thickest part, whether whole, steaks or fillets, and including any stuffing. For each measured 1 inch of thickness, cook the fish at high heat, regardless of the cooking method, for the following indicated times:

Fresh/fully thawed	*10 minutes*
Partially thawed	*12 to 15 minutes*

Allow more time for cooking if the fish is foil-wrapped or heavily sauced.
2. When the fish is properly cooked, the juices run clear, and the flesh is opaque and flakes easily when pierced with a fork.

Salmon Baked in Foil

Each serving is topped with leek, mushroom and carrot and a little flavored butter. And there's no dirty baking pan to wash since the fish is wrapped and cooked in aluminum foil.

Bake at 500° for 8 to 9 minutes.
Makes 4 servings.

Nutrient Value Per Serving: 323 calories, 27 g protein, 21 g fat, 7 g carbohydrate, 187 mg sodium, 60 mg cholesterol.

1	**leek, washed, trimmed and cut into 2¼-inch strips**
4	**mushrooms, sliced**
1	**carrot, cut into 2 x ¼-inch strips** **Vegetable oil**
1	**pound boned fresh salmon, cut in 4 equal pieces**
4	**small bay leaves**
4	**thin lemon slices**
8	**slices of Maître d'Hôtel Butter (see box, page 229), ¼ inch thick**

1. Preheat the oven to very hot (500°).
2. Bring a medium-size saucepan of water to boiling. Add the leek and mushroom slices; blanch for 30 seconds. Remove with a slotted spoon to a colander; run under cold water to stop further cooking.
3. Return the water to boiling. Add the carrot and blanch for 1 minute. Drain. Rinse under cold water to stop the cooking and drain again. Combine the vegetables in a small bowl. Set aside.
4. Tear off 4 pieces of aluminum foil, each large enough to enclose one piece of fish and a quarter of the vegetables. Lightly oil the aluminum foil. Place 1 piece of fish on each foil sheet. Top each with a bay leaf, lemon slice, one-quarter of the vegetables and 2 slices of Maître d'Hotel Butter. Fold the foil over the fish, folding the edges of the foil together to form a tightly sealed package. Place the packages on a baking sheet.
5. Bake the fish packages in the preheated very hot oven (500°) for 8 to 9 minutes or until the fish flakes when tested with a fork. Serve 1 package of fish and vegetables per person.

Easy Boston Scrod

Scrod is young codfish. If not available, substitute cod or haddock.

Bake at 450° for 30 minutes for frozen, 10 minutes for fresh.
Makes 4 servings.

Nutrient Value Per Serving: 167 calories, 22 g protein, 5 g fat, 7 g carbohydrate, 463 mg sodium, 70 mg cholesterol.

1 **pound frozen or fresh scrod, cod or haddock fillets**
⅓ **cup fine, dry bread crumbs**
½ **teaspoon salt**
⅓ **cup milk**
4 **teaspoons butter or margarine, melted**

1. If using frozen fish, unwrap and let the fish stand at room temperature for 20 minutes.
2. Preheat the oven to very hot (450°). Grease an 8 x 8 x 2-inch square baking dish.
3. Cut or separate the fish into 4 equal portions. (Be careful cutting frozen fish, since the center will still be hard and frozen.) Combine the bread crumbs and the salt on a piece of wax paper. Dip the fish into the milk, then roll in the crumb mixture to evenly coat. Place the fish in the prepared baking dish. Drizzle the fish with the melted butter.
4. Bake the fish in the preheated very hot oven (450°) for about 30 minutes for frozen fish, or about 10 minutes for fresh fish, or until the fish flakes easily when pierced with a fork. Serve the fish immediately. (Both fresh and frozen fish may contain bones, so be sure to remove before serving or as you eat.)

Sole Meunière

Our home version of the classic restaurant dish.

Makes 8 servings.

Nutrient Value Per Serving: 238 calories, 21 g protein, 13 g fat, 8 g carbohydrate, 202 mg sodium, 68 mg cholesterol.

2 **pounds fresh flounder or sole fillets**
¼ **teaspoon salt**
⅛ **teaspoon pepper**
½ **cup all-purpose flour**
3 **tablespoons butter**
3 **tablespoons vegetable oil**
⅓ **cup sliced almonds**
¼ **cup chopped parsley**
2 **tablespoons fresh lemon juice**

1. Pat the fish fillets dry with paper toweling. Combine the salt, pepper and flour in a large bowl. Dip the fillets in the seasoned flour to coat.
2. Melt the butter with the oil in a large skillet over medium-high heat. Heat until the oil is very hot but not smoking. Fry the fish fillets, a few at a time, until golden brown, for about 1 minute per side. Remove the fillets to a warm serving platter and keep warm.
3. Add the almonds to the skillet. Lower the heat to low; sauté the almonds until lightly golden, for about 45 seconds. Add the parsley and the lemon juice; swirl to evenly combine the ingredients in the skillet. Pour the sauce over the fish. Serve immediately.

FLAVORED BUTTERS FOR BROILED FISH

To add flavor interest and to ensure moist results when broiling fish, especially with the lean varieties such as cod or sole, arrange pats of one of the following butters on the fish before broiling. For an extra flavor boost, finish with an extra pat just before serving, if you wish.

Just mix together the ingredients for the flavored butter in a bowl with a wooden spoon. Place on a sheet of wax paper and roll into an 8 x 2-inch log. Slice the butter into thin pats and use immediately, or wrap the roll without slicing and refrigerate, or freeze for later use.

Lemon Butter: *½ cup (1 stick) softened butter, 2 tablespoons fresh lemon juice and ⅛ teaspoon salt. Variation: ½ teaspoon paprika or a few drops onion juice.*

Maitre d' Hôtel Butter: *½ cup (1 stick) softened butter, 1½ tablespoons finely chopped parsley, 1 tablespoon fresh lemon juice, ¼ teaspoon salt and ⅛ teaspoon pepper.*

Herb Butter: *½ cup (1 stick) softened butter, 1 tablespoon finely chopped fresh tarragon or basil, 1 teaspoon finely chopped parsley, ¼ teaspoon fresh lemon juice and ¼ teaspoon salt.*

Mustard Butter: *½ cup (1 stick) softened butter, 2½ teaspoons prepared mustard, 1 teaspoon fresh lemon juice and ¼ teaspoon salt.*

Flounder with Watercress Mayonnaise

Bake at 400° for 12 to 15 minutes.
Makes 4 servings.

Nutrient Value Per Serving: 184 calories, 21 g protein, 9 g fat, 4 g carbohydrate, 373 mg sodium, 67 mg cholesterol.

Watercress Mayonnaise:
- **1 bunch watercress, stems removed**
- **¼ pound fresh spinach, stems removed and leaves torn into bite-size pieces**
- **½ cup reduced-calorie mayonnaise**
- **1 tablespoon lemon juice**
- **½ teaspoon Dijon-style mustard**

- **4 flounder fillets (1 pound)**
- **½ teaspoon coarsely ground pepper**

1. Preheat the oven to hot (400°). Line a 15 x 10 x 1-inch jelly-roll pan with aluminum foil.
2. Prepare the Watercress Mayonnaise: You should have about 2½ cups of watercress and 2 cups of spinach after the trimming. Dry both the watercress and the spinach very well with paper toweling. Combine the watercress and the spinach in the container of a food processor. Cover; whirl until finely chopped. Add the mayonnaise, lemon juice and the mustard; whirl until the mixture is well blended. Transfer the mayonnaise to a bowl and cover. Refrigerate until serving time.
3. Fold each fish fillet in half crosswise. Sprinkle the top of each fillet with pepper. Arrange the fillets in the prepared pan.
4. Bake the fillets in the preheated hot oven (400°) for 12 to 15 minutes or until the center of the folded fish is white and firm to the touch.
5. Transfer the fish to a serving plate. Serve the fish with the mayonnaise on the side.

Poached Salmon Steaks with Rich Tomato and Basil Butter Sauce

Makes 6 servings.

Nutrient Value Per Serving: 289 calories, 15 g protein, 24 g fat, 3 g carbohydrate, 210 mg sodium, 67 mg cholesterol.

> 1   **tablespoon butter**
>   **Court Bouillon (recipe follows)**
> 1   **pound salmon steaks**
>   **Rich Tomato and Basil Butter Sauce**
>   **(recipe follows)**

1. Butter a deep skillet or similar pan large enough to hold the salmon steaks in a single layer without touching.
2. Pour enough of the Court Bouillon into the skillet so the fish will be just barely covered when added to the skillet. Bring the liquid to boiling.
3. Add the fish to the liquid in the skillet. Return the liquid to simmering. Adjust the heat to maintain the simmer. Cover the top of the fish with a piece of buttered wax paper, buttered-side down.
4. Cook the fish for 10 minutes per measured inch of thickness. Do not let the liquid boil.
5. Lift the cooked fish from the poaching liquid with a slotted spatula, draining the fish well over the skillet. Drain the fish briefly on paper toweling. Keep the fish warm, loosely covered with aluminum foil, in a very slow oven (175°) while making the Rich Tomato and Basil Butter Sauce.
6. To serve, arrange the salmon on 4 dinner plates. Spoon the sauce over the fish. Serve with hot cooked rice sprinkled with chopped walnuts, and snow peas, if you wish.

Rich Tomato and Basil Butter Sauce: Boil 2 cups of the fish poaching liquid in a medium-size saucepan over high heat until reduced to ¼ cup. Remove the saucepan from the heat. Whisk in 6 to 8 tablespoons of butter cut into small pieces, bit by bit, incorporating each piece, but not allowing it to melt completely before adding the next bit. The sauce should be creamy and frothy. Stir in 1 small tomato, peeled, seeded and chopped, and ¼ cup chopped fresh basil.

Poached Salmon Steaks

Court Bouillon

Makes about 2 quarts.

Nutrient Value Per 1 Cup: 10 calories, 3 g protein, 0 g fat, 2 g carbohydrate, 8 mg sodium, 0 mg cholesterol.

> 1   **large onion, sliced**
> 1   **large carrot, scraped and sliced**
> 1   **stalk celery, sliced**
> 2   **green onions, trimmed and sliced**
> 6   **sprigs parsley**
> 1   **teaspoon leaf thyme, crumbled**
> 1   **bay leaf**
> 6   **cups water**
> 2   **cups dry white wine***
> 6   **white peppercorns**

1. Combine the onion, carrot, celery, green onion, parsley, thyme, bay leaf and water in a 4-quart nonaluminum saucepan or pot. Bring to boiling. Lower the heat and simmer 10 to 15 minutes.
2. Add the wine. Simmer for 15 minutes. Add the peppercorns for the last 5 minutes of simmering. Skim off any foam and discard.
3. Strain the court bouillon through a strainer or colander lined with a double thickness of dampened cheesecloth or paper toweling. Discard the solids.

4. Refrigerate the court bouillon for up to 3 days, or freeze in freezer bags or ice cube trays for up to 6 months.

Note: This amount of wine added halfway through the simmering process produces a slightly acidic stock good for poaching strongly flavored fish such as swordfish, salmon, tuna and mackerel. For a milder stock, add the wine at the very beginning of the simmering.

Ocean Perch Creole

Bake at 450° for 8 to 10 minutes.
Makes 8 servings.

Nutrient Value Per Serving: 257 calories, 23 g protein, 15 g fat, 7 g carbohydrate, 367 mg sodium, 62 mg cholesterol.

Creole Sauce (recipe at right)
2 **pounds fresh or frozen ocean perch or pollock fillets***
2 **tablespoons olive oil**
2 **tablespoons dry white wine OR: water**
2 **teaspoons lemon juice**
1 **clove garlic, crushed**
½ **teaspoon leaf tarragon, crumbled**
⅛ **teaspoon pepper**

1. Prepare the Creole Sauce.
2. Preheat the oven to very hot (450°).
3. Place the fish fillets in a single layer in a 13½ x 8½ x 2-inch baking dish. Combine the olive oil, white wine or water, lemon juice, garlic, tarragon and pepper in a small bowl; mix until well blended. Pour the liquid over the fish; turn the fish over to coat. Cover the baking dish with aluminum foil.
4. Bake the fish in the preheated very hot oven (450°) for 8 to 10 minutes or until the fish flakes easily when pierced with a fork. Carefully remove the fish with a slotted spatula to paper toweling to drain. Transfer the drained fish to a warmed serving platter; keep warm. Reserve the cooking liquid for the Creole Sauce.
5. Add the reserved fish cooking liquid to the Creole Sauce. Bring to boiling; boil for 3 minutes.
6. Spoon the Creole Sauce over the fish on the platter. Serve immediately.

Creole Sauce: Sauté ⅔ cup chopped sweet green pepper, ⅔ cup chopped onion and 2 cloves garlic, finely chopped, in 3 tablespoons olive oil in a large skillet over medium heat until soft, for about 8 minutes. Add 1 can (16 ounces) whole peeled tomatoes with their juice, chopped, ⅓ cup dry white wine or water, ⅓ cup tomato paste, 2 teaspoons chopped fresh or canned seeded green chilies, 1½ teaspoons leaf tarragon, crumbled, ¼ teaspoon salt and ⅛ teaspoon pepper. Lower the heat and simmer for 15 minutes. Add ½ cup sliced pitted ripe olives; simmer for 10 minutes longer or until the sauce is lightly thickened.

Note: If using frozen fillets for this recipe, unwrap the frozen fish packages and let stand at room temperature for 20 minutes. Cut the fish into 8 chunks. (Be careful cutting the fish since the center core is still hard and frozen.) Bake the fish as above in Steps 2 through 4, but for 25 to 30 minutes. Drain and discard the fish cooking liquid. Eliminate Step 5.

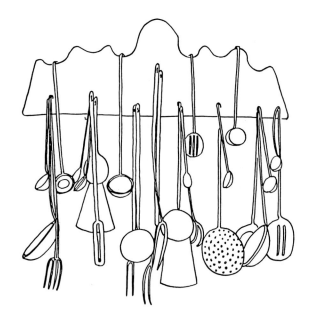

Food for thought . . .

Fish Oil — Nature's Health Food

Cutting back on the amount of fat you consume is a health-smart move — except when it comes to fatty fish. In that case, more is better. Research indicates that fish, rich in Omega-3 fatty acids, may be one of the best health foods. The reasons:

• Cholesterol cleanser. After a four-week study comparing the benefits of fish oil versus vegetable oil, the people receiving fish oil had cholesterol levels up to five times lower than those in the vegetable-oil group.

• Artery unclogger. By making platelets (the clotting factor in the blood) less "sticky" and, therefore, less likely to adhere to vessel walls, Omega-3s may prevent heart attacks and strokes.

• Migraine minimizer. According to a study at the University of Cincinnati, 8 out of 15 chronic migraine sufferers reduced both the intensity and frequency of their headaches on a diet supplemented with Omega-3 fish oil. The research, however, is still preliminary.

TYPE OF FISH (3½ OZ. RAW)	GRAMS OF OMEGA-3 FATTY ACID*
Anchovy	.9
Catfish	.3
Chinook Salmon	1.4
Clams	.4
Cod	.3
Crabs	.4
Haddock	.2
Halibut	.4
Herring	1.6
Mackerel	2.5
Mussels	.5
Oysters	.4
Red Snapper	.2
Sardines	1.3
Smelt	.7
Sockeye Salmon	1.2
Striped Bass	.8
Trout	.5
Tuna	1.3

*These are average figures; the Omega-3 content varies with different species.

Breaded Sole With Creamy Horseradish-Dill Sauce

The secret of the rich-tasting sauce is the imitation sour cream dressing.

Bake at 400° for 5 to 7 minutes.
Makes 4 servings.

Nutrient Value Per Serving: 229 calories, 24 g protein, 8 g fat, 13 g carbohydrate, 549 mg sodium, 126 mg cholesterol.

1   **egg**
3   **tablespoons water**
½   **cup packaged seasoned bread crumbs**
4   **fillets of sole (1 pound)**

Creamy Horseradish-Dill Sauce:
½   **cup imitation sour cream dressing***
1   **tablespoon bottled horseradish, drained**
1   **tablespoon chopped fresh dill**
1   **egg white**

1. Preheat the oven to hot (400°). Line a 15 x 10 x 1-inch jelly-roll pan with aluminum foil.
2. Beat the whole egg and the water together in a small pie plate. Pour the bread crumbs onto a piece of wax paper. Dip the fish first into the egg mixture; then coat the fish with the bread crumbs on both sides. Place the fish on the prepared pan.
3. Bake the fish in the preheated hot oven (400°) for 5 to 7 minutes or until the fish is white and firm to the touch.
4. Prepare the Creamy Horseradish-Dill Sauce: Stir together the sour cream dressing, horseradish and dill in a small bowl. Beat the egg white in a second small bowl until soft peaks form; fold the whites into the dressing mixture. Serve the sauce with the fish.

***Note:** Imitation sour cream dressing is available in the refrigerated dairy case.

Salmon Cakes

Bake at 400° for 10 minutes.
Makes 4 servings.

Nutrient Value Per Serving: 212 calories, 25 g protein, 8 g fat, 7 g carbohydrate, 517 mg sodium, 107 mg cholesterol.

1   **can (15½ ounces) red salmon, flaked**
1   **cup soft fresh bread crumbs (2 slices)**
¼   **cup chopped green onion**
1   **egg, lightly beaten**
2   **tablespoons fresh lemon juice**
1   **teaspoon Worcestershire sauce**

1. Preheat the oven to hot (400°). Spray a cookie sheet with nonstick vegetable cooking spray, or use a nonstick cookie sheet.
2. Combine the salmon, bread crumbs, green onion, egg, lemon juice and Worcestershire sauce in a medium-size bowl; stir the mixture well to combine. Shape the mixture into 4 equal patties. Place the patties on the prepared cookie sheet.
3. Bake the patties in the preheated hot oven (400°) for 5 minutes on each side or until the patties are golden and heated through.

Tuna Provolone Pita Pockets

Makes 4 servings.

Nutrient Value Per Serving: 219 calories, 19 g protein, 7 g fat, 22 g carbohydrate, 771 mg sodium, 35 mg cholesterol.

1   **can (7 ounces) solid white tuna, packed in water and drained**
½   **cup diced cucumber**
½   **cup cubed Provolone (2 ounces)**
½   **cup coarsely chopped seeded tomato**
¼   **cup thinly sliced pitted black olives**
¼   **cup reduced-calorie bottled Italian salad dressing***
2   **cups shredded romaine lettuce**
2   **regular-size whole-wheat pita breads, halved**
½   **cup shredded carrot**

1. Break the tuna with a fork into bite-size pieces. Combine the tuna, cucumber, Provolone, tomato and olives in a large bowl. Stir in the salad dressing. Let the tuna mixture marinate in the refrigerator for several hours. Stir the mixture occasionally.

2. Place the lettuce in each pita pocket half, dividing equally. Spoon the tuna mixture over the lettuce; top with the carrots.

Note: We used dressing with a label indicating 2 to 16 calories per tablespoon.

Burrida

A rich stewlike soup, thick with 3 different kinds of fish in a winey-tomato broth.

Makes 8 servings.

Nutrient Value Per Serving: 261 calories, 23 g protein, 16 g fat, 6 g carbohydrate, 330 mg sodium, 66 mg cholesterol.

1   **pound fresh or frozen cod fillets**
½   **pound fresh or frozen salmon***
½   **pound fresh or frozen mackerel fillets**
½   **cup chopped onion**
1   **clove garlic, finely chopped**
¼   **cup olive oil**
1   **can (16 ounces) peeled whole tomatoes, with their liquid and finely chopped**
1   **cup white wine**
3   **tablespoons finely chopped walnuts**
3   **tablespoons chopped parsley**
1   **tablespoon tomato paste**
1   **bay leaf**
½   **teaspoon salt**
⅛   **teaspoon ground hot red pepper**

1. If using frozen fish, unwrap the fish and let it stand at room temperature for 20 minutes. Cut the fish into 2¼ x 1½-inch chunks. (Be careful cutting the frozen fish since the center core will still be frozen.)
2. Sauté the onion and the garlic in the oil in a large nonaluminum skillet over medium heat until tender, for 5 to 8 minutes. Add the tomatoes, wine, walnuts, parsley, tomato paste, bay leaf, salt and red pepper. Boil the mixture, uncovered, for 5 minutes or until slightly thickened. Add the fish. Lower the heat and cook, covered, for 7 to 10 minutes for fresh fish, 18 to 20 minutes for frozen fish, or until the fish flakes easily when tested with a fork. If using a combination of fresh and frozen fish, place the frozen fish in the skillet first; cook for 10 minutes. Then add the fresh fish and continue cooking until both flake easily when tested with a fork. Remove the bay leaf. Serve the burrida with toasted garlic bread, if you wish.

Note: If salmon is unavailable, use 1 pound of mackerel rather than ½ pound.

Food for thought . . .

S K I N N Y   S U B S T I T U T I O N S

Food/Calories	Substitute/Calories	Calories saved
Butter on potatoes (2 pats), 80	Yogurt on potatoes (2 Tbs.), 15	65
Ice cream (1 cup), 330	Sherbet (1 cup), 260	70
Whole milk (1 cup), 160	Skim milk (1 cup), 90	70
Potato chips (10), 115	Popcorn (1 cup), 24	91
Toast with butter (1 pat), 120	Dry toast, 80	40
Cake with icing, 445	Angelfood cake, 110	335
Doughnut, cake, 125	Muffin, bran or blueberry, 110	15
Jelly (1 Tbs.), 55	Apple butter (1 Tbs.), 33	22
French fries, 210	Baked potato, 100	110
Beer (12 ounces), 151	Dry wine (3½ ounces), 90	61
Cashews (1 ounce), 160	Peanuts (1 ounce), 110	50
Tuna, in oil (1 ounce), 81	Tuna, in water (1 ounce), 36	45
Chicken, dark meat, 250	Chicken, white meat, 230	20
Chocolate chip cookie, 50	Vanilla wafer, 18	32
Corn (½ cup), 70	Green beans (½ cup), 15	55
Banana, 85	Cantaloupe (½), 50	35
Hamburger with bun, 305	Haddock (7 ounces), 188	117
Italian salad dressing (1 Tbs.), 55	Lemon and vinegar, 5	50
Chocolate candy, 1 piece, 50	Hard candy, 20	30
Tonic water (12 ounces), 113	Club soda (12 ounces), 0	113
Pecan pie (⅛ pie), 490	Pumpkin pie (⅛ pie), 275	215
Egg, fried, 110	Egg, soft- or hard-cooked, 80	30
Yogurt, fruit (8 ounces), 290	Yogurt, vanilla (8 ounces), 200	90
Apple pie (1/7 pie), 350	Baked apple, 195	155
Bagel, 165	Rye toast (1 slice), 65	100
Coffee, cream and sugar, 45	Coffee, black, 0	45

P·A·S·T·A

Fettuccine with Ham and Vegetables

Cream cheese makes the sauce rich with fewer calories than a heavy cream sauce, and turkey-ham provides flavor and protein with less fat than regular salami or another cold cut.

Makes 4 servings.

Nutrient Value Per Serving: 276 calories, 10 g protein, 10 g fat, 37 g carbohydrate, 471 mg sodium, 16 mg cholesterol.

- 6 **ounces fettuccine**
- 2 **cloves garlic, finely chopped**
- 3 **teaspoons olive oil**
- 1 **medium-size carrot, peeled and cut into thin julienne strips**
- 1 **small zucchini, cut into thin julienne strips**
- 2 **ounces turkey-ham (2 or 3 slices), cut into thin julienne strips**
- 1 **ripe tomato, halved and diced, reserving any juice**
- 2 **teaspoons chopped capers, rinsed**
- ¼ **teaspoon pepper**
- 1 **chicken bouillon cube**
- ¼ **cup boiling water**
- ¼ **cup cream cheese, cut into small pieces and at room temperature**

1. Cook the fettucine in a large pot of boiling water following package directions.
2. Sauté the garlic in 2 teaspoons of the olive oil in a large nonstick skillet over medium heat until browned. Add the remaining teaspoon of olive oil. Add the carrot and sauté for 1 minute. Stir in the zucchini and sauté for 1 minute, adding a little water if necessary to prevent any sticking. Add the turkey-ham, tomato with any juices, capers and pepper.
3. Dissolve the bouillon cube in the boiling water in a small saucepan.
4. Move the vegetables to one side of the skillet. Stir in the bouillon and the cream cheese. Heat the mixture over low heat, stirring constantly, until the mixture is smooth. Stir the vegetables and the cream sauce together in the skillet over low heat until the sauce is smooth and slightly thickened, for 1 to 2 minutes. Serve the sauce immediately over the hot fettuccine.

Fettuccine with Vegetables and Basil

Makes 6 servings.

Nutrient Value Per Serving: 405 calories, 17 g protein, 11 g fat, 61 g carbohydrate, 84 mg sodium, 3 mg cholesterol.

- 1 **package (1 pound) whole-wheat fettuccine**
- ¼ **cup olive oil**
- 1 **cup steamed broccoli flowerets**
- 1 **cup steamed sliced carrots**
- 1 **cup steamed baby zucchini, trimmed**
- 1 **cup steamed yellow patty pan squash, trimmed**
- 1 **cup steamed snow peas**
- ¼ **cup grated Parmesan cheese**
- 2 **tablespoons chopped fresh basil**

1. Cook the whole-wheat fettuccine in a large pot of boiling salted water following package directions. Drain the pasta. Toss the pasta with the olive oil.
2. Divide the pasta among individual plates; top with the broccoli, carrots, zucchini, squash and snow peas, dividing evenly. Sprinkle each serving with grated Parmesan cheese and chopped fresh basil.

Spaghetti with Spinach Pesto

A quick and easy pasta dish that has fewer than 300 calories per serving, with a delicious Spinach-Pesto.

Makes 6 servings.

Nutrient Value Per Serving: 289 calories, 10 g protein, 8 g fat, 44 g carbohydrate, 231 mg sodium, 3 mg cholesterol.

Spinach Pesto:
- 3 **tablespoons pine nuts (pignoli)**
- 2 **cloves garlic**
- 1 **cup firmly packed torn spinach leaves (about 1½ ounces)**
- 2 **tablespoons olive oil**
- ¼ **cup grated Romano cheese**
- ½ **teaspoon salt**
- ¼ **teaspoon pepper**

- ¾ **pound spaghetti**

1. Prepare the Spinach Pesto: Place the pine nuts in the container of an electric blender or food processor. Cover; whirl until the nuts are finely ground. Add the garlic and the spinach to the blender, whirl until finely chopped. Add the oil, cheese, salt and pepper; whirl until all the ingredients are evenly mixed and very finely chopped. Reserve.

2. Bring a large pot of water to a rolling boil over high heat. Add the spaghetti. Cook the spaghetti, stirring occasionally, until *al dente,* firm but tender, 10 to 12 minutes. Reserve about ½ cup of the boiling pasta water. Drain the pasta, reserve some of the cooking water.

3. Combine the pesto and enough of the pasta cooking water in a large serving bowl to make a smooth sauce. Add the pasta and toss to mix well. Serve immediately

the chicken livers and sauté until the livers are brown and no pink remains. Remove the livers to a large bowl with a slotted spoon and keep warm.

3. Sauté the onion in the pan drippings for 3 minutes or until golden. Add the mushrooms and sauté for 2 minutes. Remove the vegetables to the bowl with the chicken livers. Season with salt, if you wish, and pepper. Keep warm.

4. Combine the wine, the remaining ⅓ cup chicken broth and cornstarch in a small cup. Stir until smooth. Stir the mixture into the skillet until blended. Cook over medium heat, stirring constantly until the mixture thickens and bubbles, about 1 minute. Pour the sauce over the chicken liver mixture. Stir in the brandy, sherry and the cooked rice; toss gently. Turn out onto a heated serving dish.

Chicken Liver Risotto

A festive party dish with brown rice and herbs that's also very nutritious.

Makes 6 servings.

Nutrient Value Per Serving: 262 calories, 19 g protein, 6 g fat, 30 g carbohydrate, 369 mg sodium, 332 mg cholesterol.

1   cup brown rice
2⅓ cups chicken broth
½   teaspoon leaf thyme, crumbled
½   teaspoon leaf basil, crumbled
4   tablespoons (½ stick) reduced-calorie margarine
1   pound chicken livers
1   medium-size onion, chopped (½ cup)
½   pound small mushrooms
1   teaspoon salt (optional)
     Freshly ground black pepper
⅓   cup dry white wine
1   teaspoon cornstarch
1   tablespoon brandy
1   tablespoon dry sherry

1. Combine the rice, 2 cups of the chicken broth, the thyme and basil in a large heavy saucepan. Cover; cook over low heat for 45 minutes or until the liquid is absorbed by the rice. Remove the saucepan from the heat. Let stand, covered, for 10 minutes.

2. Melt 3 tablespoons of the margarine in a large skillet over medium-high heat until foaming. Add

Linguine Alla Carbonara

The preparation time for this delicious pasta dish is scarcely longer than the time it takes to boil water.

Makes 6 servings.

Nutrient Value Per Serving: 285 calories, 13 g protein, 12 g fat, 29 g carbohydrate, 278 mg sodium, 195 mg cholesterol.

1   package (8 ounces) linguine
¼   pound bacon, diced
1   clove garlic, halved
4   eggs
1   teaspoon salt (optional)
¼   teaspoon seasoned pepper
½   cup grated Parmesan cheese
2   tablespoons finely chopped parsley

1. Cook the linguine in boiling salted water in a large kettle. Drain.

2. Brown the bacon and garlic in a small skillet.

3. Beat together the eggs, salt, if you wish, and the pepper in a bowl until frothy.

4. Return the drained pasta to the kettle. Add the bacon, 2 tablespoons of bacon fat and the egg mixture. Toss the mixture over low heat with 2 forks until thickened, about 3 minutes; don't let the eggs scramble.

5. Sprinkle with the cheese and the parsley. Toss again to coat evenly. Serve immediately.

4. Add the Homemade Spaghetti Sauce to the kettle. Toss over low heat until well blended and bubbly hot. Add the parsley and spoon the pasta onto a heated serving platter.

Food for thought . . .

Cholesterol, a fat-like substance, is obtained through the diet as well as manufactured by the body. It is necessary for hormones and cell membranes. High levels of serum cholesterol are a risk factor for hardening of the arteries and heart disease. Cholesterol comes from animal sources such as egg yolks, organ meats, whole milk products, butter and lard. The American Heart Association recommends no more than 300 milligrams of cholesterol daily for the healthy adult male and female.

Pasta and Seafood Marinara

Pasta can be part of your diet plan; just keep the portion small and toss with a low-calorie sauce.

Makes 6 servings.

Nutrient Value Per Serving: 290 calories, 23 g protein, 4 g fat, 40 g carbohydrate, 670 mg sodium, 107 mg cholesterol.

1   **large onion, chopped (1 cup)**
1   **clove garlic, finely chopped**
2   **tablespoons reduced-calorie margarine**
1   **bag (1 pound) frozen shelled and deveined raw shrimp, OR: 1 pound fresh or frozen sea scallops, sliced, OR: 2 cans (10 ounces each) minced clams**
1   **can (1 pound) tomatoes**
1   **can (6 ounces) tomato paste**
1   **can (6 ounces) sliced mushrooms**
1½   **teaspoons leaf oregano, crumbled**
1   **teaspoon salt** (optional)
¼   **teaspoon lemon pepper**
1   **bay leaf**
1   **package (8 ounces) thin spaghetti**

1. Sauté the onion and the garlic in the margarine in a large skillet until softened.
2. Add the shrimp or scallops, or the clams with their liquid.
3. Stir in the tomatoes, tomato paste, mushrooms with their liquid, the oregano, salt, if you wish, lemon pepper and bay leaf. Simmer for 20 minutes or until the sauce is rich and flavorful.
4. While the sauce cooks, cook the spaghetti in a large pot of boiling salted water, following label directions. Drain; keep hot until ready to serve.
5. Spoon the spaghetti onto a heated serving plate. Top with the seafood sauce. Toss before serving. Garnish with chopped watercress, if you wish.

Primavera Pasta

Fresh vegetables, such as broccoli, toss well with pasta for a nutritious entrée.

Makes 4 servings.

Nutrient Value Per Serving: 306 calories, 14 g protein, 2 g fat, 62 g carbohydrate, 347 mg sodium, 00 mg cholesterol.

1   **package (8 ounces) thin spaghetti**
1   **bunch broccoli (about 2 pounds)**
1   **medium-size sweet red pepper, halved, seeded and cut into chunks**
2   **cups Homemade Tomato Sauce (see recipe, page 238)**
¼   **cup chopped parsley**

1. Cook the spaghetti in a large kettle of boiling salted water until tender, following the label directions. Drain the spaghetti and return to the kettle.
2. While the spaghetti cooks, soak the broccoli in warm salted water in a large bowl. Drain and trim the tough ends. Cut the stems and the flowerets into 2-inch pieces.
3. Cook the broccoli and the red pepper separately in a small amount of boiling water, salted, if desired, in a medium-size saucepan: 5 minutes for the broccoli and 5 minutes or less for the red pepper, or until crispy-tender. Drain well and add the broccoli and red pepper to the hot drained spaghetti in the kettle.

LOWERING CHOLESTEROL IN YOUR DIET

- *Reduce your intake of saturated fats such as butter, cheese, heavy cream and fatty meats.*
- *Increase your consumption of complex carbohydrates and foods with fiber.*
- *Satisfy your snack cravings with fruit and other naturally sweet foods. Avoid candy, cakes, pies and soft drinks for snacking.*
- *Cut down on the amount of fat you use for cooking by using nonstick vegetable cooking spray and nonstick cookware and utensils.*
- *No fried or deep-fried foods.*
- *Broil, roast on a rack, steam, poach or stir-fry with very little oil.*
- *Trim fat before and after cooking and remove poultry and fish skin.*
- *Chill soups and stews so the excess fat rises to the top; remove fat with a spoon and discard.*

Homemade Tomato Sauce

Makes 5 cups.

Nutrient Value Per Cup: 86 calories, 4 g protein, 1 g fat, 19 g carbohydrate, 1,036 mg sodium, 00 mg cholesterol.

- 1 **can (2 pounds, 3 ounces) Italian plum tomatoes**
- 1 **large onion, chopped (1 cup)**
- 1 **clove garlic, finely chopped**
- 1 **can (6 ounces) tomato paste**
- 2 **teaspoons leaf basil, crumbled**
- 1 **teaspoon leaf rosemary, crumbled**
- 1 **teaspoon salt** (optional)
- 1 **cup dry red wine OR: beef broth**

1. Drain the liquid from the tomatoes into a large saucepan. Reserve the tomatoes. Add the onion and garlic to the saucepan. Bring to boiling over medium heat. Lower the heat and simmer until the onion is tender, about 3 minutes.
2. Stir the tomatoes into the saucepan. Add the tomato paste, basil, rosemary, salt, if you wish, and the red wine or beef broth. Bring to boiling. Lower the heat and simmer, uncovered, until the sauce thickens, about 1 hour.
3. Pour the sauce into clean plastic containers. Cool. Cover and refrigerate. Use within 4 or 5 days. The sauce also freezes well.

Manicotti Roll-Ups

One lasagna noodle per serving satisfies the craving for pasta without causing dietetic disaster!

Bake at 350° for 30 minutes.
Makes 8 servings.

Nutrient Value Per Serving: 238 calories, 14 g protein, 7 g fat, 29 g carbohydrate, 344 mg sodium, 89 mg cholesterol.

- 8 **lasagna noodles (from a 1-pound package)**
- 1 **container (15 ounces) part-skim ricotta cheese**
- ¼ **cup chopped parsley**
- 2 **eggs, slightly beaten**
- 1 **teaspoon mixed Italian herbs, crumbled**
- ½ **teaspoon salt** (optional)
- ¼ **teaspoon pepper**
- 3 **cups Homemade Tomato Sauce (see recipe, this page)**
- ½ **cup shredded part-skim mozzarella cheese**

1. Preheat the oven to moderate (350°).
2. Cook the lasagna noodles in boiling water, salted if you wish, in a large kettle just until barely tender. Drain and place the noodles in a large bowl of cold water.
3. Combine the ricotta, chopped parsley, eggs, mixed Italian herbs, salt, if you wish, and pepper in a medium-size bowl; mix until well blended.
4. Remove the lasagna noodles from the cold water, one at a time, and drain on paper toweling. spread a scant ¼ cup of the cheese mixture on each noodle. Roll up each noodle, jelly-roll style.
5. Spoon the Homemade Tomato Sauce into the bottom of a shallow 10-cup casserole. Arrange the roll-ups spiral ends up, in the sauce. Cover with aluminum foil.
6. Bake in the preheated moderate oven (350°) for 20 minutes. Remove the foil and sprinkle mozzarella over the top. Bake 10 minutes longer or until the sauce is bubbly hot and the cheese is melted.

V·E·G·E·T·A·B·L·E·S
A·N·D S·A·L·A·D·S

Stir-Fried Vegetables and Tofu

Tofu (bean curd) and broccoli are excellent, as well as delicious, sources of calcium. And there's no cholesterol in this dish.

Makes 4 servings.

Nutrient Value Per Serving: 251 calories, 16 g protein, 16 g fat, 17 g carbohydrate, 638 mg sodium, 0 mg cholesterol.

3   tablespoons vegetable oil
2   cloves garlic, finely chopped
2   tablespoons chopped peeled, fresh
     gingerroot
¼   teaspoon crushed red pepper flakes
3   celery stalks, sliced diagonally
1   sweet red pepper, halved, seeded and cut
     into ½-inch-wide strips
5   cups broccoli flowerets (about 1½ bunches)
1   bunch green onions, sliced diagonally into
     1-inch pieces
1   pound firm tofu (bean curd), cut into
     1-inch cubes (see Note)
2   tablespoons soy sauce
¼   cup chicken broth OR: water
1   teaspoon cornstarch
     Hot cooked brown rice

1. Heat the oil in a wok or skillet. Stir in the garlic, gingerroot and red pepper flakes. Add the celery, red pepper, broccoli and green onions.
2. Stir-fry over high heat for 3 to 4 minutes or until the vegetables are coated with oil. Add the tofu.
3. Combine the soy sauce, chicken broth or water and the cornstarch in a cup until the mixture is smooth. Add to the wok.
4. Cook, stirring, for 8 to 10 minutes or until the vegetables are crisp-tender. Serve with hot cooked brown rice and additional soy sauce, if you wish.

Note: Only tofu processed with calcium sulfate provides calcium.

Two-Pepper Crustless Quiche

Try this for a summer lunch or a light first course, made even lighter with low-fat cottage cheese and skim milk, and no crust.

Bake at 400° for 15 minutes; then at 350° for 10 to 15 minutes.
Makes 12 servings.

Nutrient Value Per Serving: 125 calories, 12 g protein, 6 g fat, 5 g carbohydrate, 337 mg sodium, 169 mg cholesterol.

1   container (16 ounces) 1% low-fat cottage
     cheese
7   whole eggs
3   egg whites
½   cup skim milk
¼   cup all-purpose flour
1   teaspoon baking powder
¼   teaspoon salt
3½ ounces jalapeño Jack cheese, shredded
1   medium-size sweet green pepper, cored,
     seeded and chopped
1   medium-size sweet red pepper, cored,
     seeded and chopped

1. Preheat the oven to hot (400°).
2. Place the cottage cheese in the container of an electric blender. Cover; whirl until the cheese is fairly smooth. Transfer the cottage cheese to a large bowl.
3. Combine the whole eggs, egg whites and skim milk in the container of the electric blender. Cover; whirl until the mixture is fluffy. Add the flour, baking powder and salt; whirl until the mixture is smooth. Stir the egg mixture into the cottage cheese in the large bowl until well blended. Stir in the Jack cheese and the green and red peppers. Pour the mixture into a 13 x 9 x 2-inch metal baking pan.
4. Bake the quiche in the preheated hot oven (400°) for 15 minutes. Reduce the oven temperature to moderate (350°). Bake the quiche an additional 10 to 15 minutes or until the custard is set and the top is lightly browned.

Food for thought . . .

VEGETABLE KNOW-HOW

Here's the nutrition lowdown on some of the most popular vegetables, with cooking tips to preserve maximum flavor, color and nutrients.

Asparagus: Iron and vitamins A and C; 11 calories per ½ cup. *Steam in a covered skillet over medium heat, 5-10 minutes until asparagus bends slightly.*

Beans (green and yellow): Vitamin A; 15 calories per ½ cup. *Steam or stir-fry until crisp-tender.*

Beets: Vitamins A and C; 40 calories per ½ cup. *Microwave; grill; steam or serve raw. Wash first; leave nutrient-packed skin intact.*

Bok Choy: Vitamin C and calcium; 15 calories per cup. *Stir-fry; sauté; or serve raw. Separate leaves from stem; cook separately.*

Broccoli: Vitamins A and C, calcium, fiber; 32 calories per stalk. *Blanch to crisp-tender stage; microwave; steam; or stir-fry.*

Carrots: Vitamin A; 50 calories per cup, sliced. *Steam; stir-fry; microwave.*

Cauliflower: Vitamin C and iron; 27 calories per cup. *Microwave; steam; stir-fry.*

Cucumbers: Some vitamins and minerals; 25 calories each. *Scrub skin or peel if waxed.*

Lettuce: Darker leaves contain vitamins A, C and E; about 15 calories a head. *Best served raw.*

Mushrooms: Trace vitamins and minerals; 20 calories per cup. *Best served raw. May be sautéed.*

Onions: Some vitamin C; 40 calories per dry-skinned onion; 9 calories per green onion. *Cook chopped onion, covered, to mellow flavor.*

Peas: Protein, iron, vitamins A and C; snow peas: 40 calories per ½ cup; garden peas: 60 calories. *Stir-fry snow peas or blanch in boiling water 1 minute; hold blanched peas under cold running water to stop cooking process. Steam fresh peas.*

Peppers (sweet): Vitamins A and C, phosphorous, iron; one contains 15 calories. *Best raw, unpeeled.*

Potatoes: Vitamins, C, B1, iron, protein; average-size potato contains approx. 90 calories. *Best to cook (and serve) potatoes in skin.*

Spinach: Vitamins A and C, iron, calcium; 14 calories per cup. *Cook briefly in non-aluminum pan to retain color.*

Zucchini: Vitamins A and C; 14 calories per ½ cup. *Serve raw, unpeeled.*

Food for thought . . .

Recent research indicates that olive oil, a monounsaturated oil, tends to lower damaging LDL (low-density lipoprotein) cholesterol and preserves beneficial HDL (high-density lipoprotein) cholesterol in the blood. This research suggests that olive oil may lower your chances of heart disease.

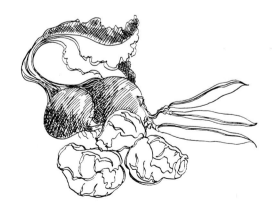

Food for thought . . .

CALCIUM CONSCIOUSNESS: DID YOU KNOW. . . ?

- One out of every four women over the age of 60 suffers from osteoporosis, a degenerating bone disease caused by the depletion of calcium. It can lead to a loss in height, back pain, "dowager's hump" and hip fractures.
- After the age of 35, the body's ability to absorb calcium decreases and much of the mineral is lost through the kidneys.
- A sedentary life can contribute to bone damage. Regular exercise not only strengthens your bones but helps their absorption of calcium.
- Postmenopausal women are especially prone to osteoporosis because the body's production of the bone-protecting hormone, estrogen, decreases measurably during menopause.
- Medical experts recommend 1,000 milligrams (mgs) of calcium daily. If you cannot get enough from food, take a calcium supplement.
- Teenagers, pregnant and breast-feeding women and postmenopausal women require more calcium — 1,500 mgs daily.
- If you're suffering from high blood pressure, thyroid problems, peptic ulcers, gastritis or have any other medical problems you should consult your physician about your calcium needs.

Food for thought . . .

SELECTED CALCIUM-RICH FOOD SOURCES

Milk Group	mgs calcium
Buttermilk, 1 cup	285
Cheese, American, 1 oz.	174
Cheese, Cheddar, 1 oz.	204
Cheese, ricotta, part skim, 1 oz.	337
Cheese, Swiss, 1 oz.	272
Ice cream, vanilla, ½ cup	88
Milk, 1 cup	291
Milk, lowfat (2%), 1 cup	297
Milk, skim, 1 cup	302
Yogurt, fruit, lowfat, 1 cup	345
Yogurt, plain, lowfat, 1 cup	415

Meat Group	
Beans, dried, cooked, 1 cup	90
Oysters, raw, 7-9	113
Salmon, canned with bones, 3 oz.	167
Sardines, with bones, 3 oz.	372
Shrimp, canned, 3 oz.	99
Tofu (bean curd), 4 oz.	240

(Note: Only tofu processed with calcium sulfate is a source of calcium.)

Fruit-Vegetable Group	
Beet greens, ½ cup	72
Bok choy, ½ cup	126
Broccoli, stalk, ½ cup	68
Collards, from raw, ½ cup	179
Collards, from frozen, ½ cup	149
Kale, from raw, ½ cup	103
Kale, from frozen, ½ cup	79
Mustard greens, ½ cup	97
Spinach, ½ cup	84

Grain Group	
Cornbread, 2½" x 2½" x 1½"	94
Pancakes, 4-inch diameter, 2	116
Waffles, 7-inch diameter	179

Information courtesy of the National Dairy Council

Mushroom-Stuffed Mushrooms

To help mushrooms retain their color, follow the technique given here.

Bake at 400° for 10 minutes.
Makes 15 appetizers.

Nutrient Value Per Appetizer: 26 calories, 2 g protein, 1 g fat, 2 g carbohydrate, 47 mg sodium, 19 mg cholesterol.

- *1 pound (about 15) mushrooms with large caps*
- *1 lemon*
  Boiling water
- *1 medium-size onion, finely chopped (½ cup)*
- *1 tablespoon diet margarine*
- *¼ cup plain lowfat yogurt*
- *1 egg yolk*
  Pinch salt
  Pinch white pepper
- *¼ cup freshly grated Parmesan cheese*
  Sweet Hungarian paprika

1. Preheat the oven to hot (400°).
2. Separate the mushroom caps from the stems. Place the mushrooms and the stems in a large bowl. Slice the lemon in half and squeeze the juice onto the mushrooms. Cover the mushrooms with boiling water and let stand for 1 minute. Drain the mushrooms well and pat dry with paper toweling. (The acidulation helps the mushrooms retain their color.)
3. Finely chop the mushroom stems. Sauté the onion and the mushroom stems in the diet margarine in a medium-size skillet for 10 minutes or until the vegetables are soft. Remove the skillet from the heat and stir in the yogurt and the egg yolk. Reheat the mixture gently, but do not let boil or the mixture will curdle. Season the mixture to taste with salt and white pepper.
4. Level each mushroom cap by cutting a thin, horizontal sliver from the rounded edge of each cap. Mound each cap with the mushroom filling. Sprinkle with the grated cheese and dust with the paprika. Place the caps on an aluminum foil-lined jelly-roll (or other low-rimmed) baking pan.
5. Bake the mushroom caps in the preheated hot oven (400°) for 10 minutes or until bubbly and hot. Remove the caps to paper towel-lined plates to cool slightly. Serve warm.

Cherry Tomatoes Stuffed with Blue Cheese

Use the largest cherry tomatoes you can find; they're easy to scoop out, yet still bite-size.

Makes 1½ dozen.

Nutrient Value Per Tomato: 19 calories, 2 g protein, 1 g fat, 1 g carbohydrate, 73 mg sodium, 3 mg cholesterol.

- *1 pint large cherry tomatoes*
- *1 container (8 ounces) small-curd cottage cheese*
- *2 tablespoons blue cheese*
- *2 teaspoons finely chopped onion*
- *1 tablespoon plain lowfat yogurt*
  Pinch salt
  Few grains white pepper

1. Cut the tops from the tomatoes, using a serrated knife; reserve the tops.
2. To level the tomatoes so they stand upright, cut a thin horizontal slice from the bottom of each tomato. Discard the bottoms.
3. Using the small end of a melon baller, scoop out the pulp and seeds from each tomato. Discard the pulp and seeds. Invert the hollow tomatoes on a double thickness of paper toweling to drain.
4. Meanwhile, blend the cottage cheese and the blue cheese, onion, yogurt, salt and white pepper in a small bowl.
5. Place the cheese mixture into a pastry bag with a ¼-inch opening. Pipe the cheese mixture into the prepared tomato shells, or fill the shells using a small spoon. Replace the tomato tops, leaving a little cheese mixture exposed for contrast.

Ham 'n Fruit Bites

Here's the low-calorie finger food variation of prosciutto-wrapped melon.

Makes 36 appetizers.

Nutrient Value Per Appetizer: 13 calories, 1 g protein, 0 g fat, 2 g carbohydrate, 58 mg sodium, 3 mg cholesterol.

6 ounces 95% lean smoked cooked ham, thinly sliced
½ cantaloupe, seeded
¼ honeydew melon, seeded

1. Cut the ham slices into 4 x 1-inch strips.
2. Cut the cantaloupe half into 4 wedges, lengthwise. Remove the rind. Cut the honeydew in half lengthwise. Remove the rind. Cut each melon wedge into ½-inch-thick slices, crosswise to yield 36 pieces.
3. Wrap a ham strip around each melon piece; secure with a small wooden pick.

Variation: Canned pineapple chunks or 1-inch fresh pineapple chunks may be substituted for the cantaloupe or the honeydew.

Food for thought . . .

20 GOOD-FOR-YOU SNACKS

150 CALORIES OR FEWER

Celery (3 stalks) **10**
Broccoli, raw (3 stalks) **96**
Carrot, raw **30**
Peach, raw **40**
Graham cracker (1 whole) **50**
Orange juice (½ cup) **55**
Cantaloupe (half) **60**
Bread, whole wheat (1 slice) **65**
Apple **80**
Egg (1 boiled) **80**
Cottage cheese, 1% fat
    (½ cup) **80**
Peanuts (2 Tbs.) **105**
Cheese, Cheddar (1 oz.) **115**
Muffin **120**
Milk, lowfat (1 cup) **125**
Tuna, in water (½ cup) **130**
Turkey, white meat (3 oz.) **135**
Potato, baked **140**
Yogurt, plain (8 oz.) **140**
Chicken breast, broiled
    (½ breast) **150**

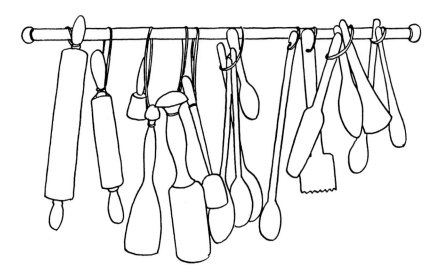

As delicious as it is lovely: Papaya Chicken Salad.

🗝️ LS

Papaya-Chicken Salad

Not a salad in the usual sense, but rather a lovely arrangement of strips of chicken, papaya and red pepper on a bed of red leaf lettuce.

Bake at 350° for 10 minutes.
Makes 4 servings.

Nutrient Value Per Serving (without dressing): 258 calories, 29 g protein, 4 g fat, 26 g carbohydrate, 86 mg sodium, 66 mg cholesterol.

- **4   boneless, skinned chicken breasts (4 ounces each)**
- **¹⁄₃ cup freshly squeezed orange juice**
- **1   tablespoon grated orange rind**
- **2   teaspoons leaf basil, crumbled**
-     **Dash liquid red-pepper seasoning**
-     **Unbleached all-purpose flour**
- **2   teaspoons safflower oil**
-     **Papaya-Orange Dressing (recipe follows)**
-     **Red leaf lettuce**
-     **Watercress**
-     **Seedless red grapes**
-     **Sweet green pepper strips**
- **1   large papaya, sliced into thin wedges**
- **1   large sweet red pepper, halved, seeded and cut into strips**

1. Place the chicken in a shallow dish. Combine the orange juice and rind, the basil and red-pepper seasoning in a cup. Pour the juice mixture over the chicken; turn to coat the chicken. Cover the bowl with plastic wrap. Marinate the chicken in the refrigerator for 2 to 4 hours.
2. Preheat the oven to moderate (350°).
3. Drain the chicken well, reserving the marinade. Dust the chicken with the flour.
4. Heat the oil in an ovenproof skillet. Add the chicken and lightly brown on both sides. Add the reserved marinade to the skillet.
5. Bake the chicken in the skillet in the preheated moderate oven (350°) for 10 minutes or until tender. Remove the chicken from the skillet. Cool the chicken. Strain the skillet juices and reserve for the Papaya-Orange Dressing.
6. Prepare the Papaya-Orange Dressing.
7. Line 4 individual plates with the red leaf lettuce, watercress, red grapes and sweet green pepper strips. Cut the chicken into strips and arrange the strips in the middle of the plates with the strips of papaya and red pepper.

7. Ladle the Papaya-Orange Dressing over the chicken. Serve the salad with a sprig of cilantro, if you wish.

🗝️ 🗝️ LS

Papaya-Orange Dressing

Excellent with duck or lobster salads, as well as chicken salad.

Makes 1½ cups.

Nutrient Value Per Tablespoon: 43 calories, 0 g protein, 5 g fat, 1 g carbohydrate, 1 mg sodium, 0 mg cholesterol.

- **¹⁄₃ cup finely diced fresh papaya**
- **¹⁄₃ cup freshly squeezed orange juice**
- **3   tablespoons lime juice**
- **1   tablespoon red wine vinegar**
- **1   tablespoon water**
- **1   tablespoon chopped shallot**
- **1   tablespoon grated orange rind**
-     **Liquid red-pepper seasoning**
- **¹⁄₂ cup peanut oil**
-     **Strained pan juices (from Papaya-Chicken Salad recipe, this page)**

1. Place the diced papaya in a mixing bowl. Add the orange and lime juices, the red wine vinegar, water, shallot, grated orange rind and a few drops of red-pepper seasoning. Whisk vigorously until blended.
2. Add the peanut oil and mix vigorously until well blended and the mixture thickens slightly. Stir in the strained pan juices.
3. Sprinkle with sprigs of fresh cilantro, if you wish, before ladling the dressing over the Papaya-Chicken Salad.

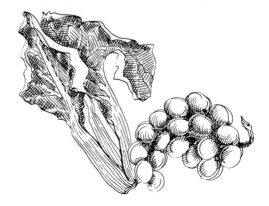

Apple and Turkey-Ham Salad

Lower-fat turkey-ham and reduced-calorie mayonnaise make this salad with its creamy dressing less fattening than you might expect.

Makes 4 servings.

Nutrient Value Per Serving: 179 calories, 8 g protein, 9 g fat, 16 g carbohydrate, 417 mg sodium, 17 mg cholesterol.

- 1 medium-size firm, tart apple
- 1 or 2 boiling potatoes (8 ounces), cooked, cooled, and peeled
- 1 piece (2 ounces) hot pepper cheese OR: Monterey Jack cheese
- 2 ounces sliced turkey-ham (95% fat-free)

Creamy Mustard Dressing:
- ¼ cup reduced-calorie mayonnaise
- 4½ teaspoons white wine vinegar
- ¼ teaspoon Dijon-style mustard
- 1 medium-size green onion, both white and green parts, coarsely chopped
- ⅛ teaspoon salt
- ⅛ teaspoon pepper
- ½ head romain lettuce, shredded

1. Halve and core the apple; leave the skin on. Cut the apple into ½-inch-thick slices; cut the slices into matchsticks, 1 inch long. Do the same with the potatoes and the cheese. Slice the turkey-ham into 1 x ½-inch strips. Combine the apple, potatoes, cheese and turkey-ham all in a large bowl.
2. Prepare the Creamy Mustard Dressing: Combine the mayonnaise, vinegar, mustard, green onion, salt and pepper in the container of a food processor. Cover; whirl until the onion is finely chopped and the mixture is well blended.
3. Add the dressing to the salad ingredients in the large bowl; toss gently to coat all the salad ingredients well.
4. Arrange the shredded lettuce on a serving plate. Mound the salad on top.

Oriental Chicken Salad Platter

Makes 4 servings.

Nutrient Value Per Serving: 237 calories, 31 g protein, 7 g fat, 12 g carbohydrate, 1,452 mg sodium, 72 mg cholesterol.

- 4 cups packed spinach leaves, torn into bite-size pieces
- ¾ pound cooked chicken breast meat, cut into 2 x ¼-inch strips
- 5 ounces snow peas, strings removed
- 2 carrots, peeled and sliced diagonally into ½-inch-thick slices
- 2 medium-size sweet red peppers, halved, cored, seeded and cut into 2 x ½-inch strips
- ¼ cup red wine vinegar
- ¼ cup soy sauce
- 1 tablespoon Oriental sesame oil*

1. Line a large shallow salad platter with the spinach leaves. Arrange the chicken, snow peas, carrots and red pepper attractively over the spinach.
2. Stir together the vinegar, soy sauce and oil in a 1-cup glass measure. Drizzle the dressing over the salad.

***Note:** Oriental sesame oil has more flavor and is darker than regular sesame oil. It can be found in the Oriental food section of your supermarket or in a specialty food store.*

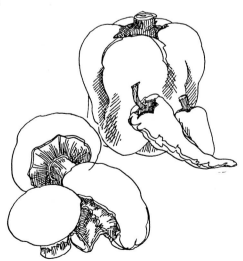

Wild Rice Tuna Salad

A luncheon entrée is enhanced by the addition of crunchy water chestnuts and cashews, bound with a tangy dressing.

Makes 10 half-cup servings.

Nutrient Value Per Serving: 283 calories, 18 g protein, 14 g fat, 25 g carbohydrate, 388 mg sodium, 36 mg cholesterol.

1	**cup raw wild rice, washed and drained**
2½	**cups water**
1	**cup low-calorie mayonnaise**
½	**cup skim milk**
½	**cup lemon juice**
1	**small onion, grated (¼ cup)**
1	**teaspoon chopped chives**
3	**cans (6½ ounces each) tuna, packed in water, drained**
1	**can (8 ounces) water chestnuts, drained and chopped**
½	**teaspoon curry powder**
½	**teaspoon pepper**
½	**pound seedless grapes, halved**
1	**cup cashew nuts**

1. Combine the rice and the water in a medium-size saucepan. Heat to boiling. Lower the heat; cover the saucepan and simmer for 1 hour or until the rice is tender.
2. Combine the mayonnaise, milk, lemon juice, onion and chives in a large bowl, blending well. Stir in the drained tuna, water chestnuts, curry powder and pepper, mixing well. Stir in the cooked rice. Refrigerate the salad for 2 hours or until chilled.
3. At serving time, fold the halved grapes into the salad. Spoon the salad onto a serving platter, lined with lettuce, if you wish. Top with the cashew nuts.

S·W·E·E·T·S

Beautiful, delicious and low in calories: Apple-Pineapple Sorbet.

Apple-Pineapple Sorbet

The flavors of apple, pineapple, lemon and lime make a sorbet that is hard to resist.

Makes 12 half-cup servings.

Nutrient Value Per Serving: 45 calories, 0 g protein, 0 g fat, 12 g carbohydrate, 1 mg sodium, 0 mg cholesterol.

4   **medium-size to large apples (Golden Delicious, Granny Smith or Pippin), peeled, cored and cut into wedges (about 3½ cups)**
1½ **cups unsweetened pineapple juice**
2   **tablespoons lime juice**
2   **teaspoons grated lemon rind**
    Diced papaya, watermelon and kiwifruit

1. Place the sliced apples and the pineapple and lime juices in the container of an electric blender. Cover; whirl until smooth. Stir in the grated lemon rind.
2. If you have an electric ice-cream maker, transfer the mixture to the machine and follow the manufacturer's instructions for making sherbet. OR: Transfer the mixture to a stainless-steel bowl. Freeze for 2 hours or until the mixture is frozen solid. Using a wire whisk, beat the mixture every 15 to 20 minutes to break up the chunks.
3. To serve, scoop the sorbet into chilled wine glasses. Garnish with the diced papaya, watermelon and kiwifruit.

Note: If the sorbet has been frozen for more than 2 hours, let it thaw for 10 minutes before serving.

Pear Flan aux Amandes

Pear Flan aux Amandes

Luscious fresh fruits in season garnish a pear flan. If you wish, serve with a coulis (purée sauce).

Bake at 350° for 25 minutes.
Makes 12 small servings.

Nutrient Value Per Serving: 75 calories, 2 g protein, 2 g fat, 12 g carbohydrate, 27 mg sodium, 47 mg cholesterol.

3   **to 4 ripe Bartlett pears, peeled, halved and cored**
2¼ **cups water**
1   **tablespoon honey**
3   **whole cloves**
2   **whole eggs**
1   **egg white**
1   **cup lowfat milk, scalded**
½   **teaspoon almond extract**
2   **tablespoons frozen apple juice concentrate**
2   **teaspoons orange-flavored liqueur**
2   **tablespoons ground almonds**

Garnish:
    Raspberries, blueberries, red grapes, sliced kiwifruit, orange twists, julienned orange rind
    Raspberry Coulis (optional; recipe follows)

1. Poach the pears in the water with the honey and cloves in a medium-size saucepan for 8 to 10 minutes or until the pears are tender. Remove the saucepan from the heat and cool the pears in the poaching liquid.
2. Preheat the oven to moderate (350°).
3. Beat the eggs and egg white in a medium-size bowl until blended. Add the scalded milk, almond

extract and apple juice concentrate, blending well. Strain the mixture through a fine sieve.

4. Spray a 9-inch quiche dish or pie pan with nonstick vegetable cooking spray. Using a slotted spoon, remove the cooled pears from the poaching liquid (reserve 1 to 2 tablespoons of the poaching liquid for the Raspberry Coulis, if you wish). Pat the pears dry with paper toweling. Slice the pears to make a fan shape. Arrange the pears in the prepared dish. Pour the strained milk mixture over the pears. Sprinkle with the orange-flavored liqueur, then the ground nuts. Place the dish in a larger baking pan on the middle rack of the oven. Pour in water to come 1 inch up the side of the dish.

5. Bake the flan in the preheated moderate oven (350°) for 25 minutes or until the filling is set. Cool the flan on a wire rack. Garnish with the fresh fruits and serve with the chilled Raspberry Coulis, if you wish.

Raspberry Coulis: Place 1 cup of fresh raspberries or 8 ounces of frozen raspberries, thawed, in the container of an electric blender or food processor. Add 3 tablespoons of frozen apple juice concentrate, 1 tablespoon of orange-flavored liqueur and the reserved 1 to 2 tablespoons of liquid from the poached pears in the above recipe. Cover; whirl just until smooth. Strain through a fine sieve and chill. Makes 1 cup.

Peanut Butter Chewies

These bite-size cookies are peanutty-rich.

Bake at 350° for 15 to 18 minutes.
Makes 50 cookies.

Nutrient Value Per Cookie: 85 calories, 2 g protein, 4 g fat, 12 g carbohydrate, 113 mg sodium, 11 mg cholesterol.

- *1/3 cup smooth peanut butter*
- *1/2 cup (1 stick) margarine*
- *1 cup firmly packed brown sugar*
- *2 medium-size eggs*
- *1/2 cup all-purpose flour*
- *1/2 cup whole-wheat flour*
- *1/3 cup molasses*
- *2 tablespoons baking powder*
- *1/2 teaspoon salt*
- *3 cups quick oats*
- *1/4 cup raisins*

1. Preheat the oven to moderate (350°). Lightly grease cookie sheets.
2. Beat together the peanut butter, margarine and brown sugar in a medium-size bowl until smooth and fluffy. Beat in the eggs until blended.
3. Beat in the all-purpose and whole-wheat flours, molasses, baking powder and salt.
4. Stir in the oats and raisins. Drop the batter by teaspoonfuls, 1 inch apart, onto the prepared cookie sheets.
5. Bake the cookies in the preheated moderate oven (350°) for 15 to 18 minutes or until browned. Cool the cookies on the cookie sheets on a wire rack before removing the cookies from the sheets.

Frozen Yogurt In Vacherins

Vacherins are meringue "dessert holders," shaped into diamonds or circles, then baked.

Bake meringue at 225° for 1 hour.
Makes 6 servings.

Nutrient Value Per Serving: 142 calories, 3 g protein, 0 g fat, 32 g carbohydrate, 17 mg sodium, 0 mg cholesterol.

- *2 egg whites*
- *1/8 teaspoon cream of tartar*
- *1/2 cup sugar*
- *1 1/2 cups low-fat frozen yogurt (60 to 115 calories per 1/4 cup)*
- *1/4 cup low-sugar raspberry or strawberry jam or preserves, stirred well*

1. Preheat the oven to very slow (225°).
2. Cover a large cookie sheet with heavy brown paper. Draw six 2-inch diamond shapes, about 3 inches apart from each other, on the paper.
3. Beat the egg whites with the cream of tartar in a small bowl until foamy. With an electric mixer on high speed, beat in the sugar, a tablespoon at a time, until the meringue forms stiff, glossy peaks.
4. Spread or pipe the meringue through a pastry bag fitted with a decorative No. 5 (plain or star) tip, following the diamond outlines. Repeat to make a second layer, building up a rim.
5. Bake the meringues in the preheated very slow oven (225°) for 1 hour. Turn off the oven and leave the meringues in the oven with the door closed until cool.
6. Place the vacherins on dessert plates. Scoop 1/4 cup frozen yogurt into each and spoon about 2 teaspoons jam over each. Serve immediately.

Very Healthy Breakfast Cookies

Very Healthy Breakfast Cookies

The nutritive content is relatively high for these cookies, thanks to wholesome ingredients.

Bake at 400° for 8 to 12 minutes.
Makes 48 cookies.

Nutrient Value Per Cookie: 60 calories, 2 g protein, 3 g fat, 8 g carbohydrate, 47 mg sodium, 6 mg cholesterol.

½ **cup smooth peanut butter**
⅓ **cup granulated sugar**
⅓ **cup firmly packed brown sugar**
2 **tablespoons margarine, at room
    temperature**
½ **teaspoon vanilla**
1 **egg**
1 **cup rolled oats**
⅓ **cup all-purpose flour**
½ **cup whole-wheat flour**
1½ **teaspoons baking soda**
1 **apple, peeled, cored and shredded**
1 **carrot, peeled and shredded**
½ **cup dark raisins**
½ **cup chopped pecans**

1. Preheat the oven to hot (400°). Grease cookie sheets.
2. Beat together the peanut butter, granulated and brown sugars, the margarine and vanilla in a medium-size bowl until smooth and fluffy. Beat in the egg until blended.
3. Blend in the oats, the all-purpose and whole-wheat flours and the baking soda until thoroughly combined.
4. Stir in the shredded apple and carrot, the raisins and chopped nuts until blended. Roll the dough into 1-inch balls and place on the prepared cookie sheets. Flatten each ball with a fork.
5. Bake the cookies in the preheated hot oven (400°) for 8 to 12 minutes or until lightly browned. Cool the cookies on wire racks.

"Light" Whipped Cream

You should make this topping just moments before serving.

Makes enough for 12 servings.

Nutrient Value Per Serving: 78 calories, 1 g protein, 7 g fat, 2 g carbohydrate, 16 mg sodium, 27 mg cholesterol.

½ **pint (1 cup) heavy cream**
2 **tablespoons 10X (confectioners') sugar**
2 **tablespoons instant dry milk powder**
1 **egg white**
1 **teaspoon vanilla**

1. Place ½ cup of the heavy cream in the container of a food processor fitted with the steel blade. Add the 10X sugar, dry milk powder, egg white and vanilla. Process until the mixture is frothy.
2. With the motor running, add the remaining ½ cup heavy cream slowly through the feed tube; process until the mixture is smooth and fluffy, but not granular in appearance.

Homemade Fudge Syrup

Drizzle a little of this low-calorie syrup over frozen yogurt, a small slice of pound cake or a small dish of strawberries.

Makes 2½ cups.

Nutrient Value Per Tablespoon: 35 calories, 1 g protein, 1 g fat, 6 g carbohydrate, 11 mg sodium, 9 mg cholesterol.

1 **cup sugar**
1 **cup Dutch-processed unsweetened cocoa
    powder**
1 **cup skim milk**
1 **egg, slightly beaten**
2 **tablespoons unsalted butter, cut into
    tablespoons**
1 **teaspoon vanilla**

1. Mix together the sugar and the cocoa powder in a large, heavy-bottomed saucepan until no lumps remain. Add the milk and the egg, stirring until the mixture is smooth.
2. Place the saucepan over very low heat. Bring the syrup just to boiling, stirring constantly; do not boil. Remove the saucepan from the heat; cool the mixture slightly. Stir in the butter until melted. Stir in the vanilla. Cool the syrup to room temperature. The syrup can be refrigerated, covered, for up to several weeks.

Chocolate Roll with Orange-Ginger Meringue

Bake at 375° for 10 to 12 minutes. Makes 12 servings.

Nutrient Value Per Serving: 98 calories, 3 g protein, 2 g fat, 18 g carbohydrate, 85 mg sodium, 69 mg cholesterol.

Chocolate Roll:
Nonstick vegetable cooking spray
½ cup sifted cake flour
3 tablespoons unsweetened cocoa powder
¾ teaspoon baking powder
3 eggs, separated
¼ cup sugar plus 3 tablespoons
2 tablespoons water
1 egg white
⅛ teaspoon salt
1 tablespoon 10X (confectioners') sugar

Orange-Ginger Meringue Filling (recipe follows)

1. Prepare the Chocolate Roll: Spray a 15 x 10 x 1-inch jelly-roll pan with nonstick vegetable cooking spray. Line bottom of pan with wax paper; spray.
2. Preheat the oven to moderate (375°).
3. Sift together the cake flour, unsweetened cocoa powder and baking powder onto clean wax paper.
4. Beat the egg yolks in a large bowl at high speed until foamy. Gradually beat in the ¼ cup sugar, 1 tablespoon at a time, until very thick, for 3 minutes. Add the water and beat well. Stir in the flour mixture until smooth.
5. Beat the 4 egg whites with the salt in a large bowl with clean beaters until foamy. Gradually beat in the 3 tablespoons sugar until soft peaks form. Fold one-third of the whites into the batter to lighten. Fold in the remaining whites until no streaks remain. Spread evenly in the pan.
6. Bake in the preheated moderate oven (375°) for 10 to 12 minutes or until the center springs back when pressed.
7. Spray a sheet of wax paper with cooking spray. Loosen cake around edges with a knife; invert onto the wax paper. Peel the paper from the cake. Starting at the short end, roll up cake and wax paper together; place the roll, seam-side down, on a wire rack. Cool completely.
8. Unroll the cake; discard the paper. Spread with the Orange-Ginger Meringue Filling. Reroll the cake. Sprinkle the cake with 10X (confectioners') sugar and garnish with orange twists, if you wish.

Note: If you make the roll a day ahead, you will have a slightly "wetter" cake.

Orange-Ginger Meringue Filling: Beat 3 egg whites with ¾ teaspoon cream of tartar in a large bowl until foamy. Gradually beat in 3 tablespoons sugar, a tablespoon at a time, until firm peaks form. Gently fold in 2 tablespoons orange marmalade and 1 tablespoon (½ ounce) chopped preserved candied ginger.

Lemon Bavarian Cream

Makes 10 servings (½ cup).

Nutrient Value Per Serving: 110 calories, 5 g protein, 4 g fat, 14 g carbohydrate, 73 mg sodium, 141 mg cholesterol.

1 envelope gelatin
½ cup lemon juice
1½ cups whole milk
1 tablespoon grated lemon rind
5 egg yolks
⅓ cup sugar plus ¼ cup
⅛ teaspoon salt
4 egg whites
⅛ teaspoon cream of tartar

1. Sprinkle the gelatin over the lemon juice in a glass measuring cup to soften.
2. Meanwhile, combine the milk and lemon rind in a heavy, large saucepan. Bring to boiling. Remove the saucepan from the heat and cool slightly.
3. Beat the egg yolks with the ⅓ cup sugar and salt in a medium-size bowl with an electric mixer on high speed until thick and lemon colored. Gradually whisk in the milk, stirring constantly. Stir back into the saucepan.
4. Heat, do not boil, over medium-low heat, stirring constantly, until the custard is thick enough to coat the back of a spoon, about 3 to 5 minutes. Strain the custard through a strainer into a bowl. Add the gelatin mixture; stir to dissolve.
5. Set the bowl in a large pan of ice and water to speed the setting. Stir occasionally until the mixture begins to thicken.
6. When the gelatin mixture begins to set, beat the egg whites with the cream of tartar in a large bowl until foamy. Gradually beat in the remaining ¼ cup of sugar until soft peaks form.
7. Fold the whites into the gelatin mixture. Spoon into a glass serving bowl, mounding the top. Cover lightly and chill until just set, up to 4 hours.

Lime Cheesecake

Bake the crust at 350° for 2 minutes; then bake the cake for 40 to 50 minutes.
Makes 12 servings.

Nutrient Value Per Serving: 141 calories, 9 g protein, 3 g fat, 19 g carbohydrate, 323 mg sodium, 49 mg cholesterol.

Nonstick vegetable cooking spray
½ **cup finely crushed zwieback biscuits**
2 **tablespoons reduced-calorie margarine**
3 **cups 1% low-fat cottage cheese**
¾ **cup sugar**
3 **tablespoons all-purpose flour**
2 **eggs, slightly beaten**
¾ **cup skim milk**
1 **to 2 tablespoons lime juice**
½ **teaspoon grated lime rind**
¼ **teaspoon salt**
Limes, for garnish

1. Spray only the tight-fitting removable bottom of a 9 x 3-inch springform pan with the nonstick vegetable cooking spray.
2. Combine the zwieback crumbs and margarine with fingers in a bowl until well blended. Scatter the mixture over the bottom of the prepared pan; press down slightly.
3. Bake the crust in the preheated moderate oven (350°) until crisp, 2 minutes. Leave the oven on. Cool the crust on a wire rack while preparing the cheesecake.
4. Place the cottage cheese in a food processor. Whirl, scraping down the sides, until smooth (no lumps), 3 to 5 minutes. Add the sugar and flour; whirl until blended. Add the eggs, one at a time, whirling after each addition. Add the milk, lime juice, rind and salt; whirl just until well blended.
5. Place the prepared springform pan on a cookie sheet. Then ladle the cheesecake mixture into the crust; do not pour, or else air bubbles will form on top.
6. Bake in the preheated moderate oven (350°) for 40 to 50 minutes or until a wooden pick inserted near the center comes out clean. Do not overbake.
7. Cool the cake in the pan on a wire rack. Refrigerate, covered, for several hours until chilled. Run a sharp knife around the edge of the cake; loosen and remove the side of the pan. Garnish with lime slices cut into quarters and strips of lime rind, if you wish.

Chocolate Sponge Cake

The more gently you fold the egg whites in Step 3, the higher and lighter your cake will be.

Bake at 350° for 40 to 45 minutes.
Makes 16 servings.

Nutrient Value Per Serving: 115 calories, 3 g protein, 5 g fat, 16 g carbohydrate, 46 mg sodium, 57 mg cholesterol.

7 **egg whites**
⅛ **teaspoon cream of tartar**
¾ **cup sugar**
3 **egg yolks**
1 **teaspoon vanilla**
1 **cup sifted cake flour**
3 **tablespoons butter, melted and cooled to lukewarm**
1½ **ounces semisweet chocolate**
2 **tablespoons vegetable shortening**

1. Preheat the oven to moderate (350°).
2. Beat the egg whites with the cream of tartar in a large bowl until foamy. Beat in the sugar, 1 tablespoon at a time, until the meringue forms stiff, but not dry, peaks.
3. Stir together the egg yolks and vanilla in another large bowl. Fold in one-third of the beaten egg whites. Fold in the remaining whites until no streaks of white remain. Sprinkle the cake flour over the top of the mixture; fold in. Very gently fold in the melted butter; do not overfold. Turn the batter into a 9-inch tube pan, spreading evenly.
4. Bake in the preheated moderate oven (350°) for 40 to 45 minutes or until a wooden pick inserted near the center comes out clean.
5. Invert the cake onto a large funnel or bottle; let the cake hang until it is completely cooled, for at least 1½ hours.
6. Run a knife around the inner and outer edges of the cake. Turn out onto a rack; cool completely, with the crusty portion up.
7. Melt the chocolate together with the vegetable shortening in the top of a double boiler over hot, not boiling, water, stirring occasionally, until smooth. Cool slightly. Spoon the melted chocolate evenly over the top of the cake, letting the excess run down the sides.

Food for thought . . .

Fat is the most concentrated source of food energy and is made up of cholesterol and 3 types of fatty acids.
- *Saturated fat: primarily from animal sources but also includes palm and coconut oils; saturated fats are usually in a solid form and generally high in cholesterol.*
- *Polyunsaturated fat: primarily from vegetable sources.*
- *Monounsaturated fat: primarily from plant sources; recent research indicates these oils may help to lower the chance of heart disease.*

The American Heart Association and the National Academy of Science recommends for the average healthy female a daily fat intake of no more than 66 grams, and for the male, 90 grams.

Hot Banana and Ginger with Papaya in Blueberry Sauce

The recipe name says it all! Although apple juice will work, papaya juice will give this dessert a beautiful golden color.

Makes 8 servings.

Nutrient Value Per Serving: 78 calories, 1 g protein, 0 g fat, 20 g carbohydrate, 3 mg sodium, 0 mg cholesterol.

4   bananas, peeled, halved and trimmed
2   teaspoons chopped crystallized ginger
1   cup papaya juice OR: apple juice
½ cup fresh or frozen blueberries
2   tablespoons julienned orange rind

1. Place the bananas, crystallized ginger and papaya juice or apple juice in a medium-size skillet. Cover and steam the bananas for 2 to 3 minutes. Turn the bananas over; steam for 2 to 3 minutes longer or until the bananas are tender.
2. Remove the skillet from the heat. Let stand, covered, for 5 to 6 minutes or until the sauce thickens slightly.
3. Stir in the blueberries just until warmed. (Do not allow the berries to burst.) Serve immediately, topped with the julienned orange rind.

CALORIE-CUTTING AND SUBSTITUTIONS

Butter and Oils
- A tablespoon of butter has the same calorie count as a tablespoon of margarine. But substitute an equal amount of diet margarine and you'll shave off up to 50% of the calories.
- Look for margarine with "liquid oil" as the first ingredient instead of "hydrogenated oil" or butter. Use corn, soybean, safflower or sunflower oil instead of peanut, palm, coconut or olive oil.
- "Sauté" foods in a little chicken broth instead of oil.
- Use only nonstick skillets for sautéing — you'll need less oil. Drain the fat when possible.

Dairy and Eggs
- Part-skim milk products can often be substituted for their whole milk cousins without affecting a recipe. You'll find part-skim or lowfat milk, cheeses and yogurt at supermarkets.
- Substitute lowfat plain yogurt for sour cream.
- Create lowfat "cream cheese" by blending 1½ cups of ricotta cheese (part-skim) with ¼ cup of plain yogurt. Refrigerate.
- Substitute 2% or skim milk for whole milk. If you've never been able to get used to the taste of skim milk, mix half whole with half skim; you'll cut 36 calories from each 8-ounce glass.
- Substitute cream with evaporated skim milk in recipes.
- Know where calories come from: 1 tablespoon of sour cream on a baked potato adds more calories than 1 tablespoon of sugar sprinkled over a grapefruit half. (Fat provides double the calories compared to carbohydrates and protein.)
- Make a two-egg omelet using one whole egg with just the white of the other egg. By eliminating the second yolk, you'll save more than 250 mg of cholesterol and 65 calories.
- Instead of American cheese as your omelet filling, substitute leftover steamed vegetables and herbs. You'll save about 210 calories and 16 grams of fat per 2 ounces of cheese.
- Try some of the lowfat varieties of these cheeses: Edam, Gouda, mozzarella, Parmesan, ricotta, Monterey Jack, cottage, Cheddar.
- Make a mock mayonnaise by blending 2 tablespoons of low-calorie mayonnaise with 1 cup of yogurt.

Poultry and Meats
- Trim fat from beef and poultry. Avoid marbled meat.
- Instead of legs or thighs, use *skinless* chicken breasts for chicken salads, pot pies, curries, stews

and soups. White meat has fewer calories than dark meat and most of the fat is in the skin.

• To keep chicken moist cook it with the skin on, but remove the skin before serving.

• Roast, bake or broil meats and poultry on a rack to ensure maximum fat runoff. Then remove the skin and all visible fat before eating.

• Eliminate bacon in stews, casseroles and soups and avoid cooking with bacon fat.

• Try some of the new lower-fat products now available: sausage-rice breakfast links, chicken and turkey franks and lower-fat luncheon meats.

• If you're a tuna fish fan, save 300 calories per 6½-ounce can by using tuna packed in water rather than oil.

Fruits, Vegetables and Grains

• Choose fresh fruit and vegetables in season instead of canned or frozen.

• Try reducing sugar and salt in recipes by half.

• Substitute whole-wheat or spinach pasta for white pasta.

• Use brown instead of white rice.

• Try lentils, bulgur or kasha as alternatives to rice, noodles and mashed potatoes.

• Make French fries without the oil: Cut a raw potato into 16 wedges. Place on a cookie sheet and bake at 400°. Sprinkle with garlic, onion or chili powder.

Desserts

• When baking, substitute whole-wheat flour for half of the white flour.

• Forego crumb toppings, icings and glazes on home-baked goods.

• Garnish desserts with slices of fresh fruit and fresh mint leaves rather than with a dollop of whipped cream.

• Try substituting a low-calorie whipped topping mix in a recipe that calls for sweetened whipped cream.

Snacks

• Try two shredded wheat biscuits with 4 ounces of skim milk for a filling, lowfat, high-fiber, 225-calorie lunchtime meal.

• Have a low-calorie California-style salad: Slices of oranges and fresh spinach leaves make a salad with lots of eye appeal that is also high in iron and vitamin C. Sprinkle with lemon, vinegar or a low-calorie dressing.

Beverages

• Mix ½ cup of tangy buttermilk with ½ cup of tomato juice — just 67 calories.

• Mix ½ cup of buttermilk with ½ cup of low-calorie borscht. It's only about 60 calories and a refreshing summer soup, too.

• Boost your calcium intake by adding a tablespoon of dry skim milk powder to a glass of skim milk — only 23 extra calories.

• Create a healthful, low-calorie thirst-quencher by mixing ½ cup of mineral water with ⅓ cup of your favorite juice.

• Another low-calorie, healthful drink: 2 ounces of orange juice mixed with a squeeze of lime and enough cold water to make 1 cup — only about 30 calories.

• Have a spritzer — equal parts of wine and club soda. If you use just 2 ounces of wine, it's about 35 to 45 calories.

• Rule of thumb for alcoholic beverages: The "proof" determines the calories — 80-proof vodka instead of 100-proof, for example, saves you about 25 calories per 1½ ounces or jigger.

• Sip your cocktail from a large glass filled with ice. There will be less room for liquid.

• Opt for lower-calorie dry wines over sweet ones. (Champagne is a good choice.)

• If you prefer no alcohol at all, sip a glass of mineral water with a slice of lemon, lime or orange. It will help take the edge off your appetite.

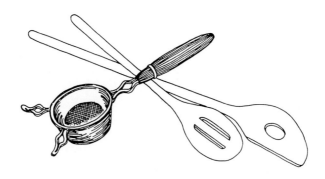

M·I·C·R·O·W·A·V·E M·A·G·I·C

Now this is real microwave magic: Pork Tenderloin Oriental (page 274) with steamed snow peas and julienned carrots.

7

*T*he microwave oven is here to stay — more than half the households in America say so! And why?

Microwaves are fast, *and* energy-efficient. No preheating time is required and cooking times are much shorter (and the kitchen stays cooler!). Plus, few vitamins and minerals are cooked away. Not to mention cleanup is a breeze! But most importantly, microwave ovens can make the most of your time — a real plus for today's busy lifestyle.

But if you're a skeptic who still thinks a microwave oven is only good for reheating coffee, melting chocolate (which it does very well), rewarming leftovers and cooking frozen entrées, this chapter is for you. Even before you try the recipes, take a look at "How to Get the Most From Your Microwave" on pages 258-259. This, along with the recipes, will convince you that you can orchestrate entire meals in the microwave.

And the recipes are diverse. From Salmon Appetizer Spread *(page 261)* to Sausage-Stuffed Onions *(page 263)* to Best-Ever Veal Parmesan *(page 273)*, the dishes are really terrific. And let's not forget about desserts: Try the Almond Cheesecake *(page 290)* or the Rocky Road Bars *(page 293)*. There's even an unbelievably quick (and delicious) Plum Pudding *(page 297)*.

So welcome to the 21st Century — space-age cooking has arrived!

How to Get the Most From Your Microwave

These tips will help you use your microwave oven to its full potential.

GENERAL TIPS

• To test whether a dish is microwave-safe or not, place it in the microwave oven next to a glass measuring cup half full of water. Heat on Full Power (100%) for 1 minute. If the dish is hot, it should not be used in the microwave oven. If it is warm, use only for reheating. If the dish is at room temperature, it is safe to use for all microwave cooking.

• Pay attention to standing times in recipes! Internal heat finishes the cooking after the dish is removed from the oven.

• Make sure the cooking utensil rests on a solid heatproof surface during the standing or resting time specified in the recipe.

• Set a timer for the minimum cooking time called for in a recipe. Check the doneness of food, then microwave for the additional time, if necessary.

• To prevent messy boil-overs, use a cooking container two to three times larger than the volume of the sauce, soup, drink or other liquid dish you are preparing.

• If cooking uniform pieces of food, such as meatballs or chicken wings, arrange in a circle in the cooking utensil for even cooking.

• Place tougher or thicker parts of food toward the outside edges of the cooking pan or tray.

• Do not use gold- or silver-trimmed dishes in a microwave oven; arcing may occur. Arcing is an electrical current that flows from the oven wall to metal in the oven, causing a light flash and popping sound. This may cause damage to the magnetron tube, the interior oven wall or the cooking utensil.

• If arcing occurs, turn the power off immediately.

• If there are small children in your house who might reach the controls and accidently turn the microwave oven on, keep a glass measure or bowl containing about 1 cup of water in the oven to prevent damage to it.

• A microwave oven works especially well with foods that have a naturally high moisture content, such as fish, poultry, fruits and vegetables.

• Dense foods, such as a potato, will take longer to cook in a microwave oven than lighter-textured foods, such as a cake.

MEATS & FISH

• Cook clams and mussels right in their shells for an easy-to-prepare appetizer. Arrange on a pie plate, hinged-side toward the outside of the plate, and cover loosely with wax paper. For three 5-ounce clams, microwave on Full Power for 3 to 5 minutes or until the shells open.

• If your roast beef is too rare, microwave the slices right on the dinner plate until the desired doneness.

• For one-step cooking and draining of excess fat, crumble ground meat into a microwave-safe plastic colander set in a casserole. The fat will drain into the casserole during cooking.

• No-fuss, fancy hors d'oeuvres: Wrap pineapple chunks or water chestnuts in bacon and fasten with a wooden pick. Place on paper toweling and microwave on Full Power until the bacon is thoroughly cooked.

• For an instant hot dog in a warm bun, lightly score a fully cooked frankfurter and place in the bun. Wrap loosely in paper toweling and microwave on Full Power for 30 to 45 seconds.

• For barbecued spareribs and chicken, first microwave until tender. Then grill long enough for a charcoal flavor and a crisp exterior.

• Remember: Boneless meats cook more evenly than meats on the bone because bones attract more microwave energy than meat.

FRUITS AND VEGETABLES

• To get the maximum amount of juice from citrus fruits, microwave on Full Power for 15 to 30 seconds before squeezing.

• Peel, core and pierce whole fruit, such as apples, before microwaving to allow steam to escape and avoid spattering.

• When microwaving cabbage-family vegetables, such as fresh broccoli or cauliflower, cover loosely with wax paper for better flavor and color.

• For an easy, quick single serving of frozen vegetables: Put ½ cup of frozen vegetables with 1 tablespoon of water in a custard cup. Cover with wax paper. Microwave on Full Power for 1½ to 2 minutes.

- To plump raisins and other dried fruits, place in a small bowl and sprinkle with a few drops of water. Microwave on Full Power for 15 to 30 seconds.
- Use your microwave to dry fresh herbs. Wash and pat dry on paper toweling. Measure 1½ cups of leaves (without stems). Spread on a double thickness of paper toweling and microwave on Full Power for 4 to 5 minutes, stirring several times.
- Shortcut acorn squash: Pierce the skin of a medium-size (1¼ pounds) squash and microwave on Full Power for 4 minutes. Cut in half, remove the seeds and microwave for another 4 minutes. Let stand for 5 minutes.
- Cook broccoli or asparagus with the tender flower ends pointing toward the center and with the tougher stem ends pointing out.

KITCHEN HELPS
- To separate cold bacon in its package: Microwave on Full Power for 30 to 45 seconds.
- To soften solidly frozen ice cream for easier scooping, microwave the container on Low Power (30%) for 20 to 40 seconds.
- Soften 1 stick of butter on Half Power (50%) for 45 to 55 seconds. Remove any foil wrapping before microwaving.
- To soften a block of cream cheese, remove the metallic wrapper and loosely wrap in wax paper. Microwave on Low Power for 1½ to 2 minutes for the 3-ounce size and 3 to 4 minutes for the 8-ounce size.
- Use doubled paper muffin-pan liners for microwaving muffins — the liners will help absorb any excess moisture.
- To melt chocolate, microwave in a microwave-safe cup on Full Power for 45 to 60 seconds per ounce of chocolate.
- To make chocolate curls, place an unwrapped square of chocolate on a microwave-safe plate. Heat on Half Power for 8 to 12 seconds. Scrape off the curls with a vegetable peeler.
- "Toasted" coconut: To brown 1 cup of shredded coconut, spread out on a microwave-safe pie plate. Microwave on Full Power for 2 to 3 minutes, stirring several times.
- Make your own chocolate syrup for milk: Combine 1¼ cups of granulated sugar, 1 cup of unsweetened cocoa powder, ¾ cup of water and ⅛ teaspoon of salt in a 1-quart microwave-safe measuring cup. Microwave on Full Power for

2 minutes or until the mixture boils. Stir. Continue cooking for 2 minutes longer, stirring every 30 seconds; don't let the mixture boil over. Stir in ½ teaspoon of vanilla. To serve, stir 2 tablespoons of the syrup into an 8-ounce glass of milk. The syrup will keep for up to 1 month when tightly covered in the refrigerator.
- For fried or poached eggs, always pierce the yolks with a wooden pick *before* microwaving to prevent bursting.
- Quick cup of tea, instant coffee or cocoa: Heat the water directly in the cup instead of boiling a large kettle of water conventionally. A cup with 6 ounces of water microwaved on Full Power will be steaming after 1¼ to 2 minutes. Two cups will take 2½ to 3 minutes.

WARMING UP FOODS
- Microwave dinner rolls in a napkin-lined straw serving basket on Full Power for 15 to 30 seconds, depending on the number and size of the rolls.
- Wrap a sandwich in paper toweling and microwave — the paper absorbs excess moisture.
- Heat gravy in a serving bowl or gravy boat on Full Power for 1 minute per cup.
- To warm a 12-ounce jar of sundae or fruit sauce topping, remove the lid and microwave on Full Power for 45 to 60 seconds.
- Reheat take-out fast food in its own paper wrapping on Full Power. If a container has a foil top, remove and cover loosely with wax paper.
- Reheat a fast-food double-decker hamburger in its plastic package on Full Power for 20 to 40 seconds.
- To crisp and renew the fresh flavor of day-old cookies, crackers or potato chips, microwave on Full Power for 5 to 15 seconds.
- Warm a slice of apple pie with "melty" cheese on top by microwaving on Full Power for 15 to 20 seconds.
- Popped corn can be reheated on Full Power for 15 to 20 seconds per cup.

F·I·R·S·T C·O·U·R·S·E·S

Microwave olé: All-In-One Tex-Mex Filling.

All-In-One Tex-Mex Filling

Microwave extra filling to keep on hand for last-minute meals or snacks. This filling keeps well in the freezer. Perfect for burritos, enchiladas or tacos.

Microwave on Full Power for 26 to 31 minutes. Makes 6 cups.

Nutrient Value Per ½ Cup: 447 calories, 27 g protein, 24 g fat, 32 g carbohydrate, 1,439 mg sodium, 75 mg cholesterol.

2 **pounds ground pork sausage**
1 **large onion, chopped (1 cup)**
2 **envelopes (1¼ ounces each) taco seasoning mix**
1 **can (28 ounces) whole tomatoes, cut up**
2 **cans (16 ounces each) red kidney beans, drained**
2 **cans (4 ounces each) chopped green chilies, drained**
8 **taco shells**
   Shredded lettuce
   Chopped tomatoes
   Shredded Cheddar cheese

1. Place the sausage and onion in a 2-quart microwave-safe bowl. Cover with vented heavy-duty microwave-safe plastic wrap.
2. Microwave on Full Power for 8 to 9 minutes, stirring twice to break the sausage into small chunks. Pour off the excess fat through the vented area.
3. Combine the taco seasoning mix, tomatoes, kidney beans, chilies and cooked sausage mixture in a 3- to 4-quart microwave-safe bowl, mixing well. Cover the bowl with vented microwave-safe plastic wrap.
4. Microwave on Full Power for 18 to 22 minutes, stirring every 5 minutes. Let the mixture stand, covered, for 5 minutes.
5. Divide the filling in half (about 3 cups each). Spoon half of the filling into a serving bowl. Freeze the other half. Serve as a filling for tacos with shredded lettuce, chopped tomatoes and shredded Cheddar cheese. Garnish with lime wedges and green chili peppers, if you wish.

Salmon Appetizer Spread

Vary the shape and/or the go-withs — your guests will always come back for more.

Microwave on Full Power for 30 to 45 seconds; then on Half Power for 1 to 1½ minutes. Makes 2½ cups.

Nutrient Value Per Tablespoon: 53 calories, 3 g protein, 4 g fat, 0 g carbohydrate, 76 mg sodium, 15 mg cholesterol.

1 **small onion, chopped (¼ cup)**
1 **tablespoon butter or margarine**
1 **package (8 ounces) cream cheese**
2 **cups shredded Cheddar cheese (8 ounces)**
1 **can (7½ or 7¾ ounces) salmon, drained and flaked**
¼ **cup chopped parsley**
   Dash liquid red-pepper seasoning
   Chopped parsley for garnish (optional)
   Thinly sliced pumpernickel

1. Microwave the onion and the butter or margarine in a small microwave-safe bowl, covered, on Full Power for 30 to 45 seconds or until the onion is tender.
2. Microwave the cream cheese in a large microwave-safe bowl on Half Power for 1 to 1½ minutes or until softened. Stir in the onion-butter mixture, blending well.
3. Add the shredded Cheddar cheese, salmon, ¼ cup chopped parsley and the liquid-red pepper seasoning, blending well. Shape the mixture into a ball. Wrap in plastic wrap and chill for at least 2 hours.
4. Roll the bottom of the ball in additional chopped parsley, if you wish. Serve with triangles of thinly sliced pumpernickel.

Salmon Appetizer Spread

Puff Pastry Sticks

Microwave on Medium-High Power for
5 to 7 minutes.
Makes 36.

*Nutrient Value Per Stick: 65 calories, 1 g protein, 4 g fat,
5 g carbohydrate, 110 mg sodium, 8 mg cholesterol.*

1 **package (17¼ ounces) puff pastry,
    partially thawed**
1 **egg yolk**
1 **teaspoon water**
2 **tablespoons sesame seeds**
2 **tablespoons poppy seeds**
2 **tablespoons caraway seeds**
¾ **teaspoon salt**

1. Unfold the sheets of partially thawed pastry; cut lengthwise into ½-inch-wide strips using a very sharp knife. Brush one side of the pastry with the egg yolk mixed with the 1 teaspoon water.
2. Place the sesame, poppy and caraway seeds in separate piles on a piece of wax paper. Sprinkle each pile with ¼ teaspoon of the salt.
3. Dip 12 pastry strips, yolk-side down, into the sesame seeds, coating the pastry strips well. Twist each strip several times; place on a wax paper-lined microwave-safe dish. Repeat with the remaining pastry strips and the poppy and caraway seeds.
4. Microwave on Medium-High Power for 5 to 7 minutes or until the puff pastry sticks turn lightly golden. (Watch for burning.)

EQUIVALENTS IN MICROWAVE COOKING TIMES

600- to 700-watt oven	500- to 600-watt oven	400- to 500-watt oven
15 seconds	18 seconds	20 seconds
30 seconds	35 seconds	45 seconds
1 minute	1 minute, 15 seconds	1 minute, 30 seconds
2 minutes	2 minutes, 30 seconds	2 minutes, 50 seconds
3 minutes	3 minutes, 30 seconds	4 minutes, 15 seconds
4 minutes	4 minutes, 50 seconds	5 minutes, 45 seconds
5 minutes	6 minutes	7 minutes
6 minutes	7 minutes, 15 seconds	8 minutes, 30 seconds
8 minutes	9 minutes, 30 seconds	11 minutes, 15 seconds
10 minutes	12 minutes	14 minutes

T·H·E M·A·I·N T·H·I·N·G·S

Savory Sausage-Stuffed Onions

Sausage-Stuffed Onions

Sweet onions make the perfect containers for a savory sausage and cornbread mixture.

Microwave onions on Full Power for 12 minutes; sausage for 8 minutes; green pepper for 6 minutes; stuffed onions for 2 minutes. Makes 8 servings.

Nutrient Value Per Onion: 340 calories, 9 g protein, 21 g fat, 27 g carbohydrate, 1,268 mg sodium, 53 mg cholesterol.

  8 *medium-size sweet onions*
 ½ *cup water*
  1 *teaspoon salt*

  1 *package (1 pound) bulk sausage*
1½ *cups water*
 ½ *cup (1 stick) butter or margarine*
  1 *small sweet green pepper, halved, seeded and diced*
  1 *package (8 ounces) cornbread stuffing mix*
     Fresh basil leaves and sweet red pepper for garnish (optional)

1. Peel the onions and arrange in a large shallow microwave-safe casserole. Add the ½ cup water to the casserole and sprinkle with the salt. Cover the casserole with heavy-duty microwave-safe plastic wrap.
2. Microwave on Full Power for 12 minutes,

rotating the dish one-half turn after 6 minutes. Remove the onions from the microwave and allow to stand while making the stuffing.

3. Shape the sausage into 8 equal-size patties and arrange in a 2-quart shallow microwave-safe casserole.

4. Microwave the patties on Full Power for 8 minutes, rotating the dish one-half turn after 4 minutes. Remove from the microwave and let stand while preparing the stuffing.

5. Place the 1½ cups water, butter or margarine and diced green pepper in a 6-cup microwave-safe casserole; cover.

6. Microwave the green pepper on Full Power for 6 minutes. Stir in the cornbread stuffing mix until well blended. Let stand while preparing the onions.

7. Loosen and remove the inner rings from the onions and reserve for another recipe. Drain the water from the casserole and return the onions to the dish.

8. Drain the sausage on paper toweling. Crumble the sausage and toss with the stuffing. Spoon into the onions, dividing evenly.

9. Microwave the onions, uncovered, on Full Power for 2 minutes or until heated through. Garnish with fresh basil leaves and red pepper, if you wish.

PRINCIPLES OF MICROWAVE COOKING

Starting temperature: *Whether you're cooking, heating or defrosting, the warmer the food, the shorter the cooking time. Starting with room temperature food is advisable.*

Positioning: *Before microwaving, arrange unevenly shaped food with the larger, thicker portions toward the outside of the dish, and the smaller, thinner portions toward the center.*

Volume: *Small amounts take less time to cook than large ones. For example, one potato cooks in about 4 minutes, four potatoes in 12 minutes.*

Piece size: *Not only will small pieces of food cook faster than large ones, but those which are similar in size will cook more evenly.*

Density: *Potatoes and other dense foods, as well as massive roasts, cook at a slower rate than light, porous foods such as bread.*

Height in oven: *The portion of food that is higher than 3 inches cooks faster than parts farther from the source of energy. Shield the protruding portion with thin strips of aluminum foil for more even cooking.*

Boiling: *Liquids may boil over before the cooking time indicated in the recipe — so set the probe which will shut off the oven when the liquid reaches the desired temperature.*

Stirring: *Because microwaves cook foods from outside in, it is necessary to redistribute the heat by stirring the cooked portion to the center.*

Standing time: *Since cooking continues after you remove the dish from the microwave, let internal heat finish the job. Standing time can account for about one-third of the cooking time.*

Meat and Vegetable Pie

A vegetable pie with a bottom layer of zesty ground meat. Serve with cinnamon-flavored applesauce and whole-wheat Italian bread.

Microwave vegetable mixture on Full Power for about 10 minutes; meat for 8 minutes; potato mixture for about 4 minutes; pie for 2 minutes.
Makes 6 servings.

Nutrient Value Per Serving: 422 calories, 25 g protein, 23 g fat, 27 g carbohydrate, 649 mg sodium, 130 mg cholesterol.

Vegetable Mixture:

1 **package (16 ounces) frozen mixed vegetables in small pieces**
¼ **cup water**
1 **tablespoon butter or margarine**
1 **tablespoon all-purpose flour**
½ **cup beef broth**
½ **teaspoon leaf thyme, crumbled**
   Pinch pepper

Meat Mixture:

½ **cup fresh bread crumbs**
1 **tablespoon grated onion**
1 **egg, slightly beaten**
2 **tablespoons catsup**
2 **tablespoons milk**
1½ **teaspoons Dijon-style mustard**
¾ **teaspoon salt**
½ **teaspoon leaf thyme, crumbled**
¼ **teaspoon pepper**
1½ **pounds ground beef**

Potato Topping:

1 **cup water**
½ **cup milk**
1 **tablespoon butter**
6 **tablespoons instant mashed potato granules**
2 **tablespoons grated Parmesan cheese**

1. Prepare the Vegetable Mixture: Place the frozen vegetables in a microwave-safe 8 x 8 x 2-inch square baking dish. Pour in the ¼ cup water. Cover the dish with pleated plastic wrap. Microwave at Full Power for 7 minutes, stirring once. Drain the vegetables in a colander.

2. Place the butter in a 4-cup microwave-safe measure. Microwave, uncovered, on Full Power for 45 seconds to melt. Stir in the flour until smooth. Mix in the beef broth, thyme and pepper. Microwave, uncovered, at Full Power for 2 to 2½ minutes or until boiling. Whisk until smooth. Mix the broth mixture with the vegetables in a small bowl. Set aside.

3. Prepare the Meat Mixture: Combine the bread crumbs, grated onion, egg, catsup, milk, mustard, salt, thyme, pepper and meat in the same 8-inch square dish; mix well. Pat the meat mixture into an even layer over the bottom of the dish. Cover the meat with wax paper.

4. Microwave the meat at Full Power for 8 minutes. Carefully drain off the liquid. Set aside.

5. Prepare the Potato Mixture: Combine the 1 cup water, ½ cup milk and 1 tablespoon butter in the same 4-cup measure used above. Microwave, uncovered, at Full Power for 4 to 4½ minutes just to boiling. Mix in the instant potato granules and the Parmesan cheese.

6. To assemble the pie: Spread the potatoes in an even layer over the meat. Top with the vegetable mixture, spreading evenly. Cover the top with wax paper. Microwave the pie at Full Power for 2 minutes to heat through. Let the pie stand for 5 minutes before serving.

You're going to love this: Mexicali Chicken with Sassy Salsa.

Mexicali Chicken

There's a taste of olé in every bite, thanks to the extra spicy seasoning blend.

Microwave on Full Power for 12 to 14 minutes. Makes 4 servings.

Nutrient Value Per Serving: 253 calories, 30 g protein, 11 g fat, 7 g carbohydrate, 97 mg sodium, 90 mg cholesterol.

- *1 broiler-fryer (2½ pounds), cut up and skin removed*
- *2½ to 3 tablespoons extra spicy salt-free 14 herb and spice seasoning blend*
- *1 tablespoon vegetable oil*
- *1 fresh lime, cut into wedges*
- *Jalapeño peppers (optional)*
- *Sassy Salsa (recipe follows)*
- *Tostada chips (optional)*

1. Arrange the chicken, bone-side up, in a shallow microwave-safe baking dish. Sprinkle with 1 teaspoon of the extra spicy seasoning blend. Loosely cover the chicken with wax paper.
2. Microwave on Full Power for 8 minutes. Turn each piece of chicken over; drizzle with the oil and sprinkle with the remaining extra spicy seasoning blend. Rotate the dish one-quarter turn. Re-cover.
3. Microwave on Full Power for 4 to 6 minutes or until the chicken is tender. Let stand, covered, for 5 minutes. Garnish with the lime and fresh jalapeño peppers, if you wish. Serve with the Sassy Salsa and tostada chips, if you wish.

Sassy Salsa

A great accompaniment to chicken and grilled fish, or as a dip.

Makes about 2 cups.

Nutrient Value Per ¼ Cup: 15 calories, 1 g protein, 0 g fat, 3 g carbohydrate, 5 mg sodium, 0 mg cholesterol.

- *2 medium-size ripe tomatoes, chopped (1½ cups)*
- *1 medium-size onion, chopped (½ cup)*
- *1 clove garlic, finely chopped*
- *1 tablespoon chopped, seeded jalapeño pepper*
- *1 tablespoon extra spicy salt-free 14 herb and spice seasoning blend*

1. Combine the chopped tomatoes, onion, garlic, jalapeño pepper and extra spicy seasoning blend in a small bowl, blending well. Let stand for at least 15 minutes to allow the flavors to develop.
2. Serve with the Mexicali Chicken, grilled fish or as a dip with tostadas.

TIPS FOR MICROWAVING CHICKEN

Chicken cooks quickly on the Full (100%) Power Setting and retains its natural juices. In general, a 3-pound whole chicken takes 1 to 1½ hours to roast in a regular oven, but will cook in less than 30 minutes in a microwave. Here are some tips for cooking chicken in a microwave oven:

- *To brown chicken, coat it with butter (not margarine), or use soy sauce, paprika, herbs or a commercial browning sauce.*
- *Do not salt chicken before cooking. Add salt during the standing time.*
- *Chicken parts cook best on Full Power, but use Half Power (50%) for whole birds.*
- *Choose chicken pieces (breasts, thighs or drumsticks) of equal size so that they will cook evenly.*
- *When cooking parts, place the larger, thicker parts near the outside and the thinner parts toward the center of the baking dish. Place giblets under the breast.*
- *Place a whole chicken, breast-side down, on a microwave-safe roasting rack in a shallow pan.*
- *Cover the chicken lightly with wax paper to prevent spattering.*
- *Microwave on Half Power for 9 minutes per pound or until a drumstick moves easily, turning the chicken breast-side up after half the cooking time.*
- *When in doubt about whether the chicken is done, undercook rather than overcook. It's easy to return the chicken to the microwave oven for more cooking. Remember, chicken will continue to cook during the standing time.*
- *Allow to rest for 10 minutes, then carve.*
- *Because chicken cooks so quickly, added flavors are absorbed more fully if the chicken is marinated before cooking.*

MICROWAVE COOKING DIRECTIONS FOR TURKEY

If frozen, thaw the turkey first. Thawing in the microwave is not recommended.

First Steps

1. Free the legs from the tucked position. Do not cut the band of skin.
2. Remove the neck and giblets from the neck and body cavities. To microwave, place 3 cups of water, ½ teaspoon of salt, the neck, gizzard and heart in a 2-quart microwave-safe casserole and cover. Microwave on Half Power (50%) for 35 minutes. Add the liver, cover and microwave for 10 minutes more. The cooked neck, giblets and stock may be used in making gravy or stuffing.
3. Rinse the turkey and drain well.
4. If desired, stuff the neck and body cavities lightly. Cover the exposed stuffing with plastic wrap.
5. Turn the wings back to hold the neck skin in place. Return the legs to the tucked position. No trussing is necessary.
6. Make Browning Sauce: Microwave ½ stick of butter in a microwave-safe bowl on Full Power (100%) for 30 to 40 seconds until melted. Blend in ¼ teaspoon paprika and ⅛ teaspoon browning and seasoning sauce. Stir well before each use.

To Cook

1. Place the turkey, breast down, in a microwave-safe dish. If the turkey tips, level with a microwave-safe item to cook evenly.
2. Brush the back of the turkey with 1 tablespoon of the Browning Sauce.
3. See the Microwave Cooking Schedule for cooking time. Use the Cooking Schedule closest to the weight of the turkey. Follow Part I and Part II Cook Times without any delay interruptions.
4. Microwave on Full Power for Time 1. Rotate the turkey a half turn. Microwave for Time 2. Remove and discard the drippings.
5. Turn the turkey, breast up. If stuffed, remove the plastic wrap. Brush with the Browning Sauce. Level if the turkey tips.
6. Microwave on Half Power for Times 3, 4 and 5. At the end of each time, rotate the turkey a quarter turn; discard the drippings. Brush the turkey with the Browning Sauce. If over-browning occurs, shield with small pieces of foil after Time 5; check for doneness. A meat thermometer inserted in the thickest part of the thigh (not touching bone) should register 180° to 185° F; in the thickest part of the breast, 170° F; in the center of the stuffing, 160° to 165° F. If *all* these temperatures have not been reached, cook for Time 6. Recheck the temperatures; cook longer if necessary.
7. Cover the turkey with foil. Let stand for 15 minutes before carving.

Microwave Cooking Schedule for Stuffed or Unstuffed Turkey
Approximate cooking time in 625- to 700-watt microwave ovens

Times	4 lb.	5 lb.	6 lb.	7 lb.	8 lb.	9 lb.	10 lb.	11 lb.	12 lb.
					Weight				
	Part I — Breast down on Full Power (100%)								
1	8 min.	10 min.	12 min.	14 min.	16 min.	18 min.	20 min.	22 min.	24 min.
2	8 min.	10 min.	12 min.	14 min.	16 min.	18 min.	20 min.	22 min.	24 min.
	Part II — Breast up on Half Power (50%)								
3	8 min.	10 min.	12 min.	14 min.	16 min.	18 min.	20 min.	22 min.	24 min.
4	8 min.	10 min.	12 min.	14 min.	16 min.	18 min.	20 min.	22 min.	24 min.
5*	8 min.	10 min.	12 min.	14 min.	16 min.	18 min.	20 min.	22 min.	24 min.
6	8 min.	10 min.	12 min.	14 min.	16 min.	18 min.	20 min.	22 min.	24 min.
Total Cook Time	48 min.	1 hr.	1 hr., 12 min.	1 hr., 24 min.	1 hr., 36 min.	1 hr., 48 min.	2 hrs.	2 hrs., 12 min.	2 hrs., 24 min.

*Check for doneness after Time 5.

Arroz Con Pollo — a Cuban version of chicken with rice (page 270).

Arroz con Pollo

This microwave version of the Cuban classic cooks without spattering, so cleanup is fast and easy.

Microwave on Full Power for 43 to 50 minutes. Makes 8 servings.

Nutrient Value Per Serving: 426 calories, 31 g protein, 10 g fat, 50 g carbohydrate, 813 mg sodium, 72 mg cholesterol.

* 4 **pounds chicken, skin removed and cut into serving pieces**
* 1¼ **teaspoons coarse (kosher) salt**
* ½ **teaspoon black pepper**
* ¼ **teaspoon sweet paprika**
* 1 **package (10 ounces) frozen peas OR: artichoke hearts**
* 1 **medium-size onion, finely diced (½ cup)**
* 2 **cloves garlic, finely chopped**
* 2 **tablespoons olive or peanut oil**
* 1 **can (28 ounces) Italian plum tomatoes**
* 2 **cups chicken broth**
* 1 **bay leaf**
* 2 **tablespoons flat-leaf parsley, chopped Pinch leaf thyme, crumbled**
* 2 **cups uncooked rice**
* ½ **teaspoon saffron, steeped in 2 tablespoons hot water**
* 1 **jar (2 ounces) sliced pimiento, drained**

1. Season the chicken with the salt, pepper and paprika. Cook the peas or artichokes following the manufacturer's directions for microwaving.
2. Microwave the onion and garlic in the oil in a 3- to 4-quart microwave-safe casserole, covered with a lid or heavy-duty microwave-safe plastic wrap, on Full Power for 5 minutes or until the onion is transparent. Add the chicken.
3. Microwave, covered, on Full Power for 6 to 7 minutes, turning the chicken pieces over halfway through the cooking time.
4. Add 2½ cups of the tomatoes with their liquid, the chicken broth, bay leaf, parsley, thyme, rice and steeped saffron and its liquid. Cover tightly.
5. Microwave on Full Power for 10 minutes. Stir; microwave for 10 minutes more. Stir again. (If the rice seems hard, add the remaining tomatoes and their liquid.) Microwave for 10 to 15 minutes more or until the rice is tender. Stir in the peas or artichokes.
6. Microwave for 2 to 3 minutes or until the vegetables are heated through. Garnish with the pimiento.

Chicken with Lemon and Olives

Be sure to marinate the chicken overnight for maximum flavor. The finished dish is even better reheated the second day.

Microwave on Full Power for 3 minutes; then for 15 to 17 minutes. Microwave gravy on Full Power for 1 minute.

Nutrient Value Per Serving: 545 calories, 49 g protein, 35 g fat, 7 g carbohydrate, 541 mg sodium, 154 mg cholesterol.

* 1 **lemon**
* 2 **cloves garlic, finely chopped**
* ¼ **teaspoon ground ginger**
* ¼ **teaspoon ground cumin**
* ¼ **teaspoon ground cinnamon**
* ¼ **teaspoon black pepper**
* ⅛ **teaspoon ground hot red pepper**
* 2 **tablespoons olive oil**
* 1 **broiler-fryer chicken (about 3½ pounds), cut into 8 serving pieces**
* 1 **medium-size onion, finely chopped (½ cup)**
* 1 **medium-size sweet red pepper, halved, cored and cut into ¼-inch-wide strips**
* ¼ **cup dry white wine OR: water**
* 1 **tablespoon water**
* 1 **tablespoon flour**
* 20 **oil-cured black olives, pitted**
* 1 **tablespoon chopped flat-leaf Italian parsley**

1. Remove just the outer yellow rind with a swivel-bladed vegetable peeler from half of the lemon. Coarsely chop the rind; reserve. Squeeze and measure out 2 tablespoons of juice from the lemon.
2. Place the rind and the juice in a 12 x 8-inch microwave-safe baking dish. Stir in the garlic, ginger, cumin, cinnamon, black pepper, red pepper and olive oil. Add the chicken, turning to coat well. Cover the dish and refrigerate overnight, turning the chicken once or twice.
3. Remove the chicken and set aside. Add the onion to the marinade and stir to mix. Cover the dish with wax paper. Microwave on Full Power for 3 minutes. Stir the sweet red pepper into the dish. Add the chicken pieces, arranging the meatier portions toward the outside of the dish. Pour the wine over all.

4. Cover the dish with wax paper. Microwave on Full Power for 15 to 17 minutes; rotate the dish after 10 minutes. Remove the chicken along with the sweet red pepper to a serving dish. Reserve the cooking liquid.
5. Stir together the water and the flour in a microwave-safe 2-cup glass measure until smooth; stir in the wine-cooking mixture. Microwave, uncovered, on Full Power for 1 minute to boiling. Sprinkle the olives and parsley over the chicken. Pour the gravy over all.

Quick Old-Fashioned Shepherd's Pie

Quick Old-Fashioned Shepherd's Pie

One of Grandmother's cherished recipes is easily adapted for use in the microwave.

Microwave on Full Power for 10 to 15 minutes. Makes 6 servings.

Nutrient Value Per Serving: 265 calories, 20 g protein, 7 g fat, 32 g carbohydrate, 504 mg sodium, 42 mg cholesterol.

 2 **cups cubed cooked turkey, chicken or beef**
 1 **package (20 ounces) frozen broccoli, cauliflower and carrot mix**
 ¼ **cup frozen chopped onion**
 1 **can (10¾ ounces) condensed cream of chicken soup**
 ½ **cup milk**
 ¼ **cup dry sherry OR: water**
 ½ **teaspoon leaf tarragon, crumbled**
   Pepper, to taste
   Frozen hash brown potatoes, cooked following package directions OR: 2 cups mashed potatoes

1. Layer the turkey, chicken or beef with the frozen vegetable mix and onion in a 2-quart microwave-safe dish.
2. Combine the soup, milk, sherry or water, tarragon and pepper in a bowl, blending well. Pour the liquid over the vegetable layer. Arrange the hash browns or mashed potatoes evenly over the top.
3. Microwave on Full Power for 10 to 15 minutes or until heated through.

Delizioso: Chicken Italia.

Chicken Italia

Cook 4 servings and freeze to reheat later. The chicken and Italian-flavored sauce are delicious the first and second time around.

Microwave on Full Power for 16 to 18 minutes.
Makes 4 servings.

Nutrient Value Per Serving: 351 calories, 32 g protein, 6 g fat, 38 g carbohydrate, 437 mg sodium, 68 mg cholesterol.

2   **tablespoons all-purpose flour**
1   **jar (15½ ounces) spaghetti sauce with**
      mushrooms
1   **medium-size tomato, chopped**
¼   **cup rosé wine OR: water**
4   **chicken breast halves, skin removed**
      Salt and pepper, to taste
      Garlic powder
1   **small onion, thinly sliced**
½   **small sweet green pepper, halved, seeded**
      and cut into strips
2   **cups hot cooked spaghetti**
      Grated Parmesan cheese

1. Shake the flour into a 16 x 10-inch oven cooking bag. Place the bag in a 12 x 8 x 2-inch microwave-safe dish. Roll down the top of the bag. Add the spaghetti sauce, chopped tomato and wine or water. Squeeze the bag gently to blend the ingredients.
2. Sprinkle the chicken lightly with the salt, pepper and garlic powder. Place the chicken in the bag and turn the bag gently to coat the chicken. Top the chicken with the onion and green pepper. Close the bag with a nylon tie. Make six ½-inch slits in the top.
3. Microwave the chicken on Full Power for 16 to 18 minutes or until the chicken is done, rotating the dish after half the cooking time. Let stand for 3 minutes.
4. To serve, spoon the chicken and sauce over the hot cooked spaghetti. Sprinkle with the grated Parmesan cheese.

To Freeze: Place 2 servings of the Chicken Italia on a square of heavy-duty aluminum foil. Bundle wrap by bringing the 4 corners up together into a pyramid shape; then fold the edges together in a series of locked folds. Label, date and freeze.

To Reheat: Remove the frozen food from the foil. Place in a 1½-quart microwave-safe casserole. Cover the casserole with vented heavy-duty microwave-safe plastic wrap. Microwave on Half Power for 10 to 12 minutes or until the chicken is heated through. Serve over hot cooked spaghetti. Sprinkle with the Parmesan cheese.

Best-Ever Veal Parmesan

Best-Ever Veal Parmesan

This veal dish shows the convenience and efficiency of the microwave oven.

Microwave on Full Power for 45 seconds; then on Medium-High Power for 8 minutes.
Makes 8 servings.

Nutrient Value Per Serving: 348 calories, 21 g protein, 24 g fat, 13 g carbohydrate, 676 mg sodium, 97 mg cholesterol.

½   **cup (1 stick) butter or margarine**
¾   **cup packaged unseasoned bread crumbs**
⅓   **cup plus 3 tablespoons grated Parmesan**
      cheese
¾   **teaspoon leaf basil, crumbled**
¾   **teaspoon leaf oregano, crumbled**
¾   **teaspoon paprika**
½   **teaspoon salt**
¼   **teaspoon pepper**
1¼ **pounds veal cutlet, pounded ¼ inch thick**
1   **cup bottled spaghetti sauce**
1   **cup shredded mozzarella cheese**

1. Microwave the butter or margarine in a large shallow microwave-safe dish on Full Power for

45 seconds or until melted.

2. Combine the crumbs with ⅓ cup of the Parmesan cheese, the basil, oregano, paprika, salt and pepper on a piece of wax paper.

3. Cut the veal into serving-size pieces; dip in the melted butter to coat, then in the crumb mixture until well covered. Place in a microwave-safe plastic dish and cover with wax paper.

4. Microwave the veal on Medium-High Power for 5 minutes or until the juices are no longer pink. Drain the meat. Top with the spaghetti sauce. Sprinkle with the mozzarella and remaining 3 tablespoons Parmesan cheese. Cover the dish.

5. Microwave on Medium-High Power for 3 minutes or until heated through. Serve the veal with vermicelli and roasted sweet red and green peppers, if you wish.

Pork Tenderloin Oriental

Microwave on Medium-Low Power for 5 to 6 minutes; then on Full Power for 4 to 6 minutes. Makes 4 servings.

Nutrient Value Per Serving: 165 calories, 27 g protein, 3 g fat, 8 g carbohydrate, 372 mg sodium, 74 mg cholesterol.

1   pound pork tenderloin
2   tablespoons low-sodium soy sauce
1½ teaspoons ground ginger
1   package (1 pound) Oriental-style frozen
        vegetable combination

1. Cut the pork into ¼-inch-thick slices. Combine the soy sauce and the ginger in a 9-inch microwave-safe pie plate. Dip both sides of the pork into the mixture; arrange the pieces in a microwave-safe baking dish, with the larger pieces to the outside of the dish. Cover the dish with a sheet of vented heavy-duty microwave-safe plastic wrap.

2. Microwave the pork on Medium-Low Power for 3 minutes. Turn the meat, rearranging the least cooked parts to the outside of the dish.

3. Microwave the meat on Medium-Low Power for 2 to 3 minutes longer or until the meat looks cooked. Let the meat stand, covered, while preparing the vegetables.

4. Microwave the frozen vegetables in a microwave-safe bowl on Full Power for 4 to 6 minutes.

5. Check the pork for final doneness by slicing in the center of the largest piece. If not done, microwave the pork on Medium-Low Power for

30 to 60 seconds longer. Season to taste. Stir the undrained vegetables into the pork, coating the vegetables with the drippings.

6. To serve, spoon the vegetables onto a serving platter; arrange the pork on top.

Note: In the photo on page 256, we show pork with steamed snow peas and julienned carrot. Here's how: Lay 1 cup *each* snow peas and julienned carrot in the center of separate sheets of microwave-safe paper toweling; fold all the sides toward the center to enclose the food. Hold the packet under running water until soaked. Place on a microwave-safe plate. Microwave on Full Power for 3 to 5 minutes or until tender. Let stand for 3 minutes.

Quiche Lorraine

This main-dish pie calls for cooking the filling and crust separately.

Microwave on Full Power for 7½ minutes. Makes 6 servings (9-inch pie).

Nutrient Value Per Serving: 369 calories, 18 g protein, 26 g fat, 16 g carbohydrate, 655 mg sodium, 229 mg cholesterol.

1   cup shredded Swiss cheese
1   cup diced fully-cooked canned ham
1   tablespoon finely chopped green onion
1   frozen 9-inch pie shell, baked following
        package directions
1   cup half-and-half OR: light cream
4   eggs, beaten
⅛   teaspoon pepper
     Pinch ground nutmeg

1. Sprinkle ⅔ cup of the Swiss cheese, the diced ham and the green onion evenly over the baked pie shell.

2. Combine the half-and-half or light cream with the eggs, pepper and nutmeg in a 1-quart microwave-safe bowl.

3. Microwave, uncovered, on Full Power for 4½ minutes, stirring after 3 minutes. Stir again and pour into the prepared crust. Cover with wax paper.

4. Microwave the quiche on Full Power for 3 minutes, rotating the quiche halfway through. The quiche is done when a knife inserted in the center comes out clean; otherwise heat for 1 minute more. Sprinkle the pie with the remaining Swiss cheese. Cover the top with wax paper and let stand for 5 minutes. Garnish with strips of cooked ham, if you wish.

Real cooks do *make this quickie Quiche Lorraine*.

Something different with franks: Sweet and Sour Devil Dogs.

Sweet and Sour Devil Dogs

Ideal for snacking, surrounded with Jalapeño Corn Bread (page 292). This dish can be made in advance and reheated.

Microwave on Full Power for 8 to 10 minutes.
Makes 6 servings.

Nutrient Value Per Serving: 418 calories, 10 g protein, 22 g fat, 47 g carbohydrate, 1,416 mg sodium, 38 mg cholesterol.

1	**pound hot dogs (about 10)**
1	**can (20 ounces) pineapple chunks in pineapple juice**
2	**tablespoons cornstarch**
1	**cup catsup**
1	**large onion, thinly sliced**
3	**tablespoons light brown sugar**
2	**tablespoons honey**
4	**cloves garlic, finely chopped**
¼	**teaspoon salt**
¼	**cup fresh lemon juice**

1. Slice the hot dogs crosswise into thirds. Drain the pineapple, reserving ½ cup of the juice. Blend the juice with the cornstarch.
2. Combine the catsup, the onion rings, brown sugar, honey, garlic, salt and lemon juice in a 2-quart microwave-safe casserole. Stir in the pineapple juice and cornstarch mixture. Add the hot dogs, stirring to coat. Cover with the casserole lid or vented heavy-duty microwave-safe plastic wrap.
3. Microwave on Full Power for 5 to 6 minutes or until the sauce is bubbly and hot. Add the pineapple chunks. Cover the casserole.
4. Microwave on Full Power for 3 to 4 minutes or until heated throughout. Garnish the top of the casserole with a lattice of mustard, if you wish.

Salmon Supreme

A dish for special occasions — fresh salmon fillets served on microwaved asparagus, topped with a hollandaise sauce.

Microwave on Medium-High Power for
8 minutes.
Makes 6 servings.

Nutrient Value Per Serving: 463 calories, 41 g protein, 11 g fat, 4 g carbohydrate, 441 mg sodium, 99 mg cholesterol.

6   salmon fillets (about 6 ounces each)
   Salt and white pepper to taste
3   tablespoons fresh lemon juice
   Microwave Asparagus (recipe follows)
   Hollandaise Sauce (recipe, page 278)

1. Arrange the salmon fillets in a single layer in a shallow microwave-safe dish. Season with the salt and pepper. Sprinkle with the lemon juice. Cover the dish with vented microwave-safe plastic wrap.
2. Microwave on Medium-High Power for 8 minutes or until the fish flakes easily, turning the fillets and basting after 4 minutes. Serve with the Microwave Asparagus and Hollandaise Sauce.

Salmon Supreme

MICROWAVE OVEN METHOD FOR FISH

Fish cooks quickly in a microwave oven and retains its natural flavor because of its high moisture content. Fish tests done the moment it becomes opaque and easily flakes when pierced with a fork. The fish will continue to cook during the standing time, so test for doneness at the earliest moment.

Directions for fresh fish:
1. Place the thicker portion of the fish and large pieces toward the outside of a microwave-safe baking dish.
2. Season with ½ teaspoon salt, pepper to taste, 1 tablespoon fresh lemon juice and 1 tablespoon butter per 1 pound of fish. Cover the dish with a glass lid or cover tightly with microwave-safe plastic wrap.
3. Microwave at Full Power for 6 to 7 minutes for 1 pound of fillets, or 8 to 9 minutes for 2 pounds of fillets. Do not overcook.
4. Let the fish stand, covered, for 5 minutes.

Directions for frozen fish:
Thaw fish fillets in their original package in a microwave-safe baking dish. Microwave at defrost setting for 10 to 12 minutes for 1 pound. Let stand for 5 minutes. Proceed with cooking directions for fresh fish in Steps 1 through 3 above.

Microwave Asparagus

Asparagus microwaves to perfection.

Microwave on Full Power for 10 to 15 minutes.
Makes 6 servings.

Nutrient Value Per Serving: 17 calories, 2 g protein, 0 g fat, 3 g carbohydrate, 184 mg sodium, 0 mg cholesterol.

2   pounds fresh asparagus
½   cup water
½   teaspoon salt

1. Wash the asparagus. Snap off the tough ends. Arrange the asparagus, buds toward the center, in a large shallow microwave-safe dish with the water and salt. Cover the dish with vented heavy-duty microwave-safe plastic wrap.
2. Microwave on Full Power for 10 to 15 minutes until tender, rearranging once so the spears on the outside are brought to the middle. Serve with the Hollandaise Sauce spooned over.

Hollandaise Sauce

Microwave on Medium-High Power for
2 minutes.
Makes about ½ cup.

*Nutrient Value Per Tablespoon: 75 calories, 1 g protein, 8 g fat,
0 g carbohydrate, 129 mg sodium, 118 mg cholesterol.*

**¼ cup (½ stick) butter
Juice of ½ lemon
3 egg yolks
¼ teaspoon salt**

1. Microwave the butter in a 1-cup microwave-safe
   measure on Medium-High Power for 1 minute or
   until melted. Beat in the lemon juice, egg yolks
   and salt, in that order, until the mixture is
   smooth.
2. Microwave on Medium-High Power for 1 minute,
   stirring every 15 seconds. For a thicker sauce,
   cook for 15 seconds longer.

Cold Salmon with Herb Mayonnaise

Microwave salmon on Full Power for
6 minutes.
Makes 2 servings.

*Nutrient Value Per Serving: 755 calories, 52 g protein, 59 g fat,
2 g carbohydrate, 376 mg sodium, 110 mg cholesterol.*

**2 salmon steaks (8 ounces each)
1 tablespoon dry white wine (optional)
Salt and pepper, to taste
⅓ cup mayonnaise
1 tablespoon chopped flat-leaf Italian
   parsley
1 tablespoon chopped fresh basil OR:
   ½ teaspoon leaf basil, crumbled
½ teaspoon leaf marjoram, crumbled
2 teaspoons lemon juice
Pinch ground hot red pepper**

1. Place the salmon steaks in a microwave-safe
   9-inch pie plate. Sprinkle with the white wine, if
   you wish, and the salt and pepper to taste. Cover
   the plate with microwave-safe plastic wrap,
   pleated at one side to allow for expansion.
2. Microwave at Full Power for 6 minutes or until
   the fish flakes easily when touched with a fork;
   rotate the dish one-quarter turn after the first
   3 minutes of cooking time. Cool the fish in the
   refrigerator.
3. Stir together the mayonnaise, parsley, basil,
   marjoram, lemon juice and red pepper in a small
   bowl. Add more salt, if you wish. Refrigerate for
   at least 2 hours for flavors to blend.
4. To serve, place a dollop of mayonnaise in the
   middle of each salmon steak.

Now this is eating: Chunky Vegetable Gumbo with Shrimp.

Chunky Vegetable Gumbo with Shrimp

The microwave oven helps to retain the vitamins of fresh vegetables.

Microwave on Full Power for 32 to 38 minutes.
Makes 6 servings.

Nutrient Value Per Serving: 394 calories, 21 g protein, 27 g carbohydrate, 942 mg sodium, 102 mg cholesterol.

6   slices bacon, diced
3   cups chopped fresh okra OR: 1 package
**   (10 ounces) frozen okra, chopped**
¹/₃ cup vegetable oil
¹/₃ cup all-purpose flour
1¹/₄ cups diced celery
³/₄ cup chopped green onion
1   medium-size onion, chopped (¹/₂ cup)
3   cloves garlic, finely chopped
1   small yellow squash, thinly sliced
1   small zucchini, thinly sliced
1   cup diced sweet green pepper
2   bay leaves
3¹/₂ cups chicken broth
¹/₄ cup finely chopped parsley
¹/₂ teaspoon salt
¹/₂ teaspoon pepper
¹/₂ teaspoon leaf thyme, crumbled
¹/₄ teaspoon ground hot red pepper, or to taste
1   teaspoon Worcestershire sauce
1   pound medium-size shrimp, shelled and
**   deveined**
³/₄ teaspoon filé powder (optional)

1. Microwave the diced bacon, uncovered, in a 2-quart microwave-safe dish on Full Power for 3 minutes or until crisp. Remove the bacon with a slotted spoon and reserve.
2. Microwave the okra in the bacon drippings on Full Power for 7 minutes or until tender, stirring occasionally.
3. Microwave the oil in a 3-quart microwave-safe casserole, uncovered, on Full Power for 2 to 3 minutes or until hot. Stir in the flour until blended.
4. Microwave the flour mixture on Full Power for 7 to 8 minutes or until cinnamon-colored, stirring often. Stir in the celery, onion and garlic.
5. Microwave, uncovered, on Full Power for 4 minutes or until crisp-tender, stirring once. Stir in the okra mixture, the squash, zucchini, green pepper and bay leaves. Add the chicken broth, parsley, salt, pepper, thyme, red pepper and Worcestershire sauce, blending well. Cover the dish with vented heavy-duty microwave-safe plastic wrap.
6. Microwave on Full Power for 7 to 9 minutes or until the vegetables are tender, stirring occasionally. Stir in the reserved bacon and the shrimp. Cover.
7. Microwave on Full Power for 2 to 4 minutes or until the shrimp just begins to curl. Stir in the filé powder, if you wish. Remove the bay leaves. Taste and adjust the seasonings. Serve over hot cooked rice, if you wish.

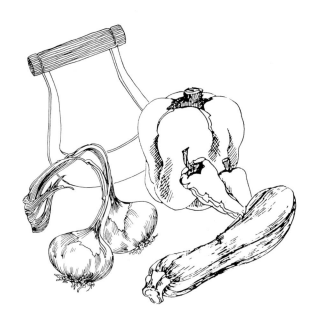

There's a delicious crab filling inside these Rainbow Stuffed Peppers.

Rainbow Stuffed Peppers

Colorful peppers encase a savory crab meat filling.

Microwave on Full Power for 15 minutes.
Makes 6 servings.

Nutrient Value Per Serving: 337 calories, 10 g protein, 18 g fat, 36 g carbohydrate, 772 mg sodium, 70 mg cholesterol.

- 6 **large sweet green, red or yellow peppers**
- ½ **cup (1 stick) butter or margarine**
- ¼ **cup diced celery**
- 1 **small onion, finely chopped (¼ cup)**
- ½ **cup water**
- ¼ **cup lemon juice**
- 1 **package (8 ounces) herb-seasoned stuffing mix**
- 1 **can (6 ounces) crab meat**
- 1 **jar (2 ounces) pimiento, drained and chopped**

1. Cut a thin slice from the pepper tops; scoop out the membrane and seeds. Arrange the peppers, cut-side down, in a large shallow microwave-safe dish. Cover the peppers with heavy-duty microwave-safe plastic wrap.
2. Microwave on Full Power for 7 minutes or until the peppers have softened. Remove the peppers with a slotted spoon to paper toweling.
3. Drain the liquid from the baking dish. Add the butter or margarine, the celery and onion to the dish.
4. Microwave on Full Power for 3 minutes, stirring twice. Add the water, lemon juice, stuffing, crab with its liquid and the pimiento. Spoon the stuffing into the peppers.
5. Microwave the peppers on Full Power for 5 minutes or until the filling is heated through.

Saucy Kabobs

A tasty bite of shrimp and chicken, basted with a sweet and sour marinade.

Microwave on Full Power for 8 to 10 minutes.
Makes 8 servings.

Nutrient Value Per Serving: 129 calories, 12 g protein, 1 g fat, 18 g carbohydrate, 77 mg sodium, 50 mg cholesterol.

- 1 **can (8 ounces) pineapple chunks in natural juice**
- ½ **cup salt-free steak sauce**
- ¼ **cup honey**
- 1 **teaspoon salt-free lemon and herb seasoning blend**
- ½ **pound medium-size shrimp, shelled and deveined**
- 1 **chicken breast, boned, skinned and cut into 16 pieces**
- 1 **large sweet red pepper, halved, seeded and cubed**
- 2 **teaspoons cornstarch**

1. Drain the pineapple juice into a shallow baking dish. Add the salt-free steak sauce, honey and seasoning blend. Add the shrimp, chicken and red pepper, turning to coat. Cover and marinate the chicken mixture in the refrigerator for at least 1 hour.
2. Alternately skewer the pineapple, chicken, shrimp and red pepper on eight 8-inch bamboo skewers; reserve the marinade. Arrange the skewers hanging on the rim of a 11 x 7-inch microwave-safe baking dish. Cover the skewers with wax paper.
3. Microwave on Full Power for 5 to 7 minutes or until the chicken and the shrimp are just tender, rotating the dish once. Let stand, covered, for 3 minutes.
4. Combine the reserved marinade with the cornstarch in a 2-cup microwave-safe measure, blending well.
5. Microwave on Full Power for 3 minutes or until thickened. Serve the sauce over the kabobs.

MICROWAVABLE VEGETABLES

Microwave ovens have made vegetable cooking simpler than boiling water. Tender-crisp, brightly colored, perfectly cooked vegetables are ready in just seconds. Less water and cooking time is required to microwave vegetables so textures, flavors, vitamins and minerals remain intact. Vitamin C, especially, is sensitive to overcooking.

Microwaving fresh vegetables requires no special equipment, but a few easy rules apply. Always use microwave-safe containers that allow microwave energy to pass through.

Glass, pottery, china, paper and thermoplastic are the most common materials used in the microwave. Plastic cooking bags, but not those from the produce department, may be used. Tie bags shut with a string, not twist ties.

Paper toweling, napkins, plates and bags make convenient disposable cooking containers. Be careful to use plastic or wax-coated plates at low temperatures; high temperatures may melt the wax or cause colors to run into the food. Also, be sure the paper toweling is all paper and does not contain synthetics that may not withstand high heat.

Glass, ceramic lids and heavy-duty microwave-safe plastic wrap make good covers for containers for most vegetables because they hold in steam. Do not use lightweight plastic wraps that have a tendency to split during cooking and melt into the food. Use caution when uncovering a cooked dish.

Wax paper works best for covering mushrooms, onions, tomatoes and moist vegetables. It allows some steam to escape so the vegetables do not become soggy.

Microwave potatoes, squash and yams whole. Remember to pierce to allow steam to escape.

Microwave Techniques for Vegetables

There are a few basic techniques used in microwave cooking. Use this as a reference guide:
- *All vegetables should be cooked on Full Power. Remember that microwave ovens do vary in wattage output.*
- *Cooking time depends on the quantity, size, freshness and moisture content of the vegetables. Standing time is as important as actual cooking time, especially when microwaving vegetables. They will continue to cook even after the heat generated by microwaves has ceased. Overcooked vegetables turn dry and tough.*
- *Vegetables should be cooked only until bright and tender-crisp when pierced. Potatoes, yams and squash should give slightly when pressed.* Test for doneness after *the recommended standing time.*

- *In general, estimate cooking time of about 6 to 7 minutes per pound of vegetables. Stir or rotate after 3 minutes; bring the center portion toward the outside of the dish for more even cooking.*

  After the minimum cooking time, let stand, then check for doneness. If necessary, cook in 1-minute intervals.

  Note: *Dried peas and beans are better cooked in a conventional oven or on a range.*
- *To cook several large individual vegetables (potatoes or squash), place them in a circle for more even cooking, leaving about one inch between. Arrange them in a single layer rather than on top of each other.*

  Cut vegetables into uniform sizes and shapes. Potatoes should be placed with the thickest portions to the outside. Those with thick, tough stalks, such as broccoli, should be arranged with the tips toward the center.
- *Stir and rotate vegetables (especially large quantities) midway through the cooking time to prevent uneven cooking.*
- *Salt vegetables only* after *they've cooked because salt draws liquid out of food and interferes with the microwave cooking pattern. Other seasonings may also be used.*

Tips For The Cook

- *To blanch vegetables for crudité platters or to add to casseroles: Slightly undercook the vegetables and let stand, covered, for 1 minute. Place the vegetables in ice water to stop cooking. Spread the vegetables on paper toweling to absorb any excess moisture.*
- *To soften the tough skins of winter squash, place the squash on the oven floor. Microwave, uncovered, on Full Power for 1 minute. Let stand for 1 minute before cutting.*
- *Easy mashed potatoes: Cube the potatoes. Add a small amount of water. Cook, tightly covered, until soft. Season and mash with milk or cream.*
- *For softer vegetables, increase the amount of water and the cooking time.*
- *Recipes made with sour cream, eggs or cream should be cooked at a slightly lower setting to avoid curdling.*
- *Add butter or margarine with water before cooking vegetables. For soft moist vegetables, such as mushrooms and spinach, substitute equal amounts of butter or margarine for water.*
- *Sprinkle vegetables with grated or shredded cheese during the standing time and toss before serving.*
- *Don't hesitate to experiment with fresh herbs. Add to vegetables during standing time.*
- *Substitute beef, chicken or vegetable broth for water. The result is richer-tasting vegetables.*

VEGETABLE	QUANTITY	WATER	PREPARATION TIPS	COOKING TIME	STANDING TIME
Artichoke	1 medium-size	¼ cup	Turn upside down in small dish or custard cup. Cover with plastic wrap.	5-7 min. (Stem should be fork tender)	5 min. covered.
Asparagus Spears	1 pound	3 Tbs.	Snap off tough ends. Arrange buds toward center of dish, cover with plastic wrap.	5 min.	5 min. covered.
Beans (green wax)	1 pound	½ cup	Snap ends and pull off strings. Cover with plastic wrap or lid.	12-15 min. Stir every 5 min.	5 min. covered.
Beets	6	1½ cups	Wash. (*Do Not Peel.*) Cover with lid or plastic wrap.	14-16 min. Turn after 7 min.	5 min. covered. Let cool, peel.
Broccoli Spears	1½ pounds	—	Place buds toward center of plate. Cover with lid or plastic wrap.	8-10 min. Rotate dish or plate after 5 min.	4 min. covered.
Brussels Sprouts	1 pound	2 Tbs.	Cover with lid or plastic wrap.	6-7 min. Stir after 3 min.	3-5 min. covered. Stem ends should be fork tender.
Cabbage	1 pound	2 Tbs.	Discard wilted outer leaves. Cover with lid or plastic wrap.	4-6 min. (shredded) 6-8 min. (wedges) Stir or turn ½ way through cooking.	3 min. covered.
Carrots	1 pound	¼ cup	Slice in uniform size or leave whole. Cover with lid or plastic wrap.	6-7 min. (slices) 8-9 min. (whole) Stir or rotate ½ way through cooking.	5 min. covered.
Cauliflower	1½ pounds	2 Tbs.	Remove outer leaves. Trim stem end. Separate flowerets *or* leave head whole. Cover with lid or plastic wrap.	6-8 min. (flowerets) 10-11 min. (whole) Stir or rotate head ½ way through cooking.	4-5 min. covered.
Corn on the Cob	1 ear	—	Secure husk closed with string. (Or shuck and wrap in plastic.) Place on paper toweling on microwave floor.	3-4 min. per ear. Turn each ½ way through cooking.	2-3 min. per ear.
Greens (kale & mustard)	1¼ pounds	—	Rinse and coarsely chop. Cover with lid or plastic wrap.	7-8 min. Stir after 3 min.	2 min. covered.
Mushrooms	1 pound	2 Tbs. *or* 2 Tbs. butter	Cut to even shapes. Cover with wax paper.	4-6 min. Stir after 2 min.	2 min. covered.
Onions	1 pound	—	Quarter, slice or leave whole. Cover with wax paper.	4-6 min. Stir after 2 min.	5 min. covered.
Peas	2½ pounds (3 cups)	¼ cup	Shell and rinse. Cover with lid or plastic wrap.	9-13 min. Stir after 5 min.	5 min. covered.
Potatoes (baking, sweet potatoes, yams)	1	—	Pierce skin on 4 sides with fork. Place on paper toweling on microwave floor. Arrange 1 on floor; 2 side by side; 4 more in spoke fashion.	4-5 min. Add 2-3 min. per potato. Turn each ½ way through cooking.	5-10 min. covered. Should give to slight pressure.
Spinach	1 pound	—	Rinse; shake excess water. Cover with lid or plastic wrap.	5-7 min. Stir after 3 min.	2 min. covered.
Squash (winter)	1 medium-size	—	Cut and remove seeds. Place on plate with hollow side up. Cover with plastic wrap.	10-12 min. Rotate after 5 min.	5 min. covered.
Squash (summer)	1 pound	2 Tbs.	Cover with lid or plastic wrap.	6-7 min. Stir after 3 min.	3 min. covered.
Turnips	1 pound	3 Tbs.	Cut into cubes. Cover with lid or plastic wrap.	7-9 min. Stir after 3 min.	3 min. covered.

Antipasto Salad

3. Separate the green beans under cold running water. Arrange the beans in a single layer on a microwave-safe plate. Cover with a double thickness of damp microwave-safe paper toweling.
4. Microwave the beans on Full Power for 4 minutes. Rinse the beans under cold water and drain.
5. Slice the beef into ¼-inch-thick strips, cutting across the grain. Place the beef in a bowl with the beans, red pepper, onion, Parmesan cheese, dressing, salt, oregano and pepper; toss to mix well. Serve immediately.

Antipasto Salad

Microwave on Full Power for 5½ minutes, then on Half Power for 3 minutes.
Makes 4 servings.

Nutrient Value Per Serving: 243 calories, 15 g protein, 16 g fat, 10 g carbohydrate, 544 mg sodium, 33 mg cholesterol.

1   piece london broil (10 ounces), cut about 1½ inches thick, trimmed
1   package (9 ounces) frozen Italian-style green beans
1   medium-size sweet red pepper, cut in ¼-inch-thick rings
1   small onion, thinly sliced (½ cup)
¼   cup grated Parmesan cheese
5   tablespoons Italian salad dressing
½   teaspoon salt
¼   teaspoon leaf oregano, crumbled Pepper, to taste

1. Microwave the beef on a microwave-safe plate, uncovered, on Full Power for 1½ minutes. Turn the meat over.
2. Microwave on Half Power for 3 minutes or until an instant-reading meat thermometer reads 120° when inserted in the center of the beef. Cover the beef with plastic wrap and let stand for 5 minutes.

Sweet and Sour Chicken and Cabbage

Microwave on Full Power for 10 to 12 minutes.
Makes 4 servings.

Nutrient Value Per Serving: 290 calories, 43 g protein, 3 g fat, 21 g carbohydrate, 240 mg sodium, 103 mg cholesterol.

3   chicken breasts, boned and skinned
1   teaspoon sesame seeds
4   cups coarsely shredded red cabbage
1   medium-size red onion, thinly sliced (about 1½ cups)
1   cup halved seedless green grapes (about 45)
5   tablespoons sweet-and-sour reduced-calorie salad dressing
¼   to ½ teaspoon liquid red-pepper seasoning
¼   to ½ teaspoon curry powder
⅛   teaspoon ground cinnamon Red and green cabbage leaves

1. Flatten the chicken slightly with a mallet between 2 pieces of wax paper. Arrange the cutlets around the outside of a microwave-safe plate. Cover the chicken with a double thickness of damp microwave-safe paper toweling.
2. Microwave on Full Power for 7 minutes, rotating the plate after 4 minutes if the chicken is cooking unevenly. Cover the chicken completely with heavy-duty microwave-safe plastic wrap and let stand for 2 minutes.
3. Place the sesame seeds in a single layer on a small microwave-safe plate.
4. Microwave the seeds on Full Power for 3 to 5 minutes or until the seeds turn golden, stirring frequently. Set aside.
5. Cut the chicken into ¼-inch-wide strips. Toss

with the shredded red cabbage, the sliced onion, halved grapes, salad dressing, liquid red-pepper seasoning, curry powder and cinnamon in a medium-size bowl until well blended.

6. Spoon into a salad bowl lined with red and green cabbage leaves. Sprinkle with the reserved toasted sesame seeds. Serve immediately.

Sweet and Sour Chicken and Cabbage

Mediterranean Salad

Mediterranean Salad

Sole and the luscious produce of the South of France are combined for a light, yet satisfying, main dish.

Microwave on defrost for 6 minutes; then on Full Power for 12 minutes.
Makes 4 servings.

Nutrient Value Per Serving: 315 calories, 16 g protein, 22 g fat, 16 g carbohydrate, 1,087 mg sodium, 40 mg cholesterol.

  1   **package (12 ounces) frozen sole fillets**
 ½   **pound small new red potatoes, sliced**
        ¼ inch thick
  3   **plum tomatoes (½ pound), cut into wedges**
 20   **Niçoise olives, halved and pitted OR: 1 can**
        (8 ounces) pitted ripe olives, halved
        if large
  2   **tablespoons chopped green onion**
  1   **clove garlic, finely chopped**
  1   **tablespoon chopped fresh basil OR:**
  1   **teaspoon leaf basil, crumbled**
 ¼   **teaspoon leaf thyme, crumbled**
 ½   **teaspoon salt**
  5   **tablespoons vinaigrette salad dressing**

1. Remove the fish from the package. Arrange in the center of a microwave-safe plate.
2. Microwave the fish, uncovered, on defrost for 6 minutes, turning the fish over after 3 minutes. Cover the defrosted fish with a double thickness of damp microwave-safe paper toweling.
3. Microwave on Full Power for 5 minutes, rotating the dish after 3 minutes if the fish is cooking unevenly. Cover the fish completely with heavy-duty plastic wrap and let stand for 5 minutes.
4. Arrange the sliced potatoes on a microwave-safe plate in a single layer. Cover with a double thickness of wet microwave-safe paper toweling.
5. Microwave on Full Power for 7 minutes; rearrange the potatoes after 5 minutes if cooking unevenly. Rinse the potatoes under cold water; drain and pat dry.
6. Flake the fish into a medium-size salad bowl. Add the potatoes, tomato wedges, halved pitted olives, chopped green onion, garlic, basil, thyme, salt and vinaigrette salad dressing; toss until well blended. Chill for 1 hour before serving. Garnish with carrot curls, if you wish.

HOW TO BAKE POTATOES IN A MICROWAVE OVEN

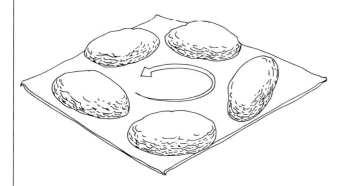

Scrub, dry and prick the potatoes. Place them 1 inch apart on microwave-safe paper toweling in the oven. Microwave on Full Power following these guidelines: one potato cooks for 5 to 6 minutes; two for 6 to 8; three for 8 to 10; four for 10 to 12; and five for 12 to 14. Remember to turn the potatoes over after the total cooking time. (Note: Microwave oven cooking times and instructions vary. Check the manufacturer's manual.)

HOW TO BLOSSOM A BAKED POTATO

Make an "x" with fork tines.

Push skin from both ends, forcing the "meat" to blossom.

Dilly Oil and Vinegar Topping for baked potatoes.

Dilly Oil and Vinegar Topping

This topping gives a nostalgic "potato salad" flavor to microwaved potatoes.

Microwave on Full Power for 1 to 3 minutes. Makes 1½ cups (enough topping for 4 to 6 potatoes).

Nutrient Value Per Serving: 293 calories, 0 g protein, 32 g fat, 1 g carbohydrate, 441 mg sodium, 0 mg cholesterol.

- ¾ **cup olive oil**
- ½ **cup chopped green onion, including some of the green top**
- ⅓ **cup red wine vinegar**
- ½ **cup chopped dill pickle**
- ½ **teaspoon dillweed**
- ½ **teaspoon salt**
- ⅛ **teaspoon pepper**

1. Microwave 1 tablespoon of the olive oil and the green onion in a 1-quart microwave-safe casserole on Full Power for 1 to 3 minutes or just until the green areas have brightened and the white areas are slightly softened.
2. Add the remaining olive oil, the vinegar, chopped pickle, dillweed, salt and pepper, blending well. Spoon into the microwave-baked potatoes which have been slashed open.

Taco Topping

Placing the sour cream and cheese in the center of the potatoes and covering with hot meat sauce allows these ingredients to melt without additional microwaving.

Microwave on Full Power for 7 to 9 minutes. Makes enough filling for about 4 medium-size potatoes.

Nutrient Value Per Serving: 370 calories, 26 g protein, 26 g fat, 8 g carbohydrate, 1,070 mg sodium, 93 mg cholesterol.

1 **pound lean ground beef**
1 **medium-size onion, chopped (½ cup)**
¼ **cup chopped sweet green pepper**
1 **can (8 ounces) tomato sauce**
2 **tablespoons, or more to taste, chopped canned mild green chilies**
1 **teaspoon salt**
½ **cup shredded sharp Cheddar cheese (2 ounces)**
½ **cup dairy sour cream**
   Diced tomatoes and shredded lettuce

1. Microwave the beef, onion and green pepper in a 2-quart microwave-safe casserole on Full Power for 7 to 9 minutes, breaking up and stirring every 2 minutes, until the meat is no longer pink and the vegetables are tender. Drain off the fat.
2. Stir in the tomato sauce, chilies and salt, blending well.
3. Just before serving, slash the tops of the potatoes and divide the Cheddar cheese and the sour cream evenly into the centers. Cover with the hot meat sauce. Garnish with the diced tomatoes and shredded lettuce.

Taco Topping for baked potatoes.

Cottage Cheese Topping for baked potatoes.

Cottage Cheese Topping

A medium-size baked potato has approximately 90 to 100 calories. The cottage cheese topping has about 90 calories a serving. This combination makes a satisfying lunch or light supper for under 200 calories per serving.

Microwave on Low Power for 3 to 4 minutes. Makes enough topping for about 4 potatoes.

Nutrient Value Per Serving: 92 calories, 14 g protein, 1 g fat, 5 g carbohydrate, 601 mg sodium, 5 mg cholesterol.

2 **cups (1 pint) small-curd, low-fat cottage cheese**
½ **cup finely grated carrot**
¼ **cup finely grated radish**
¼ **cup finely chopped sweet green pepper**
¼ **cup thinly sliced green onions, including some green tops**
¼ **teaspoon salt**
¼ **teaspoon black pepper**

1. Microwave the cottage cheese in a 1-quart microwave-safe bowl on Low Power for 3 to 4 minutes, stirring every minute, until the cottage cheese is just warmed to room temperature. (Heating the cottage cheese avoids cooling off the hot potatoes. Watch carefully, however, because over-heating can cause the cheese to separate.)
2. Stir in the grated carrot, radish, chopped green pepper, green onion, salt and pepper, mixing well. Divide the topping evenly over the opened potatoes.

P·I·E·S & O·T·H·E·R·S

A favorite-to-be: Delicious Apple Pie.

Delicious Apple Pie

Microwave on Full Power for 12 minutes; then bake at 425° for 20 minutes.
Makes 6 servings (9-inch pie).

Nutrient Value Per Serving: 447 calories, 4 g protein, 19 g fat, 68 g carbohydrate, 353 mg sodium, 45 mg cholesterol.

- **6** red Delicious apples, peeled, cored and sliced (about 6 cups)
- **½** to 1 cup firmly packed light brown sugar, depending on sweetness of apple
- **1½** tablespoons cornstarch
- **¼** teaspoon ground cinnamon
- **¼** teaspoon ground nutmeg
- **2** frozen 9-inch deep-dish pie crusts, slightly softened
- **1** egg yolk
  Pinch of salt

1. Preheat the oven to hot (425°).
2. Microwave the sliced apples, brown sugar, cornstarch, cinnamon and nutmeg in a 1½-quart microwave-safe bowl on Full Power for 12 minutes or until the apples are soft and the mixture is thick.
3. Bake one crust in the preheated hot oven (425°) for 10 minutes, following the package directions for an empty pie shell.
4. Using a leaf shape or other decorative cutter, make cutouts on the second crust; brush with a mixture of the beaten egg yolk and a pinch of salt. Place the shapes on a cookie sheet in the conventional oven with the partially baked pie crust.
5. Bake the cutouts and the crust in the hot oven (425°) for 10 minutes longer or until the crust and the cutouts are golden brown.
6. Spoon the apple mixture into the pie shell. Arrange the cutouts over the top.

Banana Cream Pie

Cream fillings are always done better by microwave cooking. Also, you'll find that by making the filling and crust separately, the finished pie will have a less soggy bottom crust.

Microwave on Full Power for 5 minutes.
Makes 6 servings (9-inch pie).

Nutrient Value Per Serving: 474 calories, 7 g protein, 26 g fat, 56 g carbohydrate, 252 mg sodium, 185 mg cholesterol.

- **2** cups milk
- **⅔** cup sugar
- **½** cup cornstarch
- **3** egg yolks, beaten
- **2** tablespoons butter or margarine, melted
- **2** teaspoons vanilla
- **1** frozen 9-inch deep-dish pie crust, baked following package directions
- **2** ripe bananas, sliced
- **½** cup heavy cream, whipped

1. Place the milk, sugar and cornstarch in a 1½-quart microwave-safe bowl; stir to blend.
2. Microwave on Full Power for 5 minutes or until the mixture thickens.
3. Add 1 cup of the milk mixture to the beaten egg yolks in a large bowl, stirring constantly until blended. Add the remaining milk mixture, then the butter or margarine and the vanilla, beating until the butter is melted and the mixture is smooth.
4. Line the baked pie crust with the bananas; pour the custard over the bananas. Cool. Garnish the pie with dollops of whipped cream.

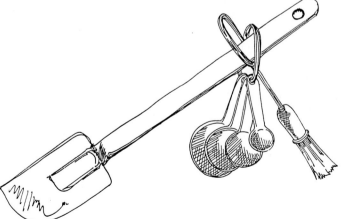

Mmmm . . . Almond Cheesecake.

Almond Cheesecake

Cheesecakes are a natural for the microwave. This one's smooth and creamy, with a gingersnap crust.

Microwave on Full Power for 1 to 1½ minutes; then on Medium-High Power for 13 to 15 minutes.
Makes 12 servings.

Nutrient Value Per Serving: 375 calories, 9 g protein, 24 g fat, 33 g carbohydrate, 242 mg sodium, 130 mg cholesterol.

 1   **cup gingersnap cookie crumbs**
½   **cup ground almonds**
1¼ **cups sugar**
¼   **cup (½ stick) butter or margarine, melted**
 1   **cup ricotta cheese**
 2   **packages (8 ounces each) cream cheese, softened**
 1   **teaspoon almond extract**
 3   **eggs**
¼   **cup all-purpose flour**

1. Combine the gingersnap cookie crumbs, ground almonds and ¼ cup of the sugar in a medium-size bowl, mixing well. Stir in the melted butter or margarine, blending until crumbly.
2. Cut a piece of cardboard to fit the bottom of a 9-inch round microwave-safe dish and place the cardboard in the dish. Spread the cookie crumb mixture onto the bottom and up the side of the prepared dish.
3. Microwave on Full Power for 1 to 1½ minutes or until just set; cool the dish directly on a heat-resistant countertop.
4. Beat the ricotta cheese in the large bowl of an electric mixer until smooth. Add the cream cheese, the remaining 1 cup sugar and the almond extract, beating until well blended. Add the eggs, one at a time, beating well after each addition. Stir in the flour. Pour the mixture into the cooled crust.
5. Microwave on Medium-High Power for 13 to 15 minutes or until the cake pulls away from the side of the dish. (The center will be soft but will firm upon chilling.) Cool the cheesecake in the dish for 1 hour. Remove the cake from the dish by carefully lifting under the cardboard with 2 spatulas. Chill the cake thoroughly before cutting into wedges.

Jalapeño Cornbread

Make with or without the jalapeño peppers, depending on your liking for hot.

Microwave on Full Power for 8 minutes.
Makes 9 generous pieces.

Nutrient Value Per Piece: 210 calories, 6 g protein, 5 g fat, 36 g carbohydrate, 490 mg sodium, 91 mg cholesterol.

 1   **can (16 ounces) white corn**
 1   **can (4 ounces) whole green chilies, drained (optional)**
 2   **cups plus 2 tablespoons stone-ground yellow cornmeal**
 2   **tablespoons sugar**
 2   **teaspoons baking powder**
 1   **teaspoon salt**
 3   **eggs, separated**
 3   **tablespoons unsalted margarine, melted**

1. Drain the liquid from the corn into a 4-cup measure; reserve the corn. Add enough water to the corn liquid to measure 2 cups.
2. Finely chop half of the drained chilies, if using. Cut the remaining chilies into strips. Reserve.
3. Measure the cornmeal, sugar, baking powder and salt into a bowl. Add the egg yolks, slightly beaten, to the bowl. Stir in the melted margarine and the corn liquid. Beat with a wooden spoon until the mixture is blended. Stir in the reserved corn and the finely chopped green chilies, if using.
4. Beat the egg whites with a pinch of salt in a large bowl until stiff, but not dry peaks form. Fold the whites into the batter until no streaks of white remain. Pour the batter into a greased 9½-inch round or square microwave-safe pie plate. Arrange the strips of chilies on top in lattice fashion, if using.
5. Microwave the cornbread on Full Power for 8 minutes. Cool the dish directly on a heatproof surface. Cut the cooled cornbread into 3-inch squares.

Apricot-Oatmeal Squares

So easy, even kids can bake these snack squares. So good, it will become a family favorite.

Microwave on Full Power for 7 minutes.
Makes 16 squares.

Nutrient Value Per Square: 232 calories, 3 g protein, 9 g fat, 36 g carbohydrate, 101 mg sodium, 23 mg cholesterol.

1½ **cups unsifted unbleached all-purpose flour**
1 **teaspoon baking powder**
½ **teaspoon salt**
1½ **cups old-fashioned rolled oats**
½ **cup firmly packed light brown sugar**
¾ **cup (1½ sticks) unsalted butter or margarine, cut into tablespoon-size chunks**
1 **jar (12 ounces) apricot preserves**
1 **to 2 teaspoons lemon juice**

1. Sift together the flour, baking powder and salt into a large mixing bowl. Stir in the uncooked oats, then the brown sugar.
2. Using your hands or a pastry blender, cut in the softened butter or magarine until the mixture is crumbly. Place 3 cups of the mixture in a greased 8 x 8 x 2-inch square microwave-safe baking dish, pressing down to form an even layer.
3. Blend the preserves with the lemon juice in a small bowl. Using a spatula, spread the preserves over the crust. Sprinkle the remaining oatmeal mixture over the filling, pressing down gently. (This prevents the crust from crumbling when you cut the squares.)
4. Microwave on Full Power for 7 minutes, rotating once. (The preserves will bubble up during the cooking. The crust may appear somewhat mushy, but it will solidify and harden within 15 minutes.) Cool the dish. Cut into squares or bars with a sharp or serrated knife.

Note: The crust mixture may be prepared ahead and refrigerated in a plastic bag.

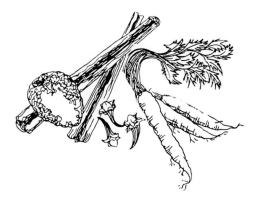

Fresh Carrot Loaves

Spices add fragrance as well as flavor to this carrot cake.

Microwave on Full Power for 14 minutes; then on Medium-High Power for 2 to 3 minutes.
Makes 2 loaf cakes (12 slices each).

Nutrient Value Per Slice: 180 calories, 2 g protein, 8 g fat, 25 g carbohydrate, 128 mg sodium, 44 mg cholesterol.

4 **cups grated carrot**
1½ **cups sugar**
1 **cup (2 sticks) unsalted butter or margarine, cut into tablespoon-size chunks**
½ **cup water OR: orange juice**
2½ **cups unsifted all-purpose flour**
1 **tablespoon ground cinnamon**
2 **teaspoons baking soda**
2 **teaspoons ground cloves**
¾ **teaspoon ground allspice**
¾ **teaspoon ground nutmeg**
½ **teaspoon salt**
2 **eggs, at room temperature**
10X (confectioners') sugar (optional)

1. Lightly butter the bottom and sides of two 8¼ x 4½ x 2⅝-inch microwave-safe loaf dishes. Line the bottom and sides of each with pieces of wax paper cut to fit.
2. Place the grated carrots, sugar, butter or margarine and water or orange juice in a microwave-safe 1½-quart bowl. Cover loosely with wax paper.
3. Microwave the carrot mixture on Full Power for 5 minutes or until the mixture begins to boil.
4. Stir the mixture. Microwave on Medium-High Power for 2 to 3 minutes longer. Remove from the microwave and cool.
5. Sift the flour with the cinnamon, baking soda, cloves, allspice, nutmeg and salt onto a piece of wax paper. Sift again.
6. Beat the eggs in the large bowl of an electric mixer at medium speed until very thick and lemon colored. Add the cooled carrot mixture, then the flour mixture, stirring until the batter is just combined. Divide the batter evenly between the 2 prepared dishes; shield the corners with triangles of aluminum foil.
7. Microwave on Full Power for 9 minutes or until a wooden pick inserted into the center of the cake comes out clean. Cool the cakes on wire racks. Dust with 10X sugar, if you wish.

Apple Upside-Down Cake

Family and guests alike will enjoy nibbling on this sweet snack.

Microwave on Full Power for 14 minutes.
Makes 16 squares.

Nutrient Value Per Square: 187 calories, 2 g protein, 7 g fat, 30 g carbohydrate, 118 mg sodium, 56 mg cholesterol.

Glaze:
- ¼ cup (½ stick) unsalted butter or margarine, cut up
- ½ cup firmly packed light brown sugar
- ½ cup granulated sugar
- 3 tablespoons all-purpose flour
  Pinch salt
- 1 teaspoon ground cinnamon

Topping:
- 2 pounds (about 5 large) firm apples (Miltons, Gravensteins, McIntosh or Golden Delicious)
  Juice of ½ medium-size lemon

Batter:
- 1 cup plus 2 tablespoons unsifted unbleached all-purpose flour
- 2 tablespoons granulated sugar
- 1 teaspoon baking powder
- ½ teaspoon salt
- ¼ cup (½ stick) unsalted butter, softened
- 2 extra-large eggs
- 1 teaspoon vanilla
- ¼ cup milk OR: orange juice
  Grated rind of ½ lemon

1. Prepare the Glaze: Using your fingertips, blend the ¼ cup butter or margarine, the brown and granulated sugars, 3 tablespoons flour, salt and cinnamon in a medium-size bowl until crumbly. Pat the mixture evenly into a greased 8 x 8 x 2-inch square microwave-safe dish.
2. Prepare the Topping: Wash, peel, quarter and slice the apples into a large bowl. (You should have 6 cups.) Sprinkle the apples with the lemon juice. Arrange the apple slices over the sugar mixture in 5 overlapping rows. Repeat with the remaining apples.
3. Prepare the Batter: Sift together the 1 cup plus 2 tablespoons flour with the 2 tablespoons granulated sugar, the baking powder and salt onto a piece of wax paper. Sift together 2 more times.
4. Beat the ¼ cup butter in a medium-size bowl with an electric mixer at high speed until light and fluffy. Beat in the eggs, one at a time, and the vanilla until well blended. (The mixture may appear curdled.)
5. Using a wooden spoon, alternately stir in the flour in 3 portions and the milk or juice in 2 portions. Stir in the grated lemon rind. (The batter will be thick.) Spread the batter evenly over the apples.
6. Microwave the cake on Full Power for 14 minutes or until the cake springs back when lightly touched with your fingertip. Invert the cake immediately onto a platter, spooning the hot glaze over the top. (The glaze will thicken as it cools.) Serve the cake hot or cold.

Note: As the cake stands, the juice exuded by the apples will dissolve the sugar crystals.

Peanutty Caramel Corn

Peanutty Caramel Corn

Prepare popping corn conventionally or in the microwave. You'll need about two 3.5 ounce pouches, regular or salt-free.

Microwave on Full Power for 10 minutes; then on Low Power for 15 minutes.
Makes about 4 quarts.

Nutrient Value Per ½ Cup: 295 calories, 3 g protein, 15 g fat, 39 g carbohydrate, 146 mg sodium, 16 mg cholesterol.

- 3 to 4 quarts freshly popped corn
- 1 cup (4 ounces) unsalted raw Spanish peanuts
- ½ cup (1 stick) unsalted butter
- ½ cup (1 stick) unsalted margarine
- 2 cups firmly packed light brown sugar
- ½ cup light corn syrup
- 1 teaspoon vanilla
- ½ teaspoon baking soda
- ¾ teaspoon salt

1. Place the popped corn and the nuts in a 13 x 9 x 2-inch glass baking dish. Keep warm in a preheated very slow oven (250°).
2. Cut the butter and the margarine into chunks and place in a 3- or 4-quart microwave-safe bowl. Using a wooden spoon, stir in the brown sugar and the corn syrup.
3. Microwave, uncovered, on Full Power for 5 minutes or until the mixture boils; stir to blend.
4. Microwave on Full Power for 5 minutes more. (The syrup should read 250° on a microwave candy thermometer.)
5. Using potholders, remove the bowl containing the hot syrup to a shielded countertop. Stir in the vanilla. (The mixture will sputter.) Stir in the baking soda. (The mixture will become opaque.) Stir in the salt.
6. Remove the warmed popped corn from the conventional oven. Stir in the caramel, coating the popped corn evenly.
7. Microwave, uncovered, on Low Power for 15 minutes, stirring once. Remove the dish to a shielded countertop for the popcorn to cool and crisp.

Rocky Road Bars

An irresistible confection for anyone who loves chocolate!

Microwave on Full Power for 13 to 16 minutes. Makes 48 bars.

Nutrient Value Per Bar: 90 calories, 1 g protein, 5 g fat, 10 g carbohydrate, 60 mg sodium, 20 mg cholesterol.

1½ cups all-purpose flour
6 tablespoons unsweetened cocoa powder
¾ teaspoon baking soda
¼ teaspoon salt
¾ cup (1½ sticks) butter or margarine
¾ cup sugar
2 eggs
1 cup chopped walnuts OR: pecans
¾ cup multicolored milk chocolate candies
⅔ cup miniature marshmallows

1. Combine the flour, cocoa, baking soda and salt in a small bowl, mixing well.
2. Beat the butter or margarine and the sugar in the large bowl of an electric mixer until light and fluffy. Add the eggs, one at a time, beating well after each addition. Stir in the dry ingredients just until blended; stir in ½ cup of the nuts. Spread the batter into a greased 12 x 8-inch

microwave-safe baking dish. Shield the corners with small pieces of aluminum foil.
3. Microwave on Full Power for 10 to 12 minutes or until the cake is not quite set in the center. Remove the foil. Sprinkle the multicolored candies, miniature marshmallows and remaining ½ cup nuts over the cake, pressing in lightly.
4. Microwave on Full Power for 3 to 4 minutes or until the marshmallows are soft. Cover the top with aluminum foil. Cool the dish directly on a heat-resistant countertop for 15 minutes. Then cool completely on a wire rack before cutting into 2 x 1-inch bars.

Chocolatey Rocky Road Bars.

Perfect Poached Pears are perfectly delicious!

Perfect Poached Pears

These pears are poached in a syrup flavored with a vanilla bean. If a vanilla bean is unavailable, substitute vanilla extract, adding the extract to the recipe after the syrup has been cooked; otherwise, the flavor of the vanilla extract will evaporate during cooking.

Microwave on Full Power for 10 minutes, 25 seconds.
Makes 2 servings.

Nutrient Value Per Serving: 402 calories, 1 g protein, 1 g fat, 103 g carbohydrate, 1 mg sodium, 0 mg cholesterol.

- 2 **cups water**
- ¾ **cup sugar**
- 1 **vanilla bean (1 inch long) OR: ¾ teaspoon vanilla extract**
- 2 **medium-size Bosc pears (7 ounces each)**
- 1 **wedge of lemon**

1. Combine the water, sugar and vanilla bean in a microwave-safe 1-quart measure. Microwave on Full Power for 2 minutes, 25 seconds or until the mixture boils. Stir to blend.
2. Microwave, uncovered, on Full Power for 5 minutes more. Using pot holders, transfer the quart measure of hot syrup to a shielded countertop. Remove the vanilla bean. (If using the vanilla extract, stir in at this point.)
3. Using a swivel-bladed vegetable peeler, peel the skin from the pears, leaving the stems intact. Place each pear in a microwave-safe dessert dish. Squeeze lemon juice over each whole pear. Pour half the syrup over each pear. Loosely cover each with wax paper.
4. Microwave the pears on Full Power for 3 minutes. Using pot holders, transfer the dishes containing the pears to a shielded countertop.

Note: If you wish, place the dried used vanilla bean in a canister of sugar to flavor it for baking or desserts.

Pear Sundae with Almond Fudge Sauce

Canned pear halves and a few other stock ingredients make a spectacular dessert with remarkable speed in the microwave.

Microwave on Full Power for 2 minutes.
Makes 4 servings.

Nutrient Value Per Serving: 342 calories, 3 g protein, 21 g fat, 42 g carbohydrate, 73 mg sodium, 18 mg cholesterol.

- 1 **package (6 ounces) semisweet chocolate pieces**
- ¼ **cup milk OR: half-and-half**
- 2 **tablespoons butter or margarine**
- ½ **teaspoon almond extract**
- 1 **can (16 ounces) Bartlett pear halves, drained**
  Vanilla ice cream
  Blanched almond slices (optional)

1. Place the chocolate, milk or half-and-half, butter or margarine and almond extract in a 4-cup microwave-safe measure.
2. Microwave on Full Power for 2 minutes or until the mixture comes to boiling, stirring every minute. Cool.
3. For each serving, place 2 pear halves in a dessert dish. Top with a scoop of ice cream and the warm sauce. Garnish with almond slices, if you wish.

Plum Pudding: A speedy version of the holiday classic.

Plum Pudding

Once a time-consuming dish to steam (2 hours or more), plum pudding cooked in the microwave is ready in just 15 minutes.

Microwave on Half Power for 15 minutes.
Makes 8 servings.

Nutrient Value Per Serving: 435 calories, 8 g protein, 14 g fat, 71 g carbohydrate, 322 mg sodium, 101 mg cholesterol.

- 2   **cups unseasoned bread crumbs**
- 1   **cup all-purpose flour**
- ¼   **cup firmly packed light brown sugar**
- ¼   **cup dark molasses**
- 1   **teaspoon baking soda**
- 1   **teaspoon ground cinnamon**
- ½   **teaspoon ground nutmeg**
- ½   **cup orange juice concentrate**
- ½   **cup (1 stick) unsalted butter or margarine, softened**
- ½   **cup brandy OR: dry sherry**
- 2   **eggs**
- 1½ **cups raisins**
  Candied pineapple and red and green cherries (optional)
  Hard Sauce Balls (recipe follows)

1. Combine the bread crumbs with the flour, brown sugar, molasses, baking soda, cinnamon, nutmeg, orange juice concentrate, butter or margarine, brandy or sherry, eggs and raisins in a large bowl, blending well.
2. Place the mixture in a 1½-quart microwave-safe bowl, pushing down slightly. Cover the top of the mixture with aluminum foil to prevent drying. Cover the bowl completely with heavy-duty microwave-safe plastic wrap. (Do not vent.)
3. Microwave on Half Power for 15 minutes or until the pudding starts to pull away from the side of the bowl and a skewer inserted into the center of the pudding comes out clean. Let the pudding stand for 10 minutes. Remove the plastic wrap and foil.
4. Place a serving platter on top of the bowl; invert. Garnish the pudding with the candied pineapple and red and green cherries, if you wish. Serve with chilled Hard Sauce Balls.

Hard Sauce Balls: Soften 1 cup (2 sticks) butter or margarine in a medium-size bowl. Knead in 1½ cups 10X (confectioners') sugar and 1 tablespoon brandy or rum. Shape the mixture into balls, using about 2 tablespoons for each. Spread 1 cup toasted flaked coconut on a piece of wax paper. Roll the balls in the coconut. Chill. Makes 10.

MANY OF YOUR STOVETOP RECIPES CAN BE ADAPTED FOR USE IN YOUR MICROWAVE OVEN

- *Follow the order of cooking just as it's described in the conventional recipe. Heat, scald, sauté or whatever the instructions say, only do it in the microwave. However, the oil may be eliminated.*
- *Brown meat, if indicated, but do it in your microwave. The microwave cooks ground meat to perfection every time. After microcooking a roast or other large cut of meat, however, you can achieve a crisper outer surface by placing it in a conventional oven or under a broiler for a short period of time.*
- *When a recipe calls for a large amount of liquid, reduce the specified amount by half. That's because there is less evaporation of liquid in a microwave oven than on the stovetop.*
- *For more even cooking, salt vegetables after microwaving.*
- *When preparing soup cook the solid ingredients first in the microwave. Then add stock that has been cooked on top of the range and heat until flavors are absorbed.*
- *Estimate the time needed for cooking. For roasts, poultry, casseroles and stews, figure about one-quarter to one-half the time indicated in a conventional recipe. Keep in mind that an extra minute in the microwave can mean a burnt offering. If in doubt, cook for just less than a quarter or half of the time indicated in the conventional recipe. You can always return the dish to the microwave oven if it's underdone.*

  If you are comparing a conventional recipe to a similar sounding one developed for the microwave, use the microwave cooking time indicated less about 20%. Then check the dish for doneness.
- *Test and taste the dish during cooking to determine the flavor, texture and tenderness. You as a microcook must stir, poke, taste, test, adjust, improvise and do all the other things you do when cooking over a hot stove.*
- *If a recipe calls for lots of water in order to cook the dish, don't try to make it in your microwave oven. Pasta, for example, is one food that turns out better when cooked on the stovetop. Soups and stews, however, in which liquid is a small part of the recipe, can be made in the microwave with much success.*

UPDATE ON MICROWAVE OVENS

Whether you're buying your first microwave or want to move up to a new model, check out this information. It goes from the basics, such as oven sizes, to state-of-the-art special features.

WHICH MODEL SIZE SHOULD YOU CHOOSE?

• Microwaves run the gamut from no-frills models (great for mainly defrosting and reheating foods) to full-featured (for a lot of cooking). Decide how much and for what purpose you'll be using your microwave before buying it.

• Always compare interior sizes — the oven capacity. *(See "Guide to Countertop Microwave Ovens," page 299, for more details.)* Check the manufacturer's booklet to find out if the oven can handle (cook) the amount of food you need and if it's large enough for your favorite microwave-safe cookware. A rule of thumb: the larger your family, the larger capacity you need. Some compact models are designed to hold only frozen food entrés and may not have enough room for one of your dinner plates.

• Where you'll place your microwave also affects your choice. Countertop ovens range from full-size to subcompact. Under-the-cabinet models come in all sizes except full-size. Some ovens can be mounted on, or built into, the wall. There's even an over-the-range microwave oven (1.0- to 1.3-cu. ft. interior) that goes above the cooktop in place of a range hood — but functions as a hood as well!

MICROWAVE PLUS!
MULTI-FUNCTION OVENS

These three types of microwave ovens perform additional cooking functions. All are able to brown and crisp food.

• *Microwave Convection Oven* Bakes, roasts, broils and toasts or cooks with microwaves alone or with convection cooking. (For the latter method, a fan forces hot air throughout the oven cavity.) Available in full- and mid-size with deluxe features and in over-the-range units.

• *Microwave Thermal Oven* Has upper and lower heating elements like a conventional range. Bakes, roasts, broils and toasts or cooks with microwaves alone or in combination with thermal energy. Compact in size, some can be mounted under the cabinet to free up counter space.

• *Microwave Oven With Browner* An upper heating unit can be turned on after the microwave cooking is completed for final top browning. This feature is available in full-size models only.

EASY-ON-THE-COOK
SPECIAL FEATURES

It pays to comparison-shop and see what different model microwave ovens have to offer. Special features are becoming more sophisticated, making less work for the cook! Following are some of the features available.

• *Automatic systems* These give you the ultimate in "computer" cooking! You simply enter the category of food, weight or amount and desired doneness. The oven automatically calculates the correct cooking time and sets power levels to either cook or defrost. Some ovens even have preprogrammed times and power levels for certain foods and recipes.

• *Temperature probes* The probe measures the temperature of a food as it cooks, and then turns the oven off or to a holding temperature when the preset temperature is reached.

• *Special defrost cycles* Provide faster, more even thawing.

• *Electronic controls* Make it easier to set precise times.

• *Rotating antennas, turntables and stirrer fans* These distribute microwaves throughout the oven cavity to insure more even cooking of the food.

GUIDE TO COUNTERTOP MICROWAVE OVENS

These ovens come in four sizes; interior capacity is given in cubic feet. **Full-size** (1.1- to 1.6-cu. ft.) hold the largest cookware and amounts of food; they also have the most deluxe features. **Mid-size** (.8- to 1.0-cu. ft.) take up less space than full-size models, but are still roomy inside. Come with many special features. **Compact** (.6- to .7-cu. ft.) and **Subcompact** (.3- to .5-cu. ft.) Both are ideal if you're cooking for one or two. Also perfect in a small space or a family room, a dorm, vacation home or office. Subcompacts generally have a limited number of features.

Note: Ovens of the same total cubic foot capacity from different manufacturers can have different interior dimensions, since some are more space efficient than others.

How to interpret wattage numbers on microwaves

Each microwave oven has an output wattage, which tells you the amount of microwave energy the oven has for cooking. Wattage is related to an oven's interior size, so, in general, the more cubic feet, the higher the wattage. Ovens range from 400 to 700 watts. Lower wattage ovens (400 to 500) take from a few seconds to a few minutes longer to cook food than higher wattage ovens (600 to 700 watts). Most recipes in magazines, newspapers and cookbooks are written for the high-wattage ovens.

Cooking Glossary

A

À la In the manner of, as in *à la maison:* in the style of the house — "the house specialty."

Al dente An Italian phrase meaning "to the tooth," used to describe spaghetti or other pasta at the perfect stage of doneness — tender, but with enough firmness to be felt between the teeth.

Antipasto Italian word meaning "before the meal." A selection of hors d'oeuvres, such as salami, marinated mushrooms, tuna or anchovies.

Au gratin Usually a creamed mixture topped with bread crumbs and/or cheese and browned in the oven or broiler.

B

Barbecue To roast meat, poultry or fish over hot coals or other heat, basting with a highly seasoned sauce. Also, the food so cooked and the social gathering.

Baste To ladle pan fat, marinade or other liquid over food as it roasts in order to add flavor and prevent dryness.

Blanch To plunge foods, such as tomatoes and peaches, quickly into boiling water, then into cold water, to loosen skins for easy removal. Also, a preliminary step to freezing vegetables.

Bone To remove the bones from meat, fish or poultry. This is usually done to make eating, carving or stuffing easier.

Bouillon A clear stock made of poultry, beef or veal, vegetables and seasonings.

Bouquet garni A small herb bouquet, most often sprigs of fresh parsley and thyme plus a bay leaf, tied in cheesecloth. Dried herbs can be used in place of the fresh. The *bouquet garni* is dropped into stocks, stews, sauces and soups as a seasoner and is removed before serving — usually as soon as it has flavored the dish.

Braise To brown in fat, then to cook, covered, in a small amount of liquid.

Broil To cook under a broiler or on a grill by direct dry heat.

Broth A clear meat, fish, poultry or vegetable stock made of a combination of them.

C

Calorie The measure of body heat energy produced by the burning (oxidation) of the food we eat.

Candy To cook fruit, fruit peel or ginger in a heavy syrup until transparent, which is later drained and dried. Also to cook vegetables, such as carrots or sweet potatoes, in sugar or syrup.

Caramelize To melt sugar in a skillet, over low heat, until it becomes golden brown.

Chantilly Heavy cream whipped until soft, not stiff; it may or may not be sweetened.

Coat the spoon A term used to describe egg-thickened sauces when cooked to a perfect degree of doneness; when a custard coats a metal spoon, it leaves a thin, somewhat jelly-like film.

Crimp To press the edges of a piecrust together with the tines of a fork or your fingertips.

Croutons Small, fried bread cubes.

Cut in To work shortening or other solid fat into a flour mixture with a pastry blender or two knives until the texture resembles coarse meal.

Cutlet A small, thin, boneless piece of meat — usually cut from the leg of veal or chicken or turkey breast.

D

Dash A very small amount — less than $\frac{1}{16}$ teaspoon.

Deep-fry To cook in hot, deep, temperature-controlled fat.

Deglaze To loosen the browned bits in a skillet or roasting pan by adding liquid while stirring and heating. A glaze is used as a flavor base for sauces and gravies.

Demitasse French for "half cup," it refers to the small cups used for after-dinner coffee and also to the strong, black coffee served in them.

Devil To season with mustard, pepper and other spicy condiments.

Dice To cut into small, uniform pieces.

Drawn butter Melted, clarified butter or margarine; often served with boiled shellfish.

Dredge To coat with flour prior to frying.

Drizzle To pour melted butter or margarine, marinade or other liquid over food in a thin stream.

Duchesse Mashed potatoes mixed with egg, butter or margarine and cream, piped around meat, poultry or fish as a decorative border, then browned in the oven or broiler before serving.

Dutch oven A large, heavy, metal cooking pot with a tight-fitting cover; used for cooking pot roasts and stews and for braising large cuts of meat and poultry.

E

Entrée A French term applying to the third course in a full French dinner. We use the term to designate the main dish of a meal.

Escalope A thin slice of meat or fish, slightly flattened and often sautéed quickly in oil or butter.

Espresso Robust, dark Italian coffee brewed under steam pressure. It is traditionally served in small cups and, in this country (though usually not in Italy), accompanied by twists of lemon rind.

Evaporated milk Canned unsweetened milk slightly thickened by the removal of some of its water.

F

Fillet A thin, boneless piece of meat or fish.

Fillo See "Phyllo."

Fines herbes A mixture of minced fresh or dried parsley, chervil, tarragon and, sometimes, chives, used to season salads, omelets and other dishes.

Flake To break up food (salmon or tuna, for example) into smaller pieces with a fork.

Flambé, flambéed French words meaning "flaming." In the culinary sense, the verb *flamber* means to pour warm brandy over a food and set it afire with a match.

Florentine In the style of Florence, Italy, which usually means served on a bed of spinach, topped with a delicate cheese sauce and browned in the oven. Fish and eggs are often served Florentine style.

Flute To form a fluted edge with the fingers, on a piecrust edging.

Fold in To mix a light, fluffy ingredient, such as beaten egg white, into a thicker mixture, using a gentle under-and-over motion.

Frappé A mushy, frozen dessert.

Fricassee To simmer a chicken covered in water with vegetables and often wine. The chicken may be browned in butter first. A gravy is made from the broth and served with the chicken.

Fritter A crisp, golden, deep-fried batter bread, often containing corn or minced fruits or vegetables. Also, pieces of fruit or vegetable, batter-dipped and deep-fried.

G

Garnish To decorate with colorful and/or fancily cut pieces of food.

Glaze To coat food with honey, syrup or other liquid so it glistens.

Gluten The protein of wheat flour that forms the framework or structure of cakes, breads, cookies and pastries.

Goulash A beef or pork stew, flavored with sweet or hot paprika.

H

Hors d'oeuvres Bite-size appetizers served with cocktails.

Hull To remove caps and stems from berries.

I

Ice To cover with icing. Also, a frozen, water-based, fruit-flavored dessert.

Italienne, à la Served Italian style with pasta.

J

Julienne To cut food into uniformly long, thin slivers (1½ x ¼ inches).

K

Kabobs Cubes of meat, fish or poultry and/or vegetables threaded on long skewers and grilled over coals or under the broiler.

Kasha Buckwheat groats, braised or cooked in liquid and usually served in place of rice, potatoes or another starch.

Knead To work dough with the hands until it is smooth and springy. Yeast breads must be kneaded to develop the gluten necessary to give them framework and volume.

Kosher salt A very coarse salt.

L

Lard Creamy, white, rendered pork fat.

Lyonnaise Seasoned in the style of Lyons, France, meaning with parsley and onions.

M

Macerate To let food, principally fruits, steep in wine or spirits (usually kirsch or rum).

Maître d'hôtel Simply cooked dishes seasoned with minced parsley, butter and lemon. *Maître d'hôtel* butter is a mixture of butter (or margarine), parsley, lemon juice and salt. It is most often used to season broiled fish, grilled steaks or chops or boiled carrots.

Marinade The liquid in which food is marinated.

Marinate To let food, principally meats, steep in a piquant sauce prior to cooking. The marinade serves to tenderize and add flavor.

Marzipan A confection made from almond paste, sugar and egg whites — often colored and shaped into tiny fruit and vegetable forms.

Mask To coat with sauce or aspic.

Meringue A stiffly beaten mixture of sugar and egg white.

Mince To cut into fine pieces.

Mocha A flavoring for desserts, usually made from coffee or a mixture of coffee and chocolate.

Mole A sauce of Mexican origin, containing chilies, onion, garlic and other ingredients, especially bitter chocolate. Usually served over poultry.

Mousse A rich, creamy, frozen dessert. Also, a velvety hot or cold savory dish, rich with cream, bound with eggs or — if cold — with gelatin.

Mull To heat a liquid, such as wine or cider, with whole spices.

N

Niçoise Prepared in the manner of Nice, France — with tomatoes, garlic, olive oil and ripe olives.

Nouvelle Cuisine A French cuisine established by classically trained younger chefs with a new and lighter twist on classic French dishes and preparation techniques. It has been adapted by many other cuisines.

O

Oil To rub a pan or mold with cooking oil.

P

Panbroil To cook in a skillet in a small amount of fat; drippings are poured off as they accumulate.

Parboil To cook in water until about half done; vegetables to be cooked *en casserole* are usually parboiled.

Pasta The all-inclusive Italian word for all kinds of macaroni, spaghetti and noodles.

Pastry A stiff dough, made from flour, water and shortening, used for piecrusts, turnovers and other dishes; it is also a rich cookie-type dough used for desserts.

Pastry bag A cone-shaped fabric, parchment or plastic bag with a hole at the tip for the insertion of various decorating tubes. Used to decorate cakes, pastries, etc.

Pâté A well-seasoned mixture of finely minced or ground meats and/or liver. *Pâté de foie gras* is made of goose livers and truffles.

Pectin Any of several, natural gelatinous substances found in the cellular structure of different fruits and vegetables. It is also manufactured in syrup form to use in helping jellies to jell.

Petits fours Tiny, fancily frosted cakes.

Phyllo (fillo) Greek term for a flaky, tissue paper-thin pastry used in many Greek dishes.

Pilaf Rice cooked in a savory broth, often with small bits of meat or vegetables, herbs and spices.

Pinch The amount of a dry ingredient that can be taken up between the thumb and index finger — less than ¼ teaspoon.

Pipe To press frosting, whipped cream, mashed potatoes or other soft mixtures through a pastry bag fitted with a decorative tube to make a fancy garnish or edging.

Plank A well-seasoned (oiled) hardwood plank used to serve a broiled steak or chop, usually edged with Duchesse potatoes.

Plump To soak raisins or other dried fruits in liquid until they are softened and almost returned to their natural state.

Poach To cook in barely simmering liquid, as fish fillets, for example.

Polenta A cornmeal porridge popular in Italy. Usually cooled, sliced or cubed, then baked or fried with butter and Parmesan cheese.

Pot cheese A soft uncured cheese from strained milk curds, almost identical to cottage cheese but perhaps a bit drier.

Purée To reduce food to a smooth, velvety texture by whirling in an electric blender or pressing through a sieve or food grinder. Also, the food so reduced.

R

Ragoût A stew.

Ramekin A small, individual-size baking dish.

Reduce To boil a liquid, uncovered, until the quantity is concentrated.

Render To melt solid fat.

Rice To press food through a container with small holes. The food then resembles rice.

Risotto An Italian dish made with short-grain rice browned in fat and cooked with chicken broth or other liquid until tender but firm. Mixture is creamy, not dry or runny.

Roast To cook meat or poultry in the oven by dry heat.

Roe The eggs of fish, such as sturgeon, salmon (caviar) or shad; considered delicacies.

Roulade A slice of meat, most often veal or beef, rolled around any number of fillings. Also, a jelly-roll cake.

Roux A cooked, fat-flour mixture used to thicken sauces and gravies.

S

Sauté To cook food quickly in a small amount of hot fat in a skillet.

Scald To heat a liquid just until small bubbles form around the pan, but the liquid does not boil.

Scallop To bake small pieces of food *en casserole,* usually in a cream sauce. Also a thin, boneless slice of meat, such as veal.

Score To make shallow, crisscross cuts over the surface of a food with a knife.

Scrape To remove fruit or vegetable skin by scraping with a knife.

Shirr To bake whole eggs in ramekins with cream and crumbs.

Short An adjective used to describe a bread, cake or pastry that has a high proportion of fat and is ultra-tender or crisp.

Shortening A solid fat, usually of vegetable origin, used to add tenderness to pastry, bread, cakes or cookies.

Sift To put flour or another dry ingredient through a sifter. (*Note:* In this book, recipes that call for sifted flour require that you sift the flour and then measure it, even if you use a flour that says "sifted" on the bag.)

Simmer To cook in liquid just below boiling.

Skewer To thread food on a long wooden or metal pin before cooking. Also, the pin itself.

Skim To remove fat or film from the surface of a liquid or sauce.

Sliver To cut in long, thin strips.

Soufflé A light, fluffy, baked combination of egg yolk, sauce, purée and flavoring, with stiffly beaten egg whites folded in.

Spit To thread food on a long rod and roast over glowing coals or under a broiler. Also, the rod itself.

Steam To cook, covered, on a trivet over a small amount of boiling water.

Steep To let food soak in liquid until the liquid absorbs its flavor, such as tea in hot water.

Stew To cook, covered, in simmering liquid.

Stir-fry To cook in a small amount of oil, in a wok or skillet, over high heat, stirring or tossing constantly for a short period of time.

Stock A liquid flavor base for soups and sauces made by long, slow cooking of meat, poultry or fish with their bones. Stock may be brown or white, depending on whether the meat and bones are browned first.

Stud To press whole cloves, slivers of garlic or other seasoning into the surface of a food.

T

Terrine A type of container used for baking dishes such as pâtés. The prepared dish may also be referred to as a terrine.

Thicken To make a liquid thicker, usually by adding flour, cornstarch or beaten egg.

Thin To make a liquid thinner by adding liquid.

Timbale A savory meat, fish, poultry or vegetable custard, baked in a small mold. Also, pastry shells made on special iron molds.

Torte A very rich, multilayered cake made with eggs, and, often, grated nuts. Usually it is filled, but frequently it is not frosted.

Toss To mix, as a salad, by gently turning ingredients over and over in a bowl, either with hands or with a large fork and spoon.

Truffles A type of underground fungi considered a real delicacy. Black, dark brown or white in color and quite expensive because of their rarity and the method of obtaining them. Also, a term for a rich chocolate candy.

Truss To tie into a compact shape before roasting.

Turnover A folded pastry usually made by cutting a circle or square, adding a dollop of sweet or savory filling, folding into a semicircle or triangle, then crimping the edges with the tines of a fork. Most turnovers are baked, but some are deep-fat fried.

Tutti-Frutti A mixture of minced fruits used as a dessert topping.

V

Variety meats Organ and muscular meat, such as liver, heart, kidneys and tripe.

Véronique A dish garnished with seedless green grapes.

Vinaigrette A sauce, French in origin, made from oil, vinegar, salt, pepper and herbs; usually served on cold meat, fish or vegetables.

W

Whip To beat until frothy or stiff with an eggbeater or an electric mixer.

Wok A round-bottomed, bowl-shaped Chinese cooking utensil used for stir-frying.

Z

Zest The oily, aromatic, colored part of the rind of citrus fruits.

INDEX

ITALICIZED PAGE
NUMBERS REFER TO
PHOTOGRAPHS

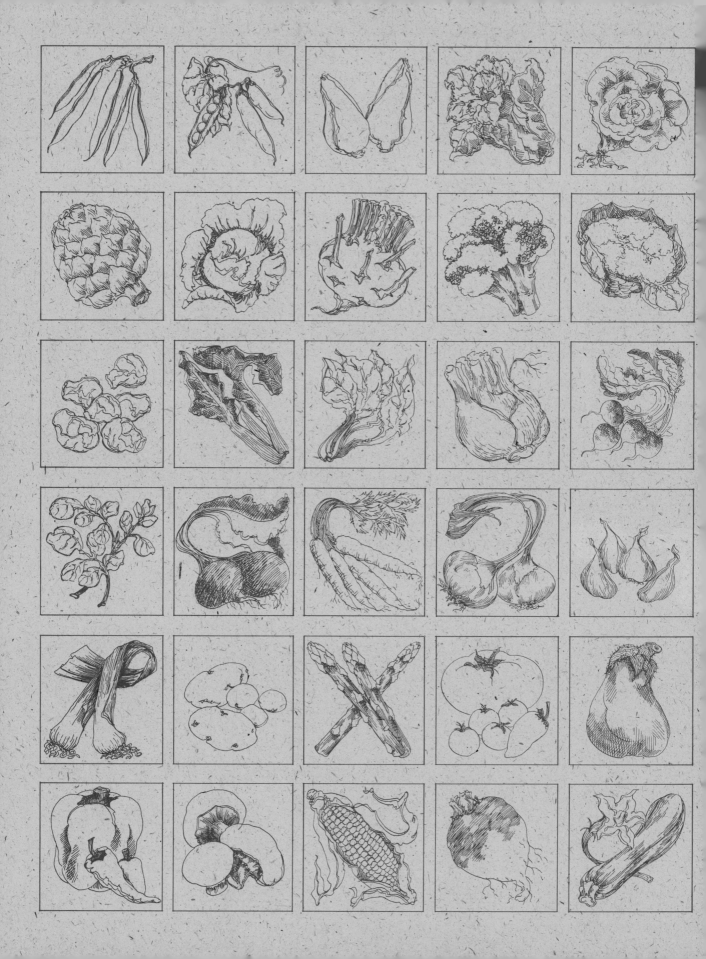